Thomas Keating

■

FOUNDATIONS FOR CENTERING PRAYER AND THE CHRISTIAN CONTEMPLATIVE LIFE

Open Mind, Open Heart

Invitation to Love

The Mystery of Christ

■

CONTINUUM
New York · *London*

2002

The Continuum International Publishing Group Inc
370 Lexington Avenue, New York, NY 10017

The Continuum International Publishing Group Ltd
The Tower Building, 11 York Road, London SE1 7NX

Open Mind Open Heart © 1986, 1992 by St. Benedict's Monastery
Invitation to Love © 1992 by St. Benedict's Monastery
The Mystery of Christ © 1987 by St. Benedict's Monastery
This arrangement © 2002 by St. Benedict's Monastery

Printed in the United States of America

ISBN 0-8264-1397-8

Library of Congress Catalog Card Number 2002 141136

CONTENTS

■

PREFACE

■

PEOPLE INTERESTED IN Centering Prayer often ask, "Which of Father Keating's books should I read first?" This single volume contains the three basic books of the Centering Prayer practice and its conceptual background. The trilogy develops the material presented in the first Ten Day Intensive workshop in which the method of Centering Prayer was taught along with its conceptual background. The homilies which were given during the liturgy attempted to integrate the method and its conceptual background into the mystery of Christ. The three basic books that summarize this material are contained in this trilogy.

Open Mind, Open Heart deals with how to do the Centering Prayer practice. *Invitation to Love* deals with its conceptual background rooted in the Christian contemplative heritage, and *The Mystery of Christ,* following the principal feasts of the liturgical year, incorporate the first two elements into the theological principles on which Centering Prayer, and indeed any practice leading to Christian contemplative prayer is based.

Centering Prayer as a practice is an effort to present the traditional practices leading to contemplative prayer in an up-to-date manner using the device of a method because this seems to appeal to people of our time. Moreover, since methods are very prominent in the spiritualities of the various world religions, practitioners of Centering Prayer can easily enter into inter-religious dialogue at this level and perhaps learn from the experience of the East without abandoning the belief system of their youth.

Centering Prayer is thus an attempt to renew the Christian contemplative tradition by drawing on the insights of the great Christian writers down through the centuries. It also serves as a point of unity between the various Christian denominations since it fosters the experience of the living Christ that gradually builds a bond of unity beyond doctrinal differences. These of course, remain important to resolve. At the same time, the experience of bonding together in the shared faith experience of the Divine Indwelling can bring Christians together in a new way and hopefully more profoundly than ever before.

Invitation to Love is a presentation of the Christian contemplative tradition in dialogue with contemporary science especially developmental psychology and anthropology. The experience of the stages of contemplative prayer bring people into deep respect and greater understanding of the methods and conceptual backgrounds of the advanced wisdom teachings of other spiritualities, especially the Buddhist, Hindu, Taoist, Sufi, and Jewish traditions.

The bonding of the different world religions through their common search for God will hopefully result in a common commitment and concern for human needs, rights, and values, as well as for world peace and justice issues.

Thus the Centering Prayer practice is not a privatized journey but through the pursuit of union with God and with everyone in the human family opens our minds and hearts to the kind of service and love that our contemporary world longingly awaits.

The Mystery of Christ develops the theological principles on which Centering Prayer is based using the liturgical year as a primary channel of instruction. The liturgy as applied scripture intends to communicate an experience of what the theological principles of the Christian religion contain. This instruction is embodied in the principal feasts of the year that celebrate the theological themes of divine light, life, and love. The Eucharist itself is a sacrament of transformation. The liturgy unpacks the divine riches contained in the celebration of these theological realities over the course of the year, especially through the principal themes just mentioned. Thus the teaching of the trilogy transcends the details of the method and its conceptual background in order to communicate the experience of the living Christ through the growth of theological virtues of faith, hope, and charity, the Fruits of the Spirit and the seven-fold Gifts of the Spirit.

Thomas Keating
March 2002

OPEN MIND, OPEN HEART

■

The Contemplative Dimension
of the Gospel

CONTENTS

∎

3

PRAYER TO THE HOLY SPIRIT

■

Inspired by the Latin hymn
Veni Sancte Spiritus

Come, Holy Spirit, pour out of the depths of the Trinity a ray of Your Light—that Light which enlightens our minds and, at the same time, strengthens our wills to pursue the Light.

Come, Father of the poor, the poor in spirit, whom You love to fill with the fullness of God.

You are not only Giver of gifts, but Giver of Yourself, the supreme Gift—*the* Gift of the Father and the Son.

You are the best consoler! What a charming Guest You make! Your conversation, though all in silence, is sweetness itself. How refreshing Your consolation! Soothing like a caress. In an instant You dissipate all doubt and sadness.

In the labor of fighting temptation, you are there promising victory. Your presence *is* our victory. You gently coax our timid hearts to trust in You.

In the greatest of labors, the struggle of self-surrender, You are our repose—our peace in the depth of our souls.

In the heat of battle, Your breath is cooling, calming our rebellious passions, quieting our fears when it looks like defeat. You dry our tears when we fall. It is you who give the grace of compunction and the sure hope of pardon.

Oh deliriously happy Light! Fill to the uttermost recesses the hearts of Your faithful children!

Without You, there is no divine life in us, no virtue at all. If Your breath is cut off, our spirit perishes; nor can it live again until You press Your lips to our mouths and breathe into them the breath of life.

Your touch is as dew, but You act with a strong hand. Gentle as the softest breeze, You are also in the whirlwind.

Like a giant furnace blast, You dry up all our faculties—but only to melt the hardness of our hearts.

You cast us before You like dead leaves in the winter's gale—but only to set our feet upon the narrow way.

Now, as a mighty Wind coming, pour down torrents to wash away our sins. Drench with grace our dried out hearts. Soothe the wounds You have cauterized.

Give to all who trust in You—with that true trust which only You can give—Your seven sacred Gifts.

Grant the reward of virtue; that is, Your very Self! Grant perseverance to the end! And then, everlasting joy!

Amen

INTRODUCTION

■

TODAY THE CHRISTIAN CHURCHES find themselves with a marvelous opportunity. Many sincere believers are eager to experience contemplative prayer. Along with this aspiration, there is a growing expectation that the leaders of local communities be able to reach the Gospel out of personal experience of contemplative prayer. This could happen if the training of future priests and ministers places formation in prayer and spirituality on an equal footing with academic training. It could also happen if spiritual teaching becomes a regular part of the lay ministry. In any case, until spiritual leadership becomes a reality in Christian circles, many will continue to look to other religious traditions for the spiritual experience they are not finding in their own churches. If there were a widespread renewal of the preaching and practice of the contemplative dimension of the Gospel, the reunion of the Christian churches would become a real possibility, dialogue with the other world religions would have a firm basis in spiritual experience, and the religions of the world would bear a clearer witness to the human values they hold in common.

Centering Prayer is an effort to renew the teaching of the Christian tradition on contemplative prayer. It is an attempt to present that tradition in an up-to-date form and to put a certain order and method into it. Like the word *contemplation,* the term *Centering Prayer* has come to have a variety of meanings. For the sake of clarity it seems best to reserve the term *Centering Prayer* for the specific method of preparing for the gift of contemplation (described in Chapter Three) and to return to the traditional term *contemplative prayer* when describing its development under the more direct inspiration of the Spirit.

This book has grown out of a number of seminars on the practice of Centering Prayer and incorporates the specific questions of participants coming from different levels of experience. The concerns expressed by the participants spring from the developing practice of Centering Prayer. Thus the questions that arise after some months of daily practice are different from those that arise in the first few weeks.

The questioner is often asking more than the actual question contains. The responses are aimed at facilitating the listening process initiated by the method of Centering Prayer. Together with the presentations, they gradually weave a conceptual background for contemplative practice.

Contemplative prayer is a process of interior transformation, a conversation initiated by God and leading, if we consent, to divine union. One's way of seeing reality changes in this process. A restructuring of consciousness takes place which empowers one to perceive, relate and respond with increasing sensitivity to the divine presence in, through, and beyond everything that exists.

1

WHAT CONTEMPLATION IS NOT

■

THERE IS MUCH POPULAR MISINFORMATION in people's minds about what contemplation is. Saying what it is not may help to put a perspective on what it is.

The first thing contemplation is not is a relaxation exercise. It may bring relaxation, but that is strictly a side effect. It is primarily relationship, hence, intentionality. It is not a technique, it is prayer. When we say, "Let us pray", we mean, "Let us enter into a relationship with God", or, "Let us deepen the relationship we have", or, "Let us exercise our relationship with God". Centering Prayer is a method of moving our developing relationship with God to the level of pure faith. Pure faith is faith that is moving beyond the mental egoic level of discursive meditation and particular acts to the intuitive level of contemplation. Centering Prayer is not designed to bring you to a "high" such as you might obtain by ingesting Peyote or LSD. It is not a form of self-hypnosis. It is simply a method leading to contemplative prayer. In this perspective, it is the first rung on the ladder of contemplative prayer.

The second thing that contemplative prayer is not is a charismatic gift. The charisms enumerated by Paul have been renewed in our time. These gifts are designed for the building up of the community. One may be a contemplative and a charismatic at the same time. And one may not be a contemplative and still have one or more of the charismatic gifts. In other words, there is not necessarily a connection between the two. Contemplative prayer depends on the growth of faith, hope, and divine love, and deals with the purification, healing, and sanctification of the substance of the soul and its faculties. The charismatic gifts are given for the building up of the local community and may be given to people who are not necessarily advanced in the spiritual journey. The gift of tongues is the one gift that may be given primarily for one's personal sanctification. It is a kind of introduction to contemplative prayer because, when praying in tongues, one doesn't know what one is saying.

9

Another gift is the ability to communicate the experience of *resting in the Spirit*. If you have already had some experience of contemplation, you would recognize it as the gift of infused recollection or perhaps even the prayer of quiet. You can resist it if you want to. If you accept it, you feel a mild suspension of your ordinary sense faculties and you slip to the floor. If people have never experienced this kind of prayer before, they go down with great delight and stay down as long as they can. I once saw a young man fall backwards horizontally as if he were doing a back dive into a swimming pool. He bounced off a little bench, landed on the floor with a terrific crash, and jumped up, completely unhurt.

Apart from the gift of tongues, the charismatic gifts are clearly given for the good of others. They include the interpretation of tongues, prophecy, healing, administration, the word of wisdom, and inspired teaching. Prophecy can exist in people who are not holy at all. A classical example is the prophet Balaam, who prophesied what the King wanted to hear rather than what God had commanded him to say. There were many false prophets in Old Testament times. Since charismatic gifts are frequent in our time and people tend to get excited about them, it is important to realize that they are not an indication either of holiness or of an advanced stage of prayer. They are not the same as contemplative prayer and do not automatically sanctify the people who have them. On the contrary, if one is attached to them, they are a hindrance to one's spiritual development. Even in the exercise of charismatic gifts, emotional programming is at work. According to Catholic tradition, the straight and narrow path of contemplative prayer is the surest and safest path to holiness. The charismatic gifts are accidental or secondary to that path. Obviously, if one has such gifts, one has to integrate them into one's spiritual journey. But if one doesn't have them, there is no reason to think that one is not progressing. The process of transformation depends on the growth of faith, hope, and divine love. Contemplative prayer is the fruit of that growth and furthers it. Right now the charismatic renewal is in great need of the traditional teaching of the Church on contemplative prayer so that charismatic prayer groups may move on to a new dimension in their relationship with the Holy Spirit. They should introduce periods of silence into the prayer meetings so that shared prayer becomes grounded in the practice of interior silence and contemplation. There is a movement to do precisely that in many prayer groups. If this development fails to take place, the groups risk stagnation. Nothing can stand still on the spiritual journey. These groups need the further growth that the practice of contemplative prayer is meant to provide.

The third thing that contemplative prayer is not is parapsychological phenomena such as precognition, knowledge of events at a distance, control over bodily processes such as heartbeat and breathing, out-of-body experiences, levitation, and other extraordinary sensory or psychic phenomena. The psychic level of consciousness is one level above the mental egoic stage, which is the general level of present human development.

In any case, psychic phenomena are like the frosting on a cake and we cannot survive on frosting alone. We should not overestimate psychic gifts, therefore, or think that holiness manifests itself in extraordinary psychic phenomena. Such manifestations, including levitation, locutions, and visions of various kinds, have been sensational in the lives of some of the saints. Teresa of Avila and John of the Cross, for example, had these experiences. The Christian tradition has consistently counseled avoiding extraordinary gifts whenever possible because it is difficult to remain humble when you have them. Experience teaches that the more extraordinary the gifts, the harder it is to be detached from them. It is easy to take secret satisfaction in the fact that God is giving you special gifts, especially when they are obvious to others.

I have noticed a significant increase in the number of persons experiencing psychic gifts in recent years. In one year alone, I met six people with out-of-body experiences. While asleep or praying, they experienced leaving their body and moving around the house. One man living in Colorado unwittingly found himself in his old home in Massachusetts. No matter how powerful these parapsychological phenomena may be, we should not allow ourselves to be pulled off center by them or to be distracted from our time of prayer. If we wait patiently the phenomenon will pass. If we are doing Centering Prayer, we should return to the sacred word.

There are actually methods to develop direct control over physiological functions like our breath, heartbeat, and body temperature. I once heard about a young man who had been reading about controlled breathing. Although he knew how to stop breathing, unfortunately he had neglected to read the chapter on how to start breathing again. He never woke up. If you are interested in psychic phenomena, be sure to practice them under an approved master.

Unusual physiological or psychic powers appear to be innate human capacities that can be developed by practicing certain disciplines. But they have nothing to do with holiness or the growth of our relationship to God. To regard them as a sign of great spiritual development is a mistake.

Joseph of Cupertino, a Franciscan friar, was one of the most sensational levitators of all time. He was so much in love with God that at one period in his life whenever he heard the word *God* he would start rising. When he was in church, he would go right up to the ceiling. This was a little distracting for the other brothers in the community and for those who came to worship. One incident that is well authenticated is worth mentioning. The friars were trying to place a huge cross atop a 100-foot steeple on the church. As often happens with levitators, Joseph uttered a loud cry of delight while taking off. He grabbed the cross, which weighed half a ton, flew to the top of the steeple, put it in place and then returned to earth. His superiors took a dim view of his extraordinary behavior and ordered him to desist. There is a certain amount of self in the exercise of any kind of sensational gift, including the most spiritual. When Joseph was ordered to stop levitating, he went into a deep depression. In his case this was clearly the night of the spirit. And that is what made him a saint, not his flying. Airplanes and birds can do that.

In ways often undiscernible to human beings, God allows parapsychological phenomena to operate, or not to operate, as he sees fit.

In the fourteenth century Vincent Ferrer, one of the great wonder workers of his time, was preaching that the end of the world was at hand. On one occasion a man who was being taken for burial was brought to him. Vincent had been preaching his usual doomsday message, so he took this occasion to warn his listeners that the world was coming to an end soon, and to say that as proof of his warning, he would raise this man from the dead. The dead man stood up. But the world did not come to an end. All prophecy is conditional. God does not commit himself to follow through on His threats. He reserves the right to change His mind if people respond by amending their lives. The prophet often gets left holding the bag; it's one of his occupational hazards.

The fourth thing contemplation is not is mystical phenomena. By mystical phenomena, I mean bodily ecstasy, external and internal visions, external words, words spoken in the imagination and words impressed upon one's spirit when any of these are the work of God's special grace in the soul. John of the Cross in *The Ascent to Mt. Carmel* considers every conceivable spiritual phenomenon from the most exterior to the most interior and commands his disciples to reject them all. Pure faith, according to him, is the proximate means of union with God.

External visions and voices can be misunderstood. Even saints have misunderstood what God has said to them. Divine communications of an intelligible kind have to be filtered through the human psyche and one's cultural conditioning. In those who are led by this path, such communications are probably authentic eighty per cent of the time but inauthentic the other twenty per cent. Since one can never tell which percentage group a particular communication belongs to, if one follows these communications without discretion, one can get into all kinds of trouble. There is no guarantee that any particular communication to an individual is actually coming from God. Even if it is, it is almost certain to be distorted by one's imagination, preconceived ideas or emotional programming, any one of which can modify or subtly change the communication. The story of a saint who was promised by God that she would die a martyr's death is a classical example. She did indeed die a holy death, but in bed. As she lay dying, she was tempted to think, "Is God faithful to his promise?" Of course He is faithful to His promise. But he doesn't guarantee that we understand Him correctly when He communicates on the level of the imagination or the reason. God meant that she would die with the same degree of love as a martyr of blood. Her martyrdom of conscience was the equivalent in His eyes to the martyrdom of blood. God does not bind Himself to the literal interpretation of His messages. If we take literally what is said, even when what we understand to be a voice from Heaven orders us to do so, we stand a good chance of deceiving ourselves. If we could just return to the sacred word, we would save ourselves so much trouble.

All the sacraments are greater than any vision. This is not to say that visions may not have a purpose in our lives, but as John of the Cross teaches, a genuine communication from God accomplishes its purpose instantly. Reflecting on it does not make it any better—but often distorts it—by losing its original clarity. This does not prevent one from mentioning it to a prudent spiritual director to make sure one does not take it too seriously or too lightly. If one is told by God to do something, it is especially important not to do anything without first discerning the matter carefully with an experienced spiritual director.

Much more reliable than visions, locutions, or the process of reasoning are the inner impressions that the Spirit suggests in prayer and to which we feel gently but consistently inclined. The more important the event, the more we have to listen to sound reason and consult a spiritual director. God's will is not always easy to discern; we have to observe all the indications of it and then decide. In the struggle for certitude however, we perceive more clearly what the obstacles are in ourselves to recognizing His will.

We come now to the question of mystical graces. They are the hardest to distinguish because they are so intertwined with our psyche. By mystical graces I mean the inflowing of God's presence into our faculties or the radiance of His presence when it spontaneously overtakes us. The levels of mystical prayer have been well described by Teresa of Avila and John of the Cross. They include infused recollection, the prayer of quiet, the prayer of union, the prayer of full union, and finally, the transforming union. I prefer to use the terms *contemplation* and *mysticism* to mean the same thing and to distinguish mystical graces from the essence of mystical prayer. Is it possible to be a contemplative and attain the transforming union without going through the experience of the mystical graces just described?

This is a question that has puzzled me over the years because contemplation as the experience of the inflow of God's grace has generally been considered a necessary sign of the gift of contemplative prayer. However, I continue to meet people who are very advanced in the spiritual journey who insist that they have never had the grace of contemplative prayer as a felt experience of God. Having spent thirty or forty years in a monastery or convent in order to become contemplatives, some of these people are tempted at times to feel that their lives have been a gigantic failure. They wind up in their sixties or seventies believing that since they never had such an experience, they must have done something wrong. Here are people who have given their whole lives to the service of Christ and yet have no internal assurance of having had even the least mystical grace.

The first few times I listened to these people's experiences, I thought perhaps they had never been properly instructed in contemplative prayer, or maybe they had received touches of it in their early religious life and either forgot about it or got used to it. But I have since changed my mind. I am convinced that it is a mistake to identify the *experience* of contemplative prayer with contemplative prayer itself, which transcends any impression of God's radiating or inflowing presence. I was pleased to see my experience articulated by Ruth Burroughs, a Carmelite nun who has lived her religious life without any experiential awareness of the radiance of God's presence. In *Guidelines to Mystical Prayer,* she proposes the distinction of *lights on* mysticism and *lights off* mysticism. This would explain how, for many persons, their whole contemplative journey is completely hidden from them until their final transformation. This Carmelite nun had two friends, one with a very exuberant mystical life, in an active order and the other a nun in her own cloistered convent who had never enjoyed any conscious experience of contemplative prayer although she had faithfully practiced the discipline of contemplative prayer for forty years. Both wound up in transforming union. Ruth Burroughs extrapolates that mystical grace may be a charism that certain mystics are given in order to explain the spiritual path to others. In any case, her hypothesis rests on the assumption that the essence of mysticism is the path of pure faith. Pure faith, according to John of the Cross, is a ray of darkness to the soul. There is no faculty that can perceive it. One can be having this "experience" on the deepest level beyond the power of any faculty to perceive it. One can only remark its presence by its fruits in one's life. God can be beaming that ray of darkness into someone who is faithful to prayer without his or her being conscious of it at all. In any case, the people in my experience who have the most exuberant mystical lives are married or in the active ministry. Less than five per cent of cloistered contemplatives that I know have the mystical experiences that Teresa or John of the Cross describe. They generally experience the night of sense, and a few experience the night of spirit. Their consolations are few and far between. Those who are in the world doubtless need more help in order to survive. Perhaps God does not help cloistered folks in the same way because He has decided that they have enough support from the structures of their enclosed lifestyle.

What is the essence of contemplative prayer? The way of pure faith. Nothing else. You do not have to feel it, but you have to practice it.

2

DIMENSIONS OF
CONTEMPLATIVE PRAYER

■

CONTEMPLATIVE PRAYER IS THE WORLD in which God can do anything. To move into that realm is the greatest adventure. It is to be open to the Infinite and hence to infinite possibilities. Our private, self-made worlds come to an end; a new world appears within and around us and the impossible becomes an everyday experience. Yet the world that prayer reveals is barely noticeable in the ordinary course of events.

Christian life and growth are founded on faith in our own basic goodness, in the being that God has given us with its transcendent potential. This gift of being is our true Self. Through our consent by faith, Christ is born in us and He and our true Self become one. Our awakening to the presence and action of the Spirit is the unfolding of Christ's resurrection in us.

All true prayer is based on the conviction of the presence of the Spirit in us and of his unfailing and continual inspiration. Every prayer in this sense is prayer in the Spirit. Still, it seems more accurate to reserve the term *prayer in the Spirit,* for that prayer in which the inspiration of the Spirit is given directly to our spirit without the intermediary of our own reflections or acts of will. In other words, the Spirit prays in us and we consent. The traditional term for this kind of prayer is *contemplation.*

We should distinguish *contemplative prayer* from *contemplative life.* The former is an experience or series of experiences leading to the abiding state of union with God. The term *contemplative life* should be reserved for the abiding state of divine union itself, in which one is moved both in prayer and in action by the Spirit.

The root of prayer is interior silence. We may think of prayer as thoughts or feelings expressed in words, but this is only one of its forms. "Prayer," according to Evagrius, "is the laying aside of thoughts".[1] This definition presupposes that there *are* thoughts. Contemplative prayer is not so much the absence of thoughts as detachment from them. It is the opening of mind and heart, body and emotions—our whole being—to God, the Ultimate Mystery, beyond words, thoughts and emotions—beyond, in other words, the psychological content of the present moment. We do not deny or repress what is in our consciousness. We simply accept the fact of whatever is there and go beyond it, not by effort, but by letting go of whatever is there.

According to the Baltimore catechism, "Prayer is the raising of the mind and heart to God." In using this ancient formula it is important to keep in mind that it is not *we* who do the lifting. In every kind of prayer the raising of the mind and heart to God can be the work only of the Spirit. In prayer inspired by the Spirit we let ourselves flow with the lifting movement and drop all reflection. Reflection is an important preliminary to prayer, but it is not prayer. Prayer is not only the offering of interior acts to God: it is the offering of ourselves, of who and what we are.

The action of the Spirit might be compared to a skillful nurse teaching the adopted children of a wealthy household how to behave in their new home. Like waifs pulled in off the street and seated at the banquet table in the elegant dining hall, we require a lot of time to learn and practice the proper table manners. Because of our earthy background, we tend to put our muddy feet on the table, break the chinaware and spill the soup in our laps. To assimilate the values of our new home, profound changes in our attitudes and behavioral patterns are required. For this reason we may experience our nurse as constraining in the beginning and heavy on the "don'ts". And yet she always seems to be encouraging in the midst of correction; never condemnatory, never judgmental, always inviting us to amendment of life. The practice of contemplative prayer is an education imparted by the Spirit.

Our participation in this educational process is what Christian tradition calls self-denial. Jesus said, "Unless you deny your inmost self and take up the cross, you cannot be my disciple." (Mark 8:34) Denial of our *inmost* self includes detachment from the habitual functioning of our intellect and will, which are out inmost faculties. This may require letting go not only of ordinary thoughts during prayer, but also of our most devout reflections and aspirations insofar as we treat them as indispensable means of going to God.

The nature of the human mind is to simplify what it thinks about. Thus a single thought can sum up an immense wealth of reflection. The thought itself becomes a *presence,* an act of attention rather than of understanding. If we apply this principle to the person of Jesus, we can see that this kind of attention does not in any way exclude his humanity. Our attention is simply given to the *presence* of Jesus, the divine-human being, without adverting to any particular detail of his person.

Contemplative prayer is part of a dynamic process that evolves through personal relationship rather than by strategy. At the same time a reasonable amount of organization in one's prayer and lifestyle advances the process, just as wholesome food and exercise help youngsters grow to physical maturity.

One of the first effects of contemplative prayer is the release of the energies of the unconscious. This process gives rise to two different psychological states: the experience of personal development in the form of spiritual consolation, charismatic gifts or psychic powers; and the experience of human weakness through humiliating self-knowledge. Self-knowledge is the traditional term for the coming to consciousness of the dark side of one's personality. The release of these two kinds of unconscious energies needs to be safeguarded by well-established habits of dedication to God and concern for others. Otherwise, if one enjoys some form of spiritual consolation or development one may inflate with pride; or if one feels crushed by the realization of one's spiritual impoverishment, one may collapse into discouragement or even despair. The cultivation of habits of dedication to God and of service to others is the indispensable means of stabilizing the mind in the face of emotionally charged thoughts, whether of self-exaltation or of self-depreciation.

Dedication to God is developed by commitment to one's spiritual practices for God's sake. Service to others is the outgoing movement of the heart prompted by compassion. It neutralizes the deep-rooted tendency to become preoccupied with our own spiritual journey and how we are doing. The habit of service to others is developed by trying to please God in what we do and by exercising compassion for others, beginning with those with whom we live. To accept everyone unconditionally is to fulfill the commandment to "love your neighbor as yourself". (Mark 12:31) It is a practical way of bearing one another's burdens. (Galatians 6:2). Refusing to judge even in the face of persecution is to fulfill the commandment to love one another "as I have loved you" (John 13:34) and to lay down one's life for one's friends. (John 15:13)

Habits of dedication to God and service to others form the two sides of a channel through which the energies of the unconscious can be released without submerging the psyche in the floodwaters of chaotic emotions. On the contrary, when these energies flow in orderly fashion between the banks of dedication and service, they will raise us to higher levels of spiritual perception, understanding, and selfless love.

These two stabilizing dispositions prepare the nervous system and body to receive the purifying and sanctifying light of the Spirit. They enable us to discern thoughts and emotions as they arise before they reach the stage of attachment or quasi-compulsion. As independence from the thralldom of habitual thoughts and desires grows, we are able to enter into contemplative prayer with a quiet mind.

Detachment is the goal of self-denial. It is the nonpossessive attitude toward all of reality, the disposition that strikes at the root of the false self system. The false self is a monumental illusion, a load of habitual thinking patterns and emotional routines that are stored in the brain and nervous system. Like programs in a computer, they tend to reactivate every time a particular life situation pushes the appropriate button. The false self even insinuates that its subtle purposes are religiously motivated. Genuine religious attitudes come from God, not from the false self. By means of contemplative prayer the Spirit heals the roots of self-centeredness and becomes the source of our conscious activity. To act spontaneously under the Spirit's influence rather than under the influence of the false self, the emotional programming of the past has to be erased and replaced. *The practice of virtue* is the traditional term for erasing the old programs and writing new programs based on the values of the Gospel.

Jesus in His divinity is the source of contemplation. When the presence of the Divine is experienced as overwhelming, we are inwardly compelled to contemplate. Such was the situation of the apostles on Mount Tabor when they witnessed the glory of God shining through the humanity of Jesus. They fell on their faces. Our experiences of God, however, are not God as He is in Himself. God as He is in Himself cannot be experienced empirically, conceptually or spiritually. He is beyond experiences of any kind. This does not mean that He is not *in* sacred experiences, but that He *transcends* them. To put this insight in another way, He leads us by means of sacred experiences to the experience of emptiness. Anything that we perceive of God can only be a radiance of His presence and not God as He is Himself. When the divine light strikes the human mind, it breaks down into many aspects juast as a ray of ordinary light, when it strikes a prism, breaks down into the varied colors of the spectrum. There is nothing wrong with distinguishing different aspects of the Ultimate Mystery, but it would be a mistake to identify them with the inaccessible Light. The attraction to let go of spiritual consolation in order to let God act with complete freedom is the persistent attraction of the Spirit. The more one lets go, the stronger the presence of the Spirit becomes. The Ultimate Mystery becomes the Ultimate Presence.

The Spirit speaks to our conscience through scripture and through the events of daily life. Reflection on these two sources of personal encounter and the dismantling of the emotional programming of the past prepare the psyche to listen at more refined levels of attention. The Spirit then begins to address our conscience from that deep source within us which is our true Self. This is contemplation properly so-called.

This pattern is exemplified in the Transfiguration. Jesus took with him the three disciples who were best prepared to receive the grace of contemplation; that is, the ones who had made the most headway in changing their hearts. God approached them through their senses by means of the vision on the mountain. At first they were overawed and delighted. Peter wanted to remain there forever. Suddenly a cloud covered them, hiding the vision and leaving their senses empty and quiet, yet attentive and alert. The gesture of falling on their faces accurately expressed their state of mind. It was a posture of adoration, gratitude, and love all rolled into one. The voice from heaven awakened their consciousness to the presence of the Spirit, who had always been speaking within them, but whom until then they had never been able to hear. Their interior emptiness was filled with the luminous presence of the divine. At Jesus' touch they returned to their ordinary perceptions and saw him as he was before but with the transformed consciousness of faith. They no longer saw him as a mere human being. Their receptive and active faculties had been unified by the Spirit; the interior and exterior word of God had become one. For those who have attained this consciousness, daily life is a continual and increasing revelation of God. The words they hear in scripture and in the liturgy confirm what they have learned through prayer that is contemplation.

3

THE HISTORY OF CONTEMPLATIVE PRAYER IN THE CHRISTIAN TRADITION

■

A POSITIVE ATTITUDE toward contemplation characterized the first fifteen centuries of the Christian era. Unfortunately, a negative attitude has prevailed from the sixteenth century onward. To understand the situation in which we find our churches today in regard to religious experience, an overview of the history of contemplative prayer may prove helpful.

The word *contemplation* is an ambiguous term because over the centuries it has acquired several different meanings. To emphasize the experiential knowledge of God, the Greek Bible used the word *gnosis* to translate the Hebrew *da'ath,* a much stronger term that implies an intimate kind of knowledge involving the whole person, not just the mind.

St. Paul used the word *gnosis* in his Epistles to refer to the knowledge of God proper to those who love Him. He constantly asked for this intimate knowledge for his disciples and prayed for it as if it were an indispensable element for the full development of Christian life.

The Greek Fathers, especially Clement of Alexandria, Origen and Gregory of Nyssa, borrowed from the Neoplatonists the term *theoria*. This originally meant the intellectual vision of truth, which the Greek philosophers regarded as the supreme activity of the person of wisdom. To this technical term the Fathers added the meaning of the Hebrew *da'ath,* that is, the kind of experiential knowledge that comes through love. It was with this expanded understanding of the term that *theoria* was translated into the Latin *contemplatio* and handed down to us in the Christian tradition.

This tradition was summed up by Gregory the Great at the end of the Sixth Century when he described contemplation as the knowledge of God that is impregnated with love. For Gregory, contemplation is the fruit of reflection on the word of God in scripture and at the same time a gift of God. It is a *resting* in God. In this resting or stillness the mind and heart are not actively seeking Him but are beginning to experience, to taste, what they have been seeking. This places them in a

20

state of tranquility and profound interior peace. This state is not the suspension of all action, but the mingling of a few simple acts of will to sustain one's attention to God with the loving experience of God's presence.

This meaning of contemplation as the knowledge of God based on the intimate experience of His presence remained the same until the end of the Middle Ages. Ascetical disciplines were always directed toward contemplation as the proper goal of every spiritual practice.

The method of prayer proposed for lay persons and monastics alike in the first Christian centuries was called *lectio divina,* literally, "divine reading", a practice that involved reading scripture, or more exactly, listening to it. Monastics would repeat the words of the sacred text with their lips so that the body itself entered into the process. They sought to cultivate through *lectio divina* the capacity to listen at ever deeper levels of inward attention. Prayer was their response to the God to whom they were listening in scripture and giving praise in the liturgy.

The reflective part, pondering upon the words of the sacred text, was called *meditatio,* "meditation". The spontaneous movement of the will in response to these reflections was called *oratio,* "affective prayer". As these reflections and acts of will simplified, one moved on to a state of resting in the presence of God, and that is what was meant by *contemplatio,* "contemplation".

These three acts—discursive meditation, affective prayer and contemplation—might all take place during the same period of prayer. They were interwoven one into the other. Like the angels ascending and descending on Jacob's ladder, one's attention was expected to go up and down the ladder of consciousness. Sometimes one would praise the Lord with one's lips, sometimes with one's thoughts, sometimes with acts of will, and sometimes with the rapt attention of contemplation. Contemplation was regarded as the normal development of listening to the word of God. The approach to God was not compartmentalized into discursive meditation, affective prayer and contemplation. The term *mental prayer,* with its distinct categories, did not exist in Christian tradition prior to the Sixteenth Century.

Around the Twelfth Century a marked development in religious thought took place. The great schools of theology were founded. It was the birth of precise analysis in regard to concepts, division into genera and species, and definitions and classifications. This growing capacity for analysis was a significant development of the human mind. Unfortunately this passion for analysis in theology was later to be transferred to the practice of prayer and bring to an end the simple, spontaneous prayer of the Middle Ages based on *lectio divina* with its opening to contemplation. Spiritual masters of the Twelfth Century, like Bernard of Clairvaux, Hugh and Richard of St. Victor, and William of St. Thierry, were developing a theological understanding of prayer and contemplation. In the Thirteenth Century methods of meditation based on their teaching were popularized by the Franciscans.

During the Fourteenth and Fifteenth Centuries, the Black Death and the Hundred Years' War decimated cities, towns and religious communities while nominalism and the Great Schism brought on a general decadence in morals and spirituality. A movement of renewal, called Devotio Moderna, arose in the Low Countries around 1380 and spread to Italy, France and Spain in response to the widespread need for reform. In an age when institutions and structures of all kinds were crumbling, the movement of Devotio Moderna sought to utilize the moral power issuing from prayer as a means of self-discipline. By the end of the Fifteenth Century, methods of mental prayer, properly so-called, were elaborated, becoming more and more complicated and systematized as time went on. But even while this proliferation of systematic methods of prayer was taking place, contemplation was still presented as the ultimate goal of spiritual practice.

As the Sixteenth Century progressed, mental prayer came to be divided into discursive meditation if thoughts predominated; affective prayer if the emphasis was on acts of the will; and contemplation if graces infused by God were predominant. Discursive meditation, affective prayer, and contemplation were no longer different acts found in a single period of prayer, but distinct forms of prayer, each with its own proper aim, method and purpose. This division of the development of prayer into compartmentalized units entirely separate from one another helped to further the incorrect notion that contemplation was an extraordinary grace reserved to the few. The possibility of prayer opening out into contemplation tended to be regarded as very unlikely. The organic development of prayer toward contemplation did not fit into the approved categories and was therefore discouraged.

At the same time that the living tradition of Chinese contemplation was diminishing, the Renaissance brought new challenges for the spiritual life. No longer were the social milieu and religious institutions supportive of the individual. There was the need to reconquer the world for Christ in the face of the pagan elements that were taking over Christendom. It was not surprising that new forms of prayer should appear that were ordered to an apostolic ministry. The new emphasis on apostolic life required a transformation of the forms of spirituality hitherto transmitted by monastics and mendicants. The genius and contemplative experience of Ignatius of Loyola led him to channel the contemplative tradition, which was in danger of being lost, into a form appropriate to the new age.

The *Spiritual Exercises of Saint Ignatius,* composed between 1522 and 1526, is extremely important in order to understand the present state of spirituality in the Roman Catholic Church. Three methods of prayer are proposed in the *Spiritual Exercises*. The discursive meditations prescribed for the first week are made according to the method of the three powers (memory, intellect and will.) The memory is to recall the point chosen beforehand as the subject of the discursive meditation. The intellect is to reflect on the lessons one wants to draw from that point. The will is to make resolutions based on that point in order to put the lessons into practice. Thus, one is led to reformation of life.

The word *contemplation,* as it is used in the *Spiritual Exercises,* has a meaning different from the traditional one. It consists of gazing upon a concrete object of the imagination: seeing the persons in the Gospel as if they were present, hearing what they are saying, relating and responding to their words and actions. This method, prescribed for the second week, is aimed at developing affective prayer.

The third method of prayer in the *Spiritual Exercises* is called the application of the five senses. It consists of successively applying in spirit the five senses to the subject of the meditation. This method is designed to dispose beginners to contemplation in the traditional sense of the term and to develop the spiritual senses in those who are already advanced in prayer.

Thus, Ignatius did not propose only one method of prayer. The unfortunate tendency to reduce the *Spiritual Exercises* to a method of discursive meditation seems to stem from the Jesuits themselves. In 1574 Everard Mercurian, the Father General of the Jesuits, in a directive to the Spanish province of the Society, forbade the practice of affective prayer and the application of the five senses. This prohibition was repeated in 1578. The spiritual life of a significant portion of the Society of Jesus was thus limited to a single method of prayer, namely, discursive meditation according to the three powers. The predominantly intellectual character of this meditation continued to grow in importance throughout the Society during the course of the eighteenth and nineteenth centuries. Most manuals of spirituality until well into this century limited instruction to schemas of discursive meditation.

To comprehend the impact of this development on the recent history of Roman Catholic spirituality, we should keep in mind the pervasive influence that the Jesuits exercised as the outstanding representatives of the Counter-Reformation. Many religious congregations founded in the centuries following this period adopted the Constitutions of the Society of Jesus. They received at the same time the spirituality taught and practiced by the Society. Hence they also received the limitations imposed not by Ignatius, but by his less enlightened successors.

Ignatius wished to provide a spiritual formation that was an appropriate antidote to the new secular and individualist spirit of the Renaissance and a form of contemplative prayer adapted to the apostolic needs of his time. The *Spiritual Exercises* were designed to form contemplatives in action. Considering the immense influence of the Society for good, if its members had been allowed to follow the *Spiritual Exercises* according to Ignatius' original intent, or if they had given more prominence to their own contemplative masters like Fathers Lallemant, Surin, Grou and de Caussade, the present state of spirituality among Roman Catholics might be quite different.

Other events contributed to the hesitation of Roman Catholic authorities to encourage contemplative prayer. One of these was the controversy regarding Quietism, a set of spiritual teachings condemned in 1687 as a species of false mysticism by Innocent XII. The condemned teachings were ingenious. They consisted of making once and for all an act of love for God by which one gave oneself entirely to Him with the intention never to recall this surrender. As long as one never withdrew the intention to belong entirely to God, divine union was assured and no further need for effort either in prayer or outside of it was required. The important distinction between making a one-time intention (however generous) and establishing it as a permanent disposition seems to have passed unnoticed.

A milder form of this doctrine flourished in France in the latter part of the seventeenth century and became known as Semi-Quietism. Bishop Boussuet, chaplain to the court of Louis XIV, was one of the chief enemies of this attenuated form of Quietism and succeeded in having it condemned in France. How much he exaggerated the teaching is difficult to ascertain. In any case, the controversy brought traditional mysticism into disrepute. From then on, reading about mysticism was frowned upon in seminaries and religious communities. According to Henri Bremond in his book *The Literary History of Religious Thought in France,* no mystical writing of any significance occurred during the next several hundred years. The mystical writers of the past were ignored. Even passages from John of the Cross were thought to be suggestive of Quietism, forcing his editors to tone down or expunge certain statements lest they be misunderstood and condemned. The unexpurgated text of his writings appeared only in our own century, four hundred years after its writing.

A further set-back for Christian spirituality was the heresy of Jansenism, which gained momentum during the seventeenth century. Although it, too, was eventually condemned, it left behind a pervasive anti-human attitude that perdured throughout the nineteenth century and into our own time. Jansenism questions the universality of Jesus' saving action as well as the intrinsic goodness of human nature. The pessimistic form of piety which it fostered spread with the emigrés from the French Revolution to English-speaking regions including Ireland and the United States. Since it is largely from French and Irish stock that priests and religious in this country have come, Jansenistic narrowness, together with its distorted asceticism, has deeply affected the psychological climate of our seminaries and religious orders. Priests and religious are still shaking off the last remnants of the negative attitudes that they absorbed in the course of their ascetical formation.

Another unhealthy trend in the modern Church was the excessive emphasis on private devotions, apparitions, and private revelations. This led to the devaluation of the liturgy together with the communitarian values and sense of transcendent mystery which good liturgy engenders. The popular mind continued to regard contemplatives as saints, wonder workers, or at the very least, exceptional people. The true nature of contemplation remained obscure or confused with phenomena such as levitation, locutions, stigmata, and visions, which are strictly accidental to it.

During the nineteenth century there were many saints, but few spoke or wrote about contemplative prayer. There was a renewal of spirituality in Eastern Orthodoxy, but the mainstream of Roman Catholic development was legalistic in character, with a kind of nostalgia for the Middle Ages and for the political influence that the Church exercised at that time.

Abbot Cuthbert Butler sums up the generally accepted ascentical teaching during the Eighteenth and Nineteenth Centuries in his book *Western Mysticism.*

> Except for very unusual vocations, the normal prayer for everyone including contemplative monks and nuns, bishops, priests and laypersons was systematic meditation following a fixed method, which could be one of four: the meditation according to the three powers as laid down in the *Spiritual Exercises of Saint Ignatius,* the method of St. Alphonsus (which was a slight reworking of the *Spiritual Exercises*), the method described by St. Francis de Sales in *An Introduction to the Devout Life,* or the method of St. Sulpice.

These are all methods of discursive meditation. Contemplation was identified with extraordinary phenomena, and was regarded as both miraculous and dangerous, to be admired from a safe distance by the average layperson, priest or religious.

The final nail hammered into the coffin of the traditional teaching was that it would be arrogant to aspire to contemplative prayer. Novices and seminarians were thus presented with a highly truncated view of the spiritual life, one that did not accord with scripture, tradition and the normal experience of growth in prayer. If one attempts to persevere in discursive meditation after the Holy Spirit has called one beyond it, as the Spirit ordinarily does, one is bound to wind up in a state of utter frustration. It is normal for the mind to move through many reflections on the same theme to a single comprehensive view of the whole, then to rest with a simple gaze upon the truth. As devout people moved spontaneously into this development in their prayer, they were up against this negative attitude toward contemplation. They hesitated to go beyond discursive meditation or affective prayer because of the warnings they had been given about the dangers of contemplation. In the end they either gave up mental prayer altogether as something for which they were evidently unsuited, or, through the mercy of God, found some way of persevering in spite of what seemed like insurmountable obstacles.

In any case, the post-Reformation teaching opposed to contemplation was the direct opposite of the earlier tradition. That tradition, taught uninterruptedly for the first fifteen centuries, held that contemplation is the normal evolution of a genuine spiritual life and hence is open to all Christians. These historical factors may help to explain how the traditional spirituality of the West came to be lost in recent centuries and why Vatican II had to address itself to the acute problem of spiritual renewal.

There are two reasons that contemplative prayer is receiving renewed attention in our time. One is that historical and theological studies have rediscovered the integral teaching of John of the Cross and other masters of the spiritual life. The other is the post-World War II challenge from the East. Methods of meditation similar to contemplative prayer in the Christian tradition have proliferated, produced good results, and received much publicity. It is important, according to the *Declaration on the Relationship of the Church to Non-Christian Religions* (Vatican II), to appreciate the values that are present in the teachings of the other great religions of the world. The spiritual disciplines of the East possess a highly developed psychological wisdom. Christian leaders and teachers need to know something about them in order to meet people where they are today. Many serious seekers of truth study the Eastern religions, take courses in them in college or graduate school, and practice forms of meditation inspired and taught by Eastern masters.

The revival of mystical theology in the Roman Catholic Church began with the publication of *The Degrees of the Spiritual Life* by Abbé Saudreau in 1896. He based his research on the teaching of John of the Cross. Subsequent studies have confirmed the wisdom of his choice. John of the Cross teaches that contemplation begins with what he calls the night of sense. This is a no-man's land between one's own activity and the direct inspiration of the Holy Spirit in which it becomes almost impossible to think thoughts that stir up sensible devotion. This is a common experience among those who have practiced discursive meditation over an extended period of time. One reaches the point where there is nothing new to be thought, said, or felt. If one has no subsequent direction in the life of prayer, one will not know what to do except perhaps to get up and walk out. The night of sense is a spiritual growing-up process similar to the transition from childhood to adolescence in chronological life. The emotionalism and sentimentality of childhood are beginning to be laid aside in favor of a more mature relationship with God. In the meantime, because God no longer gives help to the senses or to the reason, these faculties seem to be useless. One is more and more convinced that one can no longer pray at all.

John of the Cross says that all one has to do in this state is to remain at peace, not try to think, and to abide before God with faith in His presence, continually turning to Him as if opening one's eyes to look upon a loved one.

In a remarkable passage in *The Living Flame of Love*[1] in which John of the Cross describes in detail the transition from sensible devotion to spiritual intimacy with

1. Stanza III, 26–59.

God, he says that when one cannot reason discursively or make acts of the will with any satisfaction during prayer, one should give the situation a quiet welcome. One will then begin to feel peace, tranquillity, and strength because God is now feeding the soul directly, giving His grace to the will alone and attracting it mysteriously to Himself. People in this state have great anxiety about whether they are going backward. They think that all the good things they experienced in the first years of their conversion are coming to an end, and if they are asked how their prayer life is, they will throw up their hands in despair. Actually, if questioned further, they reveal that they have a great desire to find some way to pray and they like to be alone with God even though they can't enjoy Him. Thus, it is evident that there is a secret attraction present at a deep level of their psyche. This is the infused element of contemplative prayer. Divine love is the infused element. If it is given a quiet rest, it will grow from a spark into a living flame of love.

John of the Cross says that those who give themselves to God enter very quickly into the night of sense. This interior desert is the beginning of contemplative prayer even though they are not aware of it. The relationship between one's own activity and the infusion of grace is so delicate that one does not usually perceive it right away. Since the night of sense occurs frequently, it is important that spiritual directors be available to help Christians to appreciate and welcome this development and to recognize it by the signs suggested by John of the Cross. If one gets through this transition, one is on the way to becoming a very dedicated and effective Christian, one who is wholly under the guidance of the gifts of the Spirit.

How quickly is "very quickly" in the teaching of John of the Cross? Is it a few years, a few months, a few weeks? He doesn't say. But the idea that one has to undergo years of superhuman trials, be walled up behind convent walls or kill oneself with various ascetical practices before one can aspire to contemplation is a Jansenistic attitude or, at the very least, an inadequate presentation of the Christian tradition. On the contrary, the sooner contemplative prayer can be experienced, the sooner one will perceive the direction toward which the spiritual journey is tending. From that intuition will come the motivation to make all the sacrifices required to persevere in the journey.

As the introduction to this book indicates, the questions of participants in seminars on the practice of Centering Prayer are included in the text where appropriate. The following paragraph forms the first such question. Others appear throughout the text wherever they are thought to be helpful to the reader.

> *The Cloud of Unknowing* has a lot to say about being ready for this movement into contemplative prayer. It presupposes that not everyone is called to this. It gives signs for telling whether you are called or not. Yet today it seems to be offered to everyone, not only by teachers of Centering Prayer, but also by teachers of Eastern meditation. It is as if it is open to all.

The idea of laypeople pursuing the spiritual path is not something new. It just hasn't been popular in the past thousand years. In the spiritual traditions of the world religions, both East and West, there has been a tendency to isolate seekers, put them in special places, and juxtapose them with people leading family, professional, or business lives in the world. But this distinction is beginning to change. The sages of India, for example, have begun to share their secrets with ordinary folks. In times past one normally had to go into the forest to find a teacher. In the United States and Western Europe, we can now find outstanding teachers of different Eastern spiritual traditions offering advanced teachings to almost anyone who comes along. Lesser expressions of these traditions, unfortunately, are also available. In any case, a movement in the Eastern religions to make esoteric disciplines more available to persons living ordinary lives in the world is occurring.

With regards to the Christian tradition, Origen, a fourth-century exponent of the theological school of Alexandria, considered the Christian community in the world to be the proper place of ascesis. It was only through Anthony's example and Athanasius's report of it that the practice of leaving the world became the standard way to pursue the Christian path to divine union. Anthony had no intention of making this the only way to achieve it, but when mass movements occur, popularizations also take place, and these may fossilize or even caricature a movement. A new wave of spiritual renewal has to arise before the necessary distinctions can again be made. This may take a long time when movements have become institutionalized. The essence of monastic life is not its structures but its interior practice, and the heart of interior practice is contemplative prayer.

In *The Epistle of Privy Counseling,* written toward the end of his life, the author of *The Cloud of Unknowing* acknowledges that the call to contemplative prayer is more common than he had originally thought. In practice I think we can teach people to proceed in tandem toward contemplative prayer, that is, to read and reflect on the word of God in scripture, make aspirations inspired by these reflections, and then to rest in the presence of God. This is how *lectio divina* was practiced in the monasteries of the Middle Ages. The method of Centering Prayer emphasizes the final phase of *lectio* because it is the phase that has been most neglected in recent times.

My conviction is that if people are never exposed to some kind of nonconceptual prayer, it may never develop at all because of the overly intellectual bias of Western culture and the anticontemplative trend of Christian teaching in recent centuries. Moreover, some experiential taste of interior silence is a great help in understanding what contemplative prayer is all about. Recent ascetical teaching has been extremely cautious. There has been a strong tendency to assume that contemplative prayer was reserved for cloistered religious.

Contemplative prayer raises an important question: Is there something that we can do to prepare ourselves for the gift of contemplation instead of waiting for God to do everything? My acquaintance with Eastern methods of meditation has convinced me that there is. There are ways of calming the mind in the spiritual disciplines of both East and West that can help to lay the groundwork for contemplative prayer.

What is the difference between *lectio divina* and Centering Prayer?

Lectio is a comprehensive method of communing with God which begins with the reading of a scripture passage. Reflection on the text moves easily into spontaneous prayer (talking to God about what you have read), and finally into resting in the presence of God. Centering Prayer is a way of moving from the first three phases of *lectio* to the final one of resting in God.

> St. John of the Cross and St. Teresa advised that one should only discontinue discursive meditation when God takes away one's ability to practice it. How does Centering Prayer fit in with that tradition?

A certain amount of reflection on the truths of faith to develop basic convictions, which is the work of discursive meditation, is a necessary basis for contemplation. To the objection that we might be introducing contemplative prayer too soon, my answer is that our contemporaries in the Western world have a special problem with discursive meditation because of the ingrained inclination to analyze things beyond all measure, a mind-set that has developed out of the Cartesian-Newtonian world view and that has led to the repression of our intuitive faculties. This conceptual hangup of modern Western society impedes the spontaneous movement from reflection to spontaneous prayer and from spontaneous prayer to interior silence (wonder and admiration). I think you could do all three in tandem and still be in the tradition of *lectio divina*. If you are practicing *lectio divina,* you don't have to follow any particular order or time schedule. You can follow the inspiration of grace and mull over the text, make particular acts of the will, or move into contemplative prayer at any time. Obviously discursive meditation and affective prayer will predominate in the beginning. But this does not exclude moments of interior silence. If people were encouraged to reflect on scripture and be fully present to the words of the sacred text, and then practice a period of Centering Prayer, they would actually be in the tradition of *lectio*.

> It's much clearer to me now. Centering Prayer sort of compensates for the lack of people's ability in our time to go from *lectio* into contemplation.

Exactly. It is an insight into a contemporary problem and an effort to revive the traditional Christian teaching on contemplative prayer. But more than just a theoretical effort to revive it is required. Some means of exposing people to the actual experience is essential to get beyond the intellectual bias that exists. Having observed this bias in people who are already into contemplative prayer, I'm convinced that it is much deeper in our culture than we think. The rush to the East is a symptom of what is lacking in the West. There is a deep spiritual hunger that is not being satisfied in the West.

I have also noticed that those who have been on an Eastern journey feel much more comfortable about the Christian religion when they hear that a tradition of contemplative prayer exists. Centering Prayer as a preparation for contemplative prayer is not something that someone invented in our day. Rather it is a means of regaining the traditional teaching on contemplative prayer and of making this teaching better known and more available. The only thing that is new is trying to communicate it in a methodical way. One needs help to get into it and follow-up to sustain and grow in it.

One who has already received the grace of contemplative prayer can deepen it by cultivating interior silence in a consistent and orderly fashion. It is with a view to cultivating interior silence that the method of Centering Prayer is offered.

4

FIRST STEPS IN
CENTERING PRAYER

∎

SINCE VATICAN II the Roman Catholic Church has been encouraging Catholics to live the fullness of the Christian life without expecting priests, religious or anyone else to do it for them. That implies creativity as well as responsibility on the part of lay people to come up with structures that will enable them to live the contemplative dimensions of the Gospel without a cloister. A cloister does not resolve all the problems of life. There are pitfalls and traps for monks and nuns as well as for other people.

The monastic journey is a special kind of life with its own set of difficulties. For one thing, it puts human relationships under a microscope. Although the trials are not as big as those outside the monastery, they may be more humiliating. Monastics get upset by trifles and can't even claim a good reason for feeling that way.

Divine union is the goal for all Christians. We have been baptized; we receive the Eucharist; we have all the necessary means of growing as human beings and as children of God. It is a mistake to think that a special state of life is the only way of doing it. The persons I know who are most advanced in prayer are married or engaged in active ministries, running around all day to fulfill their duties.

A couple of years ago, I gave a conference to an assembly of lay organizations. These included marriage-encounter and social action groups, secular institutes, and new communities. My talk was based on monastic spirituality, but instead of saying "monastic," I said "Christian". I was amazed to see how most people identified with this traditional teaching. It corresponded to their own experience. This reinforced my conviction that the spiritual journey is for every Christian who takes the Gospel seriously.

Spiritual disciplines, both East and West, are based on the hypothesis that there is something that we can do to enter upon the journey to divine union once we have been touched by the realization that such a state exists. Centering Prayer is a discipline designed to reduce the obstacles to contemplative prayer. Its modest packaging appeals to the contemporary attraction for how-to methods. It is a way of bringing the procedures to be found in the contemplative teachings of the spiritual masters of the Christian tradition out of the dusty pages of the past into the broad daylight of the present. The popularity of meditative disciplines from the East is proof enough that some such method is essential today. But Centering Prayer is not just a method. It is true prayer at the same time. If you are willing to expand the meaning of contemplative prayer to include methods that prepare for it or lead into it, Centering Prayer can be identified as the first rung on the ladder of contemplative prayer, which rises step by step to union with God.

Centering Prayer is a method of refining one's intuitive faculties so that one can enter more easily into contemplative prayer. It is not the only path to contemplation, but it is a good one. As a method, it is a kind of extract of monastic spirituality. It concentrates the essence of monastic practice into two periods of prayer each day. When taking an antibiotic, you have to maintain the right dosage in order to benefit from the medication. You have to keep up the required number of antibodies in the blood stream to overcome the disease. So, too, you have to keep up a certain level of interior silence in the psyche and nervous system if you want to obtain the benefits of contemplative prayer.

Centering Prayer as a discipline is designed to withdraw our attention from the ordinary flow of our thoughts. We tend to identify ourselves with that flow. But there is a deeper part of ourselves. This prayer opens our awareness to the spiritual level of our being. This level might be compared to a great river on which our memories, images, feelings, inner experiences, and the awareness of outward things are resting. Many people are so identified with the ordinary flow of their thoughts and feelings that they are not aware of the source from which these mental objects are emerging. Like boats or debris floating along the surface of a river, our thoughts and feelings must be resting on something. They are resting on the inner stream of consciousness, which is our participation in God's being. That level is not immediately evident to ordinary consciousness. Since we are not in immediate contact with that level, we have to do something to develop our awareness of it. It is the level of our being that makes us most human. The values that we find there are more delightful than the values that float along the surface of the psyche. We need to refresh ourselves at this deep level every day. Just as we need exercise, food, rest, and sleep, so also we need moments of interior silence because they bring the deepest kind of refreshment.

Faith is opening and surrendering to God. The spiritual journey does not require going anywhere because God is already with us and in us. It is a question of allowing our ordinary thoughts to recede into the background and to float along the river of consciousness without our noticing them, while we direct our attention toward the river on which they are floating. We are like someone sitting on the bank of a river and watching the boats go by. If we stay on the bank, with our attention on the river rather than on the boats, the capacity to disregard thoughts as they go by will develop, and a deeper kind of attention will emerge.

A thought in the context of this method is any perception that appears on the inner screen of consciousness. This could be an emotion, an image, a memory, a plan, a noise from outside, a feeling of peace, or even a spiritual communication. In other words, anything whatsoever that registers on the inner screen of consciousness is a "thought". The method consists of letting go of every thought during the time of prayer, even the most devout thoughts.

To facilitate letting go, take a relatively comfortable position so that you won't be thinking about your body. Avoid positions that might cut off the circulation because then you will think of your discomfort. Choose a place that is relatively quiet in order not to be disturbed by excessive or unexpected noise. If there is no such place in your household, try to find a quiet time when you are least likely to be disturbed. It is a good idea to close your eyes because you tend to think of what you see. By withdrawing the senses from their ordinary activity, you may reach deep rest. A sudden sound or interruption, like the phone ringing, will shake you up. An alarm clock or timer, which is one way to notify yourself when the time is up, should be a quiet one. If the clock is noisy, stuff it under a pillow. Try to avoid outside noises as much as you can. If noises happen anyway, do not be upset. Getting upset is an emotionally charged thought that is likely to shatter whatever interior silence you may have reached. Choose a time for prayer when you are most awake and alert. Early in the morning before the ordinary business of the day begins is a good time.

Once you have picked a suitable time and place and a chair or a posture that is relatively comfortable, and closed your eyes, choose a sacred word that expresses your intention of opening and surrendering to God and introduce it on the level of your imagination. Do not form it with your lips or vocal chords. Let it be a single word of one or two syllables with which you feel at ease. Gently place it in your awareness each time you recognize you are thinking about some other thought.

The sacred word is not a means of going where you want to go. It only directs your intention toward God and thus fosters a favorable atmosphere for the development of the deeper awareness to which your spiritual nature is attracted. Your purpose is not to suppress all thoughts because that is impossible. You will normally have a thought after half a minute of inner silence unless the action of grace is so powerful that you are absorbed in God. Centering Prayer is not a way of turning on the presence of God. Rather, it is a way of saying, "Here I am." The next step is up to God. It is a way of putting yourself at God's disposal; it is He who determines the consequences.

You may be familiar with the gesture of folding your hands together with the fingers pointing upward. This is a symbol of gathering all the faculties together and directing them toward God. The sacred word has exactly the same purpose. It is a pointer, but a mental rather than a material one. The word should be introduced without any force: think it the way you would any thought that might arise spontaneously.

The sacred word, once it is well established, is a way of reducing the ordinary number of casual thoughts and of warding off the more interesting ones that come down the stream of consciousness. It does this not by attacking the thoughts directly but by reaffirming your intention to consent to God's presence and action within. This renewal of the will's consent, as it becomes habitual, creates an atmosphere in which you can more easily disregard the inevitable flow of thoughts.

If you are nervous about doing what may seem like "nothing" for a set period of time, let me remind you that nobody hesitates to go to sleep for six or seven hours every night. But practicing this prayer is not doing nothing. It is a very gentle kind of activity. The will keeps consenting to God by returning to the sacred word, and this is normally enough activity to stay awake and alert.

Twenty to thirty minutes is the minimum amount of time necessary for most people to establish interior silence and to get beyond their superficial thoughts. You may be inclined to remain longer. Experience will teach you what the right time is. At the end of your chosen time span, begin to think your ordinary thoughts again. This may be a good time to converse with God. You may also wish to say some vocal prayer quietly to yourself or to begin planning your day. Give yourself at least two minutes before opening your eyes. Withdrawal from the ordinary use of the exterior and interior senses brings you to a deep spiritual attentiveness, and opening your eyes right away can be jarring.

As your sensitivity to the spiritual dimension of your being develops through the daily practice of this prayer, you may begin to find the awareness of God's presence arising at times in ordinary activity. You may feel called to turn interiorly to God without knowing why. The quality of your spiritual life is developing and enabling you to pick up vibrations from a world you did not previously perceive. Without deliberately thinking of God, you may find that He is often present in the midst of your daily occupations. It is like color added to a black-and-white television screen. The picture remains the same, but it is greatly enhanced by the new diemnsion of the picture that was not previously perceived. It was present but not transmitted because the proper receptive apparatus was missing.

Contemplative prayer is a way of tuning in to a fuller level of reality that is always present and in which we are invited to participate. Some suitable discipline is required to reduce the obstacles to this expanded awareness. One way is to slow down the speed at which our ordinary thoughts come down the stream of consciousness. If this can be done, space begins to appear between the thoughts, enabling an awareness of the reality upon which they are resting.

In this discussion of Centering Prayer, I am not exploring methods that help to calm the body, mind and nervous system, such as breathing, yoga, and jogging. Such methods are fine for relaxation, but what we are concerned with is the faith relationship. This relationship is expressed by taking the time to open oneself to God every day, by taking God seriously enough to make a heavy date with Him, so to speak—a date that one would not think of breaking. Since this kind of prayer doesn't require thinking, we can keep our engagement even when we are sick.

The fundamental disposition in Centering Prayer is opening to God. Christian practice can be summed up by the word *patience.* In the New Testament patience means waiting for God for any length of time, not going away, and not giving in to boredom or discouragement. It is the disposition of the servant in the Gospel who waited even though the master of the house delayed his return till well after midnight. When the master finally came home, he put the servant in charge of his whole household. If you wait, God will manifest Himself. Of course, you may have a long wait.

> I find this practice gets me nowhere. Is it good to try to make the faculties a blank?

Please don't try to make your faculties a blank. There should always be a gentle, spiritual activity present, expressed either by thinking the sacred word or by the simple awareness that you are present to God. The experience of emptiness is the presence of your intention in a very subtle way. You cannot maintain that experience of emptiness unless your intention is at work. It may seem like no work because it is so simple. At the same time, this method of prayer takes time to learn and you need not worry about experiencing what you may interpret as a blank once in a while. This prayer is a way of resting in God. If you notice that you have a blank, that's a thought; merely return to the sacred word.

> What do you do when you realize you have been dozing?

If you doze off, don't give it a second thought. A child in the arms of a parent drops off to sleep occasionally, but the parent isn't disturbed by that so long as the child is happily resting there and opens its eyes once in a while.

> I was surprised by how fast the time went. Was it really twenty minutes?

Yes. When the time goes fast, it is a sign that you were not doing much thinking. I'm not saying it is a sign of good prayer. It is unwise to judge a prayer period on the basis of your psychological experience. Sometimes you may be bombarded with thoughts all during the time of prayer; yet it could be a very useful period of prayer. Your attention might have been much deeper than it seemed. In any case, you cannot make a valid judgment about how things are going on the basis of a single period of prayer. Instead, you must look for the fruit in your ordinary daily life, after a month or two. If you are becoming more patient with others, more at ease with yourself, if you shout less often or less loudly at the children, feel less hurt if the family complains about your cooking—all these are signs that another set of values is beginning to operate in you.

If you have no thoughts at all during Centering Prayer, you then have no awareness of time. Such an experience reveals the relativity of our sense of time. Our period of prayer, however, will not always seem short. Sometimes it will seem very long. The alternation between tranquility and the struggle with thoughts is part of a process, a refining of the intuitive faculties so that they can be attentive to this deeper level in a more and more stable fashion.

If you're drowsy or very tired, do you have fewer thoughts?

In general, yes, so long as you don't start dreaming! In the monastery we get up at 3:00 A.M., and one is often a little groggy at that hour of the morning. This seems to be part of our particular method, to be so tired that we just can't think. After working hard all day, one may have the same experience in the evening. That can be a help as long as you are alert enough to stay awake and not succumb to the pleasure of drowsing. But don't feel bad if you do fall asleep. You may need a little extra rest.

On the other hand, try to pick a time when you are most likely to be alert so you have a fuller experience of Centering Prayer rather than nodding your way through it. If you fall asleep, when you awake continue to center for a few minutes so that you don't feel that your prayer was a complete washout for the day. The kind of activity in which you are engaged in this prayer is so simple that it is easy to fall asleep unless you do the modest action that is required, which is to stay alert. Thinking the sacred word is one way of doing this. Jesus said, "Watch and pray." This is what we are doing in Centering Prayer. Watching is just enough activity to stay alert. Praying is opening to God.

Centering Prayer is not so much an exercise of attention as intention. It may take a while to grasp this distinction. You do not attend to any particular thought content. Rather, you *intend* to go to your inmost being, where you believe God dwells. You are opening to Him by pure faith, not by means of concepts or feelings. It is like knocking gently on a door. You are not pounding on the door with your faculties as if to say, "Open in the name of the law! I demand that you let me in!" You can't force this door. It opens from the other side. What you are saying by means of the sacred word is, "Here I am, waiting." It's a waiting game to the *nth* degree. Nothing flashy is going to happen, or, if it does, you should gently return to the sacred word as if nothing had happened. Even if you have a vision or hear infused words, you should return to the sacred word. This is the essence of the method.

> The mood I was in was one of expectation. Then I found myself thinking about the fact that I was expecting something to happen.

Have no expectation in this prayer. It's an exercise of effortlessness, of letting go. To *try* is a thought. That's why I say: "Return to the sacred word as easily as possible"; or, "gently place the sacred word in your awareness." To struggle is to want to achieve something. That is to aim at the future, whereas this method of prayer is designed to bring you into the present. Expectations also refer to the future; hence they, too, are thoughts.

Emptying the mind of its customary routines of thinking is a process that we can only initiate, like taking the stopper out of a bath tub. The water goes down by itself. You don't have to push the water out of the tub. You simply allow it to run out. You are doing something similar in this prayer. Allow your ordinary train of thoughts to flow out of you. Waiting without expectation is sufficient activity.

> What about feelings? Are you supposed to let them go too?

Yes. They are thoughts in the context of this prayer. A perception of any kind whatsoever is a thought. Even the reflection that one isn't having a thought is a thought. Centering Prayer is an exercise of letting all perceptions pass by, not by giving them a shove or by getting angry at them, but by letting them go. This enables you gradually to develop a spiritual attentiveness that is peaceful, quiet, and absorbing.

> Is the deeper attention a function of less thought?

Yes. You may even have no thoughts. Then you are at the deepest point that you can go. At that moment there is no sense of time. Time is the measure of things going by. When nothing is going by, there is an experience of timelessness. And it is delightful.

> What should we do about external noise?

The best remedy for a sound that you can't control is to let go of your resistance to it and let it happen. External things are not obstacles to prayer. It is just that we think they are. By fully accepting external distractions that you can't do anything about, you may get a breakthrough into the realization that you can be in the middle of all the noise on earth and still experience this deeper attentiveness. Take a positive view of external difficulties. The only thing about which to take a negative view is skipping your daily time for prayer. That's the only no-no. Even if your prayer time seems fraught with noise and you feel like a total failure, just keep doing it.

Is it really possible for people who run around all day to be contemplatives?

Yes. This is not to say that by doing nothing but running around all day people will become contemplatives. On the other hand, you only have to be a human being to be eligible to become a contemplative. It's true that there are certain life styles that are more conducive to the development of a contemplative attitude, but this method works well if you stay with it.

Can you say to people with whom you are traveling, "I'm going to do my meditation now?"

Sure. They might be happy to have a few minutes of quiet themselves.

I am conscious of trying to let thoughts pass, but what happens is that I work with images of my perception of God. They tend to be visual. Is that also a thought that should be discarded?

Any kind of image is a thought in the context of this prayer. Any perception that arises from any one of the senses or from the imagination, memory, or reason is a thought. Hence, whatever the perception may be, let it go. Everything that registers on the stream of consciousness will eventually go by, including the thought of self. It is just a question of allowing every thought to go. Keep your attention on the river rather than on what is passing along its surface.

My way of focusing on God has usually been through an image. If I remove that image, I have trouble understanding what it is that I should focus on. Is my attention simply on the word that I am repeating?

Your attention should not be directed to any particular thought, including the sacred word. The sacred word is only a means of re-establishing your intention of opening to the true Self and to God, who is at the center of it. It is not necessary to keep repeating the sacred word. Interior silence is something that one naturally likes to experience. You don't have to force anything. By forcing, you introduce another thought, and any thought is enough to prevent you from going where you want to go.

Some people find it easier to transcend with a visual image rather than with a word. If you prefer some kind of visual image, choose one that is general and not detailed; for example, turn your inward gaze toward God as if you are looking at someone you love.

> As you were speaking, it occurred to me that I use images to stop myself from a free fall.

Some people, when they are quiet, feel themselves on the edge of a cliff. But don't worry. There is no danger of falling. The imagination is perplexed by the unknown. It is so used to images, so plugged into them, that to disengage it from its habitual way of thinking is quite a job. It will take practice to feel comfortable with this prayer.

5

THE SACRED WORD AS SYMBOL

■

THE SACRED WORD, whatever one you may choose, is sacred not because of its meaning, but because of its intent. It expresses your intention to open yourself to God, the Ultimate Mystery, who dwells within you. It is a focal point to return to when you notice you are becoming interested in the thoughts that are going by.

Stick to the same word once you feel comfortable with it.[1] If you are moved to choose another word, go ahead and try it, but do not shop around during the same period of prayer. The sacred word is a sign or arrow pointing in the direction you want to take. It is a way of renewing your intention to open yourself to God and to accept Him as He is. While this does not prevent anyone from praying in other forms at other times, the period of Centering Prayer is not the time to pray specifically for others. By opening yourself to God, you are implicitly praying for everyone past, present, and future. You are embracing the whole of creation. You are accepting all reality, beginning with God and with that part of your own reality of which you may not be generally aware, namely, the spiritual level of your being.

The sacred word enables you to sink into your Source. Human beings were made for boundless happiness and peace, and when we see that we are starting to move in that direction, we don't have to push ourselves. The difficulty is that we are going in the opposite direction most of the time. We tend to identify ourselves with our false self and its concerns and with the world that stimulates and reinforces that false self.

The sacred word is not a vehicle or means to go from the surface of the river to the depths. It is rather a condition for going there. If I hold a ball in my hand and let go, it will fall to the floor; I don't have to throw it.

In similar fashion, the sacred word is a way of letting go of all thoughts. This makes it possible for our spiritual faculties, which are attracted to interior silence,

---

1. Examples of what the sacred word might be: God, Jesus, Spirit, Abba, amen, peace, silence, open, glory, love, presence, trust, etc.

to move spontaneously in that direction. Such a movement does not require effort. It only requires the willingness to let go of our ordinary preoccupations.

Since the will is designed for infinite love and the mind for infinite truth, if there is nothing to stop them, they tend to move in that direction. It is because they are all wrapped up in other directions that their freedom to go where they are naturally inclined is limited. During the time of Centering Prayer these faculties regain that freedom.

Thus the sacred word is a way of reducing the number of thoughts and of dissolving them into the single thought of opening to God. It is not the means by which we go from a noisy imagination to silence, but a condition that enables us to move into the spiritual realm to which the force of grace is drawing us.

The chief thing that separates us from God is the thought that we are separated from Him. If we get rid of that thought, our troubles will be greatly reduced. We fail to believe that we are always with God and that He is part of every reality. The present moment, every object we see, our inmost nature are all rooted in Him. But we hesitate to believe this until personal experience gives us the confidence to believe in it. This involves the gradual development of intimacy with God. God constantly speaks to us through each other as well as from within. The interior experience of God's presence activates our capacity to perceive Him in everything else—in people, in events, in nature. We may enjoy union with God in any experience of the external senses as well as in prayer.

Contemplative prayer is a way of awakening to the reality in which we are immersed. We rarely think of the air we breathe, yet it is in us and around us all the time. In similar fashion, the presence of God penetrates us, is all around us, is always embracing us. Our awareness, unfortunately, is not awake to that dimension of reality. The purpose of prayer, the sacraments, and spiritual disciplines is to awaken us.

God's presence is available at every moment, but we have a giant obstacle in ourselves—our world view. It needs to be exchanged for the mind of Christ, for His world view. The mind of Christ is ours through faith and baptism, according to Paul, but to take possession of it requires a discipline that develops the sensitivity to hear Christ's invitation: "Behold I stand at the door and knock; if anyone opens I will come in and sup with him and he with me." (Revelations 3:20) It is not a big effort to open a door.

Our ordinary preoccupations involve unconscious value systems. Some thoughts are attractive to us because we have an attachment to them springing from the emotional programming of early childhood. When such thoughts go by, all our lights start flashing because of our heavy emotional investment in the values that they stimulate or threaten. By training ourselves to let go of every thought and thought pattern, we gradually develop freedom from our attachments and compulsions.

In contemplative prayer the Spirit places us in a position where we are at rest and disinclined to fight. By his secret anointings the Spirit heals the wounds of our fragile human nature at a level beyond our psychological perception, just as a person who is anesthetized has no idea of how the operation is going until after it is over. Interior silence is the perfect seed bed for divine love to take root. In the Gospel the Lord speaks about a mustard seed as a symbol of divine love. It is the smallest of all seeds, but it has an enormous capacity for growth. Divine love has the power to grow and to transform us. The purpose of contemplative prayer is to facilitate the process of inner transformation.

It is easier for most people to let go of their thoughts with a word of one or two syllables. But if you find that a visual image is more helpful, use it, provided, of course, that you introduce it on the level of the imagination and return to it whenever you notice you are thinking some other thought. The visual image should be general, not clear and precise. Some people find it especially helpful to pray before the Blessed Sacrament. They usually keep their eyes closed and are simply aware of the presence in which they are praying.

Following one's breathing is another method of quieting the mind. There is a distinction, however, that should be carefully noted. In Centering Prayer the object is not simply to let go of all thoughts but to deepen our contact with the ground of our being. The intentionality of faith is fundamental. Centering Prayer is not just sustained attention to a special word or image or to one's breathing, but the surrender of one's whole being to God. It is not just an experience of our spiritual nature, which can be gained by concentrating on a particular posture, mantra, or mandala. It presupposes a personal relationship; there must be a movement of self-surrender. If, as a Christian, you use some physical or psychological method that is geared to quieting the mind, I suggest that you put it in the context of prayer. For instance, if you follow your exercises as a means of calming your thoughts, do so with the motive of drawing closer to God. Centering Prayer is not a relaxation exercise although it may bring relaxation. It is the exercise of our personal relationship with God.

How does the sacred word actually work?

The sacred word is a simple thought that you are thinking at ever deepening levels. That is why you accept it in whatever form it arises within you. The word on your lips is exterior and has no part in this form of prayer; the thought in your imagination is interior; the word as an impulse of your will is more interior still. Only when you pass beyond the word into pure awareness is the process of interiorization complete. That is what Mary of Bethany was doing at the feet of Jesus. She was going beyond the words she was hearing to the Person who was speaking and entering into union with Him. This is what we are doing as we sit in Centering Prayer interiorizing the sacred word. We are going beyond the sacred word into union with that to which it points—the Ultimate Mystery, the Presence of God beyond any conception that we can form of Him.

The desire to go to God, to open to His presence within us, does not come from our initiative. We do not have to go anywhere to find God because He is already drawing us in every conceivable way into union with Himself. It is rather a question of opening to an action that is already happening in us. To consent to God's presence *is* His Presence. The sacred word points us beyond our psychic awareness to our Source, the Trinity dwelling in our inmost being. Moreover, God dwells there not as a photograph or statue, but as a dynamic presence. The purpose of this prayer is to get in touch with the activity that God is constantly initiating in our inmost center.

If you keep up this practice every day for several months, you will know whether or not it is right for you. There is no substitute for the experience of doing it. It is like getting to know a new friend; if you meet and converse regularly, you get to know each other faster. That's why we recommend two periods of prayer each day, preferably the first thing in the morning and before supper. Sometimes the "conversation" is engrossing and you experience a certain peace and refreshment. At other times the conversation is like talking about baseball scores when you have no interest in the game; you put up with it because you are interested in a particular person and in whatever interests him or her. An uninspiring period of prayer won't bother you very much if your long-range goal is the cultivation of friendship. The essential discipline is to do it every day.

> What do you do when the entire prayer period consists of wave after wave of thoughts?

When you start to quiet down, you may become aware that your head is full of thoughts coming from both outside and inside. The imagination is a perpetual-motion faculty; it is always grinding out images. So you must expect that on the level of your memory and imagination, thoughts will just keep coming. The main thing is to accept the fact that this is going to happen. No one is going to fall instantly into an ocean of peace where there are no distractions. You have to accept yourself as you are and God as He is, and trust that He will lead you in a way that may not always feel comfortable but that is best for you.

In the case of unwanted thoughts, just let them go without being upset. If you make up your mind that there are going to be a lot of thoughts, you are less likely to get upset when thoughts arrive. If, on the other hand, you feel that the goal of Centering Prayer is to be free of *all* thoughts, you will be continually disappointed. When you feel disappointed, that is a thought with an emotional charge to it. It shatters whatever interior silence you may have been enjoying.

Must one say the sacred word constantly?

So long as thoughts are going by of their own accord, you don't have to think the sacred word. In the beginning it is helpful to keep returning to it in order to introduce it into your subconscious and thus to make it easier to recall when you need it during prayer. The basic rule is to let all thoughts on the river go by. As long as they are going by, you don't need to do anything about them. But when you want to look on board one of the boats to see what is hidden in the hold, think the sacred word. Do so gently, however, and without effort.

If you have just had an argument with someone or received bad news, you will need a little preparation for prayer. Reading scripture, walking or jogging around the clock, or doing yoga exercises may help to calm your emotional turmoil. One reason to pray early in the day is that events haven't had a chance to upset you yet.

Does the sacred word disappear permanently or just from time to time during a particular prayer time?

The experience of interior peace is the sacred word at its deepest level. You are experiencing the end of the journey toward which the sacred word is pointing. But this is generally not a permanent state. You keep getting bounced out and have to return again to the sacred word.

You said that it is not so much repetition of the sacred word that counts but the intention. I was wondering how to hang onto the intention without repeating the word. It seems as if they go together.

In the beginning it is hard to hang on to your intention without continually returning to the sacred word. But this does not mean that you have to keep repeating it. There are forms of Christian prayer similar to mantric practice in the Hindu tradition that consist of repeating the sacred word continuously. This is not the method of Centering Prayer. In this practice, you only return to the sacred word when you notice you are thinking some other thought. As you become more comfortable with this prayer, you begin to find yourself beyond the word in a place of interior peace. Then you see that there is a level of attention that is beyond the sacred word. The sacred word is a pointer and you have reached that to which it is pointing. Until you have that experience, you must continue to go back to the sacred word in order to reaffirm your intention when you notice you are thinking of something else.

> It seems that a word has a certain emotional quality to it, some kind of atmosphere about it. I was wondering if there was a distinction between trying to stay with the word to see what the feeling quality of that word becomes in Centering Prayer, and trying to allow everything to drop away, including the feeling quality of that word, in the hope that there is something coming from God's direction.

The meaning of the sacred word or its resonances should not be pursued. It is better to choose a word that does not stir up other associations in your mind or cause you to consider its particular emotional qualities. The sacred word is only a gesture, an expression of your intent; it has no meaning other than your intent. You should choose your word as a simple expression of that intent, not as a source of meaning or emotional attraction. The less the word means to you, the better off you are. It is not a way of going to God or a way into interior silence. Rather, it establishes an interior climate that facilitates the movement of faith. The movement of pure faith is the heart of contemplative prayer. Only God can put content into that kind of faith.

You may reach a point where you no longer think of the sacred word at all. When you sit down for prayer, your whole psyche gathers itself together and melts into God. Interior silence *is* the sacred word at its deepest level. For example, if you take a trip to New York, you buy a ticket at your starting point. But when you get to New York, you don't go to the ticket office to buy another ticket; you are already there. In the same way, use the sacred word to move into interior silence. So long as you experience the undifferentiated, general, and loving presence of God beyond any thought, don't go back to the sacred word. You are already at your destination.

> Sometimes I think that I have reached the tranquillity before I really have. I've tasted the real thing once in a while, but sometimes I think it is there before it really is, and I don't want to go back to the word. Yet I feel that I have to.

Well, don't be too sure. Stay there a few more moments. God is much more intimate and accessible than we think. If the Lord reaches up and pulls you down, great! But since He does not generally do so, there may be something you can do to make it easier for Him. Centering Prayer is a method of doing precisely that.

To what exactly is our attention directed in Centering Prayer? Is it to the sacred word? To the meaning of the word? To the sound of the word? To a vague sense of God being present?

None of them. We do not try to fix our attention on the sacred word during Centering Prayer. We do not keep repeating it or think of its meaning. Its sound is of no significance. The sacred word is only a symbol. It is an arrow pointing in the direction intended by our will. It is a gesture or sign of accepting God as He is. Exactly what that is, we don't know. Again, the sacred word is like the needle of a ship's compass pointing out the course of a storm. It is not a means, still less an infallible means, of getting to our destination. It is not within our power to bring about a vague sense of God's being present. What, then, is our principal focus in Centering Prayer! It is to deepen our relationship with Jesus Christ, the Divine-Human Being.

In discussions with others who practice Centering Prayer, I have found that they stop saying the sacred word as soon as some type of silence appears. They stay silent for about five minutes; then thoughts arise and they return to the word. They make another descent into quietness and drop the word; then thoughts arise and they return to it again. What do you think about this dropping and returning, dropping and returning to the word?

Your description sounds as if they know how to do it. Some teachers of prayer are convinced from their experience that contemporary Western minds are so active that they need to repeat a Christian mantra over and over, at least in the beginning. People leading very active lives can certainly benefit from that sort of concentration to hold their attention. The method of Centering Prayer, however, is not concentrative, but receptive. While both methods are excellent and aim at the same goal, they are not the same and produce different effects in the psyche. In Centering Prayer, the use of the sacred word is designed to foster the receptive attitude. The interior movement toward God without any word is often enough. You may sink into interior silence as soon as you sit down simply by opening yourself to the presence of God. His presence is already there, but you may not have noticed it because of other duties or occupations.

Contemplative prayer is an incredibly simple kind of attention. It is more intention than attention. As the Spirit gradually takes more and more charge of your prayer, you may move into pure consciousness, which is an intuition into your true Self. There is no way of knowing God directly in this life except by means of pure faith, which is darkness to all the faculties. This darkness is to be understood not as a blanking out of the faculties, but as a transcendence of their activity. Pure faith, according to John of the Cross, is the proximate means of union with God.

Contemplative prayer may open up into various kinds of inner experiences or nonexperiences. In either case, it is a training in being content with God as He is and as He acts. There is tremendous freedom when that disposition is finally established because then you will not look for any form of consolation from God. Spiritual consolations can be as distracting as sensible ones. God gives consolation to heal the emotional problems I was referring to previously. Someone who has been deprived of love needs a lot of affection. The Spirit knows that as well as any psychiatrist. It may be for this reason that the Spirit fills certain people with waves of love and various marks of affection. It doesn't mean that they are holier than others or that the Spirit loves them more. It means that they have more need of love. So he gives them what they need—always, however, with a view to strengthening them so that they may receive more substantial communications, which are beyond the range of psychological awareness.

6

THE ORDINARY KINDS
OF THOUGHTS

■

THE GREAT BATTLE in the early stages of contemplative prayer is with thoughts. It is important to recognize the various kinds of thoughts and thought patterns that come down the stream of consciousness and to learn the best way to handle each kind.

The easiest variety of thoughts to recognize is the ordinary wanderings of the imagination. The imagination is a perpetual motion faculty and is constantly grinding away. It is unrealistic to aim at having no thoughts. When we speak of developing interior silence, we are speaking of a relative degree of silence. By interior silence we refer primarily to a state in which we do not become *attached* to the thoughts as they go by.

Suppose you are conversing with someone on the seventh floor of a downtown office building with the windows wide open. There is a constant hum of traffic from the street. Obviously you cannot do anything to prevent the noise from continuing. If you get annoyed and say, "Why don't they keep quiet?" or get in the elevator and go downstairs and start shouting, "Why don't you people shut up?" you will only succeed in bringing your conversation to an end. If you just continue your conversation and put up with the hum, you will gradually develop a capacity to pay no attention to it. This is the best solution for the wanderings of the imagination. Make up your mind that they are going to be present as part of the reality of your inner world. If you fully accept them, they will begin to fade into insignificance.

Once in a while, however, the hubbub gets louder, say at the rush hour, and the decibels increase to an unbearable degree. You have to accept that too. Sometimes you will be persecuted from start to finish by the wanderings and ravings of the imagination. That does not mean that your prayer was no good or that you did not benefit from some degree of interior silence. As you persevere, you will gradually develop new habits and new capacities, one of which is the ability to be conscious of two levels of awareness at the same time. You can be aware of the noise in or around you, and yet you recognize that your attention is grasped by something at a deeper level that is impossible to define but is nonetheless real.

The ability to build a wall around your interior silence during this prayer is a phenomenon that you may experience fairly soon in regard to external sounds. If you fully accept the noise, it scarcely bothers you. If you fight it, struggle with it, or wish it were not there, you will get all wrapped up in particular sounds. Although you may not succeed right away, eventually you will experience a delightful silence at a deep level even though noise is going on around you.

I once visited a family who lived over the Third Avenue El in New York shortly before it was taken down. Their apartment overlooked the tracks. Every now and then a train would roar by. For me the din was absolutely shattering. I thought the train was going right through the living room. But the family seemed to be blissfully unaware of it. They would be chatting away and when a train would come, everybody just stopped talking because it was impossible to be heard. After the train went by, they took up the conversation exactly where they left off as though nothing had happened. They had built the deafening sound into their lives. But for someone who was not used to it, it was not only an interruption but the end of the conversation.

So it is with the rumbling that goes on in our heads. It is so bad sometimes that many people will not put up with it. They say, "Interior silence and contemplative prayer are for the birds. I cannot endure this barrage of tiresome thoughts going through my head." So they get up and leave. If they would just hang on and give themselves a little more time, they would get used to the noise.

The habitual practice of Centering Prayer gradually reduces the amount of interior noise. In the beginning you are bound to be bombarded by thoughts without end. Most of us, before we begin the method of Centering Prayer or some other process of quieting the mind, are not even aware of how many thoughts we actually have. But when we start to quiet down, we begin to realize the amazing amount of nonsense stored in our heads. Some people may even get a little scared by how much is going on in there. They find they would rather put up with the ordinary flow of their superficial thoughts.

We should set up conditions that are most conducive for our prayer: find a quiet time of the day away from phones and other foreseeable interruptions. Take the advice of Jesus when he speaks of praying in secret to the Father. If you have a bunch of youngsters running around the house, it may be hard to find a quiet spot or time. For some people the only quiet place may be in the bathtub. In any case, you should find a spot and a time where and when you are least likely to be interrupted. Some noises, like lawn mowers or airplane engines, can be integrated into interior silence, but noises that engage the intellect and imagination, such as loud conversation, are hard to handle.

To sum up, the best response to the ordinary wanderings of the imagination is to ignore them; not, however, with a feeling of annoyance or anxiety, but with one of acceptance and peace. Every response to God, whatever it is, must begin with the full acceptance of reality as it actually is at the moment. Since it is part of our nature to have a wandering imagination, however much you might want to be quiet, accept the fact that thoughts are certain to come. The solution is not to try to make the mind a blank. That is not what interior silence is.

During the entire course of a period of Centering Prayer, we are slipping in and out of interior silence. One's interior attention is like a balloon on a calm day slowly settling to the ground. Just as it is about to touch the ground, a zephyr comes from nowhere and the balloon starts to go up again. Similarly, in Centering Prayer there is a tantalizing moment when one feels about to slip into the most delightful silence. That is just the moment that some unwanted thought comes along. It takes great patience to accept the thought and not to be sad because one is prevented from entering that silence. Just start over. This constant starting over with patience, calm, and acceptance trains us for the acceptance of the whole of life. It prepares us for action. There should be a basic acceptance of whatever is actually happening before we decide what to do with it. Our first reflex is to want to change reality or at least to control it.

A second kind of thought that comes down the stream of consciousness during this prayer occurs when, in the course of the wanderings of the imagination, you get interested in some particular thought and notice your attention moving in that direction. You may also feel yourself getting emotionally involved in it.

Any emotionally charged thought or image, whether it comes from outside or from our imagination, initiates an automatic response in the appetitive system. Depending on whether the image is pleasant or unpleasant, you feel a spontaneous like or dislike for it. When you notice that there is curiosity in a particular thought or a clinging sensation, the proper response is to return to the sacred word. This reaffirms your original intention of opening to God and of surrendering to Him.

Our consciousness, as we have said, is like a great river on the surface of which our superficial thoughts and experiences are moving by like boats, debris, water skiers or other things. The river itself is the participation God has given us in His own being. It is that part of us on which all the other faculties rest, but we are ordinarily unaware of it because we are absorbed with what is passing by on the surface of the river.

In Centering Prayer we begin to shift our attention from the boats and objects on the surface to the river itself, to that which sustains all our faculties and is their source. The river in this analogy has no qualities or characteristics. It is spiritual and limitless because it is a participation in God's being. Suppose you get interested in some boat and find yourself looking in the hold to see what is on board. You are slipping away from your original intention. You must keep turning your attention from what is on the surface of the river to the river itself, from the particular to the general, from forms to the formless, from images to the imageless. Returning to the sacred word is a way of renewing your intention to seek God's inward presence in faith.

Let's return to the image of conversing with a friend on the seventh floor in a downtown office building. At the rush hour horns begin to honk. You start to wonder what is going on, so your attention is drawn away from the conversation with your friend. Courtesy requires that you renew your attention. So you turn your gaze toward your friend as if to say, "Excuse me," or, "As I was saying." In other words, a simple movement to reaffirm your conversation is called for. It is not a quesiton of fighting, stopping or shutting out the noise, but of returning to your original intention. In similar fashion, when, in Centering Prayer, you notice that you are thinking some other thought, simply give your attention back to God, and as a sign of your intention, think the sacred word.

There is no question of repeating the sacred word as if it were a magic formula to empty the mind or to force the word upon your consciousness. By returning to the sacred word, you reaffirm your choice to converse with God and to be united to Him. This does not demand effort but surrender. Thus whenever you return to the sacred word, do so without exasperation or desperation. Over-reacting is counter-productive. No one cuts a lawn with a bulldozer. All you need to brush away a fly is a movement of your hand. In Centering Prayer the patient renewal of your intention is sufficient activity.

There are all kinds of ways in which God speaks to us—through our thoughts or any one of our faculties. But keep in mind that God's first language is silence. Prepare yourself for silence in this prayer, and if other things happen, that is His problem, not yours. As soon as you make it your problem, you tend to desire something that is other than God. Pure faith will bring you closer to God than anything else. To be attached to an experience of God is not God; it is a thought. The time of Centering Prayer is the time to let go of all thoughts, even the best of thoughts. If they are really good, they will come back later.

What do you think of drugs as a means of inducing mystical experience?

Some seem to find spiritual experience through certain psychedelic drugs. It's much more desirable, however, to have a built-in discipline than to depend on drugs, which don't always work as desired. Like certain powerful methods of Eastern meditation, drugs may release material from the unconscious before one is able to deal with it. Some people taking LSD had bad trips because they did not have the psychological preparation to handle what emerged from their unconscious as a result of the drug.

> This afternoon I felt very heavy and tired.

You will often notice an alternation between so-called good and bad periods of prayer. Try to give up those categories altogether.

> One thought I had was, "What is the sense of all this? Get up and walk out."
> Of course, I did not go.

Good. It was just another thought. No matter how much a thought may persecute you, all you have to do is let it go by. By fighting it, you stir up other thoughts.

> I would like to clarify something I was wrestling with. In the past, I have worked determinedly to be centered. I have had a sense of pushing to concentrate versus quietly and gently centering in.

You cannot do this prayer by will power. The more effort you put into it, the less well it goes. When you catch yourself trying hard, relax and let go. Introduce the sacred word gently, incredibly gently, as if you were laying a feather on a piece of absorbent cotton.

Of course, when thoughts are flying at you like baseballs, you look around for some means to protect yourself. But swatting them out of the park is not the way to do it. You should honestly say, "Well, I am being pummeled with these thoughts," and put up with them, remembering that if you just wait, they will all pass by. Do not oppose violence with violence. This prayer is totally nonviolent. A sign of trying too hard is a feeling of tightness in the forehead or in the back of the neck. If you allow your attention to flow with that pain for a few moments, it usually goes away. In other words, accept the fact that you have the pain. Rest in the presence of the pain. Pain has a way of dissolving every other thought. It brings the mind to a single point, which is also the purpose of the sacred word. When the pain subsides, you may need your sacred word again.

> Throughout the first period of prayer there was a counseling session going on down the hall that was loud enough for me to catch bits and snatches. I felt like shouting the sacred word to overcome the noise.

In that situation there is not much you can do but keep returning to the sacred word, yet always with the acceptance of the situation just as it is. Sometimes you cannot do anything but put up with the noise. Think that you are being refreshed at a deeper level, but you just can't enjoy it.

> If at some distant future time, prayer should go beyond thirty minutes, or maybe even an hour, at some point your back may complain. Is that the time to say, "This is where the prayer should cease"? Or should you just keep going?

Your prayer should normally finish before you develop a sore back. One generally has a sense when one's normal period of prayer is over. For some people this might come after twenty minutes. For others, after half an hour or longer. I doubt that you would go for more than an hour without sensing that your prayer was over. But you are free to develop it to that point if you have the attraction and the grace to sustain it.

A better way of prolonging prayer would be set up two periods of ordinary length back to back with a slow, meditative walk around the room for five to ten minutes in between. This would help to dispel the restlessness that may develop from sitting in one position for a long time.

Length of time, however, is not an indicator of the value of one's prayer. The quality of prayer rather than its quantity is what matters. A single moment of divine union is more valuable than a long period of prayer during which you are constantly in and out of interior silence. It only takes a moment for God to enrich you. In that sense the waiting process is a preparation for moments of divine union. Union may occur for only an instant, yet you can be more enriched than someone spending an hour or two on lower forms of contemplative prayer without such a moment of absorption in God. Each of us has to figure out from practice and experimentation when our period of prayer is normally over. To prolong it simply because it is going well is not a good idea.

> As I find myself going deeper, I get frightened and pull myself out of it. I am afraid I am going to stay down there. I do not know if the fear is psychological, physical, or spiritual.

This is a common experience. When you get close to the edge of self-forgetfulness, unless the divine attraction is strong and reassuring, you may experience fear. Our imagination represents the unknown as frightening. If you ignore it and take the plunge anyway, you will find that the water is delightful.

> Last night I let myself go, but then I pulled myself out of it. I was so sorry afterward, and I did not know why I did it.

Before you begin your prayer, say to God, "If You want to pull me over to the other side, go ahead." Then relax. When you submitted to an anesthetic for the first time, you did not know what would happen. If it had not been more or less forced on you, you probably would not have taken it. This prayer is the same sort of situation. You do not know what it is going to be like when you stop reflecting. But try it.

> I was on the verge of a beautiful experience, but that fear was there, so I stopped. I do not know why I pulled myself out of it.

Try not to reflect on the experience at all while it is happening; just let go.

> Is there a way of doing this prayer too frequently so that you lapse into passivity?

Only if you do it for more than five or six hours a day over a long period of time. I do not think three or four hours a day would have any adverse effects at all. Many could pray longer if they built up to it gradually over a period of several months. If you are doing it correctly, you may notice in your activity an increase of energy rather than passivity. That is because you are being freed from a lot of emotional hang-ups that used to exhaust you.

That your superficial faculties are aware of a lot of boats and debris coming down the stream of consciousness does not mean that your other faculties, intellect, and will, are not deeply recollected in God. You may be painfully aware of unwanted thoughts going by and wish they were not there. At the same time you may be aware that something inside of you is absorbed by a mysterious presence that is completely intangible, refined, and delicate. The reason is that your psyche is developing the expanded awareness that I spoke of before, which is able to attend to two planes of reality at the same time, one superficial and the other profound. If you are wrapped up in superficial thoughts or are upset because you have such thoughts, you will not experience the deeper level. There are other times, however, when you will not experience the deeper level, no matter how open you are to it, because of the noise of the imagination or memory.

If the times goes quickly during prayer, that is a sign you were deeply absorbed, perhaps much more than you realized. When there are no objects going by in your imagination, the sense of time is disrupted. If there are no objects going by, there is an experience of timelessness. You are fully aware, yet not of time. This gives you an intuition into the fact that when the body slips away from the spirit, no great change is going to take place. In deep prayer you do not think about the body anyway. The prospect of dying is not so threatening because you have experienced a preview of what it might be like for the spirit to be separated from the body, and it is delightful.

> During prayer I sometimes have a happy-go-lucky feeling that I find most enjoyable.

You should not take prayer too seriously. There is something playful about God. You only have to look at a penguin or certain other animals to realize that He likes to play little jokes on creatures. The playfulness of God is a profound part of reality. It warns us to not take ourselves too seriously, to realize that God created us with a certain sense of humor.

> Does my guardian angel know what goes on in my Centering Prayer?

Not unless you tell him! Angels and devils cannot perceive what you are doing in contemplative prayer if it is deep enough. They can only know what is in your imagination and memory, and they can add material to these faculties. But when you are in deep interior silence, what is happening there is God's secret. Only He knows what goes on in the depths of the soul. Some people think that if you quiet the mind, you open yourself up to diabolical forces. But according to John of the Cross, you are never safer than when you are absorbed in God's presence, beyond thoughts and feelings, for there the demons cannot touch you. It is only when you come out of interior silence that they can badger you with temptations. That is why one of the best ways of handling temptation is to slip into the same attitude you take during contemplative prayer. This is what David means when he sings of God in the Psalms as "my refuge, my strength, my rock, my strong fortress, my high tower, my rampart!"[1] We do not have to be afraid of opening ourselves to unknown dangers by practicing contemplative prayer. No one can join us at that level except He who is deeper than that level, the God who dwells within us and out of whose creative love we emerge at every moment.

> During my period of prayer today, there was a thought that kept coming back. After my prayer was over, it came back again. It was a selfish thought. I brought it to the chapel and prayed before the Lord. I made a gift of it to Him and then I felt very good. I felt as though it was a splinter getting in my way and I had just taken it out. Is there an advantage in taking such things to the Lord in prayer when you can talk to Him like that?

1. Cf. Psalms 17, 27, 30, 45, 58, 61, 70, 90.

By all means follow your attraction. We should go to God with great freedom. I emphasize contemplative prayer because it is an area that has been neglected in recent centuries. The time that you devote to interior silence is not meant to be in conflict with other forms of prayer.

> In the beginning of centering, I used to find it very difficult not to break out into vocal prayer if I felt I was not getting somewhere, but now I understand that as you try to empty yourself, you make room for the Spirit to come in and pray in the innermost recesses of your being. This has helped me to put out thoughts. I see there is no need for me to pray in words, but that I should relax and let Him come in to pray.

Prayer is not designed to change God but to change us. The faster we let that happen, the better our prayer is going to be. But once we have gotten interested in God and have begun to seek Him, the best thing to do is to be silent in prayer and to let Him complete the process. Isn't that the great significance of the Blessed Virgin Mary? She could not possibly forget God. She was prayer in her very being and in every one of her actions.

What is the great thing that Our Lady has done for us? She brought the Word of God into the world, or rather let Him come into the world through her. It is not so much what we do but what we *are* that allows Christ to live in the world. When the presence of God emerges from our inmost being into our faculties, whether we walk down the street or drink a cup of soup, divine life is pouring into the world. The effectiveness of every action depends on the source from which it springs. If it is coming out of the false self, it is severely limited. If it is coming out of a person who is immersed in God, it is extremely effective. The contemplative state, like the vocation of Our Lady, brings Christ into the world.

> I would like to clarify something about using contemplative prayer in times of temptation, stress, or difficulty. I have difficulty with the idea of using prayer to bring me peace. Isn't that a selfish motive?

The principle I had in mind in suggesting slipping into contemplative prayer was to calm your thoughts and feelings, when they are getting hooked on some temptation, by practicing the same kind of letting go that you do during contemplative prayer. Temptation can be treated like any thought that comes down the stream of consciousness. If you let it go by, that is sufficient resistance. If you are unable to do that, you have to exercise other forms of resistance.

> Is the attitude that we develop in our ordinary life-style of letting go of certain things a way of preparing ourselves for prayer in a tangible, practical way, so that it will be easier to let go of the thoughts when we are at prayer?

There is a reciprocal interaction between your activity during the day and your prayer, and vice versa. They mutually support one another.

How can you pray in deep silence and peace when you are very upset about something?

In such circumstances you cannot hope to pray in silence without some kind of buffer zone. You may have to run around the block, do physical exercises, or some suitable reading. Otherwise, as soon as you sit down and try to be quiet, you will think that you are sitting under Niagara Falls instead of beside the stream of consciousness. You have to give yourself a chance to quiet down before you start to pray. Moreover, some trials are so big that they knock you flat on your face and no matter what means you take to quiet down, you will not be able to settle into interior silence. Giving yourself the usual time to pray, however, will help you to accept the problem and the emotional storm.

Why do you limit the periods of prayer to half an hour in the group?

It seems to be the normal period for prolonged attention. Longer than that might discourage people from starting or continuing. Yet it needs to be long enough to establish the sense of interior silence.

There is a great value in praying at the same time every day and for the same length of time. This will give you a stable reservoir of silence. Dividing the day between two equal periods of deep prayer gives the maximum opportunity for your reservoir of silence to affect the whole day.

The more activity in which you find yourself, the more you will need your times of prayer. Excessive activity has a way of becoming a drain. It also has a mysterious fascination. Like a treadmill or merry-go-round, it is hard to get off. Regular prayer is a real discipline. To interrupt what you are doing in order to pray can be difficult. You need to be convinced that your time of prayer is more important than any other activity apart from some urgent call of charity. You will be surprised that things you have to do fall into place and get accomplished more quickly. You will be able to see the proportionate value of your activities and what should be done first.

Why twice a day and not one longer period?

Twice a day keeps you closer to the reservoir of silence. If you get too far away from the reservoir, it is like being on the end of the water line after everybody has taken what they want from the reservoir. When you turn on the faucet, you only get a few drops. To prevent that from happening, keep the pressure up. You need to keep filling your reservoir until you eventually strike an artisian well. Then the water is always flowing.

Contemplative prayer is a preparation for action, for action that emerges from the inspiration of the Spirit in the silencing of our own agitation, desires and hang-ups. Such silence gives God the maximum opportunity to speak.

> During prayer is it all right to reflect on what is happening or is it better to let it go?

During this prayer it is not appropriate to reflect on what is happening. We should completely suspend judgment during this prayer. Afterwards it may be helpful to reflect on it. As you gain experience, you have to keep integrating your prayer into the rest of your life of faith. That requires some form of conceptualization. At the same time, you do not have to analyze your prayer to gain its benefits. It is just as well not to watch what is happening. If you are getting good fruit from it, you will spontaneously notice it. In fact, other people will say, "You do not seem to be as agitated as you used to be." There may be a certain gentleness in you that was not noticed before. You yourself may perceive that, while you used to feel like slugging somebody when you became angry, now you can be satisfied with administering a mild rebuke.

Contemplative prayer fosters a whole different attitude toward one's feelings; it puts them in a different frame of reference. Most extreme feelings come from a sense of insecurity, especially when we feel threatened. But when you are being constantly reaffirmed by the presence of God in deep silence, you are not afraid of being contradicted or imposed upon. You might be humble enough to learn something from insults and humiliations without being overwhelmed by feelings of self-depreciation or revenge. Negative feelings toward oneself tend to be prevalent in our culture due to the low self-image people develop in early childhood, possibly because of our highly competitive society. Anyone who does not win feels that he is no good in this culture, whereas in the quiet of deep water, you are a new person, or rather, you are you.

> What happens if, because it is consoling, you prolong Centering Prayer for hours?

If you overdo anything, it is bound to have some bad side effects. Too much joy as well as too much sorrow is fatiguing. The purpose of this prayer is not more prayer or more silence, but the integration of prayer and silence with activity. Consolation of a spiritual kind is so satisfying that it can be a trap. That is why by limiting contemplative prayer to a certain period of time, you have a common sense measure for what is reasonably good for you without running the risk of spiritual gluttony. It is a precious gift to come close to interior silence. Its beauty is so incomparable that it changes one's perception of what beauty is. If you are experiencing this fairly frequently, you gain strength to meet opposition and contradiction. Interior silence is one of the most strengthening and affirming of human experiences. There is nothing more affirming, in fact, than the experience of God's presence. That revelation says as nothing else can, "You are a good person. I created you and I love you." Divine love brings us into being in the fullest sense of the word. It heals the negative feelings we have about ourselves.

> I am afraid that I will stop breathing during the prayer time. I feel most secure when I am getting into my body rhythm. I pay attention to that and am afraid to let it go for too long.

Your breathing may get shallow, but when you need oxygen you will breathe automatically. The body has its own good sense, and if your breathing is getting too shallow, your body will just take a deep breath. It happens in sleep; it will happen in prayer. There is a correlation between thinking and breathing. As the breath gets shallow, thoughts diminish. But as soon as you start thinking, breathing increases too.

> I have heard that if you fast, meditation is enhanced. I guess that it's a matter of training yourself.

The ability to fast is peculiar to each person. What is recommended is that one not do centering on a full stomach. The tendency of this prayer is to reduce the metabolism. A consequence of this is that the bodily processes like digestion slow down. Wait an hour and a half after a full meal. Do not practice just before going to bed. You may experience a surge of energy that might keep you awake for a few hours.

For some, fasting will enhance the experience of Centering Prayer. It might have the opposite effect on others. If your hunger is so intense that it preoccupies you during the time of prayer, fasting is counterproductive. The principle to follow during Centering Prayer is to try to forget the body. Simplicity of life, not extremes, fits in better with this kind of practice.

> It helps to have the group for moral support. Is it better to center together or alone?

There is moral and psychological support in a group. That's why it is a help to hve a support group that meets regularly once a week. On the other hand, some prefer to do it alone because they don't have to adjust to what other people are doing. Both experiences are valuable.

> When I find that I am not thinking about anything, I find myself thinking about my breathing.

The best way to handle that is to accept it and to pay no attention. It is as if you were walking down the street to church and someone started to walk beside you. Just keep going, pay no attention to this uninvited companion, and you will wind up where you want to go. Say "yes" to everything that happens. In that way there is a better chance that the obsessive image will go by. A reaction of annoyance or of pleasure intensifies a particular thought.

All thoughts that come down the stream of consciousness are subject to time because they are moving objects, and every object has to go by. If you just wait and do not do anything about them, they will all pass by. But if you try to do something with them or to get away from them, you are stuck with them and you will start going downstream along with them. Then you will have to start over again.

Let thoughts come, let them go. No annoyance, no expectation. This is a very delicate kind of self-denial, but it is more valuable than bodily austerities, which tend to fix one's attention on oneself. Waiting for God without going away, giving the usual time to prayer, and putting up with what goes on in the imagination are the most effective practices for acquiring true devotion. The observance of them will lead to a complete change of heart.

> It seems that there are times when you are aware of something around you. The sacred word becomes a reality and you can't make yourself repeat it. This state is not like ordinary waking consciousness, but it doesn't feel like sleep either because there is some plane of awareness.

That is the awareness we're trying to awaken. It might be called spiritual attentiveness. This deep attention is aware of external factors, but they don't make any impression on it because we are captivated by a mysterious inward attention. It's like conversing with someone you love. You may not be saying anything special, but you are wrapped up in that person. If you are eating together in a restaurant, the waitresses may be coming and going, but if you are engaged in an interesting conversation, you don't even notice what they are doing. A waitress can even put down the check and you won't notice that it is the end of the meal or that everyone has left the place and it is time to go. This prayer is not a conversation in words, but an exchange of hearts. It is a higher level of communication than other levels of prayer and tends to integrate these lower levels into itself.

> I found myself dealing with certain kinds of resistance to God. I was half aware of those resistances that I found happening spontaneously. Is it proper to use this period of prayer as a time to wrestle with oneself or God?

When one is inwardly quiet, some of the conflicts that are hidden by the ordinary flow of thoughts begin to come into focus. Normally I would not wrestle with them at this time but would let them go by. The time to reflect on them is after you come out of prayer. The value of contemplative prayer is that it's a total immersion in that aspect of our relationship to God that happens to be the most important—the cultivation of interior silence. Psychological problems may come into focus as a result of periods of great peace, and a breakthrough may emerge. But generally such insights are a trick to get you to think of something. "Anything but silence" is the response of the false self to this kind of prayer. Interior silence goes totally contrary to all the inclinations of the false self. That is why you have to lure it into being still for a little while. However, there may be some special insight into a conflict that you feel inspired to work through right away. Feel free to make an exception. But if it happens too often, you might be making a mistake.

> Today I had an experience of having thoughts come and go without being concerned about them, as I usually am. I am still groping for a balance between using the sacred word and just resting in the presence. There were a few brief moments of simple presence without my doing anything. Then I would ask myself, should I use the word now?

When you are in deep interior silence, any thought acts on you as tasty bait acts on a fish resting in the deep waters of a lake. If you bite, out you go! Try not to have any expectation. That is not easy. It comes as a result of the habit of letting every thought go by. Eventually you do not care what is coming downstream because it is going by anyway, whether it is pleasurable or painful. I might add that the practice of this prayer will make the events of life easier to handle because you will be able to let them come and go also. Centering Prayer is a training in letting go.

7

THE BIRTH OF SPIRITUAL ATTENTIVENESS

■

THE CHIEF ACT of the will is not effort but consent. The secret of getting through the difficulties that arise in contemplative prayer is to accept them. The will is affectivity more than it is effectivity. To try to accomplish things by force of will is to reinforce the false self. This does not dispense us from making appropriate efforts. In the beginning the will is involved in habits that are selfish. We have to make efforts to withdraw from them. But as the will goes up the ladder of interior freedom, its activity becomes more and more one of consent to God's coming, to the inflow of grace. The more God does and the less you do, the better the prayer. In the beginning one is conscious of having to say the sacred word again and again. A better way of expressing that kind of activity is to say that one *returns* to the sacred word or that one gently places the sacred word in one's awareness. The sacred word is the symbol of the subtle spiritual movement of the will. One keeps consenting to God's presence. Since He is already present, one does not have to reach out to grab Him.

The sacred word is the symbol of consenting to God's presence. Eventually the will consents of itself without need of a symbol. The work of the will in prayer is real work, but it is one of receiving. Receiving is one of the most difficult kinds of activity there is. To receive God is the chief work in contemplative prayer.

The method of Centering Prayer is a way of opening to God at 360 degrees. Surrendering oneself to God is a more developed kind of consent. Transformation is completely God's work. We can't do anything to make it happen. We can only prevent it from happening.

As this prayer becomes habitual, a mysterious undifferentiated and peaceful Presence seems to be established inside of you. Some people say they feel that God is living within them. That tranquil Presence that is always there when they settle down becomes their method of prayer.

In the beginning we bring to prayer our false self with its expectations and preconceived ideas. That is why in teaching this prayer I do not speak of effort. The word *effort* is immediately translated in our work ethic into *trying*. Trying dilutes the basic disposition of receptivity that is necessary for the growth of contemplative prayer. Receptivity is not inactivity. It is real activity but not effort in the ordinary sense of the word. If you want to call it effort, keep in mind that it is totally unlike any other kind of effort. It is simply an attitude of waiting for the Ultimate Mystery. You don't know what that is, but as your faith is purified, you don't want to know. Of course, in a sense you are dying to know. But you realize that you can't possibly know by means of any human faculty; so it is useless to expect anything. You don't know and can't know what you are waiting for.

This prayer is thus a journey into the unknown. It is a call to follow Jesus out of all the structures, security blankets, and even spiritual practices that serve as props. They are all left behind insofar as they are part of the false-self system. Humility is the forgetfulness of self. To forget self is the hardest job on earth, but it doesn't come about by trying. Only God can bring our false self to an end. The false self is an illusion. It is our way of conceiving who we are and what the world is. Jesus said, "One who loses his life for my sake will find it." (Matthew 10:39) He also said, "If anyone will come after me let him deny himself [that is, the false self], take up his cross and follow me." (Matthew 16:24) Where is Jesus going? He is going to the cross where even his Divine-Human Self is sacrificed.

For Christians personal union with Christ is the way to come to divine union. The love of God will take care of the rest of the journey. Christian practice aims first at dismantling the false self. It is the work that God seems to require of us as proof of our sincerity. Then He will take our purification in hand, bring our deep-rooted selfishness into clear focus, and invite us to relinquish it. If we agree, He takes it away and replaces it with His own virtues.

At certain stages of human development, there are crisis points; for instance, early adolescence and the period just before young adulthood. Similarly, there is a crisis in spiritual development every time one is called to a higher state of consciousness. When the crisis begins, one hangs on to the false self for dear life. If one resists this path of growth, there is a chance that one might regress to a lower state or play ring-around-the-rosy for a while; there is the possibility of success or failure, of growing or regressing. If one regresses, one strengthens the false self. Then one has to wait until God reissues a new challenge. Fortunately, He has plans for us and does not give up too easily. We see that pattern at work in the way Jesus trained the apostles in the Gospel. He deals with us in similar ways.

The Canaanite woman is a magnificent example of someone undergoing what John of the Cross called the night of sense, the crisis that initiates the movement from dependency on sense and reason to docility to the Spirit. This woman went to Jesus as many other people had done and asked for the cure of her daughter. She didn't expect to have any trouble. She knelt down and made her petition. But Jesus didn't answer her. She prostrated herself, her face in the dust, and still got the cold shoulder. No one was ever treated so roughly by Jesus. As she was grovelling in the dust, he said, "It is not fair to take the children's bread and throw it to the dogs." (Matthew 15:26) The implication is obvious. But she came back with this incredible answer, "You are absolutely right, Lord. But even the dogs eat the crumbs as they fall from their master's table." (Matthew 15:27) Jesus was thrilled. His strange behavior was intended to raise her to the highest level of faith. At the end of the conversation he was able to say to her, "How wonderful is your faith! You can have anything you want!" To get to that place we, too, may have to experience rebuff, silence, and apparent rejection.

Some people complain that God never answers their prayers. Why should He? By not answering our prayers, He is answering our greatest prayer, which is to be transformed. That is what happened to the Canaanite woman.

> Sometimes there are no thoughts. There is only my self-awareness. I don't know whether to let go of it or to be aware of it.

That is a crucial question. If you are aware of no thoughts, you are aware of something and that is a thought. If at that point you can lose the awareness that you are aware of no thoughts, you will move into *pure consciousness*. In that state there is no consciousness of self. When your ordinary faculties come back together again, there may be a sense of peaceful delight, a good sign that you were not asleep. It is important to realize that the place to which we are going is one in which the knower, the knowing, and that which is known are all one. Awareness alone remains. The one who is aware disappears along with whatever was the object of consciousness. This is what divine union is. There is no reflection of self. The experience is temporary, but it orients you toward the contemplative state. So long as you *feel* united with God, it cannot be full union. So long as there is a thought, it is not full union. The moment of full union has no thought. You don't know about it until you emerge from it. In the beginning it is so tenuous that you may think you were asleep. It is not like the sense of felt union with the Lord that takes place on the level of self-reflection. Union on the spiritual level is a state of pure consciousness. It is the infusion of love and knowledge together, and while it is going on, it is nonreflective.

There is something in us that wants to *be aware* that we are not aware of ourselves. Even though the willingness to let go of the self is present, we can't do anything to bring it about except by continuing to let go of every thought. If we reflect on self, we start to move out again into the conceptual world.

Divine union for some might seem a bit scary. We can't imagine what such a state of being might be like. We think, "What if I lost consciousness? What if I never come back?" If we indulge the fear that we might not come back, we inhibit the process of letting go.

Centering Prayer is an exercise in letting go. That is all it is. It lays aside every thought. One touch of divine love enables you to take all the pleasures of the world and throw them in the wastebasket. Reflecting on spiritual communications diminishes them. The *Diamond Sutra* says it all: "Try to develop a mind that does not cling to anything."[1] That includes visions, ecstasies, locutions, spiritual communications, psychic gifts. These are not as valuable as pure consciousness.

It is extremely hard not to reflect on spiritual consolations, especially if you haven't had much experience of them. However, as you approach interior silence and are thrown out enough times, you begin to accept the fact that the grasping method won't work. Don't be discouraged or indulge in guilt feelings. Failure is the path to boundless confidence in God. Always remember that you have a billion chances. This God of ours is not crossing off anything on our list of opportunities. He keeps approaching us from every possible angle. He lures, draws, nudges, or pushes us, as the case may demand, into the place where He wants us to be.

Eventually you may get used to a certain degree of interior silence. The delightful peace that you may have enjoyed in the early stages of contemplative prayer becomes a normal state. Like anything in life, you can get used to contemplative prayer and not notice the great gifts you are receiving. Habitually you settle down at the beginning of prayer and move into a quiet space, and that's all there is. But that does not mean that you are no longer receiving the prayer of quiet, in which your will is in union with God. If thoughts are going by and you feel no attraction for them, you can be confident that you are in the prayer of quiet. When all the faculties are grasped by God, there is full union. That, however, is not the end of the journey.

What is the relationship of contemplative prayer to the rest of life?

The union established during prayer has to be integrated with the rest of reality. The presence of God should become a kind of fourth dimension to all of life. Our three-dimensional world is not the real world because the most important dimension is missing; namely, that from which everything that exists is emerging and returning in each micro-cosmic moment of time. It is like adding a sound track to a silent movie. The picture is the same, but the sound track makes it more alive. The contemplative state is established when contemplative prayer moves from being an experience or series of experiences to an abiding state of consciousness. The contemplative state enables one to rest and act at the same time because one is rooted in the source of both rest and action.

1. Luk, *Ch'an and Zen Teaching,* Series One, p. 173.

Some people experience a preview of divine union, lose it for a period of time, then have to climb back to it. God can start you off at any point in the spiritual life. If you get a headstart, you have to go back and fill in the gaps. Don't think that some people are lucky because they have visions when they are five or six years old. These people still have to go through the struggle to dismantle the emotional programs of early childhood. These programs are only temporarily put to sleep by the divine action. One great advantage for such persons, however, is that they know by experience what is missing in their lives and that nothing less than God can ever satisfy them. It is a mistake, however, to envy or admire someone else's path. You must be convinced that you have everything you need to reach divine union. The reason any expectation is a hindrance is that it is a form of clinging, hence a desire to control.

Let go of sensible and spiritual consolation. When you feel the love of God flowing into you, it is a kind of union, but it is a union of which you are aware. Therefore, it is not pure union, not full union. Spiritual consolation is so marvelous that human nature eagerly reaches out for it. We are not about to sit still and pretend it isn't there. We reach out for it with all our being and cry, "If I can only remember how I got here!"

So long as you are moved by such desires, you are still trying to control God. Even if you see the heavens opening and Jesus sitting at the right hand of the Father, forget it. Return to the sacred word. You have nothing to lose. Spiritual communications accomplish their purpose instantly before you have the chance to reflect on them. You have received the full benefit of the gift even if you never think of it again. Letting go of spiritual gifts is the best way to receive them. The more detached you are from them, the more you can receive or rather, the better you can receive. It takes a lot of courage to let go of the most delightful things that can be experienced.

> Why is there such an alternation in prayer between consolation and desolation, interior silence and the bombardment of thoughts, the presence of God and the absence of God?

The alternations in our relationship with God are not unlike the presence or absence of someone we greatly love. In the *Song of Solomon,* God is depicted as pursuing the soul as His beloved. The fathers of the Church had a fondness for this particular verse: "O that his left hand were under my head and that his right hand embraced me." (Song of Solomon 2:6) According to their interpretation, God embraces us with both arms. With the left He humbles and corrects us; with the right He lifts us up and consoles us with the assurance of being loved by Him. If you want to be fully embraced by the Lord, you have to accept both arms: the one that allows suffering for the sake of purification and the one that brings the joy of union. When you feel physical pain or when psychological struggles are persecuting you, you should think that God is hugging you extra tightly. Trials are an expression of His love, not of rejection.

In contemplative prayer, the distress caused by the absence of God is often compensated for by experiences of divine Union. The greater your longing for union with Christ, the more painful it is when he seems to go away. Suffering is part of the warp and woof of living. It is not an end in itself, but part of the price one has to pay for being greatly loved. Love, whether human or divine, makes you vulnerable. The alternation of joy and sorrow in the spiritual journey helps us to be detached from our psychological experiences. True lovers are more interested in being loved for themselves than for their embraces. So it is with God. He wants to be loved for His own sake, for who He is, beyond what we may experience. The tendency to seek the reward of love, which is to be loved in return, is natural. The Spirit teaches us through these alternations to love God as He is in Himself, whatever the psychological content of our experience. That kind of freedom stabilizes the spiritual journey. From then on, the vicissitudes of the journey, while painful at times on the surface, do not disturb the heart that is rooted in divine love.

There is a level in which pain is joy and joy is pain. Then it doesn't matter any more which it is because one is rooted in place where what matters is divine love. From the point of view of divine love, pain can be joy. It is a way of sacrificing ourselves completely for the sake of the Beloved. It does not cease to be pain, but it has a different quality from ordinary pain. Divine love is the source of that quality. It finds in pain a way of expressing its love with a totality that would not be otherwise possible. Jesus crucified is God's way of expressing the immensity of His love for each of us, proof that He loves us infinitely and unconditionally.

> Can the interior attraction for recollection overtake you during the day in your ordinary occupations?

Yes. I only recommend that when driving a car, you keep your eyes open! Apart from such situations, if one has the leisure, one could give way to it. You also can overdo it. The pleasurable part of prayer is not the goal; it is rather the introduction to it. If you can be united to God without the intermediary of feelings and thoughts, there is no more sense of separation. Spiritual consolation is a means of softening up the faculties and healing them of their various wounds. It gives you a completely different view of God than when you are dealing with Him solely on the basis of good and evil, right and wrong, reward and punishment. As the relationship of intimacy with God begins to deepen, you should not unduly prolong your time of prayer. When there is some duty to be performed, you have to sacrifice for the moment your attraction to interior silence. But if you have nothing urgent going on, I don't see why you can't give in to the attraction for five or ten minutes, or longer, if you have the time.

In contemplative orders there should be great respect for individual expressions of the contemplative life. At different periods of one's development God calls one to more intense community life and at other times to greater solitude. If you are in a community where only one or the other is available, the situation is not conducive to the full expression of the contemplative vocation. Institutions, even the best ones, have limitations. Sometimes God uses confining situations to bring someone to great perfection, but with the general awakening to individual needs in our time, communities will do well to remember that contemplatives have needs, too, and to provide for them in an atmosphere of support and sympathy.

Some of the greatest sufferings of contemplatives have come not from God, but from other people. When Margaret Mary Alacoque was receiving visions of the Sacred Heart of Jesus, she often entered into bodily ecstasy.[2] When the other nuns rose at the signal to leave the choir, she could not get up. Her superiors accused her of disobedience because she was not observing the rule. Some of the sisters thought she must have a devil, and they used to sprinkle her with holy water to protect themselves and the other nuns. You can imagine their faces when they were trying to exorcise the demon out of poor Margaret Mary, who just could not tear herself away from the love of God. Her prayer life was developing in a thoroughly normal way, but her senses could not sustain the strength of the graces that God was giving her. Later, when she became spiritually more mature, her senses did not give way, and then her state of prayer was no longer obvious.

Spiritual consolation that overflows into the senses and into the body is a phase in the growth of contemplative prayer. Some temperaments are more prone to it than others. Some do not experience it at all. If it is especially strong, the body cannot move a muscle and time goes by unnoticed. Centering Prayer may give you an inkling of what that might be like. When the period of prayer seems to pass quickly, you can see that if you were just a little deeper, you would have no idea of time at all. If somebody came up and touched you, you would be shaken up. If a community regards such phenomena as dangerous, from the devil, or unlikely to happen to humble religious, then such a community is a poor context for the development of the spiritual life. Unfortunately, such attitudes have been common in religious life for three hundred years because of the prevailing anti-contemplative climate. The fear of false mysticism led to extremes like the Inquisition, which regarded even the writings of Teresa and John of the Cross with suspicion. John of the Cross is not recognized as one of the greatest exponents of the mystical life that

2. Poulain, *Graces of Interior Prayer,* Chapter XIV:57.

the Roman Catholic Church has ever produced. If even he could not escape the suspicion of the Inquisition, what do you think would happen to ordinary religious who were having experiences that they could not articulate because they were not theologians or spiritual directors?

It is one thing to have the grace of interior prayer; another to be able to communicate it. They do not necessarily go together. Sometimes someone who truly has the contemplative experience expresses it in a way that upsets the more conservative element in the environment. Such a person may be labeled a heretic when he is just expressing himself clumsily.

Mystical language is not theological language. It is the language of the bedchamber, of love, and hence of hyperbole and exaggeration. If a husband says that he adores his wife, it does not mean that he regards her as a goddess. He is just trying to express his *feeling* of love in language that is powerless to do so—except through hyperbole. But if the people in your environment do not understand that kind of language, they may think you are under the influence of the devil.

> How does the Charismatic Movement fit in with this contemplative approach to prayer?

The great contribution that the Charismatic Movement has made is to reawaken among contemporary Christians belief in the dynamic activity of the Spirit, who is strengthening, consoling, and guiding us with his unfailing inspiration. Thanks to the Movement, the spontaneity of the early Christian communities described by Paul and by the Acts of the Apostles is being rediscovered in our time. The first believers gathered in communities around the risen Christ to listen to the word of God in scripture, to celebrate in the liturgy, and to be transformed into Christ by the Eucharist. The presence of the Spirit was palpably manifested in these assemblies by means of the charismatic gifts. The gift of tongues seems to have been given to encourage the individual believer; hence, its use in public worship was restricted. Interpretation of tongues, prophecy, healing, teaching, administration, and other gifts provided for the spiritual and material needs of the various local communities. The continuing work of the Spirit manifested by the development of the Christian contemplative tradition must now be integrated into this scriptural model revived by the Charismatic Renewal.

> I know a man who got into the Charismatic Movement, was having profound spiritual experiences, and didn't know what they were. His parish priest didn't either. This man was in touch with a contemplative nun in a cloistered convent who told him, "Don't worry about it; those are typical."

She referred him to the appropriate mystical text and continued to give him instruction.

The Charismatic Movement speaks to the need of Christians today for a supportive community and for a personal experience of prayer. "Baptism in the Spirit" is probably a transient mystical grace induced by the fervor of the group or by other factors that we don't know. The gift of tongues is a rudimentary form of nonconceptual prayer. Since you don't know what you are saying, you can't be thinking about what you are saying. Those in the Movement need what that man was fortunate enough to receive, namely, the help and instruction of someone who knew the Christian contemplative tradition. After you have sung the praises of God, shared prayer together, spoken in tongues, and prophesied for a few years, where do you go from there? There is a place to go. It is time to introduce periods of silence into the group, for the members are now fully prepared to move to a more contemplative expression of prayer. If some silence were introduced into the meetings, the Movement would hold more people. Groups differ according to their makeup and theological resources, but they all need help with spiritual teaching. Some Charismatics are opposed to contemplative prayer because they believe that if you are not thinking, the devil will start thinking of you. In actual fact, if you are praying in interior silence, the devil can't get anywhere near you. There is more chance of his suggesting things to your imagination when you are practicing discursive meditation. It is only when you come out of interior silence and reemerge into the world of the senses and reasoning that he can put his finger in the pie and stir things up. The Charismatic Movement has great potential. To fulfill its promise, however, it needs to be open to the Christian contemplative tradition.

8

THE MORE SUBTLE
KINDS OF THOUGHTS

■

THE FIRST KIND OF THOUGHT that regularly comes down the stream of consciousness when one begins to practice Centering Prayer is woolgathering. This may consist of things that we were doing or thinking about prior to our time of prayer. Or again, an outside sound, a vivid memory, or some plan for the future may attract and capture our attention. In the simile we have been using, these thoughts are like boats floating down the stream of consciousness. Our normal, habitual reaction is to say, "What is this? I wonder what is in the hold?" Instead, gently return to the sacred word, moving from the particular thought to the general loving attention to God that that word reaffirms. And let the boat go by. When another boat comes down, let it go by. If a whole fleet comes down, let them all go by.

At first this is bothersome because you want to remain quiet. Little by little you begin to develop two attentions at once. You are aware of the superficial thoughts. At the same time you are aware of an undifferentiated presence that mysteriously attracts you. It is a deeper attention, a spiritual attentiveness. You are aware of both levels of attention going on at once. To develop that deeper attention is more important than worrying about the superficial thoughts. They will cease to attract you after a while.

A second kind of thought that comes down the stream of consciousness might be compared to a flashy boat that captures your attention and makes you feel like climbing aboard. If you give in to the inclination and hop on board, you start heading downstream. You have identified yourself in some degree with the thought. To return to the sacred word is to reaffirm your original intention of opening to the divine presence. The sacred word is a means of liberating yourself from the tendency to get stuck on an attractive thought. If you are hooked or about to be hooked, let go promptly but with a very gentle interior movement. Any form of resisting thoughts is itself a thought. Moreover, it is a thought with an emotional charge to it. Emotionally charged thoughts hinder the basic disposition you are

71

engaged in cultivating, waiting upon God in the mystery of His Presence. So let go of all thoughts, and when tempted to pursue one of them, return to the sacred word. Do it as gently as if your attention were a drop of dew descending on a blade of grass. If you allow yourself to be annoyed at being pulled out of the silent waters that you were enjoying, you will just go farther downstream.

When you begin to quiet down and enjoy a certain peace, you don't want to think of anything. You just want to be quiet. Then another kind of thought emerges. It could be some bright light about the spiritual journey or some great psychological insight into your past life. Or you have a problem with a member of your family and suddenly see how it can be resolved. Or you discover the perfect argument for converting your friends. Of course, when you come out of prayer, you see that your brilliant ideas were utterly ridiculous. They looked wonderful in the darkness of the deep waters of silence, but in the light of day you realize that they were bait to lure you out of interior peace and quiet.

Again, you may feel an overwhelming urge to pray for someone. It is important to pray for others, but this is not the time to do it. Any effort you make at this point is counterproductive. This is God's opportunity to talk to you. It would be like interrupting someone who wants to confide something to you. You know how it is when you are trying to tell a friend something important and he keeps interrupting you with ideas of his own. In this prayer you are listening to God, listening to His silence. Your only activity is the attention that you offer to God either implicitly by letting go of all thoughts or explicitly by returning to the sacred word.

Preachers and theologians who are trying to practice contemplative prayer have a special problem with good thoughts. Just when they are quiet, they get some incredible inspiration. A theological problem they have been trying to fathom for years suddenly becomes as clear as crystal. There is a tendency for them to think, "I must reflect about this for just a second so I won't forget it after my prayer is over." That is the end of their interior silence. When they come out of prayer, they can't even remember what the bright idea was. When one is in deep quiet, one is very susceptible to brilliant intellectual lights. Most of the time they are just illusions. Human nature does not like to be empty before God. If you are making headway in this prayer, you will be tempted by the jealous demons who see that you are getting some place and try to trip you up. To hinder your progress they dangle various kinds of tasty bait in front of your imagination. Like a little fish enjoying deep waters, you feel engulfed by God on all sides when suddenly this bait is lowered into your peaceful space. You bite on it and out you go.

It may be hard to convince yourself of the value of interior silence. But if you are going to practice Centering Prayer, the only way to do it is to ignore every thought. Let it be a time of interior silence and nothing else. If God wants to speak to you in successive words, let Him do so during the other twenty-three hours of the day. He will be more pleased that you preferred to listen to His silence. In this prayer God is speaking not to your ears, to your emotions, or to your head, but to your spirit, to your inmost being. There is no human apparatus to understand that language or to hear it. A kind of anointing takes place. The fruits of that anointing will appear later in ways that are indirect: in your calmness, in your peace, in your willingness to surrender to God in everything that happens. That is why interior silence is greater than any insight. It also saves you a lot of trouble. Pure faith is the surest and straightest road to God. Human nature wants to recall spiritual experiences of one kind or another in order to be able to explain them to oneself and to others. The remembrance of spiritual experiences is okay up to a point, but such experiences are not as important as interior silence. Don't reflect on them during prayer. If they have genuine value, they will come back to you later. The deeper your interior silence, the more profoundly God will work in you without your knowing it. Pure faith consents and surrenders to the Ultimate Mystery just as He is; not as you think He is or as someone has told you He is, but as He is in Himself.

There is no greater way in which God can communicate with us than on the level of pure faith. This level does not register directly on our psychic faculties because it is too deep. God is incomprehensible to our faculties. We cannot name Him in a way that is adequate. We cannot know Him with our mind; we can only know Him with our love. That is what some mystical writers call *unknowing*. It is by *not* knowing Him in the ways that we now know Him, that we *do* know Him. Visions, locutions or ecstasies are like frosting on a cake. The substance of the journey is pure faith.

A special kind of thought occurs when our ordinary psychic self is quiet. If you have ever made wine, you know that after the new wine has been separated from the dregs, it is poured into a barrel and what is called a finer is introduced. A finer is a liquid that forms a thin film throughout the barrel and gradually sinks to the bottom in the course of two or three months, carrying with it all the foreign bodies in the wine. What is happening to your psyche in contemplative prayer is quite similar. The sacred word is the finer and the silence to which it inclines you is the process that clarifies your consciousness. As your consciousness is clarified, you resonate with spiritual values and the radiance of God's presence.

There is an immediacy of awareness in contemplative prayer. It is a path to the rediscovery of the simplicity of childhood. As an infant becomes aware of its surroundings, it is not so much *what* it sees that delights it as it is the *act* of seeing. I once heard about a little girl of wealthy parents who loved to play with her mother's jewelry. When her mother wasn't around and the nurse couldn't capture her in time, she used to gather her mother's diamonds and throw them into the toilet bowl. She loved to hear the splash as she watched the beautiful diamonds sinking in the water. As she grew older, she learned to flush the toilet. The members of the household were tearing their hair. How were they to cure the dear child of this terrible habit? The little girl had no interest in the value of the jewelry. Her mother, of course, thought they had great value. The little girl simply enjoyed the immediacy of the experience, the sparkling diamonds splashing into the water. She had the freedom and joy of true detachment.

As we grow older, it is important to develop our analytical judgment, but we shouldn't lose the enjoyment of reality as it is, the value of *just being* and of *just doing*. In the Gospel, Jesus invites us to become like little children, to imitate their innocence, confidence, and direct contact with reality. He doesn't invite us, of course, to imitate their childishness, and their tantrums. If our value system doesn't allow us to enjoy anything without putting a price on it, we miss a great part of the beauty of life. When we bring this value system into the domain of prayer, we can never enjoy God. As soon as we start enjoying Him, we have to reflect, "Oh boy, I'm enjoying God!" And as soon as we do that, we are taking a photograph of the experience. Every reflection is like a photograph of reality. It isn't our original experience; it is a commentary on it. Just as a picture only approximates reality, so every reflection is one step back from experience as it actually is. When we experience the presence of God, if we can just not *think* about it, we can rest in it for a long time. Unfortunately, we are like starving people when it comes to spiritual things, and we hang on to spiritual consolation for dear life. It is precisely that possessive attitude that prevents us from enjoying the simplicity and childlike delight of the experience.

In contemplative prayer we should ignore our psychological experiences as much as we can and just let them happen. If you are at peace, wonderful; don't think about it. Just be at peace and enjoy it without reflecting. The deeper the experience you have of God, the less you will usually be able to say about it. When you try to conceptualize, you are using your imagination, memory, and reason—all of which bear no proportion to the depth and immediacy of divine union. A childlike attitude makes sense in this situation. You don't have to *do* anything. Just rest in God's arms. It is an exercise of *being* rather than of *doing*. You will be able to accomplish what you have to do with much greater effectiveness and joy. Much of the time we run on cylinders that are out of oil or a bit rusty. Our powers of giving are pretty well used up by noon on most days. Contemplative prayer opens you to the power of the Spirit. Your capacity to keep giving all day long will increase. You will be able to adjust to difficult circumstances and even to live with impossible situations.

The third kind of thought, if consented to, prevents you from entering into your own deep space. That is why no matter how glamorous the thought or how many problems it seems to solve, you should forget it. You can always think about bright ideas later in the day, and then it may be fruitful to do so. In this prayer we are cultivating purity of motivation. In the Christian path, motivation is everything. When there are no obstacles in ourselves to receiving the light, the light that is always shining will shine in us. As long as we are under the influence of the false self and its ego trips, we have the shades drawn. Unfortunately, the false self doesn't just drop dead upon request. We can't just say, "That's the end of it," and expect it to disappear. The false self is extremely subtle. Without God's special help, we could never escape from it. In addition, the trials that come our way would flatten us.

The attitude that reinforces the false self more than anything else is our instinct to possess something, including our own thoughts and feelings. This instinct has to be relinquished. Most of us are starved for spiritual experience. When it begins to happen, everything in us reaches out for it. We can't help ourselves at first. As we learn through bitter experience that grasping for spiritual experience get us thrown out on the bank, it dawns on us that this is not the way to proceed. If we can let go of our clinging attitude toward this deep peace, we will move into a refined joy and an inner freedom where spiritual experience no longer looms so large. We can have all we want of divine consolation if we don't try to possess it. As soon as we want to possess it, it is gone. We have to accept God as He is, without trying to possess Him. Whatever we experience of Him must be allowed to pass by like every other thought that comes down our stream of consciousness. Once we know that our destination lies beyond any kind of spiritual experience, we realize that it is useless to hang on to anything along the way. Then we won't settle down under a palm tree in some oasis along the route. An oasis is refreshing, but it is not the purpose of the journey. If we keep going, even if we are only stumbling or crawling along, we will come to the interior freedom that is the ripe fruit of docility to the Spirit.

The third kind of thought occurs when we enter into deep peace, and the inclination to reach out for bright ideas lures us out of the quiet depths. The sacred word is not a mantra in the strict sense of the word. We do not keep saying it until we drill it into our consciousness. It is rather a condition, an atmosphere that we set up, that allows us to surrender to the attractive force of the divine Presence within us. Spiritual consolation is a radiance of that Presence. It is not the Presence of God as such. In this life we cannot know God directly and still live. To know Him directly is what the next life is all about. The closest way to know Him in this life is by pure faith, which is beyond thinking, feeling, and self-reflection. Pure faith is experienced best when there is no psychological experience of God. God is beyond sensible or conceptual experience. The state of pure faith is beyond anything we can imagine. We simply look around and realize that the divine Presence is everywhere. It just *is*. We have opened ourselves wide enough to be *aware* of what is without being able to *say* what it is.

The fourth kind of thought also takes place when we are in deep, all-encompassing peace, empty of thoughts and images. A mysterious fullness, a kind of luminous darkness, seems to surround us and penetrate our consciousness. We enjoy deep calm even though we are dimly aware of the ordinary flow of unwanted thoughts. They are especially distressing at such a time because we know if we get hooked on one of them, we are going to be carried out of that peace. We don't even want to return to the sacred word. We don't want to do anything except allow ourselves to be bathed in the light and love that seem to be tenderly anointing our inmost being. It is as if God planted a great big kiss in the middle of our spirit and all the wounds, doubts, and guilt-feelings were all healed at the same moment. The experience of being loved by the Ultimate Mystery banishes every fear. It convinces us that all the mistakes we have made and all the sins we have committed are completely forgiven and forgotten.

Meanwhile, into that silence, into that state of no-thinking, no-reflection, and ineffable peace, comes the thought: "At last, I'm getting somewhere!" Or, "This peace is just great!" Or, "If only I could take a moment to remember how I got into this space so that tomorrow I can return to it without delay." Out you go, as fast as lightning, right onto the bank. And then you say, "Oh, God! What did I do wrong?"

How do you let God act in this prayer?

It's difficult to let God act under all circumstances. Letting go and not reflecting on what you are doing is the correct way to conduct yourself in this prayer. The method doesn't consist in how you sit or in the length of time you give, but in how you handle the thoughts that arise. I think it can be said that the essential point of all the great spiritual disciplines that the world religions have evolved is the letting go of thoughts. Everything else is subsidary to that. The goal is to integrate and unify the various levels of one's being and to surrender that integrated and unified being to God.

Are you ever aware of God during contemplative prayer, or is it only afterwards that you can know that God was there? How is it possible to be aware of something and not reflect on it?

You can be aware of the undifferentiated presence of God and not have any explicit reflection about it. Pure awareness is the immediacy of experience. Our training and education have programmed us for reflection. But one can be so absorbed in an experience that one does not reflect. Have you ever enjoyed something so much that you didn't have time to think of what you were enjoying?

Yes, but I guess you would feel the enjoyment.

Of course. Just don't reflect on the feeling. If you do, you reduce the experience to something that you can understand, and God isn't something you can understand. The awareness of God is shot through with awe, reverence, love, and delight all at once.

We are made for happiness and there is nothing wrong in reaching out for it. Unfortunately, most of us are so deprived of happiness that as soon as it comes along, we reach out for it with all our strength and try to hang on to it for dear life. That is the mistake. The best way to receive it is to give it away. If you give everything back to God, you will always be empty, and when you are empty, there is more room for God.

The experience of God usually comes as something you feel you have experienced before. God is so well suited to us that any experience of him is a feeling of completion or well-being. What was lacking in us seems to be somehow mysteriously restored. This experience awakens confidence, peace, joy, and reverence all at the same time. Of course, the next thing that occurs to us is: "This is great! How am I going to hang on to it?" That's the normal human reaction. But experience teaches that that is exactly the worst thing to do. The innate tendency to hang on, to possess, is the biggest obstacle to union with God. The reason we are possessive is that we feel separated from God. The feeling of separation is our ordinary psychological experience of the human condition. This misapprehension is the cause of our efforts to look for happiness down every path that we can possibly envision when actually it is right under our noses. We just don't know how to perceive it. Since the security that we should have as beings united with God is missing, we reach out to bolster up our fragile self-image with whatever possessions or power symbols we can lay hold of. In returning to God, we take the reverse path, which is to let go of all that we want to possess. Since nothing is more desirable or delightful than the feeling of God's presence, that, too, has to be a thought we are willing to let go of.

Trying to hang on to God's presence is like trying to hang on to the air. You can't carve out a piece of it and hide it in your top bureau drawer. Similarly, you can't carve out a piece of the presence of God and hide it in the closet or store it in the refrigerator until the next period of prayer. This prayer is an exercise in letting go of everything. As it develops, it will help you to let go of things and events that arise outside the time of prayer. This doesn't mean that you do not use the good things of this world. It is only the clinging or addiction to things that reduces the free flow of God's grace and that hinders the enjoyment of His Presence.

Do thoughts always keep coming? It seems like I'm able to maintain a feeling of peace for a time. Then all of a sudden the thoughts roll in again. Is that always the way it happens?

To be in and out of peace is normal in every period of prayer, although there might be some periods that are uniformly quiet throughout. But in that case you are likely to find that the next time you pray, you will be filled with what airline pilots call turbulence, and you will be bounced around quite a bit by persistent and disturbing thoughts. This is not a disaster but something one has to accept. The alternation between peace and thought-barrage is an important part of the process. They are two sides of the same coin.

Please keep in mind that the method of centering is only one form of prayer and doesn't exclude other forms of prayer at other times. It is like Jacob's ladder in the Old Testament. After his vision of the Lord in the form of an angel who wrestled with him all night, Jacob fell asleep. He saw a ladder reaching from earth to heaven with angels descending and ascending. The ladder represents different levels of consciousness or of faith. We should communicate with God on every level of our being: with our lips, our bodies, our imaginations, our emotions, our minds, our intuitive faculties, and our silence. Centering Prayer is only one rung of the ladder. It is a way of giving God a chance to speak to us. While our spontaneous chats with God are good, there is a level that is even better. As in human friendship, there is a conversational level. But as friendship grows more intimate, the level of communion develops, where the two can sit together and say nothing. If they say nothing, does that mean they are not finding deep enjoyment in the relationship? There are obviously different ways and different levels of expressing one's relationship with another person and with God. God clearly deals with us in a personal way. This prayer adds a dimension to one's relationship with God that is more intimate than the other levels. There is nothing wrong with vocal prayer, but it isn't the only way or the most profound way of praying.

> Could it be that the one who practices contemplative prayer for long stretches of time every day might develop some form of illness?

If you had a lot of time for prayer and were in a particularly consoling period in your development, prayer could be so delightful that you might try to prolong it as much as possible. But to be consoled is not the object of contemplative prayer. Teresa of Avila made fun of certain nuns in her convents who practiced so much of this kind of prayer that they became sick. The reason was that by remaining in interior silence for seven or eight hours a day, and perhaps longer, their senses became so withdrawn from their ordinary occupations that they probably experienced what we call today sensory deprivation. When we spend a great deal of time in interior silence, the metabolism goes down, which means that less blood is going to the brain. This is fine for a limited period of time such as during a retreat, but if you keep it up day after day, you may get spaced-out. If you continue this practice for more than a week, you need supervision. Everything has to be done with discretion. Generally people overdo discretion on the side of making sure they do nothing that might injure their health. But there are some people who do the opposite, and they may need to be restrained.

Is there any value in prolonging the time of contemplative prayer?

To do it more than twice a day may hasten the process of self-knowledge. As a result, you may get insights into things from your past that you have not previously faced or handled. It is characteristic of the human condition to avoid seeing our own hang-ups. The development of contemplative prayer from this point of view is a process of liberation from everything that prevents us from being completely honest with ourselves. The more confidence you have in God, the more you can face the truth about yourself. You can only face up to who you really are in the presence of someone you trust. If you trust God, you know that no matter what you have done or not done, He is going to go on loving you. As a matter of fact, He always knew the dark side of your character and He is not lettng you in on thc secret like a friend confiding to a friend. Insights of self-knowledge, instead of upsetting you, bring a sense of freedom. They lead you to the point where you can ask yourself, "Why think of myself at all?" Then you have the freedom to think how wonderful God is and you care little what happens to you.

It seems paradoxical that at some point during the prayer you become aware of the fact that you are not thinking at all. What do you do with that?

If you are actually not thinking, there is not even the thought that you are not thinking. There is just pure awareness, and that is the proximate goal of contempla- tive prayer. The ultimate goal, of course, is to integrate your whole being with its active and passive, masculine and feminine, expressing and receptive aspects. If you begin to be aware of the fact that you are not thinking at all and can just not think that thought, you have it made. There is only a short step from that point to divine union. Of course, you eventually will be thrown out of that delicious silence and your mind will start wandering again. As soon as you notice that you are coming out of interior silence, go back with the gentlest kind of attention to the Presence. The thought of not having a thought is the last preserve of self-reflection. If you can get beyond self-reflection, allow yourself to be self-forgetful, and let go of the compulsion to keep track of where you are, you will move into deeper peace and freedom. There is a conviction deep inside of us that if we ever stop reflecting on ourselves, we will disintegrate or suffer some similar fate. That is not true. If we ever stop reflecting on ourselves, we will move into perfect peace.

I know when to use the sacred word, but I do not know when *not* to use it.

There is a state of no-thinking and that is where we want to go. It is elusive because of our inveterate tendency to reflect. This innate tendency to be aware of oneself is the last stronghold of self-centeredness. Anthony of Egypt is noted for this famous saying: "Perfect prayer is not to know that you are praying." What I have just described is the state of mind that Anthony is talking about. When you are in perfect prayer, the Spirit is praying in you. The surrender of the false self to God is death to the false self. This is the experience that Jesus was trying to explain to Nicodemus when he said, "You have to be reborn." (John 3:3) One has to die before one can be reborn. Nicodemus replied, "How can someone go back into the womb?" Jesus continued, "You do not understand what I am talking about. I am talking about the Spirit and I am speaking spiritually. The wind blows where it will, and you do not know where it is coming from or where it is going. So it is with everyone who is born of the Spirit." In other words, to be moved by the Spirit is an entirely new way of being in the world.

> I have been using the prayer of centering for over a year, but I have clung to the sacred word like a drowning man clinging to a tire. At one of the prayer periods today, the tire was getting in my way, so I threw it away. I thought that maybe that was a step forward.

By all means, throw away your life preserver. It's preserving the wrong life. The false self must die if you are to be reborn and live by the Spirit.

> As a person becomes more advanced in prayer, will he or she have more need of spiritual direction?

There are times when spiritual direction can be very helpful by way of encouragement and support. In contemplative prayer, every now and then you run into heavy weather. As you go deeper into the unconscious through interior silence, you may hit something like an oil well and up will come a whole stream of stuff. You may have a period of several months or years when it is rough going. These are the periods that John of the Cross calls "dark nights." In such situations, one needs reassurance. For some people, these periods of trial are tougher than they are for others. They need reassurance, and then a spiritual director can be a great help. But if the director does not have experience of this kind of prayer, he or she can do more harm than good.

Sometimes all you need is to wait and not lose heart. When that oil well runs dry, you will move to a new depth. Or again, it is like being in an elevator that gets stuck between floors. You just have to wait until whatever it is that is an obstacle has been removed.

A spiritual director should be someone who has enough experience to be able to perceive with some degree of certitude where you are on the spiritual path. A director can usually discern this from the kind of life that people are leading. If they are obviously seeking God but are having problems that make them think that they are the worst sinners that ever existed, the director has to know how to say, "Forget it! You are the luckiest person on earth!" When you are in the dark night of purification, you are a very poor judge of your own case. One of the trials you have to expect is being unable to find anyone who can help you. God may arrange it that way so that you have to put all your trust in Him.

9

THE UNLOADING OF
THE UNCONSCIOUS

A FIFTH KIND OF THOUGHT arises from the fact that through the regular practice of contemplative prayer the dynamism of interior purification is set in motion. This dynamism is a kind of divine psychotherapy, organically designed for each of us, to empty out our unconscious and free us from the obstacles to the free flow of grace in our minds, emotions, and bodies.

Empirical evidence seems to be growing that the consequences of traumatic emotional experiences from earliest childhood are stored in our bodies and nervous systems in the form of tension, anxiety, and various defense mechanisms. Ordinary rest and sleep do not get rid of them. But in interior silence and the profound rest that this brings to the whole organism, these emotional blocks begin to soften up and the natural capacity of the human organism to throw off things that are harmful starts to evacuate them. The psyche as well as the body has its way of evacuating material that is harmful to its health. The emotional junk in our unconscious emerges during prayer in the form of thoughts that have a certain urgency, energy, and emotional charge to them. You don't usually know from what particular source or sources they are coming. There is ordinarily just a jumble of thoughts and a vague or acute sense of uneasiness. Simply putting up with them and not fighting them is the best way to release them.

As the deep peace flowing from contemplative prayer releases our emotional blocks, insights into the dark side of our personality emerge and multiply. We blissfully imagine that we do good to our families, friends, and business or professional associates for the best of reasons, but when this dynamism begins to operate in us, our so-called good intentions look like a pile of dirty dishrags. We perceive that we are not as generous as we had believed. This happens because the divine light is shining brighter in our hearts. Divine love, by its very nature, accuses us of our innate selfishness.

Suppose we were in a dimly lit room. The place might look fairly clean. But install a hundred bulbs of a thousand watts each, and put the whole room under a magnifying glass. The place would begin to crawl with all kind of strange and wonderful little creatures. It would be all you could do to stay there. So it is with our interior. When God turns up the voltage, our motivation begins to take on a wholly different character, and we reach out with great sincerity for the mercy of God and for His forgiveness. That is why trust in God is so important. Without trust we are likely to run away or say, "There must be some better way of going to God."

Self-knowledge in the Christian ascetical tradition is insight into our hidden motivation, into emotional needs and demands that are percolating inside of us and influencing our thinking, feeling, and activity without our being fully aware of them. To give an example: When I was an abbot, which is a father image in a monastery, I was struck by the fact that some of the younger members of the community were unconsciously treating me as their real father. I could see that they were working out emotional hassles with authority figures from their early childhood. They were not relating to me as me. When you withdraw from your ordinary flow of superficial thoughts on a regular daily basis, you get a sharper perspective on your motivation, and you begin to see that the value systems by which you have always lived have their roots in prerational attitudes that have never been honestly and fully confronted. We all have neurotic tendencies. When you practice contemplative prayer on a regular basis, your natural resources for psychic health begin to revive and you see the false value systems that are damaging your life. The emotional programs of early childhood that are buried in your unconscious begin to emerge into clear and stark awareness.

If in your psyche there are obstacles to opening yourself to God, divine love begins to show you what these are. If you let go of them, you will gradually unfold in the presence of God and enjoy His Presence. The inner dynamism of contemplative prayer leads naturally to the transformation of your whole personality. Its purpose is not limited to your moral improvement. It brings about a change in your way of perceiving and responding to reality. This process involves a structural change of consciousness.

As you experience the reassurance that comes from interior peace, you have more courage to face the dark side of your personality and to accept yourself as you are. Every human being has the incredible potential to become divine, but at the same time each of us has to contend with the historical evolution of our nature from lower forms of consciousness. There is a tendency in human nature to reach out for more life, more happiness, more of God; but there are also self-destructive tendencies that want to go back to the unconscious and instinctual behavior of the beasts. Even though we know that there is no happiness in such regression, that aspect of the human condition is always lurking within us. Archbishop Fulton Sheen used to say, "Barbarism is not behind us but beneath us." In other words, violence and the other instinctual drives remain as seeds that can develop, if un-checked, into all kinds of evil.

We have to come to grips with these tendencies in order for the fullness of grace to flow through us. Contemplative prayer fosters the healing of these wounds. In psychoanalysis the patient relives traumatic experiences of the past and in doing so, integrates them into a healthy pattern of life. If you are faithful to the daily practice of contemplative prayer, these psychic wounds will be healed without your being retraumatized. After you have been doing this prayer for some months, you will experience the emergence of certain forceful and emotionally charged thoughts. They don't normally reveal some traumatic experience in early life or some unre-solved problem in your present life. They simply emerge as thoughts that arise with a certain force or that put you in a depressed mood for a few hours or days. Such thoughts are of great value from the perspective of human growth even though you may feel persecuted by them during the whole time of prayer.

When the unloading of the unconscious begins in earnest, many people feel that they are going backwards, that contemplative prayer is just impossible for them because all they experience when they start to pray is an unending flow of distrac-tions. Actually, there are no distractions in contemplative prayer unless you really want to be distracted or if you get up and leave. Hence, it doesn't matter how many thoughts you have. Their number and nature have no effect whatever on the geniuneness of your prayer. If your prayer were on the level of thinking, thoughts that were extraneous to your reflections would indeed be distracting. But contem-plative prayer is not on the level of thinking. It is consenting with your will to God's Presence in pure faith.

Emotionally charged thoughts are the chief way that the unconscious has of expelling chunks of emotional junk. In this way, without your perceiving it, a great many emotional conflicts that are hidden in your unconscious and affecting your decisions more than you realize are being resolved. As a consequence, over a period of time you will feel a greater sense of well-being and inner freedom. The very thoughts that you lament while in prayer are freeing the psyche from the damage that has accumulated in your nervous system over a lifetime. In this prayer both thoughts and silence have an important role to play.

To use a clumsy simile, in tenement houses where the garbage collection is unre-liable, some tenants use the bathroom to store the garbage. If you want to take a bath, the first thing you have to do is empty out the junk. A similar procedure holds in this prayer. When we commit ourselves to the spiritual journey, the first thing the Spirit does is start removing the emotional junk inside of us. He wishes to fill us completely and to transform our entire body-spirit organism into a flexible instrument of divine love. But as long as we have obstacles in us, some of which we are not even aware, he can't fill us to capacity. In his love and zeal he begins to clean out the tub. One means by which he does this is by means of the passive purification initiated by the dynamic of contemplative prayer.

Centering Prayer, insofar as it puts us at God's disposal, is a kind of request that He take our purification in hand. It takes courage to face up to the process of self-knowledge, but it is the only way of getting in touch with our true identity and ultimately with our true Self. When you feel bored, restless, and that anything would be better than just sitting still and being battered by thoughts, stay there anyhow. It's like being out in the rain without an umbrella and getting drenched to the skin. There is no use groaning because you didn't bring your umbrella. The best approach is simply to be willing to be doused by the torrent of your thoughts. Say, "I am going to get wet," and enjoy the rain. Before you reflect on whether a particular period of prayer is going well, you are having a good period of prayer. After you reflect, it is not so good. If you are drenched with thoughts and can't do anything about it, acquiesce to the fact that that's the way it is for today. The less you wiggle and scream, the sooner the work can be done. Tomorrow or a few days from now will be better. The capacity to accept what comes down the stream of consciousness is an essential part of the discipline. Cultivate a neutral attitude toward the psychological content of your prayer. Then it won't bother you whether you have thoughts. Offer your powerlessness to God and wait peacefully in His Presence. All thoughts pass if you wait long enough.

Another point that is worth remembering. During the unloading process sometimes you may want to figure out where a particular smile, itch, pain, or strong feeling is coming from in your psyche and to identify it with some earlier period in your life. That's useless. The nature of the unloading process is that it does not focus on any particular event. It loosens up all the rubbish, so to speak, and the psychological refuse comes up as a kind of compost. It's like throwing out the garbage. You don't separate the egg shells from the orange peels. You just throw the whole thing out. Nobody is asking you to look through it or try to evaluate it. You just throw everything out together in one big garbage bag.

It can also happen that external difficulties may arise in your life that have a direct connection with your spiritual growth. They are another way God uses to bring you to a deeper knowledge of yourself and to a greater compassion for your family, friends, and other people.

> I think I've been using the prayer words as a way of resisting thoughts. I'm not sure what it means to sink into a disturbing emotion without holding on to it.

One way to deal with intense restlessness, physical pain, or emotions, such as fear or anxiety, that arise at such times of unloading is to rest in the painful feeling for a minute or two and allow the pain itself to be your prayer word. In other words, one of the best ways of letting go of an emotion is simply to feel it. Painful emotions, even some physical pains, tend to disintegrate when fully accepted. Other manifestations of the unstressing experience may be an itch, tears, or laughter. Some people have been known to have a fit of laughter in the middle of Centering Prayer. Perhaps there was a joke they heard long ago that they were unable to enjoy because of some defense mechanism, and they finally were humble enough or free enough to get the point. You may also find yourself dissolved in tears for no reason at all. An old grief that wasn't allowed expression at the proper time is at last being felt. Contemplative prayer has a way of completing everything unfinished in your life by allowing the emotions to have an outlet in the form of moods or thoughts that seem but a jumble. This is the dynamic of purification. The intensity of feelings of fear, anxiety, or anger may have no relationship to your recent experience. Sitting through that kind of stuff is more useful than consoling experiences. The purpose of Centering Prayer is not to experience peace but to evacuate the unconscious obstacles to the permanent abiding state of union with God. Not contemplative *prayer* but the contemplative *state* is the purpose of our practice; not experiences, however exotic or reassuring, but the permanent and abiding awareness of God that comes through the mysterious restructuring of consciousness. At some point in your life, it could be in the middle of the night, on a subway, or in the midst of prayer, the necessary changes in the nervous system and psyche finally come to completion. That particular stage of the spiritual journey resolves itself, and you no longer have the problems that you had before. The restructuring of consciousness is the fruit of regular practice. That is why it makes no sense to aim at particular experiences. You can't even imagine a state of consciousness that you've never had before, so it is a waste of time and energy to anticipate it. The practice will eventually bring about the change of consciousness. The most significant happening at this stage of the journey is the calming of the affective system. You become free of emotional swings because the false self system on which they were based has at last been dismantled. The emotions then come through in their purity and are no longer upsetting. This is a marvelous release from inner turmoil.

When you feel restless, agitated, or pained by some emotional experience, you can't spend the time better than by waiting it out. The temptation is great when you are suffering from a distressing emotion to try to push it away. However, by allowing your attention to move gently toward the emotion and by sinking into it, as though you were getting into a nice jacuzzi, you are embracing God in the feeling. Don't think; just feel the emotion.

If you were blind and then got your sight back, even the ugliest things would be appreciated. Suppose you had no emotions and suddenly experienced one; even a disagreeable emotion would be thrilling. Actually, no emotion is really distressing;

it is only the false self that interprets it as distressing. Emotional swings are gradually dissolved by the complete acceptance of them. To put this into practice, you must first recognize and identify the emotion: "Yes, I am angry, I am panicky, terrified, restless." Every feeling has some good. Since God is the ground of everything, we know that even the feeling of guilt, in a certain sense, is God. If you can embrace the painful feeling, whatever it is, as if it were God, you are uniting yourself with God, because anything that has reality has God as its foundation. "Letting go" is not a simple term; it is quite subtle and has important nuances—depending on what you are intending to let go of. When a thought is not disturbing, letting go means paying no attention to it. When a thought is disturbing, it won't go away so easily, so you have to let it go in some other way. One way you can let it go is to sink into it and identify with it, out of love for God. This may not be possible at first, but try it and see what happens. The principal discipline of contemplative prayer is letting go.

To sum up what I have said on this fifth kind of thought, contemplative prayer is part of a reality that is bigger than itself. It is part of the whole process of integration, which requires opening to God at the level of the unconscious. This releases a dynamic that will be peaceful at times, and at other times heavily laden with thoughts and emotion. Both experiences are part of the same process of integration and healing. Each kind of experience, therefore, should be accepted with the same peace, gratitude, and confidence in God. Both are necessary to complete the process of transformation.

If you are suffering from a barrage of thoughts from the unconscious, you don't have to articulate the sacred word clearly in your imagination or keep repeating it in a frantic effort to stabilize your mind. You should think it as easily as you think any thought that comes to mind spontaneously.

Do not resist any thought, do not hang on to any thought, do not react emotionally to any thought. This is the proper response to all five kinds of thoughts that come down the stream of consciousness.

> When I came out of prayer, I found I had been crying, but I wasn't sad. I didn't perceive myself as being sad during any part of the meditation.

You might be consoled to know that Benedict of Nursia, the founder of Western monasticism, wept almost continuously. This was his characteristic response to the goodness of God. Similarly, there are times when we can't say anything, think anything, or feel anything. The only response is to dissolve in the presence of God's incredible goodness.

Tears may express joy as well as sorrow. They may also indicate the release of a whole bundle of emotions that can't find expression in any other way. In prayer if tears come, treat them as a gift, a response to God's goodness, which is both painful and joyful at the same time. Joy can be so great that it is painful.

It is good not to make too much of any experience or insight during prayer itself. Afterward you can reflect on it, but during prayer if you notice tears falling, lips smiling, eyes twitching, itches, and pains—treat them like any other thought and let them all go by. Gently return to the sacred word. This prayer is an apprenticeship in letting go of our dependency on thinking in order to know God in interior silence. The obstacles to getting there have to be unloaded in one way or another. Thoughts, moods, or feelings of depression that might last for several days are ways the psyche has of evacuating the undigested emotional material of a lifetime. When these pass, your psychological insides will feel much better. It's like being nauseated; it is disagreeable while your dinner is coming up, but afterwards you feel great.

Of course, if a physical pain lasts throughout the whole period of prayer, you may actually have some pathology and need to see a doctor. But often it is just an emotional knot rooted in your physiology that is unwinding, and it takes the form of a brief pain, tears, or laughter. I know people who were overcome by laughter in their prayer. I guess they hit something in the unconscious they never thought was funny before and finally got the joke. Through the deepening of one's trust in God, one is able to acknowledge the dark places in one's personality according to one's own natural rhythm. A good therapist will not bring up painful insights until he or she sees that the patient is ready to face them. God is the same way. As humility and trust deepen, you can acknowledge the dark side of your personality more easily. Eventually you will reach the center of your human poverty and powerlessness and feel happy to be there. Then you enter into the freedom of God's creative action because there is no longer any selfish or possessive attitude toward your personality or talents. You are completely at God's disposal. Interior freedom is the goal of this prayer. Not freedom to do what you like, but freedom to do what God likes—freedom to be your true Self and to be transformed in Christ.

> There seems to be a dimension in the prayer of quiet that is healing. At least that is my experience. Some people do not have too much to heal. But if there are big scars, the prayer of quiet seems to be a very soothing ointment for these wounds.

Yes, that is one important effect. John of the Cross taught that interior silence is the place where the Spirit secretly anoints the soul and heals our deepest wounds.

> Does the healing extend to the body as well as the soul?

Illnesses that are largely psychosomatic can certainly be healed by bringing peace to one's emotional life.

I was thinking that God has a way of concealing His work in us from our own eyes, leaving us with something like St. Paul's thorn of the flesh, to keep us humble.

Contemplative prayer doesn't establish people in glory, that's for sure, but it helps them to bear infirmities such as you mentioned. If certain types of people have too much success in their prayer, they may need a little tug to bring them down to earth once in a while.

The method of Centering Prayer is only an entrance into contemplative prayer. As one's experience of the latter develops, it becomes more difficult to speak about because it doesn't enter into the ordinary experience of the psychic life as such. Imagine the rays of the sun in a pool of water. The sun's rays are united to the water, yet at the same time they are quite distinct from it. They are coming from a different place. Similarly, one's experience of God in contemplative prayer is not easy to make distinctions about. The less you can say about it, the more likely it is present. It is in all and through all. And so it kinds of falls out of sight.

The beginning of anything is always striking, but as you get used to it or when it becomes a part of you, you begin to take it for granted. It no longer stirs up the emotional dust that it did when it was a new experience. The same thing happens at the beginning of the spiritual journey. For some people, contemplative prayer can be very mysterious indeed. They themselves can't say anything about what they experience except that it is real for them. The kind of infirmities that you mention, which are obvious both to them and to others, are a wonderful means of hiding them from themselves as well as from others. God loves to hide the holiness of His friends, especially from themselves.

As people grow in the prayer life, do they still experience an alternation of thoughts and contemplative moments?

As the unconscious empties out, the fruits of an integrated human nature and the resulting free flow of grace will manifest themselves by a significant change of attitude. The union that one discovers in contemplative prayer will not be reserved to that time. Moments of silence will overtake you in the course of daily life. Reality will tend to become more transparent. Its divine Source will shine through it.

When everything in the unconscious is emptied out, the kinds of thoughts that were passing by in the beginning will no longer exist. There is an end to the process of purification. Then the awareness of union with God will be continuous because there will be no obstacle in our conscious or unconscious life to interfere with it. There is nothing wrong with reality. The problem is with us, who cannot relate to it properly because of the obstacles in us. When all the obstacles are emptied out, the light of God's presence will illumine our spirit all the time, even when we are immersed in activity. Instead of being overwhelmed by externals, the true Self, now in union with God, will dominate them.

Perhaps the first stage in the development of contemplative prayer is the awareness of our independence from our ordinary psychological world. In other words, we are aware that we are not just our body and that we are not just our thoughts and feelings. We are no longer so identified with external objects that we can think of nothing else. We are becoming aware of our spiritual nature. Our spirit is the dwelling place of the Trinity. That realization remains part of every other reality and is no longer overwhelmed, even in the midst of great activity, by circumstances, external objects or our emotions and thoughts.

But the experience of independence and distancing from the rest of reality is not an absolute independence. It is only the affirmation of our true Self. Another awareness follows as a further development. As the unconscious is emptied out, the awareness of the deepest level in us is also an awareness of the deepest level in everyone else. This is the basis for the commandment to love one's neighbor as oneself. When you truly love yourself, you become aware that your true Self is Christ expressing himself in you, and the further awareness that everybody else enjoys this potential too. Augustine had a phrase for it: "One Christ loving himself." That is a good description of a mature Christian community. You are aware that a power greater than you is doing everything.

Then everything begins to reflect not only its own beauty but also the beauty of its Source. One becomes united to everything else in which God dwells. The insight into Christ dwelling in every other person enables one to express charity toward others with greater spontaneity. Instead of seeing only someone's personality, race, nationality, gender, status, or characteristics (which you like or do not like), you see what is deepest—one's union or potential union with Christ. You also perceive everyone's desperate need of help. The transcendent potential of most people is still waiting to be realized, and this awakens a great sense of compassion. This Christ-centered love takes us out of ourselves and brings our newly found sense of independence into relationships that are not based on dependency, as many relationships tend to be, but that are based on Christ as their center. It enables one to work for others with great liberty of spirit because one is no longer seeking one's own ego-centered goals but responding to reality as it is.

Divine love is not an attitude that one puts on like a cloak. It is rather the right way to respond to reality. It is the right relationship to being, including our own being. And that relationship is primarily one of receiving. No one has any degree of divine love except what one has received. An important part of the response to divine love, once it has been received, is to pass it on to our neighbor in a way that is appropriate in the present moment.

Is the purpose of this prayer to keep you in a state of union with God throughout the day?

Yes, but in the beginning it is not likely to be continuous. Later on, a prayer develops, a closer union in daily life becomes more evident. One can also be in union with God without any form of recollection that affects the senses. This is what I mean by preparing the body for higher states of consciousness. Physical ecstasy is a weakness of the body. When the senses are not ready to endure the intensity of God's communications, they just give way and one is rapt out of the body. Mature mystics who have passed through that stage rarely have bodily ecstasies. They have integrated spiritual communications with their physical nature and the body is now strong enough to receive them without the former inconveniences. Living the divine life becomes like living ordinary human life. If you are familiar with the *Ten Ox Pictures* of Zen, the last one represents the return to ordinary life after full enlightenment. It symbolizes the fact that there is no way to distinguish the life with which you started from what it has become, except that it is totally transformed in its ordinariness.

The triumph of grace enables people to live their ordinary lives divinely. First come moments of recollection that are absorbing. After these have been thoroughly integrated, the same graces are given without one's being absorbed by them. One is completely free for one's ordinary daily activities with the same degree (or greater) of union with God that one had before. Continuous prayer in the fullest sense of the term is present when the motivation of all our actions is coming from the Spirit. Short of that state, we have to use methods to unite us to God.

There is a difference between *being* and *doing*. Once one's being is transformed into Christ, all one's doing becomes anointed with the interior transformation of one's being. I suppose this is the mystery of Mother Teresa's great charm. She fascinates people. Cameras follow her not because she is physically beautiful, but because she is radiating the mysterious attractiveness of God. I'm sure she is not trying to do so, but because she is so, it happens. This is the kind of transformation contemplative prayer tends to produce. It is easy to bog down at lower levels of spiritual development. The challenge always comes to go farther, and if we accept, we are off to the races again.

No one every grew as much in the spiritual life as the Blessed Virgin Mary because there was no interior obstacle to hinder her growth. Growing in grace for her meant growing in the midst of the human condition with its interminable trials. She had, in fact, the heaviest kinds of trials. The transforming union should enable one to handle greater trials than those of less evolved Christians. What's the use of building this magnificent spiritual building unless you do something with it? I am sure God doesn't intend merely to look at these people who are so holy. He wants them to do something. If He liberated them from their false selves, it was precisely for some great purpose.

Suppose one has reached inner resurrection, transforming union, and no longer experiences the turmoil of one's emotions because they have all been transmuted into virtues. Christ is living in such persons in a remarkable way, and they are aware of their permanent union with him. Suppose God should then ask them to give up that state of enlightenment and to go back to the kind of trials, or worse, that they endured before. Their union with God would remain, but it would be completely hidden from them on the psychic level. This is one form of vicarious suffering. The transforming union is not a free ticket to happiness in this world. For some, this may mean a life of complete solitude full of loneliness; for others, it may mean an active apostolate that prevents them from enjoying the delights of divine union; for others again, it may mean intense suffering—physical, mental or spiritual—which they undergo for some special intention or for the whole human family. Their transformed humanity makes their sufferings of immense value for the same reason that Jesus, because of his divine dignity, became the Savior of every human being, past, present, and future.

Therese of Lisieux during her last illness could no longer think of heaven, although up until then it had been her greatest joy. Yet she had clearly reached transforming union, attested to by the piercing of her heart. As she herself was dimly aware, she was passing through another dark night for the unbelievers of her time. She lived at the crest of the rationalistic age when the arrogance of the human intellect was probably at its height.

Thus the greatest trials of the spiritual journey may occur *after* the transforming union. They would not take away the union, but the union would be so pure that, like a ray of light passing through a perfect vacuum, it would not be perceived. This would be a most profound way of imitating the Son of God, who gave up being God, as Paul said, in order to take upon himself the consequences of the human condition. Jesus relinquished the privileges of his unique union with the Father in order to experience our weakness and to make our sufferings his own. That sacrifice could only be imitated by one who has achieved divine union and who then, at God's request or insistence, gives back to God all the normal enjoyment of that state to be immersed once again in unbearable trials. This is evident in the lives of a number of mystics and saints. And I dare say God isn't going to change His way of doing things.

Life, once one is in union with God, is what God wants it to be. It is full of surprises. You can be sure that whatever you expect to happen will not happen. That is the only thing of which you can be certain in the spiritual journey. It is by giving up all your expectations that you will be led to Medicine Lake, the Native

American's term for contemplative prayer. The medicine that everyone needs is contemplation, which alone leads to transformation.

Contemplative prayer will go through various stages and vicissitudes. You may have experiences that will leave you in confusion. The Lord will bring help to you through a book, a person, or your own patience. Sometimes it is God's will to leave you alone without any help. You may have to learn to live with impossible situations. People who can live peacefully in impossible situations will make great headway in the spiritual journey. You will come up against loneliness and existential dread. You may feel as if nobody in the world understands you or could help you and that God is a billion light-years away. All these things are part of the preparation process. God is like a farmer preparing the soil of our soul to bear not just fortyfold or sixtyfold, but a hundredfold. That means that the soil has to be well tilled. It is as if God drives His tractor over the field of our soul and harrows it in one direction, then in the opposite direction, and then He goes around in a circle. He keeps doing the same thing again and again until the soil becomes as fine as sand. When all is ready, the seed is sown.

Or take the image of a growing tree. At first you see the trunk and the branches. Later comes the leaves. This makes the tree beautiful, the stage of growth that might be compared to the enjoyment that comes when you first learn how to enter into interior silence. After the leaves come the flowers, another moment of intense satisfaction. But they quickly die and fall to the ground. The fruit comes only at the end of the season, and even then it takes a while for it to ripen on the tree. So don't think when the leaves appear and the flowers come, that this is the end of the journey. The spiritual journey is a long trip.

Moreover, your experience will seem to recycle and you'll feel that you are back to where you started and haven't made any progress at all. Recycling is like climbing a spiral staircase. You seem to be returning to the point from which you started, but in actual fact you are at a higher level. An eagle rising toward the sun keeps returning to the same place on the horizontal plane, but to a higher place on the vertical plane.

The inflowing of the divine light into our souls is a ray of darkness according to John of the Cross. We see light in a dark room is because of the dust that is there. If there were no dust, the ray of light would go right through the room without being observed. This is a symbol of the full development of contemplative prayer, which is so pure that it is not perceptible to the one receiving it. It is manifest, however, in the progressive transformation of the person. Such a person manifests God more than any sacrament.

Is this not the meaning of the Feast of the Immaculate Conception? We are invited to become what Our Lady was from the beginning, a pure transmission of

God's presence and action. Contemplative prayer is the school through which we pass to come to the contemplative state, the means God normally uses to bring people to an abiding state of union. Once in that state they may not have much awareness of God's inflowing graces, but the Holy Spirit is the inspiration or motivation of all they do.

10

SUMMARY OF THE CENTERING PRAYER METHOD

■

THE METHOD OF CENTERING PRAYER is a way of reducing the ordinary obstacles to contemplation and preparing the human faculties to cooperate with this gift. It is an attempt to present the teaching of earlier times in an up-dated format and to put a certain order and regularity into it. It is not meant to replace all other kinds of prayer. But it puts the other kinds of prayer into a new perspective. During the time of prayer it centers one's attention on God's presence within. At other times one's attention moves outward to discover His presence everywhere else. Centering Prayer is not an end in itself, but a beginning. It is not done for the sake of having an experience, but for the sake of its positive fruits in one's life.

The method of Centering Prayer is designed to turn off the ordinary flow of thoughts, that reinforces our habitual way of thinking of ourselves and of looking at the world. It is like turning a radio from long wave to short wave. You may be used to a long wave set and the stations it picks up but if you want to hear stations from far away, you have to turn to the other wavelength. In similar fashion, if you turn off your ordinary thinking and emotional patterns, you open yourself to a new world of reality.

The Method

To do this systematically, take up a comfortable position that will enable you to sit still. Close your eyes. Half of the world disappears for we generally think most about what we see. In order to slow down the usual flow of thoughts, think just one thought. For this purpose choose a word of one or two syllables with which you feel comfortable.

A general loving look toward God may be better suited to the disposition of some persons. But the same procedures are followed as in the use of the sacred word. The word is a sacred word because it is the symbol of your intention to open yourself to the mystery of God's presence beyond thoughts, images and emotions.

95

It is chosen not for its content but for its intent. It is merely a pointer that expresses the direction of your inward movement toward the presence of God.

To start, introduce the sacred word in your imagination as gently as if you were laying a feather on a piece of absorbent cotton. Keep thinking the sacred word in whatever form it arises. It is not meant to be repeated continuously. The word can flatten out, become vague or just an impulse of the will, or even disappear. Accept it in whatever form it arises.

When you become aware that you are thinking some other thought, return to the sacred word as the expression of your intent. The effectiveness of this prayer does not depend on how distinctly you say the sacred word or how often, but rather on the gentleness with which you introduce it into your imagination in the beginning and the promptness with which you return to it when you are hooked on some other thought.

Thoughts are an inevitable part of Centering Prayer. Our ordinary thoughts are like boats sitting on a river so closely packed together that we cannot see the river that is holding them up. A "thought" in the context of this prayer is any perception that crosses the inner screen of consciousness. We are normally aware of one object after another passing across the inner screen of consciousness: images, memories, feelings, external impressions. When we slow down that flow for a little while, space begins to appear between the boats. Up comes the reality on which they are floating.

The prayer of centering is a method of directing your attention from the particular to the general, from the concrete to the formless. At first you are preoccupied by the boats that are going by. You become interested in seeing what is on them. But just let them all go by. If you catch yourself becoming interested in them, return to the sacred word as the expression of the movement of your whole being toward God present within you.

The sacred word is a simple thought that you are thinking at ever deepening levels of perception. That's why you accept the sacred word in whatever form it arises within you. The word on your lips is exterior and has no part in this form of prayer. The thought in your imagination is interior; the word as an impulse of your will is more interior still. Only when you pass beyond the word into pure awareness is the process of interiorization complete. That is what Mary of Bethany was doing at the feet of Jesus. She was going beyond the words she was hearing to the Person who was speaking and entering into union with Him. This is what we are doing as we sit in Centering Prayer interiorizing the sacred word. We are going beyond the sacred word into union with that to which it points—the Ultimate Mystery, the Presence of God, beyond any perception that we can form of Him.

Five Types of Thoughts

Various kinds of thoughts may come down the stream of consciousness when we start to quiet our mind. The appropriate response to each one varies according to the thought.

1. *The woolgathering of the imagination.* The most obvious thoughts are the superficial ones that the imagination grinds out because of its natural propensity for perpetual motion. It is important just to accept them and not to pay any undue attention to them. Such thoughts are like the noise in the street floating through the window of an apartment where two people are carrying on a conversation. Their attention is firmly directed to each other, but they cannot avoid hearing the street noise. Sometimes they reach a point where they don't notice it at all. At other times the honking of horns may distract them momentarily. The only reasonable attitude is to put up with the noise and pay as little attention to it as possible. In this way they give as much of their undivided attention to each other as circumstances allow.

2. *Thoughts with an emotional attraction to them.* The second kind of thought occurs when you get interested in something that is happening in the street. A brawl breaks out and attracts your curiosity. This is the kind of thought that calls for some reaction. Returning gently to the sacred word is a means of getting back to the general loving attention you were offering to God. It is important not to be annoyed with yourself if you get involved with these interesting thoughts. Any annoyance that you give in to is another thought, and will take you farther away from the interior silence that is the proximate goal of this prayer.

3. *Insights and psychological breakthroughs.* A third kind of thought arises as we sink into deep peace and interior silence. Something in our minds goes fishing. What seem to be brilliant theological insights and marvelous psychological breakthroughs, like tasty bait, are dangled in front of our mind's eye and we think, "I must take a moment to make sure I grasp this fantastic insight!" If you acquiesce to a thought of this nature long enough to fix it in your memory, you will be drawn out of the deep, refreshing waters of interior silence. Any deliberate thought brings you out.

A very intimate kind of self-denial is necessary in this prayer. It is not just an experience of refreshment—a sort of spiritual happy hour—though this can be a side-effect. It involves the denial of what we are most attached to, namely, our own inmost thoughts and feelings and the source from which they come, the false self.

This kind of asceticism goes to the roots of our attachment to the emotional programming of the false self. It is a thorough and delightful kind of self-denial, which does not have to be afflictive to be effective. The question is how to choose the most useful and appropriate kind of self-denial and how to work at it.

4. *Self-reflection.* As you settle into deep peace and freedom from particular thoughts, a desire to reflect on what is happening may arise. You may think, "At last I am getting some place!" or, "This feeling is just great!" or, "If only I could make a mental note of how I got here so that I can get back to it whenever I want!" These are examples of the fourth kind of thought. You are being offered a choice between reflecting on what is going on and letting go of the experience. If you let go, you go into deeper interior silence. If you reflect, you come out and have to start over. There will be a lot of starting over.

Reflection is one step back from experience. It is a photograph of reality. As soon as you start to reflect on an experience, it is over. Reflection on joy is an attempt to possess it. Then it is lost. The tendency to reflect is one of the hardest things to handle in contemplative prayer. We want to savor the moment of pure joy, pure experience, pure awareness. We want to reflect on moments of deep peace or union in order to remember how we got there and thus how to get back. But if you can let this temptation go by and return to the sacred word, you will pass to a new level of freedom, a more refined joy.

The presence of God is like the air we breathe. You can have all you want of it as long as you do not try to take possession of it and hang on to it.

This prayer is communion with the Spirit of God, who is Charity, pure gift. Our possessive instinct wants to hang on for dear life to what is pleasant—and nothing is more delightful than the divine Presence; it brings such a deep sense of security and tranquillity. The Presence of God does not respond to greed. It is totally available, but on condition that we accept it freely and do not try to possess it.

This method of prayer is a learning of self-surrender. It teaches us through our many mistakes not to be possessive but to let go. If, in this prayer, you can get over the inveterate habit of reflecting on what is going on, if you can have peace and not think about having it, then you will have learned how to do it.

5. *Interior Purification.* Any form of meditation or prayer that transcends thinking sets off the dynamic of interior purification. This dynamic is God's school of psychotherapy. It enables the organism to release deep rooted tension in the form of thoughts. Generally, thoughts that result from this therapy arise without one's knowing where they come from or why. They introduce themselves with a certain

force or emotional charge. One may feel intense anger, sorrow or fear without any relation to the recent past. Once again, the best way to handle them is to return to the sacred word.

Through this process, the undigested psychological material of a lifetime is gradually evacuated, the emotional investment of early childhood in programs for happiness based on instinctual drives is dismantled, and the false self gives way to the true self.

Once you grasp the fact that thoughts are not only inevitable, but an integral part of the process of healing and growth initiated by God, you are able to take a positive view of them. Instead of looking upon them as painful distractions, you see them in a broader perspective that includes both interior silence and thoughts—thoughts that you do not want, but which are just as valuable for the purpose of purification, as moments of profound tranquility.

Resting in God

As you quiet down and go deeper, you may reach a place where the sacred word disappears altogether and there are no thoughts. This is often experienced as a suspension of consciousness, a space. The next thing you are aware of is the thought, "Where was I? There was no sacred word and I wasn't thinking." Or you may experience it as a place outside of time. Time is the measure of motion. If the ordinary flow of thoughts is reduced to where there are few or no successive thoughts, the time of prayer passes like a snap of the fingers.

The experience of interior silence or "resting in God" is beyond thinking, images, and emotions. This awareness tells you that the core of your being is eternal and indestructible and that you as a person are loved by God and share his divine life. Many people habitually enjoy the clear experience of interior silence during prayer. Others habitually experience calm and tranquillity along with a trickle of thoughts at the same time. Still others rarely have such experiences. In whatever form or degree interior silence occurs, it is to be accepted but not desired, for the feeling of desire would be a thought.

Conclusion

Take everything that happens during the periods of Centering Prayer peacefully and gratefully, without putting a judgment on anything. Even if you should have an overwhelming experience of God, this is not the time to think about it. Let the thoughts come and go. The basic principle for handling thoughts in this prayer is this: Resist no thought, hang on to no thought, react emotionally to no thought.

Whatever image, feeling, reflection, or experience attracts your attention, return to the sacred word.

Don't judge Centering Prayer on the basis of how many thoughts come or how much peace you enjoy. The only way to judge this prayer is by its long-range fruits: whether in daily life you enjoy greater peace, humility and charity. Having come to deep interior silence, you begin to relate to others beyond the superficial aspects of social status, race, nationality, religion, and personal characteristics.

To know God in this way is to perceive a new dimension to all reality. The ripe fruit of contemplative prayer is to bring back into the humdrum routines of daily life not just the thought of God, but the spontaneous awareness of His abiding Presence in, through, and beyond everything. *HE WHO IS*—the infinite, incomprehensible, and ineffable One—is the God of pure faith. In this prayer we confront the most fundamental human question: "Who are you, Lord?"—and wait for the answer.

11

THE INTENSIVE CENTERING
PRAYER EXPERIENCE

■

IN A RETREAT SETTING, the length of the periods of Centering Prayer can be extended. Members of a group that regularly practices Centering Prayer together may also wish to increase the time length of the prayer periods once a week or once a month.

Following is a report of participants that reflects the usual experiences of persons after three successive periods of centering.

Lengthening or multiplying periods of Centering Prayer can help to deepen the experience of interior silence. In such a context it may accelerate the process of unloading the unconscious. The following is a report of one of these sessions in which there were three twenty-minute periods of centering separated by a five to seven minute meditative walk in single file at a very slow and deliberate pace.

RETREATANT 1: I found it to be a very peaceful experience. The continuity of three sustained periods brought about a deeper feeling of peace. There was no break at all, even though we got up and walked around. I can't overemphasize the experience of a community type of prayer. I got a deeper insight into sharing prayer, any type of prayer.

RESPONSE: Actually, the walking is meant to be part of the prayer, a first step to bringing interior silence into activity of a very simple kind.

RETREATANT 2: I found it very, very peaceful, but I was also aware of how many thoughts I was getting in the three periods. They did not disturb the peace, but I was aware of how many there were. I also had a sensation that sometimes my whole body wanted to go deeper. I found the time went very fast.

RETREATANT 3: The first insight that I had today was the fact that there was a supportive element in group prayer. I have practiced Centering Prayer for about two years alone, and I could not fathom how it could be done in a group, so I had my doubts. But they have been dissolved.

RETREATANT 4: During the first period of prayer I felt restless, more than I had before, but when I got to the third one, it was peaceful. It was an answer to a question that I have had for a long time. I have often found that my time span for prayer is on the short side, maybe twenty to twenty-five minutes. I have wondered whether it should lengthen with time. It has not and I was worried. But I can see from this experience that with this little break in between, it can be prolonged.

RETREATANT 5: I must say that the time went by very quickly and the walk tended to recharge my batteries. When I came back for the second period, the time went by even more quickly, and so for the third.

RESPONSE: The deeper the silence you have, the faster the time goes. After all, what is time? It is just the measurement of objects of perception going by. So when there are fewer objects, there is less time. At least there is less awareness of time. When nothing is going by, there is no sense of time at all, and that is when prayer is over like a flash. Such deep prayer is an intuition into what eternity is like. It is a preview of death, not death in a morbid sense, but in a delightful sense.

RETREATANT 6: In the beginning, I was deliberately trying to be quiet, and I was getting in my own way. Somehow or other, in the second or third period, I was experiencing great ease and a conscious sensation of quiet joy.

RETREATANT 7: At the beginning, it was rather tedious, but part way through the afternoon, I felt a subtle breakthrough, or just an ease of being without any interior pressure.

RESPONSE: If you keep centering long enough, your resistance gets tired and you fall into what you are supposed to be doing anyway. Thus, there is an advantage in gently tiring yourself out.

RETREATANT 8: I found the third meditation too short.

RESPONSE: Depending on one's temperament or grace, the time span can be lengthened when one is alone. But for a group of people, it is better to agree on a certain amount of time that is not too short and not too long. It must be long enough to enable your faculties to get into it and quiet down. But not so long that it discourages the faint-hearted, who will never do it if they have to face something that looks endless to them. Three successive periods with a brief, contemplative walk in between is a way of initiating ourselves into the fact that we are perfectly capable of an extended period of resting in God.

RETREATANT 9: I found a deep rest; so much so, that I was not sure if I was sleeping, at least part of the time. In the beginning, I was not sure if I could do the three of them in a row. It was not all that difficult once I got into it. I am still not sure what to do with the sacred word, whether there should be an effort on my part to repeat it, or just to let it go.

RESPONSE: The main thing to keep in mind in this prayer is that there is no effort, there is only the very gentle activity of listening. It is almost like letting the word say itself. But letting go of that activity is even better. Whenever you are uncertain what to do, you are completely free to do either, and your own experience will teach you. Just keep in mind that silence is better than the sacred word. Or to put it another way, it *is* the sacred word at the deepest level. Whenever you come back to the sacred word, it should be as easily as possible, as if it were a spontaneous thought that just came along. It does not have to be explicit or articulated. Even the thought to return to the sacred word may be enough.

RETREATANT 10: I found myself using the word less today than I have ever used it before.

RESPONSE: Its use or presence will vary from one period of prayer to the next, according to circumstances. You need great flexibility in using it. The principle is always to use it to go toward greater peace, silence, and beyond. But when one is in peace, silence, and beyond, forget it.

RETREATANT 11: I found myself going deeper and deeper in each session, and I have a question. Every morning I do my Centering Prayer, and then I offer Mass. But I find it hard to come out of it. What should I do?

RESPONSE: That's a nice problem to have.

RETREATANT 11: But should I not be thinking of the prayers of the Mass? Instead I find myself centering.

RESPONSE: If the divine Presence overtakes you and you are not leading the assembly, there is no reason why you cannot rest in the Presence of God. If you have some function to fulfill—if you are the principal celebrant, for example—obviously you have to move things along. You cannot just let the congregation wait until you come out of it.

RETREATANT 11: The problem is that I am enjoying this more than anything else.

RESPONSE: There are times in one's life when the divine action is very strong and hard to resist. There are also times when the Lord seems to forget about you. The main thing is to accept whatever comes, to adjust to what happens, to whatever He gives you. By alternating the sense of His closeness and distance, God trains our faculties to accept the mystery of His Presence beyond any kind of sensible or conceptual experience. The divine Presence is very close and immediate, when we are doing the most ordinary actions. Faith should become so transparent that it does not need experience. But it takes a lot of experience to reach that point.

As God brings the "new man" to life in interior silence, that is to say, the new *you,* with the world view that Christ shares with you in deep silence, His view of things becomes more important to you than your own. Then He asks you to live that new life in the circumstances of everyday life, in your daily routine, contradicted by noise, opposition, and anxieties. These seem to persecute you because you want to be alone to relish that silence. But it is important to allow oneself to be confronted by daily life. The alternation between deep silence and action gradually brings the two together. You become fully integrated, a contemplative and yet fully capable of action at the same time. You are Mary and Martha at once.

We all have these two capacities, but they are in different proportions. By bringing each of them to its full potential and integrating them, one becomes a mature Christian, able to bring forth out of one's tool kit old things and new. It is to be able to act and to be able not to act, to come into function and to withdraw into silence. The alternation of contemplative prayer and action gradually establishes you in the contemplative dimension of the Gospel, which is a new and transformed state of consciousness.

12

METHODS OF EXTENDING THE EFFECTS OF CONTEMPLATIVE PRAYER INTO DAILY LIFE

■

CENTERING PRAYER IS THE KEYSTONE of a comprehensive commitment to the contemplative dimensions of the Gospel. Two periods a day of twenty to thirty minutes—one in the early morning and one halfway through the day or in the early evening—maintain the reservoir of interior silence at a high level at all times. Those who have more time at their disposal might begin with a brief reading of ten or fifteen minutes from the Gospel. For those who wish to give a full hour in the morning to interior silence, start with ten minutes of Gospel reading and then center for twenty minutes. Do a slow, meditative walk around the room for five to seven minutes; sit down and do a second period of centering. You still have ten minutes for planning your day, praying for others, or conversing with the Lord.

To find time for a second period later in the day may require special effort. If you have to be available to your family as soon as you walk in the door, you might center during your lunch hour. Or you might stop on the way home from work and center in a church or park. If it is impossible to get a second period of prayer in, it is important that you lengthen the first one. There are a number of practices that can help maintain your reservoir of interior silence throughout the day and thus extend its effects into ordinary activities.

Means of Extending the Effects of Centering Prayer into Daily Life

1. *Cultivate a basic acceptance of yourself.* Have a genuine compassion for yourself, including all your past history, failings, limitations, and sins. Expect to make many mistakes. But learn from them. To learn from experience is the path to wisdom.

2. *Pick a prayer for action.* This is a five to nine-syllable sentence from scripture that you gradually work into your subconscious by repeating it mentally at times when your mind is relatively free, such as while washing up, doing light chores,

walking, driving, waiting, etc. Synchronize it with your heartbeat. Eventually it says itself and thus maintains a link with your reservoir of interior silence throughout the day. If you have a tendency to scrupulosity and feel a compulsion to say the prayer over and over or if frequent repetition brings on a headache or a backache, this practice is not for you.[1]

3. *Spend time daily listening to the Word of God* in lectio divina. Give fifteen minutes or longer every day to the reading of the New Testament or a spiritual book that speaks to your heart.

4. *Carry a "Minute Book."* This is a series of short readings—a sentence or two, or at most a paragraph—from your favorite spiritual writers or from your own journal that reminds you of your commitment to Christ and to contemplative prayer. Carry it in your pocket or purse and when you have a stray minute or two, read a few lines.

5. *Deliberately dismantle the emotional programming of the false self.* Observe the emotions that most upset you and the events that set them off, but without analyzing, rationalizing, or justifying your reactions. Name the chief emotion you are feeling and the particular event that triggered it and release the energy that is building up by a strong act of the will such as, "I give up my desire for (security, esteem, control)!"[2] The effort to dismantle the false self and the daily practice of contemplative prayer are the two engines of your spiritual jet that give you the thrust to get off the ground. The reason that Centering Prayer is not as effective as it could be is that when you emerge from it into the ordinary routines of daily life, your emotional programs start going off again. Upsetting emotions immediately start to drain the reservoir of interior silence, that you had established during prayer. On the other hand, if you work at dismantling the energy centers that cause the upsetting emotions, your efforts will extend the good effects of centering into every aspect of daily life.

6. *Practice guard of the heart.* This is the practice of releasing upsetting emotions into the present moment. This can be done in one of three ways: doing what you are actually doing, turning your attention to some other occupation, or giving the feeling to Christ. The guard of the heart requires the prompt letting go of personal likes or dislikes. When something arises independently of our plans, we spontaneously try to modify it. Our first reaction, however, should be openness to what is

---

1. Cf. Appendix A: The Active Prayer.
2. Cf. Keyes, *Handbook to Higher Consciousness*, Chapters 14 and 15.

actually happening so that if our plans are upset, we are not upset. The fruit of guard of the heart is the habitual willingness to change our plans at a moment's notice. It disposes us to accept painful situations as they arise. Then we can decide what to do with them, modifying, correcting or improving them. In other words, the ordinary events of daily life become our practice. I can't emphasize that too much. A monastic structure is not the path to holiness for lay folks. The routine of daily life is. Contemplative prayer is aimed at transforming daily life with its never-ending round of ordinary activities.

7. *Practice unconditional acceptance of others.* This practice is especially powerful in quieting the emotions of the utility appetite: fear, anger, courage, hope, and despair. By accepting other people unconditionally, you discipline the emotions that want to get even with others or to get away from them. You allow people to be who they are with all their idiosyncracies and with the particular behavior that is disturbing you. The situation gets more complicated when you feel an obligation to correct someone. If you correct someone when you are upset, you are certain to get nowhere. This arouses the defenses of others and gives them a handle for blaming the situation on you. Wait till you have calmed down and then offer correction out of genuine concern for them.

8. *Deliberately dismantle excessive group identification.* This is the practice of letting go of our cultural conditioning, preconceived ideas, and overidentification with the values of our particular group. It also means openness to change in ourselves, openness to spiritual development beyond group loyalties, openness to whatever the future holds.

9. *Celebrate the Eucharist regularly.* Participate regularly in the mystery of Christ's passion, death, and resurrection, the source of Christian transformation.

10. *Join a contemplative prayer group.* Set up or join a support group that meets weekly to do Centering Prayer and *lectio divina* together and to encourage one another in the commitment to the contemplative dimensions of the Gospel.[3]

Basic Tools for Times of Temptation

1. Determination to persevere in the spiritual journey.

2. Trust in the infinite mercy of God.

3. Continuous practice of the presence of God through prayer and openness to His inspirations.

3. Cf. Appendix B: The Weekly Support Group.

13

GUIDELINES FOR CHRISTIAN LIFE, GROWTH AND TRANSFORMATION

■

THE FOLLOWING PRINCIPLES represent a tentative effort to restate the Christian spiritual journey in contemporary terms. They are designed to provide a conceptual background for the practice of Centering Prayer. They should be read according to the method of *lectio divina*.

1. The fundamental goodness of human nature, like the mystery of the Trinity, Grace, and the Incarnation, is an essential element of Christian faith. This basic core of goodness is capable of unlimited development; indeed, of becoming transformed into Christ and deified.

2. Our basic core of goodness is our true Self. Its center of gravity is God. The acceptance of our basic goodness is a quantum leap in the spiritual journey.

3. God and our true Self are not separate. Though we are not God, God and our true Self are the same thing.

4. The term *original sin* is a way of describing the human condition, which is the universal experience of coming to full reflective self-consciousness without the certitude of personal union with God. This gives rise to our intimate sense of incompletion, dividedness, isolation, and guilt.

5. Original sin is not the result of personal wrongdoing on our part. Still, it causes a pervasive feeling of alienation from God, from other people and from the true Self. The cultural consequences of these alienations are instilled in us from earliest childhood and passed on from one generation to the next. The urgent need to escape from the profound insecurity of this situation gives rise, when unchecked, to insatiable desires for pleasure, possession, and power. On the social level, it gives rise to violence, war, and institutional injustice.

6. The particular consequences of original sin include all the self-serving habits that have been woven into our personality from the time we were conceived; all the emotional damage that has come from our early environment and upbringing; all the harm that other people have done to us knowingly or unknowingly at an age when we could not defend ourselves; and the methods we acquired—many of them now unconscious—to ward off the pain of unbearable situations.

7. This constellation of prerational reactions is the foundation of the false self. The false self develops in opposition to the true Self. Its center of gravity is itself.

8. Grace is the presence and action of Christ at every moment of our lives. The sacraments are ritual actions in which Christ is present in a special manner, confirming and sustaining the major commitments of our Christian life.

9. In Baptism, the false self is ritually put to death, the new self is born, and the victory over sin won by Jesus through his death and resurrection is placed at our disposal. Not our uniqueness as persons, but our sense of separation from God and from others is destroyed in the death-dealing and life-giving waters of Baptism.

10. The Eucharist is the celebration of life: the coming together of all the material elements of the cosmos, their emergence to consciousness in human persons and the transformation of human consciousness into Divine consciousness. It is the manifestation of the Divine in and through the Christian community. We receive the Eucharist in order to become the Eucharist.

11. In addition to being present in the sacraments, Christ is present in a special manner in every crisis and important event of our lives.

12. Personal sin is the refusal to respond to Christ's self-communication (grace). It is the deliberate neglect of our own genuine needs and those of others. It reinforces the false self.

13. Our basic core of goodness is dynamic and tends to grow of itself. This growth is hindered by the illusions and emotional hang-ups of the false self, by the negative influences coming from our cultural conditioning, and by personal sin.

14. Listening to God's word in scripture and the liturgy, waiting upon God in prayer, and responsiveness to his inspirations help to distinguish how the two selves are operating in particular circumstances.

15. God is not some remote, inaccessible, and implacable Being who demands instant perfection from His creatures and of whose love we must make ourselves worthy. He is not a tyrant to be obeyed out of terror, nor a policeman who is ever on the watch, nor a harsh judge ever ready to apply the verdict of guilty. We should relate to Him less and less in terms of reward and punishment and more and more on the basis of the gratuity—or the *play* of divine love.

16. Divine love is compassionate, tender, luminous, totally self-giving, seeking no reward, unifying everything.

17. The experience of being loved by God enables us to accept our false self as it is, and then to let go of it and journey to our true Self. The inward journey to our true Self is the way to divine love.

18. The growing awareness of our true Self, along with the deep sense of spiritual peace and joy which flow from this experience, balances the psychic pain of the disintegrating and dying of the false self. As the motivating power of the false self diminishes, our true Self builds the *new self* with the motivating force of divine love.

19. The building of our *new self* is bound to be marked by innumerable mistakes and sometimes by sin. Such failures, however serious, are insignificant compared to the inviolable goodness of our true Self. We should ask God's pardon, seek forgiveness from those we may have offended, and then act with renewed confidence and energy as if nothing had happened.

20. Prolonged, pervasive, or paralyzing guilt feelings come from the false self. True guilt in response to personal sin or social injustice does not lead to discouragement but to amendment of life. It is a call to conversion.

21. Progress in the spiritual journey is manifested by the unconditional acceptance of other people, beginning with those with whom we live.

22. A community of faith offers the support of example, correction, and mutual concern in the spiritual journey. Above all, participating in the mystery of Chirst through the celebration of the liturgy, Eucharist, and silent prayer binds the community in a common search for transformation and union with God. The presence of Christ is ministered to each other and becomes tangible in the community, especially when it is gathered for worship or engaged in some work of service to those in need.

23. The moderation of the instinctual drives of the developing human organism for survival and security, affection and esteem, control and power allows true human needs to come into proper focus. Primary among these needs is intimacy with another or several human persons. By intimacy is meant the mutual sharing of thoughts, feelings, problems, and spiritual aspirations which gradually develops into spiritual friendship.

24. Spiritual friendship involving genuine self-disclosure is an essential ingredient for happiness both in marriage and in the celibate lifestyle. The experience of intimacy with another or several persons expands and deepens our capacity to relate to God and to everyone else. Under the influence of Divine Love the sexual energy is gradually transformed into universal compassion.

25. The spiritual radiation of a community depends on the commitment of its members to the inward journey and to each other. To offer one another space in which to grow as persons is an integral part of this commitment.

26. Contemplative prayer, in the traditional sense of the term, is the dynamic that initiates, accompanies and brings the process of transformation to completion.

27. Reflection on the Word of God in scripture and in our personal history is the foundation of contemplative prayer. The spontaneous letting go of particular thoughts and feelings in prayer is a sign of progress in contemplation. Contemplative prayer is characterized not so much by the absence of thoughts and feelings as by detachment from them.

28. The goal of genuine spiritual practice is not the rejection of the good things of the body, mind, or spirit, but the right use of them. No aspect of human nature or period of human life is to be rejected but integrated into each successive level of unfolding self-consciousness. In this way, the partial goodness proper to each stage of human development is preserved and only its limitations are left behind. The way to become divine is thus to become fully human.

29. The practice of a spiritual discipline is essential at the beginning of the spiritual journey as a means of developing the foundations of the contemplative dimension of life: dedication and devotion to God and service to others. Our daily practice should include a time for contemplative prayer and a program for letting go of the false self.

30. Regular periods of silence and solitude quiet the psyche, foster interior silence, and initiate the dynamic of self-knowledge.

31. Solitude is not primarily a place but an attitude of total commitment to God. When one belongs completely to God, the sharing of one's life and gifts continually increases.

32. The Beatitude of poverty of spirit springs from the increasing awareness of our true Self. It is a nonpossessive attitude toward everything and a sense of unity with everything at the same time. The interior freedom to have much or to have little, and the simplifying of one's lifestyle are signs of the presence of poverty of spirit.

33. Chastity is distinct from celibacy, which is the commitment to abstain from the genital expression of our sexuality. Chastity is the acceptance of our sexual energy, together with the masculine and feminine qualities that accompany it and the integration of this energy into our spirituality. It is the practice of moderation and self-control in the use of our sexual energy.

34. Chastity enhances and expands the power to love. It perceives the sacredness of everything that is. As a consequence, one respects the dignity of other persons and cannot use them merely for one's own filfullment.

35. Obedience is the unconditional acceptance of God as He is and as He manifests Himself in our lives. God's will is not immediately evident. Docility inclines us to attend to all the indications of His will. Discernment sifts the evidence and then decides, in the light of the inward attraction of grace, what God seems to be asking here and now.

36. Humility is an attitude of honesty with God, oneself, and all reality. It enables us to be at peace in the presence of our powerlessness and to rest in the forgetfulness of self.

37. Hope springs from the continuing experience of God's compassion and help. Patience is hope in action. It waits for the saving help of God without giving up, giving in, or going away, and for any length of time.

38. The disintegrating and dying of our false self is our participation in the passion and death of Jesus. The building of our *new self,* based on the transforming power of divine love, is our participation in his risen life.

39. In the beginning, emotional hang-ups are the chief obstacle to the growth of our *new self* because they put our freedom into a straight jacket. Later, because of

the subtle satisfaction that springs from self-control, spiritual pride becomes the chief obstacle. And finally, reflection of self becomes the chief obstacle because this hinders the innocence of divine union.

40. Human effort depends on grace even as it invites it. Whatever degree of divine union we may reach bears no proportion to our effort. It is the sheer gift of divine love.

41. Jesus did not teach a specific method of meditation or bodily discipline for quieting the imagination, memory, and emotions. We should choose as spiritual practice adapted to our particular temperament and natural disposition. We must also be willing to dispense with it when called by the Spirit to surrender to his direct guidance. The Spirit is above every method or practice. To follow his inspiration is the sure path to perfect freedom.

42. What Jesus proposed to his disciples as the Way is his own example: the forgiveness of everything and everyone and the service of others in their needs. "Love one another as I have loved you."

APPENDICES

■

The Active Prayer

The sacred word is designed to lead into silence. Hence, it should be short—one or two syllables. The active prayer—an aspiration drawn from scripture for use in daily life—should be longer—five to nine syllables. The saying of the syllables is synchronized with one's heartbeat. While some people like to use a variety of aspirations for this purpose, it is easier to work a single aspiration into the subconscious. The great advantage of this practice is that it eventually becomes a "tape" similar to the "tapes" that accompany one's upsetting emotions. When this occurs, the aspiration has the remarkable effect of erasing the old tapes, thus providing a neutral zone in which common sense or the Spirit of God can suggest what should be done.

The active prayer has to be repeated again and again at free moments in order to work it into the subconscious. The old tapes were built up through repeated acts. A new tape can be established in the same way. It may take a year to establish one's active prayer in the subconscious. It will then arise spontaneously. One may wake up saying it or it may accompany one's dreams.

Go about this practice without anxiety, haste, or excessive effort. Do not blame yourself for forgetting to say it on some days; just start up again. It should not be repeated when your mind is occupied with other things such as conversation, study, or work requiring concentration.

Following are examples of active prayer.

> O Lord, come to my assistance.
> O God, make haste to help me.
> Holy Mary, Mother of God.
> Abide in my love.
> My God and My All.
> My Jesus, mercy.

Veni Sancte Spiritus.
I belong to you, O Lord.
Soul of Christ, sanctify me.
Take, Lord, and receive all I have.
Bless the Lord, my soul.
Open my heart to your love.
Lord, I give myself to you.
My Lord and my God.
Body of Christ, save me.
Lord increase my faith.
Not my will but thine be done.
Thy kingdom come, Thy will be done.
Open my heart to your love.
May my being praise you, Lord.
Through Him, with Him, in Him.
Jesus, my light and my love.
Our help is in the name of the Lord.
Holy Spirit, pray in me.
Lord, do with me what You will.
Speak Lord, Your servant is listening.

The Weekly Support Group

While Centering Prayer is done privately most of the time, a weekly sharing of the experience in a small group (up to fifteen) has proven to be very supportive, as well as a means of continuing education. The weekly meeting also serves as a means of accountability. Just knowing that one's support group is meeting together each week is an enormous encouragement to keep going, or an invitation to return to the daily practice of Centering Prayer if circumstances such as illness, business, family problems, or urgent duties have prevented one from carrying out one's commitment to daily practice for a time.

By sharing the experience of Centering Prayer with others, one's own discernment of the ups and downs of the practice is sharpened. The group serves as a source of encouragement and can normally solve problems that might arise regarding the method. The collective discernment of the group tends to be well balanced.

Following is the format suggested for the weekly meeting.

Setting: Chairs placed in a circle.

Format:
1. A brief scripture reading or chanting (one or two minutes).
2. Centering Prayer period. Choose one of the following:

    a. Twenty-minute sit.

    b. Two twenty-minute sits with contemplative walk in between. In both cases end with the slow recitation of "Our Father" by the leader or two minutes of silence to return to ordinary thinking.

   3. *Lectio divina:* In the beginning, the "Guidelines for Christian Life, Growth, and Transformation" (Chapter Thirteen) may be used as a means of developing a conceptual background for the practice of Centering Prayer. Discuss in the group how each guideline may relate to each one's own life experience. Or use scriptural texts or readings from books on contemplative prayer. Allow half an hour or forty-five minutes for this period of sharing. Avoid theological, philosophical, or scriptural debates.

The purpose of the meeting is spiritual refreshment and mutual encouragement in the practice.

A Meditation

We begin our prayer by disposing our body. Let it be relaxed and calm, but inwardly alert.

The root of prayer is interior silence. We may think of prayer as thoughts or feelings expressed in words. But this is only one expression. Deep prayer is the laying aside of thoughts. It is the opening of mind and heart, body and feelings—our whole being—to God, the Ultimate Mystery, beyond words, thoughts, and emotions. We do not resist them or suppress them. We accept them as they are and go beyond them, not by effort, but by letting them all go by. We open our awareness to the Ultimate Mystery whom we know by faith is within us, closer than breathing, closer than thinking, closer than choosing—closer than consciousness itself. The Ultimate Mystery is the ground in which our being is rooted, the Source from whom our life emerges at every moment.

We are totally present now, with the whole of our being, in complete openness, in deep prayer. The past and future—time itself—are forgotten. We are here in the presence of the Ultimate Mystery. Like the air we breathe, this divine Presence is all around us and within us, distinct from us, but never separate from us. We may sense this Presence drawing us from within, as if touching our spirit and embracing it, or carrying us beyond ourselves into pure awareness.

We surrender to the attraction of interior silence, tranquility, and peace. We do not try to feel anything, reflect about anything. Without effort, without trying, we sink into this Presence, letting everything else go. Let love alone speak: the simple desire to be one with the Presence, to forget self, and to rest in the Ultimate Mystery.

This Presence is immense, yet so humble; awe-inspiring, yet so gentle; limitless, yet so intimate, tender and personal. I *know* that I am *known*. Everything in my life is transparent in this Presence. It knows everything about me—all my weaknesses, brokenness, sinfulness—and still loves me infinitely. This Presence is healing, strengthening, refreshing—just by its Presence. It is nonjudgmental, self-giving, seeking no reward, boundless in compassion. It is like coming home to a place I should never have left, to an awareness that was somehow always there, but which I did not recognize. I cannot force this awareness, or bring it about. A door opens within me, but from the other side. I seem to have tasted before the mysterious sweetness of this enveloping, permeating Presence. It is both emptiness and fullness at once.

We wait patiently; in silence, openness, and quiet attentiveness; motionless within and without. We surrender to the attraction to be still, to be loved, just to *be*.

How shallow are all the things that upset and discourage me! I resolve to give up the desires that trigger my tormenting emotions. Having tasted true peace, I can let them all go by. Of course, I shall stumble and fall, for I know my weakness. But I will rise at once, for I know my goal. I know where my home is.

The Essentials of the Centering Prayer Method

Theological Background

The grace of Pentecost affirms that the risen Jesus is among us as the glorified Christ. Christ lives in each of us as the Enlightened One, present everywhere and at all times. He is the living Master who continuously sends the Holy Spirit to dwell within us and to bear witness to his resurrection by empowering us to experience and manifest the fruits of the Spirit and the Beatitudes both in prayer and action.

Lectio Divina

Lectio divina is the most traditional way of cultivating friendship with Christ. It is a way of listening to the texts of scripture as if we were in conversation with Christ and he were suggesting the topics of conversation. The daily encounter with Christ and reflection on his word leads beyond mere acquaintanceship to an attitude of friendship, trust, and love. Conversation simplifies and gives way to communing, or as Gregory the Great (sixth century), summarizing the Christian contemplative tradition, put it, "resting in God." This was the classical meaning of contemplative prayer for the first sixteen centuries.

Contemplative Prayer

Contemplative prayer is the normal development of the grace of baptism and the regular practice of *lectio divina*. We may think of prayer as thoughts or feelings expressed in words. But this is only one expression. Contemplative prayer is the opening of mind and heart—our whole being—to God, the Ultimate Mystery, beyond thoughts, words, and emotions. We open our awareness to God whom we know by faith is within us, closer than breathing, closer than thinking, closer than choosing—closer than consciousness itself. Contemplative prayer is a process of interior purification leading, if we consent, to divine union.

The Method of Centering Prayer

Centering Prayer is a method designed to deepen the relationship with Christ begun in *lectio divina* and to facilitate the development of contemplative prayer by preparing our faculties to cooperate with this gift. It is an attempt to present the teaching of earlier times (e.g., *The Cloud of Unknowing*) in an updated form and to put a certain order and regularity into it. It is not meant to replace other kinds of prayer; it simply puts other kinds of prayer into a new and fuller perspective. During the time of prayer, we consent to God's presence and action within. At other times our attention moves outward to discover God's presence everywhere else.

The Guidelines

1. Choose a sacred word as the symbol of your intention to consent to God's presence and action within.

2. Sitting comfortably and with eyes closed, settle briefly, and silently introduce the sacred word as the symbol of your consent to God's presence and action within.

3. When you become aware of thoughts, return ever-so-gently to the sacred word.

4. At the end of the prayer period, remain in silence with eyes closed for a couple of minutes.

Explanation of the Guidelines

1. "Choose a sacred word as the symbol of your intention to consent to God's presence and action within" (see Chapter Five).

    a. The sacred word expresses our intention to be in God's presence and to yield to the divine action.

    b. The sacred word should be chosen during a brief period of prayer asking the Holy Spirit to inspire us with one that is especially suitable for us.

       1. Examples: Lord, Jesus, Abba, Father, Mother.

       2. Other possibilities: Love, Peace, Shalom, Silence.

    c. Having chosen a sacred word, we do not change it during the prayer period, for that would be to start thinking again.

    d. A simple inward gaze upon God may be more suitable for some persons than the sacred word. In this case, one consents to God's presence and action by turning inwardly toward God as if gazing upon him. The same guidelines apply to the sacred gaze as to the sacred word.

2. "Sitting comfortably and with eyes closed, settle briefly, and silently introduce the sacred word as the symbol of your consent to God's presence and action within."

    a. By "sitting comfortably" is meant relatively comfortably; not so comfortably that we encourage sleep, but sitting comfortably enough to avoid thinking about the discomfort of our bodies during this time of prayer.

    b. Whatever sitting position we choose, we keep the back straight.

    c. If we fall asleep, we continue the prayer for a few minutes upon awakening if we can spare the time.

    d. Praying in this way after a main meal encourages drowsiness. Better to wait an hour at least before Centering Prayer. Praying in this way just before retiring may disturb one's sleep pattern.

    e. We close our eyes to let go of what is going on around and within us.

    f. We introduce the sacred word inwardly and as gently as laying a feather on a piece of absorbent cotton.

3. "When you become aware of thoughts, return ever-so-gently to the sacred word."

    a. "Thoughts" is an umbrella term for every perception including sense perceptions, feelings, images, memories, reflections, and commentaries.

    b. Thoughts are a normal part of Centering Prayer.

    c. By "returning ever-so-gently to the sacred word," a minimum of effort is indicated. This is the only activity we initiate during the time of Centering Prayer.

    d. During the course of our prayer, the sacred word may become vague or even disappear.

4. "At the end of the prayer period, remain in silence with eyes closed for two or three minutes."

    a. If this prayer is done in a group, the leader may slowly recite the Our Father during the additional two or three minutes while the others listen.

    b. The additional two or three minutes give the psyche time to readjust to the external senses and enable us to bring the atmosphere of silence into daily life.

Some Practical Points

1. The minimum time for this prayer is twenty minutes. Two periods are recommended each day, one first thing in the morning, and one in the afternoon or early evening.

2. The end of the prayer period can be indicated by a timer, provided it does not have an audible tick or loud sound when it goes off.

3. The principal effects of Centering Prayer are experienced in daily life, not in the period of Centering Prayer itself.

4. Physical symptoms:

    a. We may notice slight pains, itches, or twitches in various parts of the body, or a generalized restlessness. These are usually due to the untying of emotional knots in the body.

    b. We may also notice heaviness or lightness in the extremities. This is usually due to a deep level of spiritual attentiveness.

    c. In either case, we pay no attention, or we allow the mind to rest briefly in the sensation and then return to the sacred word.

5. *Lectio divina* provides the conceptual background for the development of Centering Prayer.

6. A support group praying and sharing together once a week helps maintain one's commitment to the prayer.

Extending the Effects of Centering Prayer into Daily Life

1. Practice two periods of Centering Prayer daily.

2. Read scriptures regularly and study the parts of this book that deal with the method.

3. Practice one or two of the specific practices for everyday life suggested in Chapter Twelve.

4. Join a Centering Prayer Support Group or Follow-up Program (if available in your area).

    a. The group meeting encourages the members of the group to persevere in private.

    b. It also provides an opportunity for further input on a regular basis through tapes, readings, and discussion.

Points for Further Development

1. During the prayer period, various kinds of thoughts may be distinguished (see Chapters Six through Ten):

    a. Ordinary wanderings of the imagination or memory.

    b. Thoughts that give rise to attractions or aversions.

    c. Insights and psychological breakthroughs.

    d. Self-reflections such as, "How am I doing?" or "This peace is just great!"

    e. Thoughts that arise from the unloading of the unconscious.

2. During this prayer, we avoid analyzing our experience, harboring expectations, or aiming at some specific goal such as the following:

    a. Repeating the sacred word continuously.

    b. Having no thoughts.

    c. Making the mind a blank.

    d. Feeling peaceful or consoled.

    e. Achieving a spiritual experience.

3. What Centering Prayer is not:

    a. It is not a technique.

    b. It is not a relaxation exercise.

    c. It is not a form of self-hypnosis.

    d. It is not a charismatic gift.

    e. It is not a parapsychological phenomenon.

    f. It is not limited to the "felt" presence of God.

    g. It is not discursive meditation or affective prayer.

4. What Centering Prayer is:

    a. It is at the same time a relationship with God and a discipline to foster that relationship.

    b. It is an exercise of faith, hope, and love.

    c. It is a movement beyond conversation with Christ to communion.

    d. It habituates us to the language of God which is silence.

A Brief History of Contemplative Outreach

Centering Prayer

During the first sixteen centuries of Church history, contemplative prayer was the acknowledged goal of Christian spirituality for clergy and laity alike. In the course of recent centuries, this heritage, at least as a living tradition, was virtually lost. Now in the twentieth century with the advent of cross-cultural dialogue and historical research, the recovery of the Christian contemplative tradition has begun. The method of Centering Prayer, in the context of the tradition of *lectio divina,* is contributing to this renewal.

Throughout the 1970s, a group of Trappist monks continued this search at St. Joseph's Abbey in Spencer, Massachusetts. In 1975 the contemplative practice called Centering Prayer, based on the fourteenth century classic *The Cloud of Unknowing,* was developed by Frs. William Menninger and Basil Pennington. This method of prayer was offered at the guest house in Spencer first to priests and later to lay people. The response was so positive that an increasing number of workshops was offered and an advanced workshop was developed by Fr. Thomas Keating to train teachers of the method.

Contemplative Outreach

In 1981, Fr. Keating resigned as abbot of St. Joseph's and moved to St. Benedict's Monastery in Snowmass, Colorado. Requests to share Centering Prayer in various parts of the country as well as requests for a more intensive Centering Prayer experience began to surface. In 1983 the first Intensive Centering Prayer Retreat was held at the Lama Foundation in San Cristobal, New Mexico. Since then, Intensives have been given at St. Benedict's Monastery in Snowmass and in several other locations. Two Post-Intensive Retreats are held each year and Formation Weeks are given.

Organization

Because of the growing interest in Centering Prayer in certain areas of the country, a number of local Centering Prayer support groups grew up and soon the need to organize became evident.

In 1984, Contemplative Outreach, Ltd. was established to coordinate efforts to introduce the Centering Prayer method to persons seeking a deeper life of prayer and to provide a support system capable of sustaining their commitment. In 1986, a national office of Contemplative Outreach was established.

Contemplative Outreach, Ltd.
10 Park Place, Suite 2B
PO Box 737
Butler, NJ 07405

Telephone: (973) 838-3384
Fax: (973) 492-5795
Email: office@coutreach.org
Website: www.contemplativeoutreach.org

GLOSSARY OF TERMS

∎

Apophatic/Kataphatic contemplation—a misleading distinction suggesting opposition between the two; in fact, a proper preparation of the faculties (kataphatic practice) leads to apophatic contemplation, which in turn is sustained through appropriate kataphatic practices.

a) Apophatic (darksome)—the exercise of pure faith; resting in God beyond concepts and particular acts, except to maintain a general loving attention to the divine presence.

b) Kataphatic (lightsome)—the exercise of the rational faculties enlightened by faith: the affective response to symbols, reflection, and the use of reason, imagination, and memory in order to assimilate the truths of faith.

Attention—the focusing on a particular object such as God's word in scripture, the breath, an image, or a concept.

Awareness—the act of being aware of a particular or general perception; another term for consciousness.

Beatitudes (Matt. 5:1–10)—a further development of the fruits of the Spirit.

Centering Prayer—a contemporary form of prayer of the heart, prayer of simplicity, prayer of faith, prayer of simple regard; a method of reducing the obstacles to the gift of contemplative prayer and of facilitating the development of habits conducive to responding to the inspirations of the Spirit.

Consent—an act of the will expressing acceptance of someone, some thing, or some course of action; the manifestation of one's intention.

Contemplation—a synonym for contemplative prayer.

Contemplative living—activity in daily life prompted by the Gifts of the Spirit; the fruit of a contemplative attitude.

Contemplative prayer—the development of one's relationship with Christ to the point of communing beyond words, thoughts, feelings, and the multiplication of particular acts; a process moving from the simplified activity of waiting upon God to the ever-increasing predominance of the Gifts of the Spirit as the source of one's prayer.

Contemplative walk—a slow meditative walk of five to seven minutes recommended when two or more periods of Centering Prayer are held back-to-back. Its purpose is to dissipate the restlessness that may build up as a result of remaining in one position for a longer time than one is used to, and to provide an opportunity to bring the interior peace of contemplative prayer into a simple form of activity.

Divine union—a term describing a single experience of the union of all the faculties in God or the permanent state of union called transforming union.

Ecstacy—the temporary suspension by the divine action of the thinking and feeling faculties, including at times the external senses, which facilitates the experience of divine union.

False self—the self developed in our own likeness rather than in the likeness of God; the self-image developed to cope with the emotional trauma of early childhood, which seeks happiness in satisfying the instinctual needs of survival/security, affection/esteem, and power/control, and which bases its self-worth on cultural or group identification.

Fruits of the Spirit (Gal. 5:22–24)—nine aspects of "the mind of Christ" manifesting the growth of the divine life in us.

Gifts of the Spirit—
   a. Charismatic gifts of the Spirit (1 Cor. 12:1–13)—given primarily to encourage the Christian community.
   b. Seven Gifts of the Spirit (Is. 11:2)—habitual dispositions empowering us to perceive and follow the promptings of the Holy Spirit both in prayer and action.

Intention—the choice of the will in regard to some goal or purpose.

Interior silence—the quieting of the imagination, feelings, and rational faculties in the process of recollection; the general, loving attentiveness to God in pure faith.

Lectio divina—reading or more exactly, listening to the book we believe to be divinely inspired; the most ancient method of developing the friendship of Christ by using scripture texts as topics of conversation with Christ.

Method of contemplative prayer—any prayer practice that spontaneously evolves or is deliberately designed to free the mind of excessive dependence on thinking to go to God.

a. Practices spontaneously evolving toward contemplation—*lectio divina,* the Jesus Prayer, Veneration of Icons, the Rosary, and most other traditional devotions of the Church rightly used.

b. Practices deliberately designed to facilitate contemplation—

1. Concentrative—the Jesus Prayer, mantric practice (constant repetition of a word or phrase), Dom John Main's method of contemplative prayer.

2. Receptive—Centering Prayer, prayer of faith, prayer of the heart, prayer of simplicity, prayer of silence, prayer of simple regard, active recollection, acquired contemplation.

c. On a scale of 1 to 10, some practices are more concentrative, others more receptive.

Mystical prayer—a synonym for contemplative prayer.

Mysticism—a synonym for contemplation.

Purification—an essential part of the process of contemplation through which the dark side of one's personality, mixed motivation, and the emotional pain of a lifetime stored in the unconscious are gradually evacuated; the necessary preparation for transforming union.

Spiritual attentiveness—the general loving attention to the presence of God in pure faith, whether an undifferentiated sense of unity or a more personal attention to one or other of the Divine Persons.

Thoughts—in the context of the specific method of Centering Prayer, an umbrella term for any perception at all, including sense perceptions, feelings, images, memories, reflections, commentaries, and particular spiritual perceptions.

Transformation (transforming union)—the stable conviction of the abiding presence of God rather than a particular experience or set of experiences; a restructuring of consciousness in which the divine reality is perceived to be present in oneself and in all that is.

True Self—the image of God in which every human being is created; our participation in the divine life manifested in our uniqueness.

Ultimate Mystery/Ultimate Reality—the ground of infinite potentiality and actualization; a term emphasizing the divine transcendence.

Unloading the unconscious—the coming to awareness of previously unconscious emotional material from early childhood in the form of primitive feelings or a barrage of images, especially during the time of prayer.

INVITATION TO LOVE

■

The Way of Christian Contemplations

CONTENTS

■

INTRODUCTION

■

THIS BOOK IS THE RESULT of an ongoing effort to re-present the Christian spiritual path in a way that is accessible to contemporary followers of Christ. During the first sixteen centuries of the Church's history, contemplative prayer was the acknowledged goal of Christian spirituality for clergy and laity alike. After the Reformation this heritage, at least as a living tradition, was virtually lost. Now in the twentieth century, with the advent of cross-cultural dialogue and historical research, the recovery of the Christian contemplative tradition has begun.

Throughout the early 1970s, a small group of Trappist monks at St. Joseph's Abbey, Spencer, Massachusetts, were reflecting on how they might contribute to this renewal. In 1975 the contemplative practice called Centering Prayer, based on the fourteenth-century classic *The Cloud of Unknowing,* was developed by Father William Meninger and offered at the guest house in Spencer to priest retreatants. A year later he made a series of audio tapes, which continues to be popular even to this day. The response to the method was so positive that introductory workshops were instituted on a regular basis and made available to everyone. Father Basil Pennington joined in this work and extended the introductory workshops to an ever-widening circle of places and persons.

In 1981, I resigned as abbot of St. Joseph's and moved to St. Benedict's Monastery, Snowmass, Colorado. The idea of a more intensive experience of Centering Prayer began to surface. In 1983, the first Intensive Centering Prayer Retreat was held at the Lama Foundation, San Cristobal, New Mexico. Since then, Intensives have been given at St. Benedict's Monastery and in other locations.

A number of weekly support groups grew up in various areas of the country, and the need to organize became evident. In 1984, Contemplative Outreach, Ltd. was established to coordinate efforts to introduce Centering Prayer to persons seeking a deeper life of prayer and to provide support systems and ongoing training opportunities capable of sustaining their commitment. Continuing practice also created the need for a more comprehensive conceptual background in order to understand the practice and to integrate its effects into daily life.

In the Christian tradition, contemplative prayer has never been a privatized spiritual experience in the service of "altered states of consciousness" or self-actualization. With the spiritual thirst awakened through encounter with God's presence during Centering Prayer periods, the need became more insistent for a representation of the classic Christian spiritual path in a way consistent with contemporary sciences, in particular, the insights of modern psychology.

It is my conviction that the language of psychology is an essential vehicle in our time to explain the healing of the unconscious effected during the dark nights which Saint John of the Cross describes. For one thing, it is a language that is better understood than the traditional language of spiritual theology, at least in the Western world. It also provides a more comprehensive understanding of the psychological dynamics which grace has to contend with in the healing and transforming process.

The first attempt toward providing a comprehensive frame of reference for the experience of contemplative prayer began as conferences at the two-week intensive retreat at Lama in 1983. These conferences were refined over the course of several years at other intensive workshop-retreats. In October 1986, these were filmed as a seventeen-part video cassette series called "The Spiritual Journey." Two years later, seven more parts were added. The series has become an important teaching tool, along with the resource book *Open Mind, Open Heart,* for ongoing support groups.

The present book is a selective development of material originally presented in those tapes. It is an attempt to provide a road map, as it were, for the journey that begins when Centering Prayer is seriously undertaken and to point to some of the recognizable landmarks on the journey, as well as to its ultimate destination. The latter is not so much a goal to be attained, as an ever more resolute commitment to the journey. This book also reflects the ongoing insights of many persons practicing Centering Prayer and sharing their experiences over many years.

Although this book seeks to establish a dialogue between the insights of contemporary psychology and the classic Christian spiritual masters, its primary goal is *practical:* to provide a solid conceptual background for the practice of contemplative prayer and the spiritual journey for our time. We are called to this journey not just for our own personal growth, but also for the sake of the whole human community.

As this book will show, one of the biggest impediments to spiritual growth is that we do not perceive our own hidden motivations. Our unconscious, prerational emotional programming from childhood and our overidentification with a specific group or groups are the sources from which our false self—our injured, compensatory sense of who we are—gradually emerges and stabilizes. The influence of the false self extends into every aspect and activity of our lives, either consciously or unconsciously.

Centering Prayer, and more particularly contemplative prayer for which it is a preparation, brings us face to face with this "false self" in several ways: The initial act of consent to letting go of our surface "I" with its programs, associations, commentaries, etc., in itself drives a fatal wedge into the false self. As we rest in prayer, we begin to discover that our identity is deeper than just the surface of our psychological awareness.

The regular practice of contemplative prayer initiates a healing process that might be called the "divine therapy." The level of deep rest accessed during the prayer periods loosens up the hard-pan around the emotional weeds stored in the unconscious, of which the body seems to be the warehouse. The psyche begins to evacuate spontaneously the undigested emotional material of a lifetime, opening up new space for self-knowledge, freedom of choice, and the discovery of the divine presence within. As a consequence, a growing trust in God, a bonding with the Divine Therapist, enables us to endure the process.

Thus, the gift of contemplative prayer is a practical and essential tool for confronting the heart of the Christian ascesis—namely, the struggle with our unconscious motivation—while at the same time establishing the climate and necessary dispositions for a deepening relationship with God and leading, if we persevere, to divine union.

Meanwhile, the same process of letting go (of thoughts, feelings, commentaries, etc.), first experienced during the prayer period, becomes the basis for a practice of consent that can be carried into all of life, enabling us more and more to live the values of the gospel.

This book is part of a trilogy that contains the principal aspects of the Intensive Centering Prayer Retreat. *Open Mind, Open Heart* deals with the practice of Centering Prayer as a preparation for the gift of contemplation. *Invitation to Love* offers the conceptual background for the practice and for the Christian contemplative journey in general. *The Mystery of Christ* is an attempt to integrate both the practice and the theory into the celebration of the liturgical year and the immersion in the mystery of Christ. Together they are meant to provide a comprehensive program with which to respond to the invitation of the Spirit to follow Christ in our time.

1

THE EMOTIONAL PROGRAMS
FOR HAPPINESS

■

CONTEMPLATIVE PRAYER addresses the human condition exactly where it is. This prayer heals the emotional wounds of a lifetime. It opens up the possibility of experiencing in this world the transformation into Christ to which the gospel invites us.

God wants to share with us even in this life the maximum amount of divine life that we can possibly contain. The call of the gospel, "Follow me," is addressed to every baptized person. We have within us in virtue of our baptism all the grace-given powers we need to follow Christ into the bosom of the Father. The attempt to do this—to reach more deeply toward the love of Christ within us and to manifest it more fully in the world—constitutes the heart of the spiritual journey.

The journey has been presented in Christian tradition as an ascent. Images of ladders and upward journeys abound. But for most of us who undertake the journey today, in our age when developmental psychology and a greater understanding of the unconscious is widespread, the journey might more properly be seen as a descent. The direction, at least initially, is toward a confrontation with our motivations and unconscious emotional programs and responses. Our spiritual journey does not start with a clean slate. We carry with us a prepackaged set of values and preconceived ideas which, unless confronted and redirected, will soon scuttle our journey, or else turn it into pharisaism, the occupational hazard of religious and spiritual people.

The developmental character of human life has become much better known in the last hundred years, and it has enormous implications for the spiritual journey. Our personal histories are computerized, so to speak, in the biocomputers of our brains and nervous systems. Our memory banks have on file everything that occurred from the womb to the present, especially memories with strong emotional charges. In the first years of life, there is no consciousness of a self, but there *are* needs and our emotional responses to them, all faithfully recorded in the biocomputers of our brains. Already these computers are developing emotional programs for happiness—happiness at this stage meaning the prompt fulfillment of our instinctual needs. By the time we come to the age of reason and develop full reflective self-consciousness around the age of twelve or thirteen, we have in place fully developed emotional programs for happiness based on the emotional judgments of the child—even the infant.

Of all newborn mammals none is more helpless than the human infant. Other species have all kinds of useful instincts, but the infant depends completely on the reception he or she receives from the parent(s); the best he can do is to cry loudly to make his needs known. The most crucial instinctual needs in the first year of life are survival and the sense of security. The infant enjoyed a marvelous environment in the womb where all his needs were taken care of and where he felt perfectly safe. The new environment can hardly compare with the wonderful environment of the womb. The first need of the infant is to bond with his mother. His entire world is the mother's face, smile, and the heartbeat that reminds him of the safe environment of the womb. The infant's whole concern is the prompt fulfillment of his needs, the chief of which, along with food, is affection. The baby needs to be held, kissed, and caressed. Being picked up frequently to nurse or to have his diapers changed reinforces the bonding process with the mother. The bonding force of the universe is love. We can hardly exaggerate the amount of affection that the infant needs in order to feel safe. This feeling of security enables the emotional life of the child to unfold in a healthy way.

Suppose an infant comes into the world in an environment that is not welcoming or where he experiences hesitation about his arrival. He will then have an emotional hesitation to accept the adventure of life because his most important need, the biological necessity for security, is not met.

In the second year of the child's life, a more varied repertory of emotions develops, and the child experiences need for pleasure, affection, and esteem. These are present, of course, earlier in life, but now the child is differentiating himself from the environment and is beginning to experience himself as a body distinct from the other creatures crawling around on the floor. The child needs more than ever the warmth of affection and acceptance of parents and family. Along with this development of a body-self, the child begins to want his own way, manifesting the instinctual needs for power and control.

Suppose that one of these instinctual needs, necessary for biological survival, is perceived by the child to be withheld, either through competition with other siblings or through exposure to an environment that is hazardous. Maybe he lives in a locale where the great tragedies of our time are taking place—guerrilla warfare, epidemics, destitution, starvation—where there is daily risk of losing one's parents, and where violence is the order of the day. In such situations it becomes more and more difficult for a child to consent emotionally to the goodness and beauty of life.

Again, the child may have a handicap that prevents him from taking part in games. Or, through sibling competition or a vague sense of unwantedness, he may come to feel inferior. In any case, the fragile emotional life of the child, if there are any negative influences, begins to develop compensatory needs to offset the frustration of its instinctual needs, or to repress painful memories into the unconscious. We may not remember the events of early childhood, but the emotions do. When events occur later in life that resemble those once felt to be harmful, dangerous, or rejecting, the same feelings surface. We may not be fully aware of where the force of those feelings is coming from.

Even with the most well-intentioned and capable of parents, we have to deal with the influences of the culture and peer groups. Although we may not have experienced serious traumas, all of us have experienced that emotional fragility of early childhood and hence bring with us some wounds as a result. Some have enormous wounds because of the misunderstanding or fumbling of parents or the lack of parents.

If a child is severely deprived of affection in infancy, especially during the first year or two, he has no way of discerning the cause. He has only feelings to go by. All he knows is that he is not being loved, and this deprivation may lead to deep-seated feelings of hostility or fear.

If we felt deprived of security, the particular security symbols of the culture that we grow up in will exercise an enormous attraction. Since we developed these programs for happiness before reason could provide any kind of moderation, they have no limits. When the desire for security is frustrated by some event and we cannot obtain the symbol of security that we desire, we immediately experience the afflictive emotions—grief, anger, jealousy, and so on.

The emotions faithfully identify the value system that developed in early childhood to cope with unbearable situations. These emotional programs for happiness start out as needs, grow into demands, and can finally become "shoulds." Others are then expected to respect our fantastic demands. People can grow up intellectually, physically, and even spiritually while their emotional lives remain fixated at the level of infancy, because they have never been able to integrate their emotions with the other values of their developing selves.

Persons whose emotional need for power and control has become a center of motivation like to control every situation and everyone. You may have met such persons in your family, or at work, or maybe in a religious community. Maybe you are one of them. In any case, such persons are programmed for human misery. In trying to control situations and other people, they are in competition with five and a half billion other people, many trying to do the same impossible thing. It can't possibly work; statistics are against them.

During the socialization period from ages four to eight, we absorb unquestion-ingly the values of our parents, teachers, and peer groups. We draw our identity or self-worth from what others in the particular group to which we belong think of us. Hence we have to measure up to their expectations. The emotional programs for happiness, already fully in place by age three or four, become much more com-plex. When we come to the age of reason and full reflective self-consciousness, we find ourselves at the most vulnerable point in our growth process. The human heart is designed for unlimited happiness—for limitless truth and for limitless love—and nothing less can satisfy. Hence we have to repress that desperate but unfulfilled hunger for happiness. We travel down various roads that promise happiness but can't provide it because they are only partial goods. Since the emotional programs from early childhood are already in place, our search for happiness in adult life tends to be programmed by childish expectations that cannot possibly be realized.

Here, for example, is a gentleman who has a hundred million dollars in assets. He is successful in Wall Street but not satisfied with his hundred million. He makes a million a day but still feels unsatisfied. He wants to make more money, and he wants to make more money to much that, although he already has a hundred million, he engages in fraudulent activity. His desire for more is insatiable. The nature of the emotional programs is to want to get more and more out of life, bigger and better pleasures, and more and more power over as many people as we can dominate, including God if we could get away with it. Most people are bliss-fully unaware that these emotional programs are functioning at full force inside them and secretly influencing their judgments and important decisions.

Again, someone who felt rejected in early childhood and never experienced real family life may be attracted to a religious community on the unconscious level, looking for a family he or she never had. Or children who feel deprived of affection may later choose spouses who they think can meet their dependency needs. If they choose mothers instead of wives or fathers instead of husbands, their marriages may be headed for serious trouble. This is not an impossible situation if they know what their problem is and take steps to deal with its dynamics. However, I have known people who were so dependent that they felt they could not escape from their ingrained over-dependence unless they actually separated from their spouses for a time. The dependency was so deep-rooted that it was reinforced just by living in the same house.

We come now to the heart of the problem of the human condition. Jesus ad-dressed this problem head-on in the gospel. What was his first word when begin-ning his ministry? "Repent." To repent is not to take on afflictive penances like fasting, vigils, flagellation, or whatever else appeals to our generosity. It means *to change the direction in which you are looking for happiness*. That challenge goes to the root of the problem. It is not just a bandage for one or another of the emotional programs.

If we say yes to the invitation to repent, we may experience enormous freedom for a few months or for even a year or two. Our former way of life, in some degree, is cleaned up and certain relationships healed. Then, after a year or two the dust stirred up by our first conversion settles and the old temptations recur. As the springtime of the spiritual journey turns to summer—and fall and winter—the original enthusiasms begin to wane. At some point, we have to face the fundamental problem, which is the unconscious motivation that is still in place, even after we have chosen the values of the gospel. The false self is the syndrome of our emotional programs for happiness grown into sources of motivation and made much more complex by the socialization process, and reinforced by our overidentification with our cultural conditioning. Our ordinary thoughts, reactions, and feelings manifest the false self on every level of our conduct. When the false self learns that we have been converted and will now start practicing all the virtues, it has the biggest laugh of a lifetime and dares us, saying, "Just try it!"

Now we experience the full force of the spiritual combat, the struggle with what we want to do and feel we should do, and our incredible inability to carry it out. We recall Paul's classical lament:

> I don't understand myself at all. I really want to do what is right, but I can't. I do what I don't want to do—what I hate. I know perfectly well that what I am doing is wrong, and my bad conscience proves that I agree with these laws that I am breaking. . . . No matter which way I turn, I can't make myself do right. I want to, but I can't. When I want to do good, I don't; and when I try not to do wrong, I do it anyway. . . .
>
> I love to do God's will, so far as my new nature is concerned. But there is something else deep within me, in my lower nature, that is at war with my mind, and wins the fight, and makes me a slave to sin that is still within me. . . . Oh, what a terrible predicament I am in! Who will free me from my slavery to this deadly lower nature? (Rom. 7:15–24, *The Living Gospel*)

Such insight is the beginning of the real spiritual journey. We realize, with a heavy heart, that it is going to be a long journey. We grasp that we are dealing with subtle forces that are powerful and fully in place. To dismantle these value systems in favor of the values of the gospel is not a matter of a few high spiritual experiences. These can remain merely tranquilizers of an exalted kind if we do not work to dismantle the false self and to practice the virtues. Spiritual highs give us temporary relief, but when they subside they leave us back where we were with all the same problems.

Shortly after Jesus was anointed by the Spirit in the River Jordan, he was led into the desert by the same Spirit to be tempted by the devil. Lent is our battle with the same temptations. The biblical desert symbolizes the confrontation with the false self and interior purification. Jesus was tempted regarding each one of the instinctual needs. He did not consent to them while yet experiencing them in their utmost intensity—"He was tempted in every way that we are, yet never sinned" (Heb. 4:15). When Jesus was desperately hungry, the devil maliciously suggested, "Why don't you change these stones into loaves of bread?" Jesus replied, "I choose to put my trust in Abba, my heavenly Father." Then the devil took him up to the pinnacle of the Temple and suggested that he jump off, sure of angelic protection, and thus be regarded as a wonder worker. Jesus rejected this appeal to fame out-of-hand. Finally the devil took him to the top of a high mountain and offered him power over all the nations of the world, saying, "If you bow down and worship me, you can have them all!" To this Jesus responded, "To hell with you?" Having rejected the exaggerated demands of each of the emotional programs for happiness, he invites us to do the same, saying, "Repent." This is as if he were to say, "Change the direction in which you are looking for happiness. You'll never find it in your emotional programs for happiness. Let go of your childish motivation because it can't possibly work in adult life."

Jesus' harsh sayings also cast a strong light on the false-self system. For instance, "If your eye scandalizes you, pull it out." Or, "If your hand or foot scandalizes you, cut it off." Obviously, these words are not to be taken literally. The Hebrew language uses exaggeration or the repetition of the same words to emphasize an important point. In this case, the point being stressed is our attachment to our emotional programs for happiness. We might thus paraphrase his words: "If your desire for survival/security, affection/esteem, and power/control is so dear to you, as dear to you as your eye, or your hand or your foot, cut it off! This is the only way you can be free to enter the kingdom of God."

The heart of the Christian ascesis is the struggle with our unconscious motivations. If we do not recognize and confront the hidden influences of the emotional programs for happiness, the false self will adjust to any new situation in a short time and nothing is really changed. If we enter the service of the Church, the symbols of security, success, and power in the new milieu will soon become the new objects of our desires.

Thus the false self accompanies us, implacably, into whatever lifestyle we choose. Here is the story of a macho young man from a society in which drinking his friends under the table is the symbol of domination and success. He experiences enormous satisfaction as he watches his friends slithering under the table at the local tavern. Of course, this feeling of exaltation only lasts a few minutes, and he has to go to another tavern if he wants to enjoy the same result. Whatever satisfaction comes from getting what the false self wants is always brief.

This young man hears a televangelist and is totally converted from his evil ways. Not only is he resolved never to drink again; he isn't even going to eat an ice-cream cone. He looks around for the hardest religious order he can find, and, sure enough, he discovers the Trappists. "There," he thinks, "they scarcely eat anything." He applies to a monastery and is welcomed with open arms. He evidences that great spirit of austerity that the Trappists were especially strong on in those days. So he enters the monastery and dives into all the rules of strict silence and heavy work. Lent comes and the monks are fasting on bread and water. As the weeks pass, he notices the older brethren disappearing from the refectory. They are eating in the infirmary because their health has been weakened by the severe fast. Others are catching the flu. By Holy Week he is left alone in the refectory. As the great bell rings out for the Paschal Vigil, he staggers out of the refectory. To his surprise, he feels a familiar surge of pride and self-exaltation reminiscent of his former tavern accomplishments; only now, instead of drinking all his friends under the table, he has fasted all the monks under the table.

What, I ask you, has changed in this young man? Nothing apart from his address, hairdo, and clothes. This is what the gospel means by worldliness. When John says, "Leave the world," he does not mean the world with its desperate needs that cry out to be served. He means the self-centered projects, programs, demands—rationalized, justified, and even glorified—of security, pleasure, esteem, and power, which hinder our growing up into full human personhood. Persons who take responsibility for their emotions do not project their painful emotions on other people. In fact, even if we should succeed in manipulating other people and situations to our liking, nothing really changes, for the root of the problem is not in them but in us.

2

THE FALSE SELF IN ACTION

∎

MINUS THE MACHO, that young man in the last chapter could have been myself. My conversion to Christ was extremely deep and personal prior to entering the monastery, and marked by a strong attraction for long periods of prayer and a willingness to make almost any sacrifice to follow Christ. Although there continued to be occasional periods of consolation in prayer, my early years in monastic community brought me face to face with the not-so-pleasant parts of myself, as I came to experience firsthand the false self in action. I knew that the Trappist life was going to be difficult. But what I expected would be difficult was not as hard as I expected. And what I expected would be easy proved to be difficult in the extreme.

I joined the monastic community because I was sold on the idea of spending my whole life in search of union with Christ. In my understanding, contemplative prayer was the heart of the spiritual journey. At the time, an austere regime was considered the indispensable way to contemplation; hence I looked for the most difficult order I could find. I was willing to give up everything—family, friends, and comfort—in order to follow Christ into the desert.

Newcomers to a Trappist monastery in the mid-1940s could normally speak only to the abbot and the novice master. Both had almost absolute authority over the novices, a fact that did not help to develop spontaneous relationships. The only communication allowed between the monks was a sign language limited to functional communication. As inheritors of the strict Trappist reform of the Cistercian Order instituted a century prior to the French Revolution, Trappists generally believed that the more silent you were and the more penances you performed, the closer you would draw to God and the more likely you were to make spiritual progress. Vocal prayers took up a significant part of the day. We rose ordinarily before two in the morning, an hour earlier on big feast days, and went to bed at seven at night. The work was frequently hard manual labor. The food was not very nourishing. The vegetables that we harvested in the fall were wrinkled and a bit soggy by March.

I bought into the rules hook, line, and sinker. The only way that I could survive was to get on my knees and beg God's help. I used to go to the church during every free moment, which added up to a couple of hours on most days. Since growth in contemplative prayer was my goal, I wanted to spend as much time as I could in the church. When praying privately in church, a monk was supposed to stand or kneel; sitting down was proscribed by the book of regulations. Although calluses were forming on my knees from kneeling so long, I hoped that if I persevered in extended periods of prayer, I would someday achieve my ideal of becoming a contemplative.

When I had been in the monastery for a year or so, another person entered the community who seemingly had the same idea. Like me, he came to church regularly during all the periods of free time, but he had the good sense to get permission from the abbot, who could dispense from certain regulations, to sit down during his prolonged visits. That possibility never occurred to me. I made a point of not allowing myself any relaxation in observing all the rules.

For months the newcomer spent as much time in church as I did. Often when I came in from work, washed up quickly, and hastened upstairs to kneel in church, he would be there. A general sense of uneasiness started to float through my mind along with my efforts to pray: I wondered how he was able to get here ahead of me. Whenever I took a furtive glance in his direction, he always seemed to have a beatific smile hovering about his lips. The thought came, "How is it that I am wearing out my knees while this guy who is always sitting down seems to be enjoying the Lord's special favors?"

I began to recognize that these thoughts were prompted by envy. Here I was in this holy place, in this holy position, trying to practice the holiest kind of prayer, and I was envying someone else's spiritual attainment. I had read enough about moral theology to know that this was the worst kind of envy. The thought came, "I was better before I came to this monastery. Maybe I should leave." This temptation went on for months, though not always with the same intensity. I even had thoughts that I should give up prayer altogether because whenever I tried these feelings of envy arose. Fortunately, I had enough sense to realize that I should not be governed by my own judgment in so important a matter. When I sought advice, our abbot encouraged me to persevere in prayer no matter what happened. As a man of prayer, he was aware of the purification that usually begins when one enters a life of strict silence, solitude, and prayer: one's mixed motivation emerges into clear awareness. Grace is there, but so is the false self.

The truth about ourselves is inevitable; whatever it is, it is going to come up. When the dust settles after the first fervor of religious conversion, we once again confront our old temptations. They may be worse than before because now we are more honest, open, and vulnerable. The great struggle is not to get discouraged when the divine reassurance begins to recede. It seems that God wants us to know experientially just what he has been putting up with throughout our lives. He seems to expect us to receive this information not as a reproach, but as a gift—like a friend revealing secrets to a friend. But instead of saying, "Thanks," we are ready to get up and walk out.

As I sat there day after day engulfed in horrible feelings of envy and praying for them to go away, matters got worse. Every now and then, especially on a bad day when I had been through other difficulties, these feelings translated into taste. I could virtually taste the feeling of envy in my mouth and would think to myself, "This is like sinking my teeth into a piece of juicy manure! And the manure is me!"

After three or four years of struggling with these feelings, I was thrown into a situation where I could speak with my brother monk. I discovered that he had the same problems I had in trying to find enough free time for prayer and that his periods of consoled prayer alternated with very heavy seas. As we sympathized with each other, my envy vanished and in time we became friends.

On the spiritual journey, there is usually someone in our family, business, or community whom we cannot endure, someone who has a genius for bringing out the worst in us. No matter what we do, we cannot seem to improve the relationship. This was the nature of my envy toward my brother monk. He had not done anything to cause it. God simply used him to reflect back to me what *my* problem was. Thus the person who gives us the most trouble may be our greatest gift from God.

In religious circles there is a cliché that describes the divine purification as "a battering from without and a boring from within." God goes after our accumulated junk with something equivalent to a compressor and starts digging through our defense mechanisms, revealing the secret corners that hide the unacceptable parts of ourselves. We may think it is the end of our relationship with God. Actually, it is an invitation to a new depth of relationship with God. A lot of emptying and healing has to take place if we are to be responsive to the sublime communications of God. The full transmission of divine life cannot come through and be fully heard if the static of the false self is too loud.

Once we start the spiritual journey, God is totally on our side. Everything works together for our good. If we can believe this, we can save ourselves an enormous amount of trouble. Purification of the unconscious is an important part of the journey. The decision to choose the values of the gospel does not touch the unconscious motivation that is firmly in place by age three or four, and more deeply entrenched by the age of reason. As long as the false self with its emotional programs for happiness is in place, we tend to appropriate any progress in the journey to ourselves.

The experience of God's love and the experience of our weaknesses are correlative. These are the two poles that God works with as he gradually frees us from immature ways of relating to him. The experience of our desperate need for God's healing is the measure in which we experience his infinite mercy. The deeper the experience of God's mercy, the more compassion we will have for others.

Why did I, a young man who had given up so much to come to the monastery, experience such strong feelings of envy? Evidently one of the programs in my unconscious was still in place. Was I using the time of prayer as a security blanket? Or again, since prayer before the Blessed Sacrament was held in great honor in our monastery, was I in competition with my brother monk, somewhat like the young man who fasted everyone under the table?

The work of following Christ is like working with a psychotherapist who has a clear insight into what is wrong with us. With incredible accuracy, God puts his finger on exactly the spot that needs attention at this precise time in our spiritual growth. If we are hanging on to one last shred of possessiveness, he comes along and says, often through some person or event, "Won't you give this to me?"

In the book of Deuteronomy, Moses compares God's training of his people to an eagle training an eaglet to fly. In ancient times it was believed that eaglets learned to fly by being pushed out of the nest, which was usually perched on the edge of a cliff. This is a marvelous image of what we feel is happening to us. God seems to push us into something that we feel totally incapable of doing. We wonder if he still loves us. Or again, he pushes us out of whatever nest we are in. Like the eaglet desperately flapping its wings, we seem to be heading straight for the abyss. But like the mother eagle, God swoops down and catches us just before we hit the rocks. This happens again and again until the eaglet learns to fly.

After we have been treated in this fashion a number of times, we too may realize that it is not as dangerous as we first believed. We begin to be content with these hair-raising escapes. We learn to trust God beyond our psychological experiences. And we become more courageous in facing and letting go of the dark corners of ourselves and begin to participate actively in the dismantling of our prerational emotional programs.

We cannot escape from the worldliness that is inside us, but we can acknowledge and confront it. The invitation to allow God to change our motivation from selfishness to divine love is the call to transforming union.

3

THE AFFLICTIVE EMOTIONS

■

AS WE BEGIN the difficult work of confronting our own unconscious motivations, our emotions can be our best allies. The emotions faithfully respond to what our value system is—not what we would like it to be, or what we think it is. Our emotions are perfect recorders of what is happening inside; hence they are the key to finding out what our emotional programs for happiness really are.

In a certain area of Africa, the local planters have a way of catching monkeys that raid the banana plantations. The planters split a coconut in half, scoop out the insides, and replace them with a sweetmeat they know that monkeys love. The coconut is then sealed up, leaving just a slit like one in a mailbox to allow the monkey to slip its hand in sideways. The hunters then hide in the underbrush and wait for an unsuspecting monkey to come swinging through the trees. In due time one shows up, smells the sweetmeat, and cries out, "A treat for me!" It jumps down, picks up the coconut, slips its hand through the slit, and grasps the sweetmeat.

But when it tries to remove the sweetmeat, its fist will not fit through the slit. The hunters emerge from the bush and start coming closer. With ever-increasing intensity the monkey keeps pulling as hard as it can, but to no avail. The monkey is dimly aware that the hunters are approaching and that if it does not let go of the sweetmeat, it will be captured. But it can't quite free itself from its desire to possess its newfound treasure. So the hunters catch it, roast it, and eat it.

This is a parable of the human condition. There are times when we too are dimly aware that if we think about an insult or harbor a particular desire for one more second, we will be caught by one of our afflictive emotions. We do not want to be caught, but at the same time we want to relish for a few more seconds the particular desire or the thought of revenge. Then the hunters—the afflictive emotions—catch us, roast us, and eat us! All the monkey had to do was open its hand and let go; then it could have jumped into a tree and been off to freedom. All we have to do is open our minds and hearts and let go.

146

We can learn to recognize our emotional programs for happiness by the afflictive emotions they set off. Basically, these emotions might be reduced to anger, grief, fear, pride, greed, envy, lust, and apathy. If we have an emotional investment in the instinctual needs for survival/security, affection/esteem, or power/control, the events that frustrate these desires will inevitably set off one or another of the afflictive emotions.

The imagination and the emotions work like the intermeshing wheels of an old watch; if one wheel moves, the other has to move. Along with every emotional frustration, a commentary also arises drawn from our personal history or temperament. Through this interaction the feelings grow more intense and the commentaries more violent. Even though we know that the process is making us miserable, we cannot stop, like the monkey with his hand in the sweetmeat. The body reacts by pouring chemicals into the bloodstream to prepare for action. Each wheel feeds into the other at an accelerating rate until we are on an emotional binge that may go for hours, days, weeks, or even years.

For example, here is a man who has undertaken the spiritual journey and is determined to practice the moral virtues of justice, prudence, fortitude, and temperance. In other words, he has *consciously* chosen the values of the gospel. There happens to be a secretary at his place of work whom he cannot stand; their chemistries do not agree. He makes all kinds of resolutions to love this person. Nothing helps. After a particularly fruitful retreat, he determines to forgive everything in the past and never to get angry again.

On the first day back at work, he arrives at the office with this new determination and finds that he secretary has left her dirty golf socks on his desk. A few hours later, she spills coffee all over an important letter he has just completed, and it has to be done over. At lunchtime, she disappears for a couple of hours leaving him to handle all her phone calls and interviews. In the middle of the afternoon, she rushes in saying that she met her boyfriend at lunch and has to go to the beach for the weekend, and so would he please take care of her work for the rest of the day. Without waiting for an answer or saying a word of thanks, she departs.

With each blow, the afflicted man resists his rising feelings of indignation. The brain and nervous system, as we pointed out before, are like a vast biocomputer. Many computers today, given a command to erase a program, will say, "Do you really want to erase this program?" In virtue of his good resolutions, this man's biocomputer prints a similar question: "Are you sure you really want your program of indignation?" In response to each untoward event throughout the day, he replies, "No, I don't want the program."

It is now four o'clock in the afternoon. His reservoir of interior peace, established by the retreat and renewed during his early morning period of contemplative prayer, is bone dry. Once again the computerized question flashes on his inner screen of consciousness: "Are you sure you really want your program of indignation?"

This time his answer is almost a shout: "Yes, give me the whole program!" The red lights start flashing. The computer starts to grind out the printout. Out pour all the disagreeable things he has ever suffered at the hands of this woman. Next come all the disagreeable people he has ever met, all the events that have ever upset him, all his anger and feelings of revenge toward anyone, all programmed with cross references and elaborate commentaries previously recorded in his memory bank. Moreover, the commentaries, based on his temperamental biases and personal history, are calibrated to respond to his ascending levels of emotional intensity. As his indignation crescendos into anger, the thought arises, "Why doesn't somebody fire this woman?" This commentary turns his anger into rage. The next commentary is, "Why doesn't God strike this woman with lightning?" This commentary turns his rage into fury. A state of temporary insanity takes over and he screams, "No, no! Let me strangle her with my bare hands!"

The printout may go on for hours. Eventually he gathers up all the papers and goes home in utter turmoil. His wife and children take one look at his face and head for the doors and windows. The evening is ruined. He cannot eat. He cannot sleep. He tries to look at TV, pours himself a drink, calls a friend on the telephone. Everything is a disaster. Finally he collapses on his bed and falls into a fitful sleep. He rises in the morning with a terrible headache and a feeling of utter defeat. In despair he sighs, "Oh God, what went wrong?" Indeed, what became of his conscious resolutions to be patient, kind, and forgiving?

It does not occur to him that he may be experiencing emotional turmoil because there is something seriously wrong with his unconscious value system. The facts of the situation and what might be an appropriate response are overwhelmed by the intensity of emotion generated by the emotional programs for happiness in his unconscious. He projects the cause of his pain on the other person, saying, "If only I could get rid of her, how happy I would be!" And after each emotional storm he wonders, "Why do people treat me this way? What have I done to deserve this?" Each time he gives in to his emotional programs and their expression, he is reborn into the endless cycle of desire, gratification, frustration, and the ensuing need to compensate.

This man has to modify his outrageous reactions and the value systems they reflect, if he is to begin to deal with the real problems that his coworker presents. Not every method is adequate or sufficiently comprehensive to deal with the subtleties of the false self. We need to choose one that is suitable for our state of life. We may also require some psychotherapy. Regular periods of contemplative prayer are the keystone of the whole program; they need to be reinforced by positive efforts in daily life to change our inveterate habits of acting under the influence of the emotional programs for happiness.

But having acknowledged the essential character of efforts to change, we must emphasize what Paul pointed out in the passage from Romans: The conscious resolution to change our values and behavior is not enough to alter the unconscious value systems of the false self and the behavior they engender. Only the passive purifications of contemplative prayer can affect this profound healing. Only then will the reservoir of interior silence, built up in periods of contemplative prayer, never run dry.

This man's experience, of course, is a paradigm of everyone's experience on the spiritual journey, given a little time for the process to develop. Whenever an emotional program is frustrated, we immediately experience a spontaneous feeling reaction. If something happens that undermines our need for a particular security symbol, the feeling of grief or anger instantly arises. When, for example, we arrive at work and the manager tells us that the other employees have been complaining about us and to look for another job, our instant reaction may be the feeling of hurt. Then the commentary promptly arises, "Who did this to me?" or "What will this look like on my résumé?" After one or two self-protective thoughts like this, the churning sensation accelerates.

Let us try to identify the principal emotions or combinations of emotions that announce the presence of false-self values in the unconscious. Anger responds to goods that are difficult to obtain or evils that are hard to avoid. When something perceived in this way overtakes us, we experience anger.

Apathy is pervasive boredom or bitterness resulting from recurrent frustration. It is the withdrawal from life, friendship, and community. Someone who suffers this disease might complain, "I've served this community for twenty years. You've never asked my opinion. Or if you did, you never followed it. I'm going to my room and closing the door. Don't anyone dare to knock on that door. You go your way, I'm going mine." The bottom line is, "To hell with you!" Nobody can talk to such persons because they are hurt and self-righteous, and they love it. The latter feeling nourishes their sense of self-satisfaction because they hope that their withdrawal will hurt everyone else. It does. Thus they have their revenge. Apathy is the opting out of the flow of life in order to hug one's wounds, real or imaginary.

Lust in the context of the frustration of the emotional programs refers not just to sexual misbehavior. It is the overweening desire for satisfaction, whether physical, mental, or spiritual, in order to compensate for the intolerable affronts that people have inflicted on us by not honoring our unreasonable demands. As we saw, the emotional programs gradually grow into centers of motivation around which our thoughts, feelings, and behavior circulate like planets around the sun.

Pride as an emotional reaction may be experienced in two ways. Some people experience it as self-rejection instead of self-inflation. They have to punish themselves for not measuring up to their idealized images of themselves. Instead of being angry at other people for hurting their feelings, they turn the anger against themselves and say, "I'm no good." They may even adopt self-destructive measures if the emotion becomes strong enough. They cannot bear to see themselves failing because then pride brings down the verdict of guilty. Pride, not God, suggests that they never measure up to the demands that their idealized images impose upon them.

Any upsetting emotion is warning us that an emotional program may just have been frustrated. The cause may not be somebody else's misconduct or an unpleasant event. For us to be habitually happy, nobody has to change except ourselves. If we are upset by anything, we have a problem, and we will continue to experience emotional turmoil until we change the root of the problem, which is the emotional program for happiness in the unconscious. The effort to change it is called the practice of virtue.

If we keep our desires and aversions dried out by not watering them with commentaries or acting them out, they wither like weeds in the desert.

A certain businessman used to commute to work every day on the New York subway. He regularly stopped at a newsstand along the way to buy the *New York Times* to read on the train. One day a business associate accompanied him. When they came to the newsstand, the businessman said to the attendant, "Will you kindly give me a copy of the *New York Times?*" The attendant grabbed a copy and threw it at him.

The businessman said, "Thank you. Please accept your money." The attendant grabbed the money and thrust it into the cash register with a loud grunt. The businessman said, "I wish you a very good day." The attendant glared at him and responded, "I hope you have the worst day of your life!" With that he spat right in his direction. Undisturbed, our friend walked off toward the subway. His companion, who had been getting more and more exasperated finally burst out, "How can you put up with such treatment? I wouldn't stand for it for one moment. I would walk to the other side of town to catch the train rather than be treated in such an outrageous manner!" His friend replied, "Look, I have to take the subway to work every day. That newsstand is right on my way. Why should I inconvenience myself because of the way this person treats me?"

There is no commandment that says we have to be upset by the way other people treat us. The reason we are upset is because we have an emotional program that says, "If someone is nasty to me, I cannot be happy or feel good about myself." It is true that there is psychological and sometimes physical pain involved in not being treated as a human being. In such situations, we have every right to be indignant and to take steps to remedy them. But apart from such circumstances, instead of reacting compulsively and retaliating, we could enjoy our freedom as human beings and refuse to be upset.

Once on the spiritual journey, we begin to perceive that our emotional programs for happiness prevent us from reacting to other people and their needs. When locked into our private worlds of narcissistic desires, we are not present to the needs of others when they seek help. The clarity with which we see other people's needs and respond to them is in direct proportion to our interior freedom.

4

THE HUMAN CONDITION

■

PERSONAL SIN is the ripe fruit of the emotional programs for happiness; it is not the chief problem, but the chief symptom of the problem. And the problem itself is clearly universal. It affects the entire human condition. In fact, it *is* the human condition.

The human condition is my term for the doctrine Christian tradition has referred to, since Saint Augustine of Hippo first proposed it, as original sin and its consequences. No theologian ever considered original sin the personal fault of any one of us. It was strictly reserved as the sin of our first parents. The doctrine of the Fall was an effort on the part of theologians to explain how the pervasive disease of human nature came about. Taoism, Hinduism, Buddhism, and other religions also bear witness to the experience of a universal illness that has afflicted the human family from the beginning.

Psychology is evidently coming to a similar conclusion regarding the pervasiveness of this disease. In fact, one of the great benefits of contemporary psychology is the precision that it provides regarding the nature and causes of the human condition as we experience it. The discovery of the unconscious by Freud a little over a hundred years ago has immense significance for the spiritual life. More recently, the literature about the dysfunctional family and co-dependency provides us with a diagnosis of the human condition far more detailed than that provided by the doctrine of the consequences of original sin and the capital sins that we learned about in catechism class. The science and practice of psychology greatly reinforce all that we previously understood about the dynamics of human motivation and hence are essential for moral judgments. Thus psychology has become the new "handmaid of theology." At the same time it gives new validation to the earlier insights gained through theological reflection on revelation and through contemplative prayer.

We have seen already in the first chapter how one such model—the developmental, pioneered by child psychologist Jean Piaget—helps explain the roots of our unconscious emotional programs for happiness. Each of us needs to be reassured and affirmed in his or her own personhood and self-identity. If this assurance is withheld because of lack of concern or commitment on the part of parents, these painful privations will require defensive or compensatory measures. As a consequence, our emotional life ceases to grow in relation to the unfolding values of human development and becomes fixated at the level of the perceived deprivation. The emotional fixation fossilizes into a program for happiness. When fully formed it develops into a center of gravity, which attracts to itself more and more of our psychological resources: thoughts, feelings, images, reactions, and behavior. Later experiences and events in life are all sucked into its gravitational field and interpreted as helpful or harmful in terms of our basic drive for happiness. These centers, as we shall see, are reinforced by the culture in which we live and the particular group with which we identify, or rather, overidentify.

The developmental model is actually a subset of an even more comprehensive model, the evolutionary. The infant experiences the same developmental pattern and value systems that the human family as a whole experienced. In other words, each human being is a microcosm of where the human race has been—and where it might be headed. For the evolutionary model I will follow the insightful arrangement of Ken Wilber, which he calls the Great Chain of Being.[1]

Some five million years ago, the first flicker of differentiation between animal and human life took place with the development in humans of what is now termed "reptilian consciousness." The mythological symbol of this consciousness is the serpent eating its tail, signifying the recurrence of natural processes: day and night, summer and winter, birth and death, desire and satisfaction. The most primitive humans were totally immersed in nature. They had no consciousness of a separate self. Their lives were centered on day-to-day survival activities such as the search for food and shelter and on the prompt fulfillment of instinctual needs.

The infant in the first year of life experiences reptilian consciousness and is totally immersed in matter and pleasurable sensations. The first year is an experience of unity with the mother and continuity with the life once enjoyed in the womb. If bonding with the mother takes place right away, the baby is on the road to accepting emotionally the human adventure.

About two hundred thousand years ago, reptilian consciousness moved into "typhonic consciousness." This awareness was embedded in animal life and primitive instincts, but it enabled these new humans to distinguish their bodies from other objects in the environment. This type of consciousness is usually expressed in mythology by the symbol of the Typhon, the part-human, part-animal creature, aware of a body-self but dominated by its instincts for survival, nourishment, and reproduction. Typhonic culture revolved around hunting and worship of the Great Earth Mother as nurturer and protectress.

The characteristics of typhonic consciousness are manifested by the infant between the ages of two and four. The infant experiences his body-self as separate from the objects in the environment and from his siblings. Supported by the newly developing capacity of the brain to process sensory information at a rapid rate, the child wants to explore her world and try things out. The child's consciousness participates in the part-human, part-animal world of typhonic consciousness. Her dreams are mostly about animals or animal images that personify people. The dreamlike quality of typhonic consciousness is manifested in a child's games and imagery. A block can represent a car and a closet becomes a spaceship in which to travel to the stars or to the center of the earth. A young child cannot clearly distinguish imagination from reality or the part from the whole; anything she can imagine exists or can happen. Children also suffer from the terrors that were typical of our typhonic ancestors: the dark, the unknown, the powers of nature, and the monsters created by the imagination.

The move from typhonic to "mythic membership" consciousness, accelerated by the invention of language, occurred around 12,000 B.C.E. The invention of farming facilitated this movement by providing leisure for art, reflection, ritual, and politics. The stratification of society in the form of city-states led to the acquisition of land and possessions and the struggle to defend or extend them by wars of ever-increasing proportions. At the mythic membership level, identification with the community provided the sense of belonging, protection from enemies, and the prolongation of one's life through offspring. The social self, identified with a particular city-state or family grouping, developed hierarchies for ritual sacrifice, the authority of kings and nobles, and slavery to serve the cultural expansion of the victors in war. As people became more self-conscious and hence capable of anticipating death, they sought to hide their growing fear of it. They projected into the future a life that they could not, in fact, be sure of. Ways of forgetting the proximity of death, according to some anthropologists, are one of the main thrusts in the formation of cultures.[2]

Between the fourth and eighth year, the child enters the period of socialization and accesses the mythic membership level of consciousness where possessions, competition, success, belonging to a group, and interiorizing the values of a structured society are the order of the day. The child at this age absorbs unquestioningly the values of parents, teachers, peers, and the predominant society in which he is being raised.

About 3000 B.C.E. the most dramatic leap in human consciousness took place: the emergence of reason. This level of consciousness is termed by anthropologists "mental egoic" and is symbolized in Greek mythology by Zeus slaying the dragon. Zeus represents reason; the dragon stands for the domination of the emotions and primitive levels of consciousness.

Theoretically, to continue with this paradigm, the mental egoic is the era we live in now, and the level of consciousness that we attain in the normal course of our human development after about eight years of age. It would be comforting if this were so. Then the human condition might be not a pervasive illness but a right evolution toward ever-greater participation in the possibilities of life. Unfortunately, this is not the case. For along with the emergence of full reflective self-consciousness and the sense of personal identity, there also arose a growing sense of separation from God. If humankind had enjoyed the awareness of divine union as the levels of consciousness unfolded, the emergence of full reflective self-consciousness would not have been experienced as threatening. But instead, the developing levels of consciousness brought a growing sense of alienation from God, oneself, others, and the cosmos.

Mental egoic consciousness is the movement beyond the self-centered instinctual drives and gratifications of the prerational instincts into full personhood. It is to take responsibility for ourselves as well as to respond to the needs of our families, our nations, and the human race, including the generations yet to come. But this level of consciousness is still not accessed by the vast majority of humankind. For, as we have seen, the human condition is still under the sway of the false self with its emotional programs for happiness based on the primitive stages of consciousness: security from the reptilian, affection/esteem and power/control from the typhonic. As a result, even as adults our consciousness is still in many respects infantile. And culture as a whole has not advanced beyond the mythic membership level, as we shall see in chapter ten, whose values the gospel specifically challenges.

In the reptilian and the typhonic periods of the evolutionary journey of the human family, the Great Earth Mother personified the paradisiacal innocence that remains as an archetype in every human being. Since each stage of human evolution is recapitulated in each one of us, we dimly recall how pleasant it was to be immersed in nature and to enjoy the animal functions of eating and reproducing without accountability. There is an unconscious tendency in every human being to regress to the bliss of the womb; we naturally prefer to regress to a place that was familiar rather than to go forward into the unknown.

Every movement of human growth precipitates a crisis appropriate to the level of physical, emotional, or spiritual development at which we find ourselves. Each major crisis of growth requires letting go of the physical or spiritual food that has been nourishing us up to then and moving into more mature relationships. In such a crisis we tend to seek the feeling of security. It is characteristic of reptilian and typhonic consciousness to react to frustration by choosing the line of least resistance, or whatever seems to be the easiest security blanket in which to wrap themselves. The capacity to go forward into personal responsibility is constantly challenged by the temptation to revert to lower levels of consciousness and behavior. Human growth is not the denial or rejection of any level, but the integration of the lower into more evolved levels of consciousness.

Human development depends on freeing ourselves from emotional fixations on these instinctual levels in order to grow to full reflective self-consciousness. The gospel calls for the full development of the human person and invites us to the further growth that God has in store for us: the intuitive and unitive levels of consciousness to which mature faith and love gradually raise us. Meanwhile, passing through the mythic membership stage to the mental egoic stage, we feel the undertow of primitive instincts. They remain part of us until they are thoroughly integrated by the purification of sense and spirit from the influences of the emotional programs for happiness.

At the same time, we have a vague remembrance that somewhere, back in the reptilian period, everything was unified. Indeed, during that period, there was no consciousness of a separate self, no sense of accountability. There was a mysterious wholeness. This is the experience of innocence symbolized by the Garden of Eden. As adults we yearn for the kind of un–selfconscious unity that was actually present in the first year or two of life, but was lost during the development of the separate-self sense. It is to be recovered in an immensely superior form in the transforming union.

5

MYTHIC MEMBERSHIP CONSCIOUSNESS

■

OVERIDENTIFICATION WITH THE GROUP is the dominant characteristic of mythic membership consciousness. When we derive our identity from the social unit of which we are a member, we give the group unquestioning loyalty. The sense of belonging to something important gives us feelings of security, pleasure, and power. A child may boast to his companions, "My daddy is better than your daddy." Believing that his daddy can beat up anybody on the block supports the child's need to feel secure in relating to the broader community.

The uncanny ability of an established group to resist constructive change is supported by the overidentification of its members. The first group we come in contact with is the family. There is nothing wrong with experiencing loyalty to our roots, but the influence of the emotional programs exaggerate what is reasonable in our loyalty. Peer-group pressure demands conformity whether or not our consciences fully approve of what is being done. As we identify with the group's value system, we conform more easily and resist those who challenge the group on any point. Thus conformity patterns become entrenched.

When authority functions on the mythic membership level, it easily moves from the exercise of authority to authoritarianism. Jesus' idea of authority belongs to the mental egoic level. Authority is designed to serve those whom it leads. It is exercised to elicit and encourage the creativity of the members of the Christian community. Authority in the Christian religion is designed to lead us out of the swamp of self-centered motivation into the freedom and accountability of full personhood. We can then take our place in the mystical body of Christ as a living cell responsible for the well-being of the whole body.

Jesus directs strong words to people at the mythical membership level: "If anyone comes to me without turning his back on his father and mother, his wife and his children, his brothers and sisters, indeed his very self, he cannot be my follower" (Luke 14:26). It is important to grasp the force of this saying. We can be sure he does not mean that we should cease to love or care for our parents. In Jesus' time it was the custom to make contributions to the Temple in place of supporting one's parents in their old age, a practice Jesus vigorously condemned. The text urges us to refuse to be locked into a conformity that prevents us from following the values of the gospel. As we grow, our relationships to ourselves, God, and other people change. We start life dependent on our parents, but in adulthood our relationship changes to one of equality. The old relationship of dependency dies and we form a new relationship. We continue to love them, but if they want us to do something against our values, we must be able to say, "I love you, but I can't go along with you in this matter."

The same thing goes for membership in a broader group. We may have to say, "I can't remain a member." If family, nation, or group—anyone—stands in the way of our true growth, which is in the interest of the whole human family, we have to be able to say "no" and stick to it. We may lose a few friends by modifying our way of life, because they may find the change in us threatening. The spiritual journey can be a lonely road in the beginning. Later God will give us new friends. God does not take anything away except to give us something better.

A significant influence in the life of the developing human being is the superego, which is an emotional judgment of what is right or wrong behavior. Parents and teachers give the child "do's" and "don'ts" which may be accompanied by punishments or threats. The precepts in themselves may have no real moral significance. The superego, however, treats them as "shoulds," and they become a source of guilt feelings. Later in life, when a true conscience that belongs to the age of reason is formed, we have to struggle with these parental injunctions, especially if they were laced with sanctions. Thus a significant part of genuine moral development consists in freeing ourselves from the tyranny of the superego. This is not to reject all the values we have received up to that point, but rather to reevaluate them, putting moral injunctions into the broader perspective of our relationship with God.

Some adolescents rebel against the moral straitjackets in which they were raised. The only path to freedom apparent to them may be to throw the whole thing over. If religious values have been intertwined with a tyrannical superego, there will be a reaction against a religion that was presented in an overmoralistic way. It may look as though these adolescents have given up their religion, but they may be simply struggling against heavy odds to make their own judgments about religious values. It may take a long time, however, for their rebellion to subside.

Ideas about morality may or may not be the result of a right conscience. In Northern Ireland, Catholic children are inculcated from birth to hate Protestants and vice versa. They grow up with the same hatred that their mothers, fathers, grandparents, and great-grandparents cherished. Imagine the guilt feelings that would arise if a Catholic fell in love with a Protestant. Such a couple would feel they were betraying their respective religions and families. This is the superego at work making an emotional judgment regarding right and wrong. A true conscience functions on the basis of reason and faith.

Much of the spiritual journey consists in getting rid of the effects of the superego. Nothing could be more frightening to a child than to hear that one mortal sin could catapult him into hell forever. The child unquestioningly receives religious instruction from parents and teachers. He does not evaluate the information about God or the way the information is given—or if he does, he tries to find ways of coping with disturbing information.

A five-year-old in a certain household began acting strangely. Whenever he was asked a question, he would say, "I don't know."

"Did you brush your teeth?"

"I don't know."

"Did you have breakfast?"

"I don't know."

"Did you kiss Mommy goodnight?"

"I can't remember."

The household thought it was a great joke, but after a while his conduct began to get on their nerves. His alert grandma finally intervened. "There's something wrong with this child," she said. "Take him to a psychiatrist."

The doctor discovered that the boy's nurse had said to him, "A lie is a mortal sin. If you tell one, you will go to hell." The youngster felt that he could not always be certain whether what he said was true or not, so he decided not to take any chances—and was well on the way to becoming thoroughly neurotic. This nurse thought she was faithfully reflecting the moral teaching of her religion, but if her admonitions had not been stopped, she would have caused permanent emotional damage to that child and retarded his spiritual growth, perhaps for good, by casting deep shadows on his relationship with God.

Let me give another example of how the superego works. When I entered the austere life of the monastery, fasting was held in honor. When I completed my formation and was given the job of novice master, I wanted to set a good example of fidelity for the novices. The symbol of fidelity in a monastery in those days was perfect conformity to the rule. This meant being on time for all the offices, per-forming manual labor, and observing the fasts. Because I was somewhat fragile in health, I rarely was able to get through the whole of Lent without having to be dispensed from the fasting. In the milieu of the monastery, if one could not fast, one felt like a second-class citizen. One Lent I approached the abbot to ask permis-sion to start the fast even though I had always been forced to drop out after a couple of weeks. To my surprise he said, "Do you want to know the penance that God wants you to do this Lent?" I said, "Sure." His response was, "Gain twenty pounds."

In order to reinforce this injunction, he added, "Between meals, each morning and afternoon, I want you to drink a glass of cream and eat two Hershey bars."

My first thought was, "Has the abbot gone mad? Does he think this is a country club?" Notice the commentary rising out of my hurt feelings and monastic super-ego. With a heavy heart, I withdrew from his office and reluctantly started this unusual Lenten observance.

My next thought was, "How am I going to prevent the novices from knowing about this?" I did not want them to lose confidence in my austere leadership. But there was no escape. I had to throw all self-respect to the winds. They fasted and I did not. I faithfully drank cream and ate two Hershey bars between meals every day during Lent and actually gained ten pounds.

The great gift that the abbot gave me was not the ten pounds, but his insightful perception that I was attached to the observance of fasting in a way that was not wholesome. The peculiar penance that he imposed freed me from my overidentification with what I had interiorized as the proper way to be a monk and especially a monastic superior. We all have notions of the proper way to be a husband, wife, father, mother, employee, or employer, and a proper way to be a member of our parish or religious community. These preconceived ideas lock us into one way of doing things. This is what I mean by overidentification with the values of our group. Our preconceived ideas and prepackaged value systems are obstacles to grace. Contemplative prayer increases our inner freedom, enabling us to reevaluate them in the light of the gospel.

I appeal to your own experience. Recall the undertow of guilt feelings when you tried to break out of your parental value system or early religious instruction. True guilt is the realization that you have acted against your conscience; that is to say, that you have done something against what you believe is right. The sense of guilt warns you, "Hey, you have gone against your principles." As soon as you regret your fault and say, "My God, forgive me," you should forget it. Guilt feelings that last longer than half a minute are neurotic. Pervasive, prolonged, and paralyzing guilt is the result of the superego at work. It is an emotional judgment about right and wrong, not a true judgment of conscience. Neurotic pride says, "Look what you've done! You're just no good!" It accuses us not only of having done wrong in a particular instance, but of being totally worthless. When we do not measure up to our self-images, pride brings down the verdict of guilty, and we mistakenly project that judgment onto God. Meanwhile, God is saying, "There's nothing seriously wrong with you. Everybody makes mistakes. Forget it." Or, "I forgive you. Why don't you forgive yourself?"

Loyalty to family, country, and religion, and gratitude for all the good we have received from them is a virtue, but loyalty is not an absolute value. It should be enlightened by mental egoic consciousness. This more mature level of consciousness presupposes personal responsibility for the community in which we live insofar as we can influence it for good.

The structures of government that belong to the mythic membership level of consciousness are mostly monarchical, dictatorial, and authoritarian in form. The mental egoic level of consciousness, since it involves personal responsibility for the group, is inclined toward participatory forms of government in which a broad constituency of qualified people are consulted. The final decision is thus enlightened by all the facts. In our time, the facts are more and more complex. Experts need to be consulted in important matters before a final judgment is taken if any decision is going to be an adequate one today.

One of the chief factors that tend to destroy relationships among people and nations is the emotion of fear. It also destroys the relationship between us and God. To be afraid of God, or to be afraid of other people, makes us defensive. In the case of God, we will try to stay as far away from him as our situations and the demands of respectability permit. In the case of other people, we try to control them and hold them within limits that enable us to feel secure.

The biblical term "fear of God" does not refer to the emotion of fear. Fear of God is a technical term in the Bible meaning the right relationship with God. The right relationship with God is to trust him. The right relationship with God involves reverence and awe for God's transcendence and immanence as well as trust in his goodness and compassion. To envisage what the biblical fear of God actually means, imagine a child at Christmas time in a huge department store. The top floor, the size of a whole city block, is filled with toys. When the child emerges from the elevator into this wonderland of desirable objects, her eyes grow bigger and bigger. She looks to the left and to the right, seeing everything her heart has ever desired: skis, T-bears, doll houses, toys, sleds, electric trains, computers. She wants to go in every direction at once. She is so enthralled that she does not know where to start. She wants to grasp everything and take it home. The biblical fear of God is similar. We feel ourselves invited into a mystery that contains everything our hearts could possibly desire. We experience the fascination of the Ultimate Mystery rather than fear of the unknown. We want to grasp or be grasped by the mystery of God's presence that opens endlessly in every direction.

Here is an incident that might emphasize this point. It is a story told on himself by Cardinal Basil Hume, the Primate of England. As a youngster, he was brought up in a strict English household. Wanting to discipline the children, his mother called them together one day and, pointed to a jar in the pantry, said, "You see that cookie jar? I don't want you children putting a hand in that jar between meals. It is only for dessert on feast days." And as a sanction she added: "Because God is always watching you." Naturally, the children were shaking in their shoes. Young Basil's idea of God, which had been very trusting up to that point, shifted to that of a policeman always watching for his every fault. This unhealthy fear of God seems to have retarded his spiritual growth for the next twenty or thirty years.

Parents and teachers, despite good intentions, sometimes project onto God sanctions of their own creation. God only gave us ten commandments. Let us not add any more. If people want to impose more commandments, they should blame themselves, not God.

Young Basil eventually entered the Benedictine order. There were more rules there than his mother had laid down at home. I suppose he kept them for the same reason: fear of this God ever on the watch to catch him in some fault. If I had been the vocation director when this young man presented himself at the monastery, I would have been tempted to ask him, "What is your motive for coming here? You are giving up family, friends, career, and all the other things your brilliant mind could do. Are you sure that your primary motive may not be to placate the God that you heard about in childhood and whom you identified as a policeman, a tyrant, and pitiless judge? . . ."

"One day," the cardinal said in concluding the story, "I received a very special grace that completely changed my attitude toward God. I realized that if as a child I had put my hand in the cookie jar, and if it had been between meals, and if God had really been watching me, he would have said, 'Son, why don't you take another one?' "

This, I submit, is the God of the Christians. I do not know this other god, and don't want to know him. Such a god is a caricature of the true God. Such a god is certainly not the God of Jesus Christ, whom he called "Abba," the God of infinite concern for everyone, ever present to us and enfolding us in his infinite love. That is what a child needs to hear.

6

MENTAL EGOIC CONSCIOUSNESS

■

WE SAW IN THE FIRST FIVE CHAPTERS how the gospel calls us to grow to full personhood, to grow out of our childish programs for happiness, necessary for survival during the fragile period of childhood but now an obstacle to becoming fully human. We saw as well how the gospel invites us to disidentify with the values of our cultural conditioning, whether ethnic, nationalistic, or even religious, insofar as these values hinder our personal response to Christ.

Given the prepackaged values firmly entrenched from early childhood, the arising of mental egoic consciousness at about the age of reason finds us unfree to reevaluate our enormous emotional and social investment to prerational attitudes. Thus we use our newfound intellectual powers to rationalize, justify, and even glorify our emotional programs and the false values of the culture.

Instead of developing the capacity to relate to other persons and to all reality with honesty and compassion, we use the immensely creative energy of rational consciousness to develop more sophisticated ways of controlling people, extracting greater pleasures out of life, and heaping up more security symbols. Thus we reinforce the self-centered motivation appropriate to childhood but totally inappropriate for adults.

Our pathology is simply this: we have come to full reflective self-consciousness without the enjoyment of divine union—indeed, without any awareness of it at all. Because that crucial conviction, born of experience, is missing, our fragile egos seek every possible means to ward off the painful and at times agonizing sense of alienation from God and from everyone else. As we saw, the poignant character of this sense of alienation from God is described by Augustine as the consequences of original sin.

In the story of the Garden of Eden there is a charming reference to God conversing with Adam and Eve in the cool of the evening, a lively image of intimacy with the divine and harmony with the powers of nature. This, the true garden of paradise, is not primarily a place but a state of consciousness. As long as intimacy with

God was enjoyed by our first parents, everything in creation was friendly. As soon as that intimacy was lost, briars grew up instead of crops and all the ills of fallen human nature came upon them.

These images reflect what we experience in our own psychological awarenesses. We come to full reflective self-consciousness without the easy intimacy with God that Adam and Eve enjoyed in the garden. We lack a sense of oneness with God, other people, and the cosmos. We feel incomplete and afraid and hence seek symbols of security, affection, and power to shore up our fragile self-identities.

When the gospel of John proclaims, "The word became flesh," the author is indicating that God took upon himself not human nature in its ideal state before the Fall, but human nature in its actual condition of privation, sin, and death.

Jesus on the cross is a striking symbol of the human condition when it reaches the mental egoic state of consciousness: we cannot regress to primal innocence and the irresponsibility of animal life, and we cannot rise under our own power to higher states of consciousness. We feel rejected, as it were, by both heaven and earth—like Jesus, crucified between heaven and earth. Jesus urges his disciples not to regress to earlier stages of consciousness, but to go forward into full personhood, to assume full responsibility for ourselves and our relationships, and to open to the Ultimate Reality whom he called Abba, Father.

Similarly, Jesus invites us to change the direction in which we are looking for happiness and to join the new humanity that is opening to interior freedom and self-transcendence. The primary issue for the human family at its present level of evolutionary development is to become fully human. But that, as we have seen, means rediscovering our connectedness to God, which was repressed somewhere in early childhood.

The arrival at the mental egoic stage of consciousness is characterized by basic attitudinal changes. One graduates from mere self-concern and is motivated by the larger concerns of family, country, and the world. In mythic membership consciousness our concern for others is principally motivated by personal security, esteem, and power considerations. Our personal identity is associated with our group affiliation and its response to us. The mental egoic level begins to manifest itself when the powers of the brain have developed biologically to the point of sustaining abstract thinking, somewhere around twelve to fourteen years of age. This new level of relating is established only with difficulty, because the lower levels with their value systems and selfish motivations are firmly in place and resist change in the sense of growth.

Jesus expressed this level and called everyone to it when he reaffirmed the first commandment of the Mosaic Law and stated that the second was like to it: "You shall love your neighbor as yourself." In philosophical language this first commandment means that we must respect the rights and needs of others. This was the starting point of the teaching of Jesus. His own second commandment, "Love one another as I have loved you," goes much further and presupposes a movement to higher levels of motivation.

In this connection, two Greek New Testament words have special significance in Christian revelation.[1] *Sarx* is the body and the psyche locked into survival at its present level of human development. *Soma* is the body open to transcendence. *Sarx* is the "old Adam," Saint Paul's term for the false self, the ego bent on self-preservation at any cost, including other people's rights and needs. *Soma* is the new Adam with the transcendent element that Christ has brought into the human family by taking the entire human race to himself, thus giving it a decisive thrust toward wholeness and divine union. *Soma* is the emergence of full mental egoic consciousness and opens the way to further human development.

The mental egoic level is the level of the full emergence of moral responsibility for our behavior and relationships. It is the level of true conscience, the capacity to distinguish rightly and not just notionally, between right and wrong. Hence personal sin becomes much more serious. Basically, personal sin is the ratification of the emotional programs for happiness and the values of our cultural conditioning insofar as they disregard the rights and needs of others and our own true good.

The dispositions proper to the mental egoic level reflect the growing sense of equality with other humans, accountability for the care and preservation of the earth and its living and inorganic resources, and a more mature relationship to God. Respect for others diminishes the drive to dominate and control. Cooperation replaces unbridled competition. Harmony replaces rigid value systems. Negotiating replaces exclusive self-interest or national interests. Living in peace with others becomes a more important value, though not at any price. Accessing full mental egoic consciousness is the door leading to the great adventure of recovering and developing union with God.

In this adventure, further human growth begins with the intuitive level of consciousness. The good dispositions planted in the mental egoic stage begin to bloom. The sense of belonging to the universe and being one with others takes root. Compassion moves beyond respect for the rights and needs of others. The activity of the intuitive brain increases; there are more frequent insights, spiritual consolations, and psychic gifts. But the false self can still co-opt these gifts and turn them into ego trips and motives for spiritual pride; hence the need for the purification of the unconscious and the growth of self-knowledge in order to discern the subtle workings of our emotional programs from the movements of the Spirit. Later chapters will continue the discussion of the characteristics of intuitive consciousness and will also discuss the unitive stages of consciousness in the Christian contemplative tradition.

7

THE FOUR CONSENTS

■

OUR INSTINCTUAL NEEDS gradually grew into emotional programs for happiness because in growing up we had no experience of the divine presence within, which is the true security, the deepest affirmation of our basic goodness, and the true freedom. Since we did not even know that God was actually present within us, we had to look elsewhere for the security, affirmation, and freedom that only the divine presence can provide. The spiritual journey is a training in consent to God's presence and to all reality. Basically this is what true humility is. The divine action invites us to make the consents that we were unable to make in childhood and growing up because of the circumstances that surrounded our early lives.

This brings us to a paradigm for the spiritual journey that sheds a great deal of light on the positive aspects of grace, which not only heals the emotional damage of a lifetime, but also empowers us to enter on the path of unconditional love, even from the beginning of our conversion. Jesus emphasized this approach to divine union when he said, "Love one another as I have loved you."

The theologian John S. Dunne has suggested that the stages of the spiritual journey correspond to the passage of human life from birth to death.[1] At each major stage of that development, God asks us to make an appropriate consent. Let us follow closely Dunne's insightful presentation.

In childhood, God asks us to consent to the basic goodness of our nature with all its parts. As children we experience our own faculties, develop imagination, memory, and language, and learn to relate to family and peers. In these years we are asked to accept the basic goodness of our being as a gift from God and to be grateful for it. The acceptance of our basic goodness does not refer to what we can do or do better than others, but to the goodness of our being before we do anything.

Unfortunately, if our childhood environment is filled with fear, rejection, or ambivalent signals of parental affection and caring, or if we are burdened with some physical handicap, our emotions may hesitate to give full consent to the goodness of life. The biological need to survive usually gets us through this hesitation. We develop ways to bolster our fragile self-images and to go on living, but we bring our ambivalence toward life into the next stage.

In early adolescence, God asks us to accept the full development of our being by activating our talents and creative energies. Puberty actualizes the physical side of a much broader energy: our capacity to relate to other people, to emerge out of the isolated world of a child, and to begin to assume responsibility for ourselves and for our relationships. Because of the vicissitudes of the human condition, sexual energy may be awakened before our emotions can handle it. Then our attitude toward sexual energy and its expression may be distorted. Relationships may be difficult, and we may even hesitate to give full consent to the goodness of our sexuality and creative potentialities.

When any emotion is felt to be dangerous, fear may repress that emotion into the unconscious, where it continues to express itself surreptitiously in physical illness or unhealthy forms of behavior. On the spiritual journey, we are invited to dismantle the false self. Part of that process is the dismantling of our repressive apparatus. As our trust in God grows, our defense mechanisms are no longer an essential means of survival. What has been repressed emerges from the secret hiding places of the unconscious. God allows this to happen because he is determined to give us another chance to integrate everything that is good into our ongoing development, including what we may have mistakenly perceived as not good.

The distortion of emotional development is seen in many persons on the Christian spiritual journey who suffer from the repression or rejection of their sexual feelings. Once such repression takes place, these people will have difficulty relating with genuine warmth to others. Sexual energy sustains the driving force of the motivation to serve other people with affection and warmth. People who have repressed their sexual feelings, or any other emotion for that matter, tend to repress their feelings across the board. This means that their capacity to relate to others in a supportive or affirming way is truncated. The fear that sexual energy may become uncontrollable tends to make them defensive; they avoid closeness with others because any form of expression of intimacy gives rise to an acute sense of danger. Later in life, the sexual energy may break through their defenses and present itself with twice as much force as in adolescence. The poignancy of a confrontation with overwhelming sexual feelings in midlife is obvious.

In early adulthood, God invites us to make a third consent: to accept the fact of our nonbeing and the diminutions of self that occur through illness, old age, and death. The passing of a friend or relative, or some accident, may invite us to reflect on our own death. Most cultures create means of pretending that death does not exist. When it happens, they cover it up as best they can with whatever cosmetics are available.

Acceptance of our nonbeing is directed not to the morbid side of death but rather to the consequences of dying: the letting go of everything we love in this world, whether persons, places, or things. If we have suffered some great loss in early life such as the death of a parent, we may have an excessive fear of dying. Then we hesitate to make this consent. Moreover, if we have not made the previous consents, this one is more difficult.

The fourth consent is the consent to be transformed. We might think that everybody would be eager to make this one, but even the holiest people are inclined to say, "Let's not rush into this." The transforming union requires consent to the death of the false self, and the false self is the only self we know. Whatever its inconveniences, it is at least familiar. Some of us are more afraid of the death of the false self than of physical death.

These four consents are invitations to welcome life and death as God's gracious gifts and to appreciate the vocation of being a member of the human family in this marvelous universe with all its beauty and potentialities. Our consents, however, are not directed to the good things of life for their own sake or as ends in themselves. That would be idolatry. The emotional programs for happiness seek symbols of survival/security, affection/esteem, and power/control for the sake of the symbols themselves. Because of our fixations on particular programs for happiness, we treat survival/security, affection/esteem, and power/control symbols as absolutes, that is, as substitutes for God. Instead of being content with a reasonable amount of security, pleasure, and independence, we want to squeeze from these limited goods an absolute happiness that they cannot give. We then experience immediate disappointment and frustration.

This gradual training in consent is the school of divine love in which God invites us to accept the divine plan to share the divine life with us in a way that transcends all that the human imagination can foresee. We do not make these consents as ends in themselves, but rather to the will of God present in these things. We consent to God and to his will both in the enjoyment and in the surrender of his gifts. Each consent involves a kind of death. A child has to die to childhood in order to become an adolescent. An adolescent has to die to adolescence in order to enter the adult world. Most of us do not object in principle to growing up. In practice, however, we tend to hang on to our childish values, even as we grow up physically and intellectually. Consenting to God's will does not mean that we reject the values of any period of life as we pass through it; we simply leave behind its limitations.

Thus, the child's simplicity, innocence, enchantment with sense objects, and immediacy to sense experience are qualities that we should retain all through life. Only the tantrums and the ignorance of the child are left behind. Similarly, the spirit of adventure of the adolescent and the search for personal identity and relationship are values to be kept all through life; only the emotional turmoil of adolescence and the anxiety of establishing a personal identity are left behind as we become adults.

True asceticism is not the rejection of the world, but the acceptance of everything that is good, beautiful, and true. It is learning how to use our faculties and the good things of this world as God's gifts rather than expressions of selfishness. The basic ascesis is the appreciation of all that is good on each level of our developing humanity and the integration of the genuine values of each level into the next one. Integration is the unification of experience. As we perceive reality and relationship from new vantage points, we synthesize all that went before. This pattern continues beyond the mental egoic level of consciousness into further stages of human growth. The good things proper to the beginning of our spiritual journey have significant value, but we are asked to let them go as we move into more intimate relationships with God. While we do not reject the consolations of earlier times, we no longer depend on them or react to their withdrawal as we did in the beginning. We love God by loving all that he has made and everything that he does.

If we have not succeeded in making the consents proper to childhood, adolescence, and young adulthood, we may be invited to do so in later life under the inspiration of grace. God often invites us to rethink the judgments we made in childhood and adolescence, or in the early years of our conversion, that amounted to a rejection of the goodness of his gifts. He invites us to take another look at our hesitations and to realize that our rigid attitudes were based on our inability to handle events and relationships that were emotionally traumatic. Now he asks us to accept the legitimate pleasures of life, the value of friendship, the exercise of our talents, the loveliness of nature, the beauty of art, the enjoyment of both activity and rest. God is a tremendous supporter of creation, especially of all living beings. Jesus emphasized this when he said, "I came that they might have life and have it to the full" (John 10:10). The abundant life is divine union, which includes the capacity to use all things as stepping stones to God rather than as ends in themselves. To access this state, however, requires the willingness to negotiate the first three consents.

By consenting to God's creation, to our basic goodness as human beings, and to the letting go of what we love in this world, we are brought to the final surrender, which is to allow the false self to die and the true self to emerge. The true self might be described as our participation in the divine life manifesting in our uniqueness. God has more than one way of bringing us to this point. It can happen early in adult life, but if it does not, the ongoing stages of natural life may contribute to bringing it about. In the midlife crisis, even very successful people wonder whether they have accomplished anything. Later we experience physical decline, illness, and the infirmities of old age. What happens is the process of dying may be God's way of correcting all the mistakes we made and all the opportunities we missed during the earlier part of our lives. It may also provide the greatest chance of all to consent to God's gift of ourselves.

8

BERNIE

■

THE STORY OF BROTHER BERNIE O'SHEA exemplifies what consent to the basic goodness of our own being and nature might look like in actual practice. Bernie entered the monastery at seventeen immediately after finishing high school. He was a warm, affectionate, loving young man who enjoyed close relationships. At the time, the members of the Trappist order, because of the strict rule of silence, lived like hermits in community. Whether Bernie fully realized what this meant before he entered, I do not know, but in he came with his broad smile, exuberance, and bouncing step. He immediately tried to make friends with all the other novices. Since he could only use sign language to communicate, he learned all two hundred signs in one day. He then pressed into service every available occasion to relate.

One of the best opportunities came when someone held the door for him so that he could pass from the novitiate into the cloister. Bernie would watch for this opportunity so as to be able to make the sign for "thank you." To make this sign, we brought the fingertips of our right hands to our lips and kissed them, but we were not supposed to make any noise. When anyone opened the door for him, Bernie was delighted. Like a baseball pitcher winding up to deliver a fast ball, he would rotate his right arm, bring his fingers to his lips with a great flourish and a big smack, and look into your eyes with his broadest possible smile. It was a marvelous encounter the first time, but after three or four times in one day, I, for one, had a strong inclination to go in the opposite direction when I saw him coming.

The superiors were aware that Bernie was socially inclined and decided he would do better as a lay brother. In that vocation he could find more opportunities for practical services and hence more opportunities for signs, and even an occasional spoken word if the nature of the work required it. The superiors decided that cooking would be a good job for him. This was not an easy assignment for Bernie. For him to learn to cook meant copying page after page of recipes and writing all kinds of accessory instructions to himself in the margins.

When the community prepared to move from Valley Falls, Rhode Island, to a dairy farm in Spencer, Massachusetts, Bernie was sent to cook for the two monks who were in charge of converting the cow barns into a monastery. This was Bernie's first opportunity since joining the order to relate to people outside the cloister. His innate friendliness was now given a little scope.

After the disastrous fire in March 1950 that virtually destroyed the old monastery in Rhode Island, the abbot sent me to Spencer to replace the priest in charge, who was now needed to renovate an abandoned camp for immediate occupancy by the community back home. I arrived on the premises in full monastic fervor, having been ordained a priest just a year before.

The former owner of the farm and his family were still living on the property. Bernie had already made friends with his wife. They enjoyed swapping recipes, and they both had a flare for music and loved decorative objects. One day while I was out for a walk, they got together and put some curtains in the windows, rugs on the floor, and a few knickknacks on the window sills. When I walked in, I was shocked. The Trappists at that time were noted for their simplicity of lifestyle. We used to sit on benches. There was no such thing at the old monastery as a chair with a back, a rug on the floor, or curtains at the windows. I said to myself, "This is contrary to the Trappist spirit!" I felt it was my duty as the one in charge to uphold the rule. Accordingly, a few days later when Bernie went out for a walk, I removed all the curtains, rugs, and knickknacks. When he came back and saw the devastation, his heart must have been broken, but he put up with the decision, of course, because I was in charge. Fortunately for him, he was transferred back to Rhode Island shortly afterward and escaped from my austere regime.

There was a tendency in the Trappist tradition that we had inherited to disapprove of any kind of enjoyment. Indulging in simple pleasures was considered a form of falling back into the ways of the world. Bernie could not understand what was wrong about enjoying art, music, flowers, sunsets, and people. When a new monastery was started in Colorado in the late 1950s, the abbot sent Bernie there to cook for those who were constructing it. When Bernie arrived in the beautiful Roaring Fork Valley with his big stack of cookbooks, he immediately fell in love with the mountains, the clouds, the nights full of stars, and springtime in the Rockies. Nobody ever loved that mountain valley as Bernie did. The flowers fascinated him. He could become ecstatic over a daisy. Some people used to think his reaction was a put-on. It was not! Later, when I was sent to Snowmass, he used to say to me, "God speaks to me through the flowers. Is there anything wrong with that?" I had to say, "I guess there is nothing wrong with that," but I really did not agree. I thought that his priorities were in disarray and that he should be more interested in prayer, spiritual reading, and penitential practices.

Actually Bernie was a faithful reader of the gospels, but he had little interest in reading other things. He often said that a few sentences from the gospel were enough for him. Then he liked to go out into the woods or onto a mountainside and watch the clouds, the flowers, the elk, the porcupines, and the eagles if he could spot one.

Bernie's social proclivities were severely curtailed by our strict rule of silence. He could not understand what was wrong with socializing or having an occasional party, but in those days we rarely had a feast. I can remember when it was a startling innovation to sing a few carols on Christmas day. Later our abbot, who was ahead of his time, allowed ice cream on certain great feasts, but rarely and in the silence of the refectory.

Bernie often expressed deep self-doubts because he realized the order had different ideas from his about how to be a monk. He felt that the supreme value of monastic life was the community and that loving the brothers and serving them was the best way to express this value. He could not understand the idea of hermits in community. He approved of solitude, but he thought that silence was overdone. He felt there should be more opportunities for communication. He accepted the status quo, however, and continued to cook and work hard to please the community. After three and a half years in Snowmass, I was elected abbot of the motherhouse and returned to Spencer.

Following the Second Vatican Council, religious orders were urged to review their respective observances in the light of modern conditions and the charism of their founders. Changes in the Trappist order began to take place rapidly. The rule of silence was modified, and the local superior was given discretionary powers with regard to many rules that up to then had been regarded as inviolable. In this way events like celebrations or hikes could be permitted.

Bernie experienced these changes as an affirmation of his own monastic orientation. For many years he had thought he was the only one in the order who was crazy. Now it seemed that the order was beginning to move in the direction he thought it should have espoused in the first place. This encouraged him to follow still more his attraction to serve the community and to show love in every possible way. He developed his service into an art. If genius is the art of taking pains, Bernie was a genius. He enlarged his benign sphere of influence beyond the kitchen. Not only was he concerned that the brothers and the guests had the right food, but also that they had enough blankets and clothes; that they saw a herd of elk when one was out there; and that, if they were visitors, they had the chance to see the local sights. He sponsored hikes into the mountains and the celebration of birthdays, homecomings, and anniversaries.

A party in those days consisted of a chance to chat and to enjoy a few goodies, especially ice cream. One of Bernie's favorite pranks at parties was to tease the more austere members of the community. He would make himself a bowl of ice cream beginning with four or five scoops of chocolate or vanilla. On top of that he would pour a generous helping of hot fudge sauce. On top of that would go an enormous portion of whipped cream, and finally a fistful of pecans to top it off. Then he would sit down in the presence of any number of hard-nosed ascetics and eat this concoction, smacking his lips in delight. His philosophy was, "If you are going to indulge in some legitimate pleasure, why not enjoy it?" He could not figure out why monks experience guilt feelings whenever they encounter some innocent pleasure.

In a western household, the kitchen is the center of the home, the place where everybody usually enters and leaves. This was Bernie's kingdom. From there he ruled the roost. He was the abbot's right-hand man, whether by choice or circumstance. He enjoyed complete freedom to take an interest in visitors to the monastery. He showed so much interest, in fact, that people who met him once rarely forgot him. He would even take vicarious pleasure in what the guests ate in restaurants in Aspen. If they stayed overnight in the monastery, he was concerned that they have a good breakfast. When my brother visited, he was impressed that Bernie insisted on serving him eggs and bacon, a treat the community was not permitted.

I came regularly to Snowmass in those days as the official visitor on behalf of the order, to encourage and check out the community. The visitor interviewed the members of the community for most of the day, listening to their opinions about the way the observances were going and to the difficulties they might be experiencing. Bernie perceived that this might be a fatiguing occupation, so he used to bring me a cup of tea and, of course, a few cookies to go along with it. Such things as coffee breaks were still unheard of, and I was hesitant at first about this favor, but he took such pleasure in doing this service that I could not say so. Bernie challenged us to accept his special acts of kindness by making us feel as if we were doing him a favor.

At a certain point in the process of renewal, the lay brothers' vocation was integrated with that of the choir monks, to the great dissatisfaction of many lay brothers, including Bernie. He reflected, however, that in a small community everybody has to pitch in. Although he had no inclination to join the choir, he learned how to play the organ in order to offer the gift of his presence to the common prayer. He loved every kind of music. When he accompanied the chant, he had a tendency—such was his taste—to pull out the tremolo. To someone trained in the purity of Gregorian chant, this was not exactly the last word in sacred music. But clearly his efforts were proof of his determination to serve the needs of the community.

Over the years I kept coming back for visits and could see that Bernie was growing in maturity as well as in loving kindness. He was less obtrusive in pushing his charitable intentions on others; at the same time he always seemed to be on hand when you needed something.

On one occasion, the local abbot attended a workshop and was convinced that the community would benefit from a macrobiotic diet. By dint of dogged perseverance, Bernie was at this time one of the best cooks in the order. When the community agreed to this new diet as an experiment, Bernie went along with it although it meant the disruption of all his carefully worked out and annotated recipes. All the goodies he loved to prepare and to eat were ruled out by this diet. Carrot juice, uncooked vegetables, and sugarless desserts, all totally foreign to his taste, were the order of the day. Fortunately for him, everyone starting getting sick, including the abbot. Gradually the health food diet was modified and eventually laid to rest.

Every now and then, the community had what they called an evaluation meeting. The monks could bring up matters of concern with regard to the community. On one occasion the question was raised, "Would it be all right to see a movie once in a while, or some exceptional program on TV?" Each monk, as was customary, gave his opinion. Some expressed concern that this might bring the spirit of the world into the monastery. "It is not our vocation," they said. When everyone had given his opinion, Bernie, who had originally brought up the idea, said, "What if all the people watching TV at this very moment are holier than we are?" No one was able to answer that question, and so a television set was brought in to show an occasional video. I suspect that that was what everyone wanted to do anyway. Bernie was just more honest and outspoken.

Although the occasions were rare, Bernie loved to go to Aspen and window-shop. When he heard people say, "Aspen is sin city, the Babylon of the West, the cocaine capital of America," he would defend it, saying, "I find God in Aspen." Because he had a special love for *National Geographic* specials, the abbot occasionally allowed him to drop into the local rectory when he was in town to view a documentary about whales or other nature subjects.

When I resigned as abbot of Spencer in the fall of 1981, the community in Snowmass graciously invited me to come there to live. Everyone welcomed me warmly, but I could see that Bernie's mind was working overtime. His reflections seemed to run along these lines: "This guy has been abbot of a big monastery and has been in the service of the order for twenty years. Now he is living in this insignificant little community. He must miss the big one that he left behind and all the brothers there. He needs special consideration." Instead of treating me like everybody else, he went out of his way to find out what food I liked and what food I could not eat, in addition to all his other ever-increasing activities. I remember reflecting, "This must be the way God is!" When someone treats you in such a way that it makes you think of God, that person clearly is a sacrament of God's presence.

During my first Thanksgiving celebration at Snowmass, Bernie, as was his wont, was banging on the piano and happened to play a melody that I was especially fond of. I wanted to ask him to put it on a cassette so that I could listen to it from time to time, but there was so much going on at the party that I was not able to mention my request to him.

A few weeks later, the abbot and I were attending a meeting of superiors at another monastery. While we were there, the abbot had a phone call notifying him that Bernie had dropped dead on the street in Aspen. He had gone to the dentist and was on his way to take my clerical suit to the cleaners. A final stop at the local rectory to see a video about whales had been scheduled, but he had had a massive heart attack and died instantly.

The abbot was completely broken up by the news. He flew back at once, asking me to stay to represent him at the meeting. Two days later I flew back and landed at the airport in Aspen. It was a glorious winter day and Colorado was at its best— bright blue sky, a few white clouds, snow, green fir trees, and the air as clear as crystal. I could not help thinking. "This valley is celebrating! It belongs to Bernie because he loved it so much."

When we got into the car, the brother who picked me up said, "Would you like to hear Bernie's voice again?" I said, "What do you mean? How can I hear his voice again?" He replied, "A few days before Bernie died, we made an audio cassette together for my brother's twenty-fifth wedding anniversary." Characteristically, Bernie had wanted to provide a little surprise for one of the monks' relatives with whom he had made friends. Bernie and this brother had produced a skit in which Bernie played the role of a piano player in a night club in Aspen. The other brother played the role of an announcer for the local radio station who was interviewing him. I said, "By all means, turn it on!"

The brother turned on the cassette player. What do you think came out? The piece that Bernie was playing on the piano was the tune I had wanted him to put on a cassette for me. I thought to myself, "My God, Bernie, you really are thoughtful! Here you are in glory and you are thinking of this trifling request of mine!" The coincidence was so typical of him that it was absolutely impossible for me to interpret it in any other way.

I never knew anyone who resembled sunshine more than this man. No one ever loved life so genuinely and consented to its goodness so unreservedly. Yet in one second, at God's request, he dropped everything. That is true detachment— accepting everything that God wants us to accept and letting go of everything that God wants us to let go of, at a moment's notice.

9

ANTHONY AS A PARADIGM OF THE SPIRITUAL JOURNEY

■

SAINT ANTHONY OF EGYPT, the fourth-century father of Christian monasticism, is one of the few holy people whose inner spiritual journey we know in considerable detail. His biography provides a paradigm for dismantling the false self by means of both active confrontation and passive purification. Bernie, of course, exemplifies the positive way of dismantling the false self by practicing unconditional love: selfishness cannot survive in the climate of continuous self-giving. A combination of the two ways may be the most practical response to the human condition.

In the preceding chapters, we have been looking at the dynamics involved in the development of the false self and at how the false self interferes with the proper exercise of our relationships with God, ourselves, and others. Dismantling it often feels like interior warfare—and in fact, it is! Anthony of Egypt, the champion of the ascetic life, is the perfect paradigm for this approach to the spiritual journey. By taking this inward path, he too reached perfect love, at which point he manifested the lively concern for the needs of others that Bernie manifested and practiced.

These two paths should not be presented in opposition to each other. Both are needed for a balanced spiritual development. Anthony is especially helpful in that he exemplifies the heart of the Christian journey, whether the emphasis is placed on its positive or negative aspects: namely, the struggle with unconscious motivation. The cross that Jesus invites each of us to carry is precisely the emotional wounds that we bring with us from early childhood, together with the coping mechanisms we developed to deal with them. Although original sin is not the result of personal wrongdoing on our part, it causes a pervasive feeling of alienation from God, from other people, and from our true selves.

The term *original sin* is a way of describing the universal experience of coming to full reflective self-consciousness without the certitude of personal union with God. This gives rise to our intimate sense of incompletion, dividedness, isolation, and guilt. The cultural consequences of these alienations are instilled in us from earliest childhood and passed on from one generation to the next. The urgent need to escape from the profound insecurity of this situation, when unchecked, gives rise to insatiable desires for pleasure, possessions, and power. On the social level, it gives rise to violence, war, and institutional injustice.

The particular consequences of original sin include all the self-serving habits that have been woven into our personalities from the time we were conceived; all the harm that other people have done to us knowingly or unknowingly at an age when we could not defend ourselves; and the methods we acquired, many of them now unconscious, to ward off the pain of unbearable situations. This constellation of prerational reactions is the foundation of the false self. The false self develops in opposition to the true self. Its center of gravity is the self as separate from God and others, and hence turned in on itself.

In Anthony's time, demons were familiar figures in the popular culture both within and without the Christian community. Thus, it is not surprising that Anthony's biographer, Saint Athanasius, Bishop of Alexandria, describes Anthony's ascetical life as a series of combats with Satan.[1] In fact, spiritual combat was a vivid theme for the early Church—and a recent literal memory.

Prior to the Edict of Milan in 313, which established peace between the Roman Empire and the Christian Church, the great symbol of Christian perfection was fidelity to the gospel in the face of persecution. During the first three centuries, Christians lived with the daily prospect of being thrown to the lions, sent to the mines, or ostracized and banned from any kind of public career. The Edict of Milan was an event of enormous significance for this persecuted Church whose membership was composed largely of slaves and the poor. Once martyrdom was no longer a daily prospect, fervent Christians started looking for a lifestyle that would express a similar dedication to Christ.

When Athanasius wrote *The Life of Saint Anthony* in the mid–fourth century, a few years after the death of Anthony, he affirmed that the same Spirit who prompted the generosity of the martyrs was still present in the Church and calling people to a new expression of dedication to Christ. Athanasius coined the term "the daily martyrdom of conscience" for the practice of asceticism that Anthony had inaugurated in the desert. The generosity of seeking God day after day by means of asceticism was compared to the generosity of laying down one's life in the arena. And Athanasius dared to say, "They are equal." Asceticism thus became the ideal way to lead a fervent Christian life in times of peace.

Anthony was born about 251 in a little town in lower Egypt. His well-to-do parents owned a fertile farm of about two hundred acres. We are told that Anthony was a fair-haired boy who ate what was put before him and was obedient to his parents. Tragedy hit this happy home, although we are not told exactly what happened. Perhaps Anthony's parents were killed in a chariot accident. In any event, the young man of eighteen was left in charge of the estate and of his younger sister.

One day, while thinking of how the apostles had given up everything in order to follow Christ, Anthony happened to go into the local church. The gospel text being proclaimed (Matt. 19:21–23) went right to his heart: "If you seek perfection, go, sell your possessions, and give to the poor. You will then have treasure in heaven. Afterward come back and follow me." (This is the same text that later inspired the conversion of Saint Francis of Assisi.) Anthony immediately sold everything he had, keeping back just a little to take care of his sister. Although this was surely a prudent judgment, God had other plans. A few weeks later Anthony entered the church again, and this time he heard the text, "Stop worrying, then, over questions like, 'What are we to eat, or what are we to drink, or what are we to wear?" (Matt. 6:31). Cut to the quick, he gave away the meager savings he had reserved to take care of his sister and placed her with a group of devout women.

Anthony was now free to pursue his attraction for asceticism. There was no organized form of religious life at that time, so he sought out the two chief benefits of the common life, namely, the support of good example and the advice of those who had been on the spiritual journey for a long time. Under this tutelage, he soon began to experience the springtime of the spiritual life, the first fruits of his generosity. Athanasius's text sums up Anthony's zeal in practicing the virtues:

> He observed the graciousness of one, the earnestness in prayer of another; he studied the even temper of one and the kindheartedness of another. He fixed his attention on the vigils kept by one and on the studies pursued by another. He admired one for his patient endurance, another for his fasting and sleeping on the ground. He watched closely one man's meekness and the forbearance by another. And in one and all alike he marked especially their devotion to Christ and the love that they had for one another. (*The Life of St. Anthony,* No. 4, 21)

Notice the bond that unites the members of the group amid their diversity of gifts: the love of Christ and their love for one another. The deeper the unity, the more pluralism a community can absorb. The variety of viewpoints and gifts are experienced not as threats to one's own practice and views, but as enrichments.

Now comes the statement that intones the basic theme of the first stages of Anthony's journey, which Athanasius presents as an ever-increasing struggle with the powers of evil:

> The devil, the hater and envier of good, could not bear to see such resolution in the young man, but set about employing his customary tactics against him. (*The Life of St. Anthony,* No. 5, 22)

The term "customary tactics" suggests a program of testing neophytes on the spiritual journey to see what their weak points are, and then of pressing hard on those weaknesses in order to persuade them to give up the spiritual journey and return to their former occupations. In other words, the envier of all that is good tempts us to give up following Christ and to go back to cultivating the false self.

Anthony at the time had already logged several months of intense asceticism, living in extreme privation. As a modern equivalent, we might picture him living at the edge of a town in a tiny shack overlooking the local garbage dump. The springtime of Anthony's journey had passed; interior consolation had dried up, and he was famished from fasting. Suddenly his imagination was stirred. The demon began to remind him of the pleasures he had enjoyed in his former lifestyle.

The first thing that came into his mind was the memory of his property. He saw once again the fertile land with the flowing waters of the Nile glistening in the setting sun. Everything was so peaceful. Stringed instruments played soft music in the distance. Anthony could smell the delicious perfume of flowers like hyacinth or wisteria. Sight, smell, taste, touch, and sound all combined in his imagination and memory to awaken an immense nostalgia for that beautiful property, especially on those long, lovely summer evenings. Then a voice close to his ear seemed to whisper, "Anthony, how could you leave such a gorgeous property? It's still there. It's not too late. If you leave right away, you can easily get it back!"

The spiritual entity called the devil could well be a great stage and screen producer. Cecil B. deMille was amateurish by comparison. By stirring up the senses and choosing just the right images, the devil evokes the most tender memories and the most poignant feelings in order to create the maximum impression. His purpose: to weaken one's resolve to continue the spiritual journey.

But Anthony was unmoved in his resolve. The devil's next temptation conjured up memories of intimacy with former friends and relatives. In the ascetic life, it was no longer appropriate to have any contact with them. In fact, Anthony's friends must have heard of his new lifestyle and probably did not want to go anywhere near him. The devil reminded Anthony, "No longer will you be able to see your dear little sister . . . No more affectionate embraces, no more family gatherings, no more birthday parties." The sweetest memories of family and friends came floating down the stream of his consciousness. But Anthony remained firm.

Anthony's next temptation was calculated to awaken greed for money. As we saw, Anthony had given away all his possessions for the love of Christ, even the meager funds he had thought of using to provide for his sister. Now as he sat in his poverty-stricken shack, the desire for money passed before his mind's eye. The devil suggested all the wonderful things he could use it for: pleasures, travel, studies, high finance, perhaps even investments to amass funds to give to the poor! But Anthony paid no attention to the endless procession of possibilities.

His next temptation appealed to the desire for power. This young man who had never known power over anyone began to feel the attraction to control the other ascetics. A mysterious and insidious voice whispered, "Anthony, if only you had stayed where you were, you could have had a fine job at the local fertilizer plant! It's not too late! With your talents, you could be a junior executive in no time! Perhaps even a senior executive! And in a little while you would become the president of the company! Then you could buy up all the fertilizer plants in Egypt!" Notice how this kind of temptation builds up and becomes more and more grandiose. But Anthony was prompt in letting go of each suggestion.

Next came the attraction to become famous. This form of vanity was so incongruous, given the kind of life that Anthony had chosen, that it made no impression on him at all.

His imagination and memory were then subtly directed to the amenities of life: sports, hi-fi's, movies, holidays, good housing, all the comfort of life. All that was most charming and entrancing in his early life passed in review. These memories were in sharp contrast to his tin-can shack and unobstructed view of the dump. He winced at the contrast but did not entertain these pleasureable thoughts.

Next came the memory of the pleasures of food and drink. This young man from a well-fed household had been fasting for months on one meal a day of simple vegetables, often of just bread and water. Thoughts of the good old days were dangled before his mind's eye. Perhaps he recalled those delicious crocodile burgers by the Nile. The bottom line to all these impressions was always the same: "Anthony, do not delay! You must leave. Do not think twice about it. Go back to your luxurious property! Go back to your career! Go back to your friends! Go back to those sumptuous meals!"

These worldly temptations that kept pounding him were not outside him, but inside him. That is what made them so disconcerting and confusing. What was his method of resistance? Faith, determination, and incessant prayer. Anthony was resolved not to give up the spiritual journey. This is his timeless message to those on the journey: never stop waiting for God, never stop trusting in God, never stop praying to God.

The devil was nonplussed by Anthony's steadfast resolution. He suspected that Anthony, by escaping unharmed from these temptations, might undermine his malignant influence over the local population. Though the positive attraction to return to the pleasant things of the world had failed, the demon had another card up his sleeve: to weaken Anthony's resolution to persevere in the spiritual journey by attracting him to leave under the pretext of a greater good. General followers of Christ cannot normally be tempted by the raw attraction of evil, nor will they exchange the spiritual journey for respectable mediocrity. The suggestion of a greater good is the only way to catch them.

The voice of the devil now challenged Anthony's resolution with the following considerations. "Anthony, what have you done? You have put your little sister in that community of austere, gloomy, horse-faced women! Despite their pretensions of piety, they are a bunch of old witches. They never smile. They won't let her play with her doll. They beat her whenever she commits the slightest fault. She's crying her heart out! You must leave instantly and rescue her!"

This kind of temptation is a dirty trick if there ever was one. Sometimes those we love raise a similar problem of conscience. There was a novice in my monastery whose mother used to write regularly saying, "If you do not come home, I will commit suicide!" Imagine getting that message on a cold, dark, damp fast day. The monk stayed and his mother continued to go on living.

I had a grandma who doted on me because I was named after my deceased grandfather whom she adored. We used to do many things together. After my conversion from worldly objectives to the values of the gospel, she could not understand my increasing interest in spiritual things. When I told her that I intended to enter a cloistered Trappist monastery, it was just the end. She had been brought up in a tradition that associated monks with lurid tales about finding the skulls of infants in underground passages between adjoining monasteries of men and women. Her idea of a monk was someone in the last stages of degeneracy.

In her last illness, Grandma was bedridden in an apartment in New York, attended by nurses around the clock. One day I received a letter from her which read, "Dearest Grandson, I'm lying in my bed and I miss you terribly. I still hope you will come home. Over and over I say to my nurse, 'If my grandson won't come home, won't you please throw me out of the window!'"

My first reaction was, "How can I justify causing so much suffering to someone who loves me so much?" This kind of trial tests our vocation to the roots and sifts our motives. If we came to the monastery because we wanted to be a farmer, a liturgist, or a country dweller, we would not last very long.

Here are a few contemporary scenarios for this subtle kind of temptation. The bottom line is always the same one: drop your commitment to the spiritual journey in favor of a greater good. There follows the voice of the tempter:

"Dear Soul, you were studying to be a doctor and doing so well. Doctors are badly needed. Why not return to your career? You could serve people so much more generously . . ."

"Dear Friend, your mother and father are each other's throats again. You are the only one who was ever able to bring peace to the home. If you leave now, you can make everything peaceful again . . ."

"Dearest One, your old flame is sitting in a furnished room with the tears streaming down her cheeks. Her heart is breaking. How can you do this to her?" Actually she has met a wonderful guy, has never been happier, and has not given you a second thought, but the devil never suggests another possible side to the story. He builds up a huge smokescreen of arguments to support his thesis. We are treated to a production that is compelling, absorbing, but completely unreal.

When the devil was not able to persuade Anthony to return to his former way of life, he tried to insinuate a negative attitude toward the ascetic life that Anthony had embraced. His first ploy was to suggest weakness of the body and the rigors of asceticism. "Anthony, how long do you expect to survive like this? You will soon be ill. You may die!" He reminded Anthony of the long journey still ahead and of how endless time can seem in adverse circumstances. "How can you keep up this attack against the false self month after month, year after year?"

Finally, the devil pointed to the greater labor of practicing virtue and dismantling the emotional programs of happiness. "How can you give up your desire to control things and other people? You are a superior person!" Or again, "Why give up your desire for security? You've earned it!" And as a final shot, "You entered on this path much too young. You'll never make it as a lifelong celibate!"

Every temptation is tailor-made to fit one's personal history and particular vulnerability. The rigor of virtue, the duration of time, and the great labor of practicing virtue are temptations that arise in various forms and degrees of intensity. One form is the feeling of incompatibility with one's spouse, family, or the members of one's community. When it came time for me to make a final commitment to the Trappist order, I had to face the searching question, "How am I going to live for the next fifty or sixty years with this person whose fidelity to prayer makes me unbearably envious?"

To each of his temptations Anthony gave the same basic response: determination to persevere in the spiritual journey, trust that God would give him the grace to do so, and incessant prayer. Each of these three dispositions is an exercise of faith, hope, and love.

10

THE NIGHT OF SENSE

■

Freedom from the False Self

ANTHONY'S TEMPTATIONS TO ABANDON the spiritual journey, as we saw, were of two kinds. One was the positive attraction to things he had enjoyed in his former lifestyle. The other was the feeling of aversion for the ascetical life that he had embraced. Why did he experience such strong and repeated temptations to return to the life he had so vigorously renounced when he initially committed himself to the spiritual journey?

The answer is that Anthony's emotional programs for happiness were still present on the unconscious level; it was to the hidden contents of Anthony's unconscious that the devil kept appealing. To decide consciously to follow the values of the gospel is only the first step in our commitment to Christ. The *values in the unconscious* must then be confronted. When the springtime of the spiritual journey subsides, the old temptations surface once again with the same or more force than before our conversion.

The spiritual journey is characterized by the ever-increasing knowledge of our mixed motivations, the dark sides of our personalities, and the emotional traumas of early childhood. Nothing is more helpful to reduce pride than the actual experience of self-knowledge. If we are discouraged by it, we have misunderstood its meaning.

What is our experience when we start to dismantle the false self and refuse to act out of our emotional programs? God seems to come closer. Since God is always present, it might be better to say he turns up the voltage in our interior world. A room that is well appointed and cleaned every day looks pretty clean. We are happy to sit in it. If, however, fifty ten-thousand-watt bulbs are turned on and the floor is put under a magnifying glass, the whole room would be crawling with little creatures. We would leave as fast as possible.

God responds to our generosity as if saying, "This person is serious about the spiritual journey. Let's go to work and clean out the junk." God turns up the voltage and, as a consequence, our inner world begins to crawl, so to speak; the damage that our emotional programs for happiness are doing to us and to our relationships becomes apparent. From this perspective our good deeds look like piles of dirty dishrags.

Saint John of the Cross, the sixteenth-century Spanish mystic, has distinguished this difficult period more articulately than any other spiritual writer. He calls it the night of sense. The first sign of the presence of this night is a generalized aridity in both prayer and daily life. This dryness or diminution of satisfaction in our relationships with God is the direct effect of an increase of faith and the beginning of contemplative prayer. God is beaming an increase of divine light into our inner world, but we do not have the receptive apparatus to properly interpret the experience. It feels like a great loss. What is lost? The free and easy exchanges that we had previously enjoyed with God as a result of fruitful reflection on the scriptures, reception of the sacraments, prayer, and the service of others. When we pick up the scriptures, it is an effort to sit still with the text for the time that we had agreed upon. Spiritual reading is like reading a telephone book. As sensible grace begins to fade, the lack of any feeling of benefit in spiritual exercise increases. At the same time, we do not find satisfaction in worldly things. The growth of faith, under the influence of what theology calls the gift of knowledge, one of the seven gifts of the Holy Spirit, produces this lack of satisfaction, both in things relating to God and in the emotional programs in which we had placed a heavy investment. The Holy Spirit infuses into our minds the insight that God alone can satisfy our boundless longing for happiness. This positive experience is not a dissatisfaction with anything—pleasure, power, or security. It springs from the realization that no created thing can bring us unlimited satisfaction. In the light of this intuition, we know that all the gratifications we were seeking when we were motivated by our emotional programs cannot possibly bring us happiness. This creates a period of mourning, during which all the things that we had counted on to bring us happiness are slowly relativized.

According to John of the Cross, the second sign of this growth in the spiritual journey is manifested by the fear that we are going backwards and that through some personal fault or failure we have offended God. Since there is no felt affirmation coming from grace, we can get into quite a stew. Some people mistakenly think it is the end of their relationships with God. This is not true. What has ended is their overdependence on the senses and reasoning in order to pray. God is offering them a more intimate relationship; if they would not reflect on their anxious feelings, they would begin to perceive it. In this state we are like a baby being weaned from the breast. Infants are generally opposed to this development, but once they learn to accept the situation, they enjoy the more nourishing food of meat and potatoes. It is part of growing up. The night of sense is a period of weaning from the consolations that characterized the beginning of our relationships with God. The solid nourishment of pure faith is an acquired taste, like solid food for the weaned child.

The third sign of the night of sense identified by John of the Cross is the inability or disinclination to practice discursive meditation. Discursive meditation, in which one ponders the teaching and example of Jesus, is generally prescribed as a preliminary step to contemplative prayer. Without the inclination to meditate discursively, the mind wanders far and wide. The will finds no benefit or pleasure in particular acts of love, praise, petition, or any other response to God's gifts. Still, we desire to be alone with God, even though he seems to be a million miles away and to have lost interest in us.

John of the Cross states that all three signs should be present together in discerning the night of sense. If only one and not the others is present, there could be some pathology such as a depression.

The night of sense, John of the Cross asserts, happens "fairly soon" to those who commit themselves to the spiritual journey. By the term *night* John of the Cross means the darkening of the usual ways in which we relate to God, whether through reflection or through the experience of the senses. Our ordinary ways of relating to God are being changed to ways that we do not know. This pulls the rug out from under our plans and strategies for the spiritual journey. We learn that the journey is a path that cannot be mapped out in advance. God helps us to disidentify from our preconceived ideas by enlightening us from within by the contemplative gifts of the Spirit. Through the infusion of his light and the assurance of his love, he lets us in on our weaknesses and deficiencies—not to overwhelm us with discouragement, but to encourage us to entrust ourselves completely to his infinite mercy.

11

SPECIAL TRIALS IN THE
NIGHT OF SENSE

■

WHEN THE NIGHT OF SENSE is prolonged, three particular trials may arise. Although they make this transitional period more difficult, they also accelerate its progress and enable us, once and for all, to put to rest the predominating influence and motivation of the false self. These temptations do not occur in everyone, nor do all three usually occur in the same person. They are sure signs that we are in the night of sense.

Here is how John of the Cross describes the first trial:

> For to some the angel of Satan presents himself—namely, the spirit of forni- cation—that he may buffet their senses with abominable and violent tempta- tions, and trouble their spirits with vile considerations and representations which are most visible to the imagination, which things at times are a greater affliction to them than death. (*Dark Night of the Soul*, Ch. 14, no. 1)

Anthony's experience of this temptation is thoroughly described by Athanasius. We are told that immediately after he had resisted the positive and negative temptations to return to his former lifestyle, the devil pulled this trick out of his bag. He began by lobbing pornographic images into Anthony's imagination, somewhat the way an invading army lobs mortars into a city to soften up the opposition before the troops move in. The next salvo involved the stirring up of sexual feelings. This trial apparently went on for some weeks or months. The text says that the struggle between Anthony and the demon was so intense that his colleagues could sense the battle that was going on.

When vivid temptations of this kind continue for a long time, our conscience may become confused as to whether it has consented or not. We think, "If I am really rejecting them, why do they keep coming back?" As obsessive thoughts and emotions keep returning, the full force of the sexual energy comes into focus. Since Anthony had led a withdrawn life in early childhood, he was probably not aware of its power. He had made a commitment to celibacy in order to channel his whole strength into the single-hearted pursuit of the spiritual journey. He needed to confront and accept the full force of his sexual energy in order to allow the Spirit to transmute it into zeal for the service of God and of his future disciples.

After weeks and perhaps months of constant struggling with these temptations, Anthony experienced the devil's final assault. It might be verbalized as follows: "Anthony, you have done your very best, but your best efforts are evidently not working at all. You might as well give in." Anthony responded with anger and grief, certain signs that his will was not consenting.

Anthony acted on the energy aroused by his anger in a practical way. He introduced into his mind's eye a vivid image of the fires of hell. This strategy was not designed to stir up the emotion of fear, which is counterproductive in temptations to sexual misconduct. The body responds to the feeling of fear by pouring chemicals into the blood stream and concentrating the flow of blood in the abdomen in order to prepare the body to fight or run away. Anthony's strategy was to introduce a lively image of material fire on the same level as his urgent attractions to sexual pleasure. By putting the image of material fire and its pain into his imagination, he was able to put out the fire of lust.

When Anthony came through this temptation unscathed, the devil, we are told, immediately changed his tactics. Fawning and saying Anthony was not like other people who are all easy prey to temptation, he tried to persuade Anthony to take personal credit for his victory over sensuality, and thus fall into spiritual pride. Anthony's response was, and I paraphrase, "To hell with you! . . ." "This," Athanasius says, "was Anthony's first victory over Satan."

Thus, in addition to refusing to consent to the spirit of fornication, Anthony refused to consent to the more subtle gratification of victory over his temptations. The pride of innocence is one of the most dangerous forms of pride. It attributes to oneself what only the grace of God can enable one to do. The risk at this point in the spiritual journey is that freedom from personal sin and ease in the practice of virtue may go to one's head.

The night of sense reveals the full extent of the selfishness of which we are capable. Humility is the fruit of the bittersweet experience of this intimate kind of self-knowledge. It is the peaceful acknowledgment of our faults without the reactions of blame, shame, anger, or discouragement. Self-recriminations are neurotic. They are the voice of wounded pride saying, "You've done it again, you dumb so-and-so! You always foul things up. You don't measure up to my (fantastic) standards of perfection." Humility is the balance between the truth about weakness and confidence in the infinite mercy of God.

John of the Cross describes a second temptation in the night of sense:

> At other times in this night there is added to these things the spirit of blasphemy, which roams abroad, setting in the path of all the conceptions and thoughts of the soul intolerable blasphemies. These it sometimes suggests to the imagination with such violence that the soul almost utters them, which is a grave torment to it. (*Dark Night of the Soul*, Ch. 14, no. 2)

Some persons who experience this trial conclude that they are failing God and that their former friendship is at an end. Their anxiety is thus intensified.

The sense of helplessness in the face of raw anger can occur in any lifestyle. When I emerged from the novitiate into the professed house, I was given the chore of assisting the sacristan in preparing the vestments for the celebration of the Eucharist. Because I wanted to spend all my free time in prayer, I used to rush in from work, wash up, and go directly to church. The sacristan sometimes intercepted me along the way with a sign that a visiting priest had arrived unexpectedly and wanted to say mass; it was my duty to set out the vestments and the sacred vessels of the altar for the visitor. I was in a prolonged dried-out period at this time and was very short on patience. When I saw the sacristan heading my way, I could feel the indignation rising within me along with the commentary, "Here goes my prayer time again. Why can't the superiors give this job to somebody else?" Instead of being grateful for the honor of setting out the vestments, I was inwardly grumbling and murmuring against God. Thoughts of blasphemy sometimes swept over me. By this time I had enough faith to know that God was arranging everything in my life, so I would say, "Lord, why do you do this to me? Here I am trying to pray during the little free time that I have and you foul up the few chances I get." Then guilt feelings would immediately arise: "How can I have such thoughts when God is so good to me? I guess I don't have a vocation." Here an insidious voice would chime in, "You sure don't! This is no place for you!" The tempter was only too happy to reinforce my negative thoughts.

The third trial in the night of sense is similar to, and in fact anticipates, the later purification that John of the Cross calls the night of spirit, in which one's inmost being is purged of the last traces of the false self.

> At other times another abominable spirit, which Isaiah calls *Spiritus vertiginis*, [the Spirit of Dizziness] is allowed to molest them, not in order that they may fall, but that it may try them. This spirit darkens their senses in such a way that it fills them with numerous scruples and perplexities, so confusing that, as they judge, they can never, by any means, be satisfied concerning them, neither can they find any help for their judgment in counsel or thought. (*Dark Night of the Soul*, Ch. 14, no. 3)

This uncertainty could be about one's vocation or about some serious matter of conscience. The afflicted person feels like a Ping-Pong ball batted back and forth across the net. "Yes, I'll do this. No, I better do something else. No, not that, but maybe this." Even when one goes to a spiritual advisor and is told, "Here's the solution to your problem," peace lasts about a minute, and then one is back in the whirlpool of uncertainty and may feel rejected or abandoned by God.

Why does God allow such excruciating trials? Notice that these extreme temptations, like a spotlight on a dark stage, focus on the selfishness that lies at the heart of each emotional program for happiness.

The spirit of fornication reveals the intensity of desire that fuels our instinctual need for pleasure, affection, and esteem. In the night of sense, all sensible satisfactions dry out. If this situation is prolonged, human nature craves to feel something—anything! It reaches out for any pleasurable thing it can find. Sexual activity is for most people the most pleasurable of sense experiences: hence, temptations of lust may arise with great force. In others this craving for pleasure can also express itself in overeating, listening to certain kinds of music, or endlessly entertaining or distracting themselves—anything to get away from the interminable dryness.

The spirit of blasphemy addresses the need to control. In the night of sense, we cannot control anything. All our plans, including plans for self-improvement, come to nothing. This eventually causes intense frustration that may express itself in angry thoughts bordering on blasphemy. One would like to grab God by the throat and choke him.

The spirit of dizziness spotlights the need for certitude that is rooted in our security program. In this trial, we do not feel certitude about anything. The spiritual journey is a call into the unknown. Its scriptural paradigm is the call of Abraham: "Leave your father's house, your friends, relatives, and property, and come into the land that I will show you" (Gen. 12:1). God first calls us out of our childish ways of reacting into relationships that are appropriate for full mental egoic consciousness. But after that has been stablilized, we have not the remotest idea where God is taking us. Paul says, "Eye has not seen, ear has not heard, nor has it so much as dawned on man what God has prepared for those who love him" (1 Cor. 2:9). The only way to get there is to consent not to know. The desire or demand for certitude is an obstacle to launching full sail on the ocean of trust.

These three trials are immense favors from God. The divine light puts the spotlight on the source of the problem, which is the innate selfishness that is the hard core of each of the emotional programs for happiness. We cannot bring the false self to an end by ourselves; we can only allow it to die. If we do what we can to dismantle it, God, in response to our efforts, moves in and completes the job. All we have to do then is to consent. But that is about the biggest job there is. When all our efforts have failed, we finally accept the gift of God's infinite mercy.

The night of sense enables us to perceive that the source of the emotional programs for happiness is selfishness. By letting go of our desires for satisfaction in these areas, we move toward a permanent disposition of peace. Upsetting thoughts and emotions arise, but they no longer build up into emotional binges. The immense energy that was required to bear the afflictive emotions that flared up when our programs for happiness were frustrated is now available for more useful things, such as loving the people with whom we live and whom we are trying to serve.

12

ANTHONY IN THE TOMBS

■

Freedom from Cultural Conditioning

PERIODS OF STRUGGLE move us to new levels of integration, and then we have to translate our relationships to God, ourselves, and other people into this new perspective. This may take some years. After it has been accomplished, the spiritual food that nourishes us at that level eventually becomes insipid and no longer nourishes. We find ourselves once again in a crisis of faith, and, after another extended struggle, we take the leap to the next level of faith and love. This does not mean that we are immediately well established at the new level. Rather, we must go through another lengthy period of integrating all our relationships into the new perspective.

So it was for Anthony. After the first round of battles with the demons, Anthony emerged into a period of relative tranquillity and inner equilibrium—a plateau, as John of the Cross would call it. The plateau refers to the sense of freedom that emerges after the purification of the false self. But such a purification is not the end of the journey. Anthony knew that the devil was plotting further strategies against him. Accordingly, he did not presume on any progress he had made, but began anew each day, as if he were at the very beginning of the journey.

As Anthony completed the period of integration, he began to feel within himself a further call into the unknown, an invitation to take another quantum leap of trust in God. In Anthony's story we read this simple phrase: "Anthony left for the tombs which lay at some distance from the village" (*The Life of St. Anthony*, No. 8, 26.)[1] If we were fourth-century readers, our hair would be standing on end at these words. "He's going to the tombs!" we would exclaim in disbelief. In the popular imagination, the tombs, and especially the desert, were believed to be the strongholds of the demons. No one ever stayed in the tombs longer than was necessary to lay a deceased relative or friend on a shelf.

This one sentence in Anthony's story may represent a whole year or longer during which Anthony was trying to discern whether he should take his battles with the devil into the latter's territory. In the end, Anthony decided to take the offensive. Going to the tombs was thus an expression of tremendous courage, a stepping forth from the cultural conditioning of his time and place in complete disregard of the popular mindset.

As we have seen, Anthony was probably withdrawn and timid by temperament. He may have realized that there was still some residue of timidity in his character, and felt inspired by God to confront it. The difference between Anthony and certain starry-eyed ascetics is that his decision was an inspiration of grace. Some people attempt to imitate those who are advanced in the spiritual journey before they have taken their own first steps. They want to become perfect all at once and take on penances, trials, and ministries that are beyond their capacities. They usually fall on their noses. We cannot expect God to support us if we are doing our own thing. The spiritual journey consists in doing God's thing.

The decision to take the battle into the devil's territory is a vivid symbol of the struggle to free oneself from cultural overidentification. Mythic membership consciousness, we have seen, is characterized by overidentification with the value systems of a particular group. In this case, the culture, by giving power to the devil over certain places or geographical locations, was limiting the sphere of God's love and power. To become free—that is, to move from mythic membership to mental egoic consciousness—requires a journey away from cultural expectations, stereotypes, and mindsets into an increasing trust in the goodness and power of God.

Anthony marched off alone to the tombs and asked a friend to lock him in. Notice that detail. Was he afraid that his resolution would weaken?

Anthony's courage took the devil by surprise. I paraphrase his words: "What is this guy doing here? How dare he set foot in my domain? Let's get rid of him!" With this the devil called all his cohorts together and they beat Anthony into semiconsciousness. Anthony said afterward that no human force could have beaten him so badly. His friend, when he came to bring Anthony some bread, found him lying on the ground unconscious. The friend picked Anthony up, carried him to the church, and laid him on the ground. His relatives and friends gathered around his body and mourned him as if he were a corpse.

Toward midnight, however, they all started to doze. Anthony awoke and saw that they were nodding. The questions must have risen in his mind, "What is the Spirit asking of me now? Is he saying, 'You have done enough, call an ambulance and go to the hospital'? Or is he saying, 'Anthony, it is time to bring this battle to a conclusion; go back, I'll take care of you'?"

This was Anthony's double bind. "Shall I return? Shall I not? Is this an inspiration coming from God, or is it just my idea?" He decided in favor of taking the risk. He beckoned to his friend and asked to be carried back to the tombs. His friend lifted him quietly so that no one would wake up, carried him to the tombs, laid him on the floor, and once again locked the door and departed. (One wonders what kind of friend this was.)

Anthony was too feeble to stand, so he prayed lying down. Having finished his prayer, he challenged the devil as follows: "Here I am!" he shouted. "I am not cowed by your blows. Even though you should give me more, nothing can separate me from the love of Christ." Then, as was his custom, he began to sing verses of the psalms. "If camps of enemies stand against me, my heart shall not fear" (Ps. 27:3). Notice the reference to fear, suggesting his determination to eliminate the last traces of fear so that he might be completely free to follow every movement of the Spirit.

Athanasius writes: "The hater of good marveled that after all the blows Anthony had the courage to come back." The devil called together his "dogs" (a nickname for the demons among the Desert Fathers) and, bursting with rage, shouted, "You see that we have not stopped this fellow, neither by the spirit of fornication, nor by blows. On the contrary, he even challenges us! Let us go after him in another way!"

> That night they made such a din that the place seemed to be shaken by an earthquake. It was as though the demons were bursting through the four walls of the little chamber in the form of beasts and reptiles. All at once the place was filled with the phantoms of lions, bears, leopards, bulls, serpents, asps, scorpions, and wolves. Each moved according to the shape it had assumed. The lion roared ready to spring. The bull appeared about to gore him through. The serpent writhed ready to strike him. The noises emitted simultaneously by all the apparitions were frightful, and the fury shown was fierce. Anthony, pummeled and goaded, felt even more severe pain in his body, yet he lay there fearless. (*The Life of St. Anthony*, No. 9, 27ff.)

Notice the last word "fearless," hinting that Anthony has now passed beyond the dimension of fear. The text continues:

> But he was all the more alert in spirit. He groaned because of the pain that racked his body, but his mind was master of the situation. And to mock them, he said, "If you had any power, it would have been enough for just one of you to come. You are just trying to scare me out of my wits. If you have received power against me, come at me. If you cannot, why excite yourselves to no purpose?" After many ruses, the demons gnashed their teeth against him because they were only fooling themselves and not him. The Lord was not forgetful of Anthony's struggle, but came to help him. For Anthony looked up and saw, as it were, the roof opening and a beam of light coming down to him. The demons suddenly were gone. The pain in his body ceased. The building was restored to its former condition. Anthony,

perceiving that help had come, breathed more freely and felt relieved of his
pains. (*The Life of St. Anthony*, No. 9, 27ff.)

He asked the vision the inevitable question that arises in such circumstances:

Where were *you*? Why did you not appear at the beginning to stop my pains?
And a voice came to him, "Anthony, I was right here, but I waited to see
you in action. And now because you held out and did not surrender, I will
always be your helper and I will make you renowned everywhere. (*The Life
of St. Anthony*, No. 10, 28)

The last line is reminiscent of the promises God made to Abraham after he came
through his great trial of faith on Mount Horeb.

Hearing this, Anthony rose in prayer. He was so strengthened that he felt his
body more vigorous than before. He was at this time about thirty-five years
of age. (*The Life of St. Anthony*, No. 10, 28)

The question and the Lord's answer linger in my mind with a certain uneasiness.
Is the answer "I was right here watching to see you in action" convincing? Why
could God not have come a little sooner, as Anthony suggested? Anyone in straits
such as Anthony was in would feel completely abandoned by God. Where was
God's infinite compassion? He did not seem to provide any help at all.

In the presence of immense suffering, any attempt to answer on God's behalf
sounds like a platitude. In place of an answer, I offer this parable based on a story
by Gerald Heard called "Dryness and the Dark Night":[2]

A certain scientist devoted his life to developing a strain of butterfly that would
be the most beautiful combination of colors ever seen on this planet. After years of
experimentation, he was certain that he had a cocoon that would produce his ge-
netic masterpiece. On the day that the butterfly was expected to emerge, he gathered together his entire staff. All waited breathlessly as the creature began to work
its way out of the cocoon. It disengaged its right wing, its body, and most of its left
wing. Just as the staff were ready to cheer and pass the champagne and cigars, they
saw with horror that the extremity of the left wing of the butterfly was stuck in the
mouth of the cocoon. The creature was desperately flapping its other wing to free
itself. As it labored, it grew more and more exhausted. Each new effort seemed
more difficult, and the intervals between efforts grew longer. At last the scientist,
unable to bear the tension, took a scalpel and cut a tiny section from the mouth of
the cocoon. With one final burst of strength, the butterfly fell free onto the labora-
tory table. Everybody cheered and reached for the cigars and the champagne. Then

silence again descended on the room. Although the butterfly was free, it could not fly . . .

The struggle to escape from the cocoon is nature's way of forcing blood to the extremities of a butterfly's wings so that when it emerges from the cocoon it can enjoy its new life and fly to its heart's content. In seeking to save the creature's life, the scientist had truncated its capacity to function. A butterfly that cannot fly is a contradiction in terms.

This is a mistake that God is not going to make. The image of God watching Anthony has to be understood. God holds back his infinite mercy from rushing to the rescue when we are in temptation and difficulties. He will not actively intervene because the struggle is opening and preparing every recess of our being for the divine energy of grace. God is transforming us so that we can enjoy the divine life to the full once it has been established. If the divine help comes too soon, before the work of purification and healing has been accomplished, it may frustrate our ultimate ability to live the divine life.

Anthony's battles with the devil were not yet over. Athanasius's text continues, "On the next day, Anthony went out inspired with an even greater zeal for the service of God." He headed for the desert. In the fourth century, the desert was believed to be the stronghold of the devil, his military-industrial complex, so to speak, where he devised projects to destroy lives, communities, and nations, world-wide.

Thus, Anthony marched into the devil's concentration of power. It is a mistake to think of monastic life as an escape from the world. Monasticism is the aggressive action of persons who struggle with the "evil powers in high places" that Paul writes about, in order to wrench from them their insidious ascendancy over the human family. The ascesis of solitude is not kindergarten; it is postgraduate work in the spiritual journey. Significantly, Anthony lodged in an abandoned fort, symbol of the devil's ammunition dump. As he went in, the reptiles that were living there went out as fast as they could. Anthony again asked his friend to lock him in, and there he stayed, seeing no one and continuously doing battle with the demons.

He spent the next twenty years in the fort. His friends sometimes came and, listening at the door, thought there was a riot going on inside. The demons, however, were not getting the better of Anthony; they were trying to escape from him! Anthony prayed various verses from the psalms to force them to relinquish their grip over the people they were oppressing. He loved such verses as, "Let God arise and his enemies be scattered. As the smoke vanishes, so let them vanish away," and, "All nations compassed me about. In the name of the Lord, I drove them off."

When Anthony was fifty-five years of age, his friends tore down the door of the fort. Anthony took this as the call of God to emerge from his solitude.

Anthony came forth as out of a shrine, as one initiated into the sacred mysteries and filled with the Spirit of God. When his friends saw him, they were astonished that his body had kept its former appearance. He was neither fat from want of exercise, nor emaciated from fasting and struggles. He was the same man they had known before his retirement. Again the state of his soul was pure for it was neither contracted by grief, nor dissipated by pleasure, nor pervaded by jollity. He was not embarrassed when he saw the crowd, nor was he elated at seeing so many there to receive him. He had himself completely under control, a man guided by reason and stable in his character. He exhorted all to prefer nothing in the world to the love of Christ. (*The Life of St. Anthony*, No. 14, 32)

The desert that had once belonged to the demons now became a place of peace. In a decade it was filled with thousands of monks.

Anthony's experience of the spiritual journey is a classic example of how the divine action works in our lives. When he reacted vigorously against the devil's first temptation to abandon the spiritual journey and return to a worldly life, he entered the night of sense, during which time the divine action laid to rest the unconscious motivation of his false self. Having enjoyed a plateau in which he worked his newfound freedom into ordinary daily life and his relationships, he moved into a further confrontation with the devil, which was at the same time a radical letting go of the influence of his cultural conditioning insofar as it was an obstacle to following Christ. John of the Cross calls this purification the night of spirit, a transitional period that will be considered more fully in chapter fifteen. From this decisive trial, he entered the transforming union.

13

THE FRUITS OF THE
NIGHT OF SENSE

■

THE NIGHT OF SENSE is about dismantling our immature programs for happiness, which can't possibly work in adult life. Little do we realize when we embark on the spiritual journey that our first fervor is itself immature and under the influence of these programs; it will have some growing up to do.

Thus, at some point in our journey, a pervasive sense of God's absence begins to manifest itself during prayer and spreads into other areas of one's life. This is actually the beginning of a deeper union with Christ. Most of us, however, do not experience it that way. When the biblical desert opens up within us, we worry that something is going wrong in our relationship with God.

In the night of sense, we are called to make the transition from superficial spiritual nourishment to the solid food of pure faith. The sensible consolations enjoyed during prayer, liturgy, or *lectio divina* may be compared to junk food. We are now being served much more substantial food, the dry bread of faith. The baby weaned from its mother's breast does not like the privation of its customary nourishment, but solid food will lead to more substantial growth. Similarly, God as divine mother pushes us away from the breasts of consolation so that we can adjust to the pure food of faith that will strengthen us for the rugged terrain of the spiritual journey.

The night of sense heals the malformations that took place in growing from childhood to early adolescence when we felt that our basic needs were not being met and we responded with insatiable compensatory demands. We not only experience dryness in our relationship with God, but also a lack of satisfaction in all the areas in which we previously sought happiness. When the emotional programs dry out and begin to crumble, they make a last stand to resist their demise.

The principal fruit of the night of sense is humility, which enables us to assume our places as members of the human family, enduring the ups and downs of the human condition like everybody else. Actually, God is giving us more protection than before, though in secret.

The night of sense is designed to bring about the dismantling of the emotional programs and the death of the false self. The fruit of this purifying process is the freedom to decide what to do, without interference from the compulsions and fixations of the false self. It took constant effort to keep ourselves in some semblance of peace when we were seeking fantastic goals that were constantly frustrated, setting off the afflictive emotions of anger, grief, fear, pride, lust, greed, jealousy, and the other capital sins. As the false self diminishes and trust in God increases in the night of sense, our energies can be put to better purposes.

The night of sense is doing more than dismantling the false self. In relaxing our compulsions and habitual ways of overreacting, it also releases the energies of the unconscious. This is particularly true if our journey is grounded in the regular practice of contemplative prayer by a receptive method such as Centering Prayer. Through the process of resting in God, beyond thoughts, feeling, associations, and commentaries, we are moving from the level of our physical faculties and their perceptions to the level of spiritual faculties and their intuitions, and opening to the divine presence at a deeper level still. This brings even greater rest. And this rest, in turn, loosens up the material in the unconscious that the defense mechanisms of early childhood have previously kept out of our awareness.

The energies of the unconscious may rise to awareness in either a positive or a negative way. Psychic powers and spiritual consolations generally produce positive emotions. Negative emotions arise when the dark sides of our personalities and our mixed motivations thrust themselves into our awareness, alerting us to the damage that the false self is doing.

A number of seekers have experienced a sudden upsurge of powerful energy without being adequately prepared for it. In some cases it was triggered by a mantra or set of breathing exercises specifically designed to loosen up the energies of the unconscious. If we experience spiritual consolation, psychic powers, or charismatic gifts before the purification of pride in the night of sense, we could be overwhelmed by feelings of self-exaltation; if the dark sides of our personalities arise, we could be submerged in the depths of discouragement. The antidote for this naïveté is sound spiritual teaching. All the great spiritual traditions of the world religions require both devotion to God and the service of others as two essential practices for beginners. For the Christian, devotion and dedication to God are cultivated in the practice of *lectio divina* (a sacred, attentive listening to the word of God through scripture), liturgy, and prayer. We grow in the service of others through the fulfillment of the duties of our state of life, whatever these may be. The building up of these two banks, as it were, creates a safe channel for the emergence of the positive and negative contents of the unconscious. It prepares us to benefit from the various forms of self-knowledge revealed by the night of sense and avoids the hazards of repressed material exploding into consciousness before we have established an adequate discipline and the proper attitudes to handle it.

A positive benefit derived from the energies arising from the unconscious is the development of the intuitive level of consciousness. According to Ken Wilber's model (see Appendix III), this level transcends even the mental egoic and opens up a new perspective on all reality. The human brain has potentialities that are still waiting to be actualized. If we can believe the experience of many mystics, the present level of human consciousness is the door to higher states of consciousness. In their view, our human potentialities are only fully realized in the transforming union.

In mythic membership consciousness, we absorb unquestioningly the values of parents, nation, race, and early religious education. These unquestioned assumptions become our world view, or the myth in which we live. In the night of sense, these presuppositions are challenged, though not as deeply as they will be in the night of spirit. Like the parables of Jesus, the night of sense shakes the ground on which we had felt secure and opens us to new ways of seeing reality.

At each level of human development, God offers himself to us just as we are. Thus, he is the typhonic God of primitive peoples and children, the monotheistic God of mythic membership consciousness, and the God of infinite concern for the whole human family revealed in the gospel. Each of us, in growing up, relates to God on each of these levels.

In the night of sense, our primitive ideas of God are challenged. The latter may include prejudices imposed on us in early childhood. If God was presented as a bogeyman, policeman, or implacable judge, the emotional overtones of these frightening images may remain deeply ingrained. They are emotional judgments, not true judgments, and need to be corrected. The night of sense enables us to face our distorted views of God and to lay them aside. Then we are free to relate to God as he is and to use the immense energy that this freedom releases to relate to other people with respect and love.

One way God deals with the limited ways we have of relating to him is by reducing our concepts of him to silence. As resting in God in contemplative prayer becomes habitual, we spontaneously disidentify with our emotional programs for happiness and our cultural conditioning. Already we are meeting God at a deeper level. In time we will grow from a reflective relationship with God to one of communion. The latter is a being-to-being, presence-to-presence relationship, which is the knowledge of God in pure faith.

The night of sense brings the nature of commitment into clear focus. When we take to heart Jesus' words, "Follow me," he invites us into his friendship. Friendship always involves commitment to the other person. This is the disposition that enabled Anthony to get through all his temptations and to reach transforming union.

His basic means were always the same: commitment to the spiritual journey, the practice of constant prayer, and trust that God would give him the strength to persevere.

The apparent absences of God, interior purification, and the trials of daily life challenge our commitment. In our time, models of commitment are few. People move from job to job; marriages do not last; careers end prematurely; religious life and vows of celibacy are not taken as seriously as they used to be. The supports that once helped or forced people to remain in their commitments have diminished through the cultural revolution of modern times. Whatever good has come from these social developments, the models of commitment available in earlier times have largely disappeared, at least in the Western world.

Most young married couples do not have the remotest idea of what they are getting into at the times of their weddings. When difficulties arise, they often decide that they were not cut out for each other and call it quits. They go through heart-rending divorces and seek other mates, only to repeat the same horrendous process. Of course, there are some committed relationships that do die or become harmful. Other relationships are dominated by the romantic side alone and disintegrate in the face of the demands of love that require self-sacrifice.

Actually, difficulties arise whenever a committed relationship is succeeding. Love makes you vulnerable. When you feel loved by God or by another person, you do not have to be self-protective. Your defenses relax and the dark side of your personality arises, not only into consciousness, but also into your behavior, to the dismay, perhaps, of your spouse. Hopefully, your spouse is having similar experiences. One purpose of the sacrament of marriage is to provide the grace to process each other's dark side. In this way, marriage becomes a school of purification and transformation. When a couple bears with each other's failures, dark sides, and weaknesses, they minister the love of God to each other. Human love is the symbol of God's love in the sacrament of marriage and communicates it to the other person. The commitment to marriage enables one to get through the process of self-knowledge and to reap the benefit of this enlightenment.

Suppose that you become aware that your motives for entering marriage were defective. If you are a man, maybe you were looking for the mamma that you never had or for a replica of the mamma you *did* have and saw in this capable person someone who would take care of all your needs: do the wash, put food on the table every day, and dry your tears. Suddenly, it dawns on you, precisely because of your progress in self-knowledge, that this was not the right motive to marry in the first place. So the thought comes, "The only way to gain my freedom is to sever this relationship completely." But the commitment suggests, "Why not bring your new insight back into the relationship and see if it can now work?" This is not always possible because the patterns of dependency may be too deeply ingrained. Separating may indeed be necessary when a serious mistake is made, but the commitment inclines us first to try to bring the new insight into the relationship.

No one enters a commitment, including the religious life or priesthood, with completely pure motives. Thus, it is not so much the motives we had in entering, but the motives we have for persevering that actually count the most.

God is calling us in the night of sense to take responsibility for ourselves and for our personal response to Christ's invitation to follow him. This includes our response to the people we live with and, ultimately, to the whole human family.

As the night of sense gradually turns to dust all our previous sources of strength and consolation, the temptation to give up is enormous. "This journey can't be for me. I have a family to raise, a professional life to lead. I can't deal with all this painful negativity that keeps rising within me." When dryness and temptation are prolonged, everything in us wants to call a halt to the spiritual journey and hopes we never have to start again. If we walk away from our commitment to the journey, the false self goes with us. Wherever we go, we will have to face it again under other circumstances. Commitment opposes this regressive instinct, saying, "I won't give up. I resolve for the love of Christ to go through the desert of purification no matter what happens." This is the determination that enables the night of sense to complete its work.

14

THE STAGES OF
CONTEMPLATIVE PRAYER

■

IN THE NIGHT OF SENSE, God is feeding us from within rather than engaging our faculties through the external senses, memory, imagination, and reason. In contemplative prayer these faculties are at rest so that our intuitive faculties, the passive intellect, and the will-to-God, may access the "still point," the place where our personal identity is rooted in God as an abiding presence. The divine presence has always been with us, but we think it is absent. That thought is the monumental illusion of the human condition. The spiritual journey is designed to heal it.

We translate dryness in prayer as God's absence until we perceive that God is communicating with us at a deeper level. Silence is God's first language; everything else is a poor translation. In order to hear that language, we must learn to be still and to rest in God. One of the signs of the night of sense is an inclination for solitude and silence; to be alone with God, even though we do not find any satisfaction in it. The vague but felt need for God comes from the contemplative gifts of the Spirit, especially the gift of knowledge, which relativizes all other goods and announces the onset of the night of sense.

The attraction to interior silence is the result of the food of pure faith that God is communicating, not to the senses or to reason, but to our intuitive faculties. At first we do not know what to do with this dryness; hence, the disconcerting reactions that make us want to give up the whole process of prayer in favor of relaxation or some form of engrossing work. As we accustom ourselves to the exercise of pure faith, however, we begin to experience its fruits: trust in God and humility. The latter manifests itself in an unwillingness to judge others. Our own good deeds appear so mixed with selfish motivations that we would be happy if no one would ever bring them up again. We are painfully aware of the fact that all our actions are shot through with selfishness and that, try as we may, we cannot do much about it.

At this point, the spiritual journey may begin to unfold along the lines that the sixteenth-century Spanish mystic Saint Teresa of Avila described in *The Interior Cas-*

tle. She presented the spiritual journey from the perspective of the stages of prayer. This is indeed the way that many people experience the journey. There is an alternative, but let us look first at Teresa's model.

The first grace that emerges as the night of sense nears its completion is a mysterious awakening, as if a breath of fresh air has entered one's spirit. A whiff of the divine perfume escapes from God's presence at the inmost center of our being and comes within range of our spiritual faculties. Teresa of Avila calls this grace "infused recollection." This term is confusing because every kind of prayer has an infused element—i.e., it is given to us; we do not manufacture it. God was present in the night of sense, but we had not recognized his presence and thought he was absent. Now the former dryness seems to have a delicious spiritual savor that attracts us toward the center of our being. Spiritual consolation does not come through the external senses; it wells up from a source deep within. It may overflow into the senses like a fountain, but the source of the water does not spring from sense or rational activity.

Infused recollection does not absorb us in such a way that we cannot resist; we can get up and walk away. Normally, the feeling is so pleasant that we want to prolong it. This grace may expand into the prayer of quiet in which the will is absorbed in God. The faculties of memory and imagination are free to roam around and often play with images and memories in order to keep themselves occupied. The will feels persecuted by their unwanted activity. Teresa says that we should regard the wanderings of memory and imagination as "the ravings of a madman," and pay no attention to them. Thus, we may experience a bombardment of thoughts that we do not want, while at the same time our will is attending to the presence of God, whether through an undifferentiated sense of unity or a more personal attention to one or another of the Divine Persons.

The "prayer of quiet," the next stage, is more absorbing than infused recollection. In this state the divine action seems to grasp the will in a spiritual embrace. The will could break away but does not want to. In fact, it easily becomes attached to the feeling of consolation and wants to prolong the time of prayer. When prayer is delightful, we want more of it. Thus we may fall into the trap of spiritual gluttony and try to squeeze as much pleasure as we can out of this God who has suddenly become so bountiful.

If the prayer of quiet moves to a yet deeper level, the imagination and memory are temporarily suspended. God, as it were, calls these faculties to himself. They hear the sound of his voice and are enchanted by it; they gather around and sit still to listen. While they are quiet, the will enjoys the divine presence. In that state God can communicate more of his gifts because there is no resistance or commentary on our side. This is the "prayer of union."

In all these states, we are aware of the presence of something real, but it is not a form, image, or concept. The divine presence may arise in various ways. It can come suddenly or overtake us gradually. It may seem to descend from above or arise from below. It may envelop us like a luminous cloud or well up from within. In any case, there is a sense of deep quiet as the imagination and memory grow still. When they are completely still and the will is totally absorbed in God, there is no self-reflection. This is the experience of the "prayer of full union" in which all the faculties are motionless and rest in God.

John of the Cross also describes this process, but indicates that there is another path, which he calls the path of pure faith. Both paths move toward the goal of transforming union, which is the abiding sense of rootedness in the divine presence within. John refers to the path of pure faith as a "hidden ladder." This is the path that people on the spiritual journey experience most of the time. They have the attraction for interior prayer, but do not experience the levels of absorption described by Teresa. At times they are aware that their will is resting in God, but their habitual experience is dryness accompanied by endless wanderings of the imagination. Even when the night of sense is far advanced, their prayer may continue without any noticeable change.

Certain spiritual writers have identified what might be called the "felt" experience of God with contemplative prayer to such an extent that when it is absent they presume that contemplation is also absent. John of the Cross, as well as experience, disproves this theory. There is an exuberant approach to divine union that is full of light, and there is an approach that is very dark. In other words, we may be invited to the front entrance of the interior castle, or we may be directed to the service entrance. We may be invited to climb the front stairs, or we may be led up the back stairs. The back stairs correspond to the hidden ladder of John of the Cross. Which way is better? Nobody knows. What is certain is that both paths lead to transforming union. God as he is in himself can be fully accessed only by pure faith. The purification of faith and love, not spiritual consolation, leads to transforming union.

Transforming union is a restructuring of consciousness, not an experience or set of experiences. In the course of this restructuring, as we shall see in chapter sixteen, the presence of God becomes a kind of fourth dimension to the three-dimensional world in which we have been living. In the light of transforming union, therefore, the most important element in contemplative prayer is the practice itself, not its psychological content. If we fully grasped this truth, it would make the spiritual journey much easier. At the beginning of the journey, our expectations of what should happen and our commentaries about what is happening are the causes of most of our anxiety and distress.

For those enjoying the path of exuberant mysticism, as well for those on the hidden ladder, there comes the further purification of the night of spirit. Even in the experience of the unfolding stages of prayer, the false self is at work, subtly transferring its worldly desires for satisfaction to the good things that are now available on the spiritual path. This last assertion is not meant to denigrate the value of the consolations of contemplative prayer. Some people need them, especially those who have been severely damaged in childhood. God bends over, caresses, and virtually makes love to people who have been deeply hurt, in order to convince them that it is all right to enjoy pleasures that they thought they should not enjoy, or were taught that they should not enjoy. God invites them to review the emotional judgments of childhood and to accept the good things of life with grateful hearts. Gratitude is an essential disposition in the spiritual journey.

The experience of God's love enables us to understand emotionally where true values are to be found. When we taste the goodness of God and experience the humility that arises spontaneously from that relationship, the programs glorified by the false self and our cultural conditioning diminish in size and no longer exercise the fascination that used to hold them in place.

15

THE NIGHT OF SPIRIT

■

AS HAVE SEEN, the night of sense virtually immobilizes the false self. Its residue, however, is still lingering in our spiritual faculties and manifests itself by the secret satisfaction that we find in ourselves as the recipients of God's favors or of a special vocation. It is all very well to say, "I owe everything to God." But there may still be a subtle inclination that says, "After all, he did give these gifts to *me!*" The tendency to possess even on the spiritual level requires purification. This is the work of the night of spirit.

The night of spirit, the beginning of divine union according to John of the Cross, is a further transitional stage involving a more intimate purification. John teaches that even during the experience of exuberant mysticism there are "alarms." We become aware that there are some rough spots in the unconscious that have not been corrected by the night of sense, such as habitual distractedness of mind, the lingering effects of cultural conditioning, and spiritual pride. The night of spirit is designed to free us from the residue of the false self in the unconscious and thus to prepare us for transforming union.

When the night of spirit begins, all "felt" mystical experiences of God subside and disappear, leaving persons who have been led by the path of exuberant mysticism in a state of intense longing to have them back. In proportion to the spiritual consolations that these persons previously received, they now experience the pain of privation. Perhaps the night of spirit is less painful for those who are led by the hidden ladder since they do not enjoy much, if any, of God's felt presence. In any case, the night of spirit is essential for the final movement into divine union. Without that purification, the consequences of the false self are not completely erased, and there is danger of falling into the spiritual archetypes that may arise out of the unconscious.

Those who have been led by the path of exuberant mysticism are especially susceptible to these subtle temptations. They may experience psychic or spiritual gifts and become gifted teachers or charismatic leaders. But the very gifts that attract people to them and to their teaching subtly and insidiously incline them toward a glamorous self-image. Precisely because of their spiritual attainments, the temptation arises to identify with the role of prophet, wonderworker, enlightened teacher, martyr, victim, charismatic leader—in short, God's gift to humanity. The night of spirit reduces such temptations to zero because, through its purifying action, we experience ourselves as capable of every evil. Not that we are likely to commit evil deeds, but we feel completely dependent on God in order to avoid personal sin or the habitual hangups of the false self that lead to it.

This kind of temptation is important to understand in our time when a lot of publicity is given to psychic gifts such as out-of-body experiences, channeling, levitation, control of bodily functions, various forms of healing, prophecy, and many others. Spiritually gifted people may also be empowered to impart spiritual experiences to others. The latter takes place in the charismatic renewal in the phenomenon called "slaying in the Spirit." Unfortunately, if enlightenment is only partial, success and adulation may go to some people's heads; then the temptation to identify with a particular idealized self-image takes over, and they are back in the grip of the false self.

Service is the hallmark of one who is sent by God. The true prophet, martyr, spiritual leader, or teacher does not try to dominate others. Notice how often Jesus emphasized that he was sent by his Father and that he did nothing of himself: "He can do only what he sees the Father doing" (John 5:19). His chief argument against every accusation was, "My Father is at work until now, and I am at work as well" (John 8:16).

In a ministry inspired by God, one receives a particular call and has to exercise it on God's terms. That means that the ministry will be characterized, as it was for Jesus, by opposition, rejection, failure, disappointment, persecution, and perhaps death. Jesus did not invoke his psychic powers or his prerogatives as the Son of God to defend himself or his teaching. He allowed himself to experience the utmost suffering and rejection as part of being sent, thus manifesting the inner nature of Ultimate Reality as infinite compassion and forgiveness. His death and resurrection put an enormous question mark in front of everything the false self looks upon as happiness or success.

The spiritual journey is not a success story, but a series of diminutions of self. Saint Bernard of Clairvaux, the twelfth-century Cistercian abbot, taught that humiliation is the path to humility. In those who have a low self-image, there may be some confusion between humility and the neurotic tendency to put oneself down. The latter, of course, is not humility. The language of humility can be misunderstood. Basically, it is the experiential awareness, born of the divine light, that without God's protection we are capable of every sin. The night of the spirit is an intensive course in humility.

There are five significant fruits of the night of spirit. The first is freedom from the temptation to assume a glamorous role because of our spiritual gifts or charisms. It purifies the secret satisfaction of being chosen as the recipient of God's special gifts. It allows God to treat us like everyone else and allows us to find his special love in that treatment, rather than in experiences that single us out from the rest of humanity. Christ represented us on the cross and identified with the consequences of sin, the chief of which is the sense of abandonment by God. It is in the sacrifice of his divine prerogatives that he became the savior of the world and entered into the fullness of his glory, not by earthly success of by taking to himself a role that was not given to him.

A second fruit of the night of spirit is freedom from the domination of any emotion. Characteristically, we are pushed around by emotions and by our tendency to overidentify with them, and we find ourselves forever trying to get what they want or to get away from what they do not want. The night of spirit gradually frees us from the last traces of domination by emotional swings or moods. This takes place not by repressing or unduly suppressing unwanted emotions by sheer willpower, but by accepting and integrating them into the rational and intuitive parts of our nature. The emotions will then serve and support the decisions of reason and will, which is their natural purpose. The integration of our emotional life with reason and faith and the subjection of our whole being to God constitute Saint Thomas Aquinas's definition of human happiness. In his view, human beings were meant to act in harmony with their nature and to enjoy doing so. This harmonious state is substantially restored in the night of spirit by extinguishing the last traces of our subjection to the emotional programs for happiness in the spiritual part of our nature. As for the emotional and sense levels, they were laid to rest in the night of sense.

A third fruit of the night of spirit is the purification of our idea of God, the God of our childhood or the God worshipped by the particular group to which we belong. The God we used to know no longer seems to care about us. In addition, God even purifies the idea of him that we developed through the experience of close union enjoyed during the period of exuberant mysticism (if that was our path). God reveals himself in the night of spirit in a vastly superior way—as infinite, incomprehensible, and ineffable—the way that he appeared to Moses on Mount Sinai and to Elijah on Mount Horeb. No one can describe the experience of pure faith. We know only that an immense and unnameable energy is welling up inside. This immense energy may be experienced by some as impersonal, although it certainly treats us in a personal way.

A fourth fruit of the night of spirit is the purification of what are traditionally known as the "theological virtues," which are faith, hope, and love. In the purification of faith from human props, we may experience rejection by the group from whom we have been drawing our human, religious, or spiritual identity. There may be a breakup with our spiritual director or with people on whom we depended for spiritual development and for meaning in life. Our idea of the spiritual journey and the means we should use to pursue it, and our ideas of our vocations, the Church, Jesus Christ—even God himself—may be shattered. This experience is reflected in the great personages of scripture like Job, Moses, Joseph, Mary, and Jesus himself. Jesus' life and teaching were built on his personal union with the Father, and yet, in his last moments, he seems to have experienced that relationship as a gigantic question mark. "My God, my God, why have you forsaken me?" Job, according to the biblical story, was a model of perfection and admired by everyone in his time. In the course of a few days, his property, family, reputation, and even his bodily health were swept away. What kind of God is this who permits or sends such tragedy into the lives of his friends? Job complained bitterly about his pitiful condition. But would he have learned who God is unless he had gone through the shattering experiences that brought to an end his naive conception of how God functions? The greatest fruit of the night of spirit is the disposition that is willing to accept God on his own terms. As a result, one allows God to be God without knowing who or what that is.

Total self-surrender and abandonment grow mightily, though in a manner hidden from us, in the night of spirit. The divine light is so pure that it is imperceptible to any of our faculties. According to John of the Cross, pure faith is a ray of darkness. Since there is no consolation or reassurance from God and since the props on which we used to rely have all been taken away, this surrender may be a moment of existential doubt and dread in the extreme. If we can let God be whoever God is and accept whatever he is doing, an invincible trust emerges. Such trust is not based on our good deeds, roles, or anything else. We simply trust in God's infinite mercy. Mercy of its nature reaches out to weakness and extreme need. We begin to be content with God's infinite mercy. Divine love is infused in the seedbed of total submission and self-surrender and brings us through the night of spirit into the transforming union.

A fifth fruit of the night of spirit is the longing to let go of the selfishness that still lingers in us and to be free of every obstacle that might hinder our growth in divine union. According to John of the Cross, the same fire of divine love that is experienced painfully in the night of spirit becomes gentle and full of love in the transforming union. The "I" of self-centeredness diminishes to a very small "i." The great "I AM" of Exodus looms in its place. Thus, the divine plan is to transform human nature into the divine, not by giving it some special role or exceptional powers, but by enabling it to live ordinary life with extraordinary love.

One final word of caution is in order. While we may talk of the divine "plan" and outline the stages of the spiritual journey as presented by the great teachers of our tradition, the only thing we can be absolutely sure of in the spiritual journey is that whatever we are expecting to happen will not happen. God is not bound by our ideas. Sometimes the night of sense begins at once, sometimes the night of sense and the night of spirit are reversed, and sometimes they take place at the same time. If we have read widely and expect that things are going to proceed according to our understanding, God will reverse the normal order for our benefit. One way or another, we will have to take the leap of trust into the unknown.

16

THE TRANSFORMING UNION

■

THE EXPERIENCE OF THE TRANSFORMING UNION is a way of being in the world that enables us to live daily life with the invincible conviction of continuous union with God. It is a new way of being in the world, a way of transcending everything in the world without leaving it.

In the transforming union, the domination of the emotions ceases. Emotional swings disappear. We are aware that what we thought were emotions were not the emotions as such, but our interpretations of them. The emotions are just as strong as ever and more so, but there is no backwash from them in the sense of lingering feelings or mood swings. The emotions are appropriate responses to the present moment with its specific content. Jesus in anger casting out the money changers is an example of this. When the situation is over, so is the emotional response. As a result, the emotions no longer attract us to sinful activity. We are aware that we could still sin, but there is no stimulation to do so. Freedom from the false self and emotional domination is complete.

The Fathers of the Desert had a word for this experience. They called it "apatheia," which is sometimes taken to mean "indifference." It is rather a tremendous concern for everything that is, but without the emotional involvement characteristic of the false self. We are free to devote ourselves to the needs of others without becoming unduly absorbed in their emotional pain. We are present to people at the deepest level and perceive the presence of Christ suffering in them. We long to share with them something of the inner freedom we have been given, but without anxiety and without trying to change them or to obtain anything from them. We simply have the divine life as sheer gift and offer it to anyone who wants it. The risen life of Christ through the gifts of his Spirit can then suggest what is to be done or not done in incredible detail.

This state of consciousness is not passing, but a permanent awareness that spontaneously envelopes the whole of life. The X-ray eyes of faith, which penetrate through outward appearances, perceive all things in God and God in all things.

Thus the movement from the takeoff point of sacred symbol to spiritual attentiveness, to ever-deepening absorption of the faculties in God, and to the purification of the unconscious terminates in the transforming union. The latter involves a restructuring of consciousness that perceives a new dimension to all reality. We live without the consoling spiritual experiences of the past, but with the mature awareness of a purified faith and love that is open to the divine energy of grace directly and continuously.

Whatever we experience of God, however exalted, is only a radiance of his presence. No experience in this life can be God as he is in himself because God infinitely transcends all categories and experiences. In the transforming union, the energy of faith, trust, and love is constantly being beamed to us whether we experience it or not. The body has been prepared and stabilized by the practice of virtue and the purification of sense and spirit so that it can receive the divine communications uninterruptedly. Divine love can now manifest itself in all our activities, even the most ordinary. The same all-pervasive union is present while walking down the street or brushing one's teeth as in periods of contemplative prayer. External and internal realities are unified because all are equally rooted in God and manifest God. The entire organism is sensitized to all the ways in which the divine presence manifests itself, without mistaking any one of them as the ultimate expression of God's love.

The divine energy in itself is infinite potentiality and actuality. Creatures are localized manifestations of it. If there is no obstacle in us, no false self, we become spiritual transmitters through whom the divine presence as boundless love and compassion communicates itself to others in ever-widening circles of influence.

Transforming union is the ripe fruit of dismantling the false self. As soon as the false self is reduced to zero, transforming union occurs. A nonpossessive attitude toward everything, including ourselves, is established because there is no longer a self-centered "I" to possess anything. That does not mean that we do not use the good things of life, but now they are not ends in themselves but stepping-stones to God's presence. The Spirit's energy filters down from the still point into all the other faculties, purifying the external senses so that they can perceive God's presence and action in every sense experience. What is true, beautiful, and good in everything that exists becomes transparent.

Transforming union can be manifested in various ways: patience in illness and external trials, as in Job; intense solitude, as in the case of Anthony; demanding ministries. But it has to express itself in a more than ordinary way because the energy for good that divine union releases is tremendous. From particle physics we have a description of what occurs when a particle returns to the wave pattern from which it came. The power of the wave is far greater than the localized particle. It was from his movement into the very heart of the divine love that Anthony drew his strength.

We may think of God as the Heavenly King dominating all creation, and of course he is in charge of everything. Notice, however, that he exercises that authority by serving creation all the time. He created and nurtures this planet with exquisite care, providing air, water, food, and all kinds of natural resources, all day long. Service without seeking any return characterizes the Ultimate Reality. Those in transforming union are beginning to find that out. Hence, they too become servants, not dominators.

Transforming union is the goal of the first part of the Christian spiritual journey. Despite its rarity, it should be regarded as the normal Christian life. We must then translate all our relationships—with God, ourselves, other people, and the cosmos—into this new perspective and way of being in the world. The principal means of reaching transforming union is the personal love of Christ. The next part of the journey is to learn the meaning of Jesus' words, "The Father and I are one" (John 10:30), and the consequences of his prayer, "That they may be one in us" (John 17:21).

17

THE FIRST FOUR BEATITUDES

■

THE BEATITUDES are the quintessence of the teaching of Jesus. They represent his comprehensive approach to happiness. They are the outpouring of the Spirit in the Pentecostal grace. We have within us, by virtue of baptism, the seven gifts of the Spirit: reverence, piety, knowledge, fortitude, counsel, understanding, and wisdom. These gifts are activated by dismantling the straitjacket of the false self so that the communication of the divine light and love may be received with ever-increasing clarity and fullness.

The beatitudes are wisdom sayings that express the disposition appropriate to each level of consciousness. They highlight both the goodness and the limitations of each stage of development. The object of the spiritual journey is the healing of body, mind, and spirit. Jesus said, "The healthy do not need a doctor; sick people do. I have not come to invite the self-righteous to a change of heart, but sinners" (Luke 5:31-33). A physician does not heal people by killing them. Similarly, the Spirit does not heal the wounds of early childhood and the emotional programs for happiness by destroying the instincts that gave rise to them. Rather, whatever was good in the instinctual needs must be preserved and integrated into the unfolding values of the human organism. The biological need for survival is essential to keep going in this world when the going gets tough; only the exaggerations and distortions of these instinctual needs are left behind. The grace of the Spirit heals each level of consciousness in order to enable the values proper to each level to contribute to the wholeness of the human organism with all its potentialities.

The first beatitude addresses the level of consciousness that we experienced in coming into the world, the reptilian consciousness, in which there is no awareness of a separate self. The principal focus of reptilian consciousness is food, shelter, survival, and the prompt fulfillment of physical needs. Privations during this period of childhood may later give rise to drives to possess the symbols of security in the culture. "How happy you would be," Jesus says, "if you were poor in spirit," that is, if you put your trust in God rather than in possessions or other symbols of security.

The poor in spirit are those who accept afflictions for God's sake. They are not only the materially poor, but also those who suffer any affliction, whether emotional, mental, or physical, and who accept their situation out of love of God. The poor have a special claim on the kingdom because they literally do not have anything, or if they do have possessions, they are willing to let them go as the needs of others or the will of God may require. The gift of the Spirit called "reverence" empowers the poor to place their trust in God rather than in the symbols of security that the culture provides.

The experience of happiness in the face of destitution, poverty, and affliction is the fruit of accepting what is. By accepting reality, we are free of our predetermined demands and shoulds. It is not just a passive acceptance, however. We may also be asked by God to do something to change, improve, or correct situations, including defending ourselves or others when circumstances call for it.

The part-human, part-animal typhonic consciousness characteristic of the emotional life of the child is addressed by the second and third beatitudes. At this level of consciousness, the drive for affection/esteem and pleasure and the drive for power and control may turn these instinctual needs into centers of motivation that dominate our lives. The beatitude "Happy are those who mourn, for they will be comforted" speaks to the exaggerated demand for affection/esteem and pleasure. The refusal to let go of what is being taken from us creates tension. When we let go of some person, place, or thing that we love, we automatically enter a period of mourning. If we accept the loss of what we loved, we experience freedom from what we formerly depended upon excessively and we enter into a new relationship with it, based on the new freedom that does not try to squeeze absolute happiness from passing pleasures. If we pursue particular pleasures in the name of happiness, we make them into idols. The third beatitude, "Happy are the meek," addresses the drive for power, as if to say, "How happy you would be if you did not want to control situations, other people, or you own life, and if you possessed the freedom to accept insults and injustice without being blown away."

Each one of the three emotional programs develops in the context of a self-consciousness that is increasing without the reassurance of divine union. Each time we move to a further level of self-consciousness, the separate-self sense is enhanced, and we experience a heightened feeling of alienation.

Christian tradition has suggested various disciplines to initiate the healing of the reptilian level of consciousness. As infants we were engrossed by our physical needs: eating, sleeping, being caressed, and having our bodily needs promptly serviced. By deliberately upsetting our habits of eating, sleeping, and daily living through fasting, vigils, and simplifying our lifestyle, we create a space in which to change. A situation of temporary privation can alert us to the fact that we are not as dependent on physical demands as we had thought. Bodily discipline, work in the service of the community, and manual labor develop control over physical impulses. Through such practices we can reduce our overdependency on the prompt fulfillment of our desires for pleasure.

The traditional means of overcoming the drive to control others is the practice of fraternal charity, accepting people as they are without trying to change them, and the service of others through the corporal and spiritual works of mercy: feeding the hungry, visiting the sick and those in prison, and responding to the various forms of physical, mental, and spiritual needs.

Our efforts to practice the dismantling of the emotional programs for happiness and to serve the needs of others attract the movement of the Spirit. It is in response to our efforts that God's passive purifications come to our assistance and take us far beyond anything that we could do alone to free the reptilian and typhonic levels of consciousness from their respective hang-ups.

The mythic membership level of consciousness brings our programs for happiness into contact with the social development that took place from four to eight years of age, during which time we absorbed the value systems of parents, teachers, peer groups, and television programs. A child does not have the use of reason to evaluate these influences, so he absorbs them unquestioningly, and relates his or her emotional programs for happiness to the new social situation. The emotional programs we created to cope with the difficult situations of infancy are now extended into the vast world of social relationships, making those programs far more complex.

The beatitude "Happy are those who hunger and thirst for justice; they will have their fill" addresses overidentification with our social group and frees us from the urgency to be accepted and approved by the group. In order to respond to the invitation of the gospel, we need to go beyond the behavior that may be held in honor or demanded by the particular social group to which we belong. This does not mean that we should reject our country, religion, ethnic roots, or families. While remaining grateful for the good things we have received and loyal to family and social group, we recognize that such loyalty is not an absolute. We try to improve unhealthy or unjust situations in our family or community instead of clinging to a naive loyalty that refuses to see defects or fails to suggest improvements or corrections that should be made. We have the freedom to remain within our tradition or institution, while at the same time working for its renewal. We do what we can to improve family, church, or social situations without demanding results or expecting to see the fruits of our labors. The Spirit gives us courage to make our personal response to Christ, rather than one that is based on what others say, do, or expect.

The beatitudes are directed to the growth of inner freedom. Progress toward inner freedom depends on the firmness of our commitment. The gift of fortitude is reflected in the beatitude "Happy are the meek for they shall inherit the earth." The meek are those who do not want to control anybody or to push other people around, and who are willing to be insulted and set aside without being unduly upset by such opposition. They do not draw their identity from what other people say or think, but from the values of the gospel. The fortitude that belongs to the meek is the fortitude that stands firm in the face of opposition, as Anthony did in the tombs. Thomas Aquinas says that having the patience to hold one's ground requires greater courage than fighting back. This leads to a deeper understanding of the passion of Christ, learned from our own personal struggles with life and not just from an abstract reading of the gospels.

The beatitudes are an invitation to assimilate the values proclaimed by Jesus. We struggle with the difficulties of life, depending on him and believing in his help, without demanding to feel consolation or depending on it. The first four beatitudes correspond to the commandment, "Love your neighbor as yourself." They enable us to graduate from our childish programs once and for all and to move into the freedom to which Jesus invites us. They prepare us for the continuing work of letting go of selfishness and of sensitizing ourselves to the movements of the Spirit, which invite us not only to generous efforts, but also to heroic service of God and other people.

18

THE LAST FOUR BEATITUDES

■

"'HAPPY ARE THE MERCIFUL, mercy will be shown to them" is the beatitude that corresponds to the full reflective self-consciousness of mental egoic consciousness. At this level we become fully human. Our response to life is cooperative, nonjudgmental, and accepting of others. This beatitude fulfills Christ's new commandment, "Love one another as I have loved you" (John 15:12).

The new commandment is much more demanding than the commandment to love one's neighbor as oneself. To love one's neighbor as oneself is to respect the image of God in our neighbor with all the rights which that dignity confers. To love one another as Jesus loves us is to love one another in our humanness—in our individuality and opinionatedness, in personality conflicts and in unbearable situations. It is to continue to show love, no matter what the provocation may be to act otherwise.

The merciful are those whose concern is beginning to expand beyond family and loved ones into the larger community. Their concern ultimately includes the whole human family, past, present, and to come. The ultimate goal of Jesus is to engage us in the redemption of the world. The beatitudes impart the steadfast love of God who makes the sun to shine on the good and the not-so-good, on those who respond and on those who do not respond.

In our time an important aspect of the beatitude of the merciful is to practice compassion toward ourselves. Many people come to self-consciousness with a low self-image and suffer from varying degrees of self-hatred. This disposition is pride in reverse. Instead of reaching out for self-aggrandizement, these people demean themselves because they do not measure up to the idealized image of perfection that their self-image demands. When they fail to meet this impossible standard, pride, not God, says, "You're no good!" They then feel shame for failing to measure up to the grandiose expectations of themselves that their upbringing, culture, or drive to overachieve created.

Most of us have a heavy burden of emotional junk accumulated from early childhood. The body serves as the storehouse for this undigested emotional material. The Spirit initiates the process of healing by evacuating the junk. This takes place as a result of the deep rest of mind and body in contemplative prayer. The energy formerly used up in trying to cope with current emotional stress is now available for growth. The straitjacket of the false self squeezes people into an infinitesimal use of their human potentialities. The beatitudes enable them to expand and to start to access these immense possibilities.

As prayer becomes more intimate, grace reaches down into the depths of our psyche, empowering it to unload the emotional damage and debris of a lifetime. In time we will make the transition from going to God through reason and particular acts of the will to going to him more directly through the intuitive faculties. Then God will relate to us through them instead of through the external senses, memory, imagination, reasoning, and acts of the will. This period of transition may be experienced as a crisis of faith. We are moving from the mental egoic to the intuitive level of consciousness. Once the intuitive level is established, all our relationships change—toward ourselves, God, other people, and the cosmos—and we spend a significant period of time adjusting to this new way of being in the world. The beatitude that corresponds to the intuitive level is the beatitude of the pure of heart and the promise is, "They will see God." They will see him not with their bodily eyes, of course, but with the eyes of the spirit purified by faith.

Purified in the night of sense, faith penetrates beyond appearances to the hidden reality. Rituals, sacraments, nature, art, friendship, and the service of others become transparent, and we access the Mystery that is manifesting itself through each of these symbols or events. Everything begins to speak to us of God. Happiness arises from the perception of God's closeness and our sense of belonging to the universe. The feeling of closeness may be manifested in spiritual experiences such as the stages of "felt" contemplation, as we saw in chapter thirteen. Such experiences may deepen through ever-increasing absorption in God during prayer, and alert us to his presence in daily life, events, and other people.

Having experienced the beatitude of seeing God in ourselves and others, we come to the crisis of trust called the night of spirit, during which the longing for divine union becomes acute. This is the level to which the beatitude of the peacemakers is addressed. Peace, according to the classical definition of Augustine, is the tranquillity of order. The right order of human nature consists in the effective integration of our emotional and rational lives into our intuitive faculties and the surrender of our unified nature to God in love. In divine union, the great "I" of Jesus Christ becomes our "I." Our identity becomes rooted in him rather than in our own interests. If we still have interests, we are ready to give them up at the request of the Spirit, who has become the senior partner, so to speak, of the firm.

Peace is the great gift of Jesus on the day of his resurrection. The peace that Jesus offers is not sentimental. This peace transcends joy and sorrow, hope and despair. This peace is rooted in a way of being that transcends the emotions. We are no longer blown away by the winds of persecution, nor washed away by the floods of tribulation. Our house is built on rock, and the rock is Christ. That rock is strength against every storm. Divine union has become an invincible conviction, a way of being, a fourth dimension to all reality.

Entering into union with God makes one God-like, which is quite different from becoming God. At times spiritual consolation in the states prior to the night of spirit are so fantastic that one feels "as if one were God." John of the Cross says such experiences can be even stronger after the transforming union. However, the tendency of the transforming union as an abiding state is rather to be without extraordinary experiences and to lead ordinary daily life in an unobtrusive way. If one has special gifts, these are exercised in dependence on God. One is completely free of the results and does not draw one's identity from any glamorous role, but is simply, like God, the servant of creation.

The eighth beatitude belongs to a further stage of consciousness, the stage of perfect wisdom. This is the wisdom that finds happiness in persecution. "Be happy," Jesus says in effect, "if people say the worst things they can about you, or when you suffer for the truth, for justice, or for my name. Rejoice. Dance for joy for your reward is very great in heaven." In this extraordinary world view, persecution endured for God is the peak of happiness. Those who have experienced this beatitude have moved beyond self-interest to such a degree that they no longer have a possessive attitude toward themselves. Their identity is rooted in Christ and the unique identity he wants them to have. If their vocation requires suffering, they perceive that they are then serving him more effectively. They not only enter into the peace of Christ but also become sources of the divine life and peace for others. The graced energy received from God, like an everflowing stream, is shared with those with whom they live and far beyond. Through them, God is pouring the divine light, life, and love into the human family.

19

THE ESSENCE OF
CONTEMPLATIVE PRAYER

∎

LET US BEGIN by clarifying what contemplation is not, in order to better understand what it is. Contemplative prayer is not a technique, although it makes use of methods as starting points to awaken spiritual attentiveness. It is not a magic carpet to bliss, a spiritual happy hour, a respectable substitute for mind-changing drugs, self-hypnosis, or a trance state.

Contemplative prayer should not be identified with charismatic gifts. These are enumerated by Paul (1 Cor. 12:7–11): speaking in various languages, interpreting the languages, speaking with knowledge, healing, performing miracles, speaking with wisdom, preaching, discerning spirits, administering, and others. All the charisms, according to Paul, are aimed at encouraging the local Christian community. Their primary purpose is not to benefit or sanctify the one who has them. These gifts do not necessarily indicate either the presence of contemplative prayer or holiness. Hence, our admiration for them should be measured.

Perhaps the most striking of the charisms is resting in the Spirit, formerly called "slaying in the Spirit." It is communicated by an anointing or blessing, or simply by the glance of the healer. Those who receive this gift experience the attraction to rest in God. They may resist or consent. If they consent, their external senses are slightly suspended and they sink to the floor. There is the human tendency, because the experience is so delightful, to want to prolong it by staying on the floor or by going back to the healer for more. It is important in our day, when charismatic gifts are multiplying, that a well-balanced teaching be offered to help people understand the true value of these particular gifts. They are an invitation to begin the spiritual journey, not an invitation to be blissed out as often as possible. The latter is spiritual gluttony.

Many people receive occasional mystical graces that are significant and sometimes very powerful. Since God is present within us, he may reach up and pull us down anytime, or let a wisp of the delicious perfume of his presence escape from his secret place within us. Even people who are not especially religious may have this kind of experience. Ordinary Christian instruction in our time does not usually articulate Christian mystical experience, so when these experiences arise spontaneously, most average Christians cannot understand them or articulate them. We may even be frightened by them. Actually these graces are gilt-edged invitations. Christ is saying, "Follow me"—not in words but through the experience. If we want just to lie on the floor, we might as well take a nap.

Another kind of experience, often mistaken for contemplative prayer, is the realm of psychic gifts or parapsychological phenomena. These are multiplying so much in our time that some anthropologists believe that the human family as a whole is moving from the mental egoic to the intuitive level of consciousness. We are beginning to grasp the fact that the human brain possesses potentialities not commonly tapped or explored, which are simply by-products of the process of human growth. If this energy were well grounded in the body by means of chanting, Taoist or yogic exercises, vigorous walking, moderate jogging, or light work like crafts or gardening, the body itself would normally distribute the increase of energy. If the natural energy gets stuck in the body or nervous system, however, it may manifest itself in psychic or physical phenomena.

The false self is still at work on the intuitive level of consciousness. What the intuitive level provides—and it is a significant growth of the human potential—is new energy. But energy is only energy; it is how we use it that matters. As we have seen, spiritual energies can be used for self-aggrandizement and the domination of people who may be fascinated by unusual gifts. Both charismatic gifts and psychic powers can easily go to one's head if the false self has not first been purified in some significant degree. The night of spirit is a necessary corrective before one can exercise these gifts without the danger of spiritual pride turning it into some form of self-exaltation.

Let us now look at mystical phenomena. These are psychic phenomena that are inspired by the divine presence and action, such as bodily ecstasies, locutions (words spoken externally, in the imagination, or in the spirit), and external or internal visions. The apparitions of Lourdes and Fatima, insofar as they are authentic, are probably charisms designed to encourage the Christian people in times of disaster, war, and persecution. They are a call to repentance and prayer.

In the Hindu tradition, there are over a hundred *siddhis* or psychic powers listed by Patanjali, a near contemporary of Jesus. These powers are meant to be integrated into the unfolding levels of consciousness. If one gets stuck at any stage, however spiritual, and does not continue to grow, the gifts proper to that stage may stagnate. Special gifts that started out as very beneficial can then become harmful, both for oneself if one falls into spiritual pride, and for others if one tries to exploit them for the sake of personal gratification.

One of the great levitators of all time was Saint Joseph of Cupertino, a seventeenth-century Capuchin. At a certain period in his spiritual development, Joseph was experiencing the exuberant mysticism we described earlier. He was so much in love with God that when he heard the name of Jesus he would frequently rise into the air. He sometimes rose not just a few feet like most levitators, but right up to the ceiling. For the friars trying to chant the divine office in choir, this became a problem. The superiors began to take a dim view of Joseph's gift. However, he was such an exemplary religious that they remained silent and waited to see what might develop. One day a huge cross weighing half a ton arrived at the monastery to be set in place on top of the church steeple. Derricks had not been invented, and the scaffolding was found to be defective. It was too dangerous to lug the cross to the top of the steeple. While the friars stood around wringing their hands, Joseph felt inspired by the Spirit to do the job. Letting out a little cry as he lifted off, he grabbed the huge cross, flew to the top of the steeple, and set it in place. Then he gently descended to earth. It is also recorded that when Joseph was talking with other friars and the name of Jesus was mentioned, his heart would at times be so smitten by divine love that he would interiorly melt into God. Without realizing what he was doing, he would grab the other friar and they both would rise. This was too much for the superiors. They ordered Joseph to stop levitating. He indicated that it was not in his power to resist this upward movement when it came over him, but they insisted. Since he was a very obedient religious, he kept trying to resist the upward urge. We are told that Joseph went into a "depression." Was this a euphemism for the night of spirit which sometimes manifests similar symptoms? If so, it was the experience of the night of spirit that transformed him, not levitation.

Parapsychological phenomena are only by-products of contemplation, not the essence of it. No manufacturer goes into business for the sake of by-products. If we give psychic or spiritual by-products too much emphasis, we are making a mistake; they can even become a hindrance to the spiritual journey if we have a conscious or unconscious attachment to them. It is only after the night of spirit has done its work that the secret satisfaction of being a specially chosen soul is finally reduced to zero.

In our time, spiritual guides are needed who are thoroughly familiar with the Christian contemplative tradition, the stages of prayer, and the traps along the way, so that they can encourage people who are entering the dark nights of sense. The number of such people is constantly increasing. They need the guidance that can come only from someone who has already had some experience of contemplative prayer. They need the warnings that come from spiritual wisdom about not making too much of psychic or mystical phenomena. One cannot live on the frosting of a cake; one needs the solid food of pure faith. The essence of contemplative prayer is not the way of external or internal phenomena, but the way of pure faith. This is the narrow door that leads to life.

The tendency to identify contemplative prayer with felt experience is very deeply ingrained in us, however—and, unfortunately, it keeps getting reinforced. There has been a tendency among spiritual writers in recent centuries to identify contemplation with the felt presence of God or the unfolding of the spiritual senses—the sensation, in prayer, of experiencing God's presence within as directly as experiencing the objects of the senses of smell, touch, and taste. In textbooks dealing with spiritual theology, we find the assumption, either stated or presupposed, that contemplation must be felt to be real.

Many persons on the contemplative path, including cloistered religious, are committed to the practice of contemplative prayer and yet have never experienced the inflow of divine grace according to the pattern laid out by Teresa of Avila and other mystics. But does that make them any less contemplatives? Ruth Burrows in her book *Guidelines for Mystical Prayer*[1] describes two nuns whom she knew intimately. One was a sister in a Carmelite convent; the other was an active religious with a busy and hectic ministry in the world. The active sister was the exuberant mystic. The other sister was the typical plodding, faithful, obedient religious who practiced contemplative prayer day after day for thirty or forty years, experiencing it most of the time as drudgery, boredom, and an endless bombardment of unwanted thoughts. Instead of coming out of the night of sense, she either remained in it or went into the night of spirit without any transition. Ruth Burrows says both of these nuns arrived at transforming union at about the same time.

Teresa of Avila suggested once in her writings that the prayer of full union might be a short cut to transforming union. That may indeed be its purpose. It may be a special way of hastening the ordinary process of dismantling the false self. Ruth Burrows extrapolates that exuberant mysticism may be a charism. Some persons are given the necessary psychological experience in order to explain the various stages of contemplation for the benefit of the majority contemplatives who are led by the hidden ladder described by John of the Cross.

This brings us to the remarkable insight of John of the Cross that contemplative prayer is fundamentally a ray of darkness. Again and again he identifies pure faith as the proximate means of union with God. Hence, any experience of the divine that we may enjoy is not God, but our interpretation of God, or the radiance of God's action in us. Pure faith transcends every human experience and accesses God just as God is. If a ray of light passed through a perfect vacuum, John of the Cross writes, we would have no knowledge of it, because in a perfect vacuum there are no dust particles to reflect the physical energy as light. When we accept it as it is, the divine light is constantly beaming into our whole being—body, soul, and spirit. Even the spiritual senses do not access the immense purity and power of the divine energy in its essence.

In this life it is not possible to see God just as God is and live, according to the author of the First Epistle of John. But we can consent to know him in the darkness of faith, and in that darkness the invincible conviction of the divine presence arises. If we could grasp this basic insight of John of the Cross, it would free us from an immense amount of anxiety in the journey. Most of our troubles come from expectations that are unrealistic and cannot be fulfilled.

The narrow way of pure faith leads to life. This teaching of John of the Cross might be exemplified by reflecting on the difference between taking an express elevator to the top floor of a skyscraper and taking a local. The local elevator stops at every floor, and at every stop the vista gets better. The problem is that one may never get back on the elevator because one is so entranced by the view. John of the Cross forbids his disciples to accept psychic phenomena or to desire substantial touches. "The latter," he acknowledges, "are part of divine union and can be accepted, but not desired." As for locutions, sweet odors, or visions coming from outside or from within, he strongly recommends resisting them.

The higher the gifts, the more we need the nights of sense and spirit to protect us from the residue of the false self and spiritual pride. If we get hooked on spiritual pride, progress on the journey comes to a screeching halt. The wisdom of taking the express elevator—the way of pure faith—to the top floor is that it avoids all mystical phenomena that might occur as by-products of the unloading of the unconscious. The way of pure faith is to persevere in contemplative practice without worrying about where we are on the journey, and without comparing ourselves with others or judging others' gifts as better than ours. We can be spared all this nonsense if we surrender ourselves to the divine action, whatever the psychological content of our prayer may be. In pure faith, the results are often hidden even from those who are growing the most.

Let us return to the story of the nun who affirmed that she never had any experience of the inflowing of mystical (felt) grace. She persevered in contemplative prayer when it was dull and routine, enduring severe struggles with her primitive feelings and the unloading of emotional trauma from early childhood. One day she was walking in the convent garden when suddenly she was aware that everything had changed. The "I" of her ego-identity was reduced to nothing, and the big "I AM" of Christ had moved to center stage in her awareness. The source of her identity was no longer the self that she had known, but Christ's presence within her. The risen life of Christ began manifesting itself in everything she did, sleeping or waking, and communicating to her the strength to fulfill her vocation with unwearying determination.

Thus it is commitment to the journey and fidelity to the practice that leads to transforming union, not spiritual experiences. Such experiences, of course, may help to bring us to this commitment. Sometimes we need them in order to heal the wounds and the emotional pain of childhood. But once our emotions have been healed, God gets down to business and begins to treat us like adults. Then we are initiated into the narrow path that leads to life, which is the way of pure faith.

The divine light of faith is totally available in the degree that we consent and surrender ourselves to its presence and action within us. It heals the wounds of a lifetime and brings us to transforming union, empowering us to enter Christ's redemptive program, first by the healing of our own deep wounds, and then by sharing in the healing of others.

If the divine energy of grace is penetrating our being to the roots at every moment, it is bound to have effects in our lives. Persons in transforming union manifest who they are by how they live. But the chances are good that they themselves will not perceive this. Lay people living quiet, prayerful lives in the world, who think they are not contemplatives because they never became monks or nuns, and elderly religious, who think they are not contemplatives because of the misunderstandings about contemplative prayer in recent centuries, may be so holy that they are not even upset by their apparent failure as contemplatives. This is the triumph of hiddenness.

20

FROM CONTEMPLATION
TO ACTION

■

A FEW YEARS AGO a motion picture appeared called *The Mission*. It dealt
with a historical situation that existed in the seventeenth century in South America
near the borders of what are now Paraguay, Argentina, and Brazil. Jesuit missionaries had created a community in which the natives were becoming self-supporting.
These indigenous people had been for many years the prey of political forces in
Europe vying for control of their land. The success of the Jesuit missionaries in
raising them to a certain well-being and autonomy was threatening the slave trade
in the area and the extension of the colonial aspirations of Spain and Portugal.

The Spanish and Portuguese governments were putting enormous pressure on
Church authorities to end this mission so that the dwindling slave trade could be
expanded without the opposition of the missionaries and the developing native
community. The Spanish and Portuguese agents threatened to close all Jesuit institutions in their respective countries if the Holy See did not close the mission. The
Apostolic Visitor, a former Jesuit, arrived on the scene with secret instructions from
the Holy See to close the mission in order to save the Jesuit institutions in Europe
and throughout the world. To understand the dilemma in which this man was
placed, we have to keep in mind that the Jesuits were introducing the reforms of
the Council of Trent and establishing colleges, retreat houses, and missions all over
the world. To close down all these efforts for the renewal of the Church would
have been a serious loss and even a disaster.

As the movie progresses the Apostolic Visitor witnesses the remarkable work that
the local Jesuits are doing at the mission. He meets the happy and industrious native
people who have come out of the jungle and received the enlightened social teaching of the Jesuit missionaries along with the Christian faith. After an agonizing
interior struggle and much prayer, he gives the order to close the mission. The
natives refuse to leave. Several of the Jesuit missionaries side with them, while the
founder of the mission refuses to resort to violence to defend it.

Mercenaries are hired by the European powers; they attack the helpless mission with cannons and massacre all the natives and the missionaries. In the last scene, the ambassadors of Spain and Portugal meet with the Apostolic Visitor to report what has happened. The Visitor is appalled by the extent of the massacre. "Was this massacre really necessary?" he demands with mounting indignation. One of the ambassadors, seeking to calm the Visitor's rage and horror, answers soothingly, "Your Eminence, do not feel badly. After all, such is the way the world is!"

The Visitor replied, "No! . . . Such is the way *we* have made the world!" Rising from his chair, he walks to the window, fixes his gaze on something outside, and, as if speaking to himself, adds a further precision, "Such is the way *I* have made the world!" There is the glimmer of a tear in one of his eyes.

The plot of *The Mission* focuses on the most crucial question of our time and one that is addressed to each of us. It is the question of responsibility for social injustice. What happens when the rights of the innocent interfere with the economic or territorial interests of world powers? At the mythic membership level of consciousness, the response is, "Such is the way the world is." Whoever has the most money or power wins. The national interest always comes first. The mature Christian conscience says, "No! This is unjust! The exploitation of the innocent by armed force cannot be tolerated. Oppression is a collective sin of enormous magnitude and carries with it the most serious consequences. How can I free myself from being implicated in so great an evil?"

The limitations of mythic membership consciousness, especially its naive loyalty to the values of a particular cultural or interest group, hinder us from fully responding to the values of the gospel. We bring to personal and social problems the prepackaged values and preconceived ideas that are deeply ingrained in us. The beatitude that hungers and thirsts for justice urges us to take personal responsibility for our attitudes to God, other people, the ecology of the earth, and the vast and worsening social problems of our time.

Abraham Lincoln, influenced by the cultural conditioning of his time, hesitated to sign the Emancipation Proclamation. In the first months of his administration, his primary consideration was to preserve the union. Since the Constitution provided for states' rights and slavery in the South was such a right, he favored allowing the South to maintain slavery as long as the practice was not extended to the new territories opening up in the west. It was only with time that he saw that the evil of slavery was the primary issue of the Civil War and issued the Emancipation Proclamation.

Apartheid has been a prominent global concern in recent times. The doctrine that whites are better than blacks, supported by all kinds of illusory arguments, supports a blatantly unjust political structure. But if people are brought up in such a situation, they absorb this mentality unquestioningly. The attitude is not, of course, limited to people living in South Africa. The racist tone of colonialism reflected for centuries the sick mindset of Europe. Once we give our consent to unjust situations, reason is co-opted to bring forth arguments to rationalize and justify them.

The Christian denominations sent missionaries into Asia with a chip on their shoulders, which was the colonial mentality of Europe. The missionaries preached from the viewpoint that Western culture was better than Eastern, and that the people of Asia were a bunch of pagans. Actually, the Asians in many instances had a higher culture than the medieval barbarians the Church had been trying for centuries to convert in Europe. The mindset of the missionaries did not allow them to question their preconceptions and prepackaged values. As a result, they made virtually no inroads in Asia in four centuries of evangelization. Since they had no appreciation of the local culture, it did not occur to them to try to live the gospel from inside the culture.

In our time, Abbé Monchanin, Henri LeSaux, and Father Bede Griffiths have pioneered the latter approach in India. In Father Griffiths's ashram, texts from the Hindu scriptures are incorporated into the liturgy along with the customs of the *sannyasi,* the monastics of India. The values of Christian monastic life are lived in terms that the local people can understand. That is the genius of those who are free to use their creativity in the service of God and who have graduated from excessive dependence on their early religious education and the philosophical or nationalistic values of the secular culture.

Would the Catholic population in general have acquiesced so easily to the Nazi regime if they had graduated from the mythical membership level of consciousness and had taken personal responsibility for their relationship to the Nazi movement? Franz Jagerstetter refused to be drafted into the German army because he believed that the war was unjust. He had a family he loved, but that was not his highest priority. His conscience said, "You cannot support this unjust regime or its war!" He refused to join the German army, was put into jail, and eventually was beheaded. It is because he is a martyr to conscience that he is a martyr to religion.

The seventh beatitude is "Blessed are the peacemakers." Jesus did not say, "Blessed are the peace-lovers." The latter are people who do not want to rock the boat and hence sweep embarrassing situations under the rug. Capitalistic systems are embarrassed by the homeless and try to hide them. Until very recently, communist regimes were embarrassed by dissidents and tried to hide them. Every mindset, bias, and prejudice is afraid of peacemakers. Authorities can deal with the peace-lovers by appealing to their desire not to have their lives upset by the oppression and misery of other people. Mythic membership mindsets lead to serious injustices because they tend to disregard the rights and needs of others.

The movement beyond mythical membership consciousness is essential to becoming fully human. Although humanity as a whole began to access the mental egoic level of consciousness around 3000 B.C.E., its mature vision of personal responsibility still has to be interiorized by each of us. Such maturity is vigorously opposed by the downward pull of regressive tendencies and overidentification with national, ethnic, tribal, and religious groups from which we draw our sense of belonging and self-worth. These regressive tendencies hinder us from taking responsibility for the injustices that are perpetuated in the name of our particular community.

Nations still try to solve their differences from a mythic membership level of consciousness, as the following analogy may illustrate. Here is a youngster of four or five playing with a friend in a sandbox. He suddenly gets the idea that he would like to have the sandbox all to himself. He says to his friend, "Get out of my sandbox." The other replies, "I will not"—"Yes you will"—"I will not"—"Yes you will." Finally, the boy shoves his former friend out of the sandbox. This is so much fun that he goes to all the other sandboxes on the beach and punches one child after another until they all get out of their sandboxes. Now he has ten sandboxes, a domain—an empire!

This approach to disagreements among nations is manifestly irrational, especially when weapons have become so destructive that those who use them against an enemy are likely to destroy themselves. One of the basic requirements of the Just War Theory is not to injure or kill the innocent. Given the weaponry that is available, this essential condition is now absolutely impossible. The wars of our century have destroyed many times more civilians than soldiers, and the proportion goes on increasing.

One wonders what the responsibility of the world religions is in this situation. Historically they have contributed to serious violence, war, prejudice, bigotry, and endless division. Yet more than any other institution, they have an obligation to address the problem of world peace and to emphasize the human values that they mutually share and proclaim. Their collective conscience could challenge the nationalistic interests of world powers. But as yet they have no networking process or place where they might speak with one voice on behalf of basic human values, especially justice and peace. We cannot expect the military establishment to end war. War is their profession. The only way that war can be eliminated is to make it socially unacceptable. If the world religions would speak to the human family regarding its common source and the potential of every human being to be transformed into the divine, a moral voice of great power would be introduced on behalf of the innocent and of the human family as a whole.

One cannot be a Christian without social concern. There is no reason why anyone should go hungry even for a day. Since the resources are there, why do millions continue to starve? The answer must be greed. It is, for most people, an unconscious greed stemming from a mindset that does not ask the right questions and a world view that is out of date. Those who have reached the mental egoic consciousness perceive the necessity to be persons of dialogue, harmony, cooperation, forgiveness, and compassion. The problems of our time have to be dealt with creatively—from the inner freedom to rethink ethical principles in light of the globalization of world society now taking place.

One of these problems is our relationship to the earth of which we are stewards. At the very least, we have the obligation to pass on the environment intact to the next generation. We are only brief sojourners on this planet and must consider what happens after we are gone. When we pass on, we will obviously have a new relationship to the human family, but our attitude toward it while we were alive will continue after death. That is the meaning of the parable of the Last Judgment (Matt. 25:31–46). Our humanity in some form is not going to disappear after death. What we do, or fail to do, to the least of God's little ones is going to happen to us in eternity.

In his parable Jesus identifies those who will receive the kingdom of God: "I was sick and you visited me, hungry and you fed me, in prison and you came to me" (Matt. 25:35). According to these words, Christ suffers in the needy and the afflicted. Insofar as we access the mind of Christ, we too identify with the sufferings of others and reach out to help according to our possibilities.

The realization of Christ suffering in the oppressed is the fruit of intuitive consciousness which brings to full growth the seeds sown during the mental egoic period. The average level of consciousness of people today has yet to graduate from mythic membership into the maturity of mental egoic consciousness. The contemplative journey, of its very nature, calls us forth to act in a fully human way under the inspiration of the gifts of the Spirit. These gifts provide the divine energy of grace not only to accept what is, but also to change what is unjust. The gift of fortitude creates the hunger and thirst for justice. This disposition frees us from the downward pull of regressive tendencies and from the undue influence of cultural conditioning. As in the case of Anthony, it frees us from all fear.

The human family is still immersed in the patriarchal culture that arose around 3000 B.C.E. By no stretch of the imagination can we affirm that men and women are treated equally in the present cultures of the world. This inequality is greater in some cultures than in others, depending on where a particular culture is on the scale of the evolutionary process. Only an institutional commitment to the beatitudes can offset the institutional commitment to exploitation characteristic of addictive societies. The Second Vatican Council was a movement of the Spirit to make the values of the gospel available to everyone on earth. That requires translating its message into terms that people can understand through structures adapted to mental egoic consciousness and providing practical examples of concern without which words are useless.

A delicate shift seems to be taking place in the Christian consciousness since World War II. The ideal of Nazareth—simplicity of lifestyle, the domestic virtues, unquestioning obedience to authority—has been the basic model of Christian holiness since the end of the age of martyrdom in the fourth century. With the movement of humanity as a whole toward mental egoic and intuitive consciousness, this model of holiness is changing. The will of God in important matters can no longer be discerned by simple obedience alone. Other factors have to be taken into account as well, such as the actual circumstances, expert advice, the needs of others, the interior attraction of grace, spiritual direction, and the signs of the times. Mental egoic consciousness urges us to assume personal responsibility for our response to Christ in every situation. It does not limit itself to the conventional morality of a local parish, diocese, or religious community. It feels responsible for the whole Church and for the entire human family. Its respect for authority and tradition is genuine, but its sense of responsibility impels it to initiate ways of making the challenges of the gospel better known and available, especially the contemplative dimension and the social implications.

21

CONTEMPLATION IN ACTION

■

ARCHBISHOP DOM HELDER CAMARA started what are called the "base communities" in South and Central America. These communities teach people to take responsibility both as individuals and as communities for their response to the gospel. This may mean taking political stances since the policies of certain governments are manifestly unjust. The members of base communities read the gospel as if they were part of it, identifying themselves with the characters in the text, and applying the gospel principles in their daily lives. To my knowledge, this is the first time that groups of people have addressed the question: "Can we live the beatitudes not only as individuals, but also as a community?" If there were institutions with such a Magna Carta, they would change the world.

I had the privilege of introducing Dom Helder at a meeting of World Religions held at the Cathedral of Saint John the Divine in New York on October 7, 1984. He is a tiny person, deeply wrinkled, with two huge sacks under his eyes. No one could understand his broken English, but just to look at this man was sufficient to know what he stood for. The focus of the meeting was to raise the consciousness of the participants about the necessity of a commitment to peace as an essential aspect of religion in our time. Representatives of the World Religions were speaking as one voice and proclaiming that war in our time is indefensible. Since the monumental weaponry of our time inevitably destroys vast numbers of civilians, the only alternative nations can morally make use of in the defense of their territories and interests are nonviolent means of resistance. This stance underlines the necessity of supporting and strengthening international bodies of arbitration, the United Nations in particular.

Later there was a private meeting of leaders from the different world religions at the United Nations Church Center. Dom Helder was invited to speak about the situation of the poor in Brazil. It is a misnomer to call the people that he has served all his life "the poor." They are rather the destitute. Jesus said, "You will always have the poor with you." He did not say, "You will always have the destitute."

The destitute are our responsibility. As Dom Helder started to speak about the poor, he choked up and could not continue. The bags under his eyes filled up like fountains and the tears ran down his wrinkled face. For five minutes he could not speak. His mouth twitched every now and then, and we hoped he might be able to continue. We waited in rapt attention for him to express what he was trying to say, but he could not. The memory of the destitute and the realization of their desperate plight left him with just one response: tears. Nothing has ever so convinced me of what it means to be destitute as his face at that moment.

As people begin to feel uneasiness with the mindset that treats other people as if they were of less value than themselves, and as they sense the enormity of the global problems of hunger, oppression, and peace, they ask the question. "What can I as a single individual do?" Others may put the same basic question in this way: "How can I contribute to peace and justice when I myself am under the influence of my selfish desires for more pleasures and more security symbols, and the fear of losing control of my life situation?" The same question might be put in a slightly different way. "Do I have to wait until I have been completely purified before I can begin to serve others or practice the corporal works of mercy?"

To this Jesus replies, "I was hungry and you gave me food, I was thirsty and you gave me drink. I was a stranger and you welcomed me" (Matt. 25:35). In the light of these words, the exercise of compassion does not sound like a big deal. It could mean giving someone a cup of water, a smile, or showing concern to someone suffering a loss. We do not have to wait until we can speak at the United Nations or go to Moscow for a summit conference. Somebody is in need right next door, in our family, at work, on the bus—everywhere we turn.

Jesus sent his disciples out two by two to work miracles and to preach the gospel before they were remotely prepared to do so; they were even less prepared to handle the success they achieved. When they arrived back from their journeys, they exultingly proclaimed, "The demons are subject to us in your name!" (Luke 10:17). They expected to be patted on the back. On the contrary, Jesus said, "Do not get excited about that kind of success. Anybody can work miracles with a little psychic energy and the divine assistance. What you should rejoice over is that your names are written in heaven." That is to say, "You have the destiny to enter the kingdom of God and to transmit the values of the kingdom to the people you love and to whom I am sending you."

The failure of our efforts to serve teaches us how to serve: that is, with complete dependence on divine inspiration. This is what changes the world.

22

SPIRITUALITY IN EVERYDAY LIFE

■

THE PRIMARY SPIRITUAL PRACTICE is fidelity to one's commitments in daily life. The same old routines, failures, difficulties, and temptations keep recurring endlessly and seem to take us nowhere. The journey through the desert to which God subjected the Israelites mirrors our own spiritual journey through daily life.

It is difficult to perceive daily life in terms of the biblical desert unless we practice contemplative prayer. A commitment to the contemplative dimension of the Gospel is the keystone to accepting the guidance of the Holy Spirit both in prayer and in action. The soil of our souls is like hardpan; it does not easily let go of the emotional weeds. We need the deepest kind of physical and mental rest in order to restore to our bodies their natural capacities to evacuate the harmful material that blocks the free flow of grace.

Contemplative prayer is addressed to the human situation just as it is. It is designed to heal the consequences of the human condition, which is basically the privation of the divine presence. Everyone suffers from this disease. If we accept the fact that we are suffering from a serious pathology, we possess a point of departure for the spiritual journey. The pathology is simply this: we have come to full reflective self-consciousness without the experience of intimacy with God. Because that crucial reassurance is missing, our fragile egos desperately seek other means of shoring up our weaknesses and defending ourselves from the pain of alienation from God and other people. Contemplative prayer is the divine remedy for this illness.

Anthony of Egypt discovered and organized the four basic elements of the contemplative lifestyle: solitude, silence, simplicity, and a discipline for prayer and action. Monastic life is an environment designed to support the practice of these essential elements of spiritual health.

Contemplative prayer combines these four elements in a capsule that can be taken twice a day. The period of deep prayer, like a capsule, acts like an antibiotic to heal the psychotoxins of the human condition. There are ways in which we can work the effects of contemplative prayer into daily life and thus maximize the benefits of the prayer itself. Following are some suggestions as to how this might be done.

Dismantling the Emotional Programs

The disease of the human condition as we saw, is the false self, which, when sufficiently frustrated, is ready to trample on the rights and needs of others, as well as on our own true good, in order to ease its own pain or to obtain what it wants. By dismantling the emotional programs, we are working to heal the disease and not just the symptoms. The emotional programs were developed by repeated acts. With God's help, they can be taken down by repeated acts.

A good practice for daily life is the deliberate dismantling of our chief emotional program for happiness. By noticing the emotion that most often disturbs us and the particular event or memory that triggered the emotional upset, we can usually identify the program that is its source. If we then deliberately let go of the desire to avoid something or to have something, we have made a choice that undermines the habitual emotional reaction. This practice is not just a matter of lopping off dead branches, but also aims at changing the roots of the tree, which in this metaphor are our basic motivations. If we are bearing a grudge, we will continue to become angry at every provocation until we change the value system in the unconscious that is the source of the frustration which our anger is faithfully recording. All the resolution in the world not to get angry will not change anything until we deliberately address the source of the problem. That is the heart of the ascesis of contemplative prayer. When the root of the problem is healed, the afflictive emotions no longer go off in response to the frustration of our emotional programs for happiness, whether conscious or unconscious.

To summarize the practice once again: when you notice a particular upsetting emotion recurring frequently in daily life, name it without analyzing or reflecting on it. Then identify the event that triggered the emotion. In this way you can sleuth back to the emotional program that has been frustrated. Sometimes more than one program is involved at the same time. Then, say, "I give up my desire to control . . . I give up my desire for approval and affection . . . I let go of my desire for security . . ."

Obviously this practice is not going to dismantle the false self all at once, but by consistently letting go of our principal program for happiness, we begin to see how often it goes off and how much it influences our reactions, judgments, and behavior; as a result, we become more deeply motivated to let go of the emotion as soon as it arises.

It is important to let go of the emotion before it sets off our customary set of commentaries. Once our commentaries are activated, they reinforce the afflictive emotions, and once the emotional pot starts boiling, we may have a long wait for it to simmer down. The afflictive emotions release chemicals in the body, which may require the liver several hours to filter out.

If we have a duty to correct someone like a child or a friend, this is best done when our emotions are calm. Times when we are upset are not good times to correct a situation, unless the need to do something at once is very urgent. We only reinforce our habitual patterns by blasting our friends or shouting at the children.

Moving beyond Group Loyalty

Another practice is that of disengaging ourselves from overidentification with the cultural conditioning we received and toward which we feel deep loyalties or special ties. These dispositions are basically good in themselves, but as we move into interior freedom, God calls us to take personal responsibility for more and more of our decisions and actions. As we saw, the characteristics of the mental egoic consciousness are taking personal responsibility for our emotional life, no longer projecting our difficulties on others, and reappraising the parental or peer-group values that we accepted without question in early life.

The Active Prayer Sentence

Another practice for daily life is to work an active prayer sentence of six to twelve syllables into our subconscious memory by saying it at moments when we are not engaged in a kind of activity that requires our attention. It can be a sentence from scripture or words of our own choice. The hesychastic practice of saying the "Jesus Prayer" in Orthodox Christianity is a model for this discipline. According to the teaching of *The Way of the Pilgrim,* when the "Jesus Prayer" has been repeated day after day for a long time, it enters the heart and starts to repeat itself. The Desert Fathers used to say verses from the psalms. Several of their favorites have been enshrined in the divine office: "Oh God, come to my assistance! Oh Lord, make haste to help me!" Or, "Our help is in the name of the Lord." It takes a lot of determination and time to work a sentence into our subconscious memory by saying it again and again, but these times will present themselves if we are alert to make use of them. Most people spend a couple of hours a day in more or less mindless activity—taking a shower, doing the dishes, driving a car, walking to work, waiting for a bus or for the phone to ring.

Once worked into the subconscious memory, this new "tape" tends to erase the prerecorded tapes already in place. Whenever one of the emotional programs is frustrated, a painful emotion promptly records the fact, and an appropriate commentary arises from our store of prerecorded tapes: "How can this happen to me? . . . How cruel everybody is to me! . . . I'm no good." If we have worked a sentence into our subconscious memory that is about the same length as our normal commentaries, it erases the former tapes and thus reduces the force of the upsetting emotions. If there is no commentary, the process of building up emotional binges is less likely to take place. That gives us a neutral zone in which we can decide what to do.

The following story exemplifies the effects of the active prayer sentence. A certain woman was driving down a country road, hugging the center to avoid hitting a boy on a bicycle. A man drove up behind her, who was in a great hurry and wanted to pass her. He did not see the boy on the bicycle and did not understand why the woman was nudging the center of the road. He kept honking the horn, meaning, "Get out of the way!" When she did not move over to let him pass, his program of rage and accompanying commentaries took over. Pushing the accelerator to the floor, he zoomed around her and, as he passed, rolled down the window, shouted obscene words at her, and spat right in her face! Anger, shame, hurt feelings, and grief all started to surface in the woman. At the same time, her store of commentaries also began to arise: "How could someone be so cruel? How could God allow this to happen? . . . All men are beasts!"

Just as she was about to lose control, up came her active prayer sentence: "How sweet and pleasant it is for people to live together in unity!" The new tape erased the old tapes, and she entered into a neutral zone where she was not preprogrammed to react one way or the other. Into that empty space rushed the Holy Spirit saying, "Love the guy!" A wave of peace flooded her whole being. She was filled with love, joy, and all the other fruits of the Spirit. She forgave the man from the bottom of her heart and drove on down the road as if she had just received a bouquet of roses.

This example points in a special way to the practical purpose that all the various means of bringing the effects of contemplative prayer into everyday life actually serve. They cultivate a neutral zone or open space within us from which we can *decide* what to do. That is true freedom. The neutral zone enables God, according to circumstances, to manifest all the fruits of the Spirit in and through us: charity, joy, peace, patience, gentleness, goodness, self-control, and meekness.

Self-Acceptance

Another practice for daily life is to cultivate the loving acceptance of ourselves. Encounter groups made a great contribution in the sixties and seventies by teaching people who had never really experienced their feelings to begin to do so. If certain levels of our being have been damaged in early life, a program such as the encounter groups provide can be helpful. The mistake would be to glorify the program as if it were able to heal every problem. In the sixties and seventies, encounter groups opened people to feelings that had previously been repressed for ethnic, cultural, or other reasons. People found the liberating of their emotions from repression so wonderful that they almost made a religion out of process. A program designed to heal one level of consciousness cannot heal every other level all by itself. Other levels need their special remedies too.

Compassion for ourselves is an important disposition because all our emotional programs are fully in place by the time we are four or five, certainly by the age of seven or eight, and hence are not our fault. The more we were damaged as children by inconsiderate treatment, the greater our compensatory needs, and the more firmly our emotional programs are likely to be in place. For instance, there is an 80 percent chance that physically abused children will, in turn, abuse their own children. Child battering is the chief cause of death of children under seven in this country. Without deep therapy, those who were abused perpetuate the same horrors on their children that they endured. Those with repressed rage may find in an infant the first helpless person on whom that rage can be expressed. The tendency seems to be strong to repeat what was done to us—to project our own problems on someone else and then to offer that helpless person as a victim sacrifice to satisfy our rage.

When we suffer some great loss or feel that our conduct has damaged our children or experience an important relationship breaking apart, we may find ourselves overwhelmed with guilt feelings. This is the time to say, "I accept it all. I will try with God's help to learn from this experience." When there is no way to correct the damage, as is often the case, we have to turn it over to God and ask him to reduce the consequences. Then we can work to dismantle the emotional programs that were the cause of the tragedy. That is the best contribution we can make to righting the wrongs that may have occurred in our lives. When we try to bring about change in ourselves, we are guaranteeing that it will not happen again. And it is the only guarantee we can have.

Sometimes we need to sit with feelings instead of trying to get away from them. We may be experiencing guilt, loneliness, or the boredom that goes with loneliness. If we sit with painful emotions, name them, feel them, and accept them, saying, "Yes, I feel guilt . . . anger . . . panic; I accept them, I embrace them," then we can stare down our feelings. What we are embracing in these painful emotions is not the suffering itself, but the God of love who dwells somehow at the bottom of them. In this way, grace is released and begins to reduce the pain. To sit with our suffering is one of the fastest ways to work through it. We may need a friend to confide in, and, in certain cases, medication or psychotherapy. Every kind of help can be pressed into service, but the radical healing is the acceptance of the situation, because in some way God is present there.

God always offers a way out. If we sit still, we are more likely to see what it is. If we act out our feelings to get away from the pain, we end up back where we started. Around and around we go. Human misery keeps evil alive. As soon as we accept the situation and forgive the people involved, the devil drops dead. The devil and his influence can exist and thrive only on our refusal to love and our unwillingness to forgive.

Guard of the Heart

Another practice to bring the effects of contemplative prayer into daily life is traditionally known as "guard of the heart." This consists of letting go of every emotional disturbance as soon as it arises and before we start to think about it. This is a more sophisticated method than dismantling the emotional programs for happiness because it deals with the whole of life. Guard of the heart is based on the sense of interior peace that comes when our wills are united by intention with God's will. Whenever that basic sense of peace is disturbed, we reaffirm our intention to be united with God's will by some simple but appropriate act. The attentiveness to abide in this union of wills might be compared to a radio beam that guides an airplane. If the plane moves off course, the signal changes, warning the pilot to readjust his direction.

Following are three ways of keeping ourselves on course in everyday affairs: the first is to cast disturbing thoughts as soon as they arise into the lap of God, or to give them to Jesus as a gift. The second is to give our entire attention to whatever we are doing when we notice disturbing thoughts; we concentrate on the activity of the moment and refuse to think of them. Finally, if we find ourselves unoccupied when disturbing thoughts arise, we may grab a book or take up some prearranged project and thus avoid thinking about the upsetting situation and setting off the commentaries that initiate or reinforce interior turmoil.

Lectio Divina

Another practice for daily life is *lectio divina,* listening to the word of God in scripture as a means of deepening our relationship with him on the levels of reflection and spontaneous prayer. Daily *lectio divina* is especially important since it leads to the contemplative practice of resting in God and provides an ongoing conceptual background for it. In fact, contemplative prayer was traditionally seen by the Fathers of the Church as the final stage of *lectio divina,* the natural result of reading and reflecting on the word of God with a listening heart. Other forms of spiritual reading also contribute to our knowledge and motivation to sustain the journey.

In addition many find it helpful to keep "minute books." They write down a few sentences from scripture that they like or find helpful. While waiting for the phone or bus, instead of doing nothing or looking around to no purpose, they take their "minute books" from their purses or pockets and read a few lines. It is astonishing how quickly our best resolutions are forgotten. We need to propagandize ourselves throughout the day—to give ourselves short commercials, so to speak—to remind ourselves of what we really want to do.

Joining a Support Group

A weekly support group that practices some form of contemplative prayer has the advantage of pooling silence, which is a kind of liturgy, as well as providing encouragement to each other. Such a group helps to renew our resolution to persevere in prayer if we have slipped for a good or not-so-good reason. Sharing prayer together, especially silent prayer, increases faith. In addition, if it is customary in our tradition, we should participate in a worshiping community and receive the Eucharist.

Conclusion

What is described here is not just a smorgasbord of practices intended to bring the effects of contemplation into daily life; nor is it just a method of prayer and a conceptual background to motivate us to persevere in it. What is being proposed in this book and in the other two books of the trilogy, *Open Mind, Open Heart,* and *The Mystery of Christ,* is a commitment to the contemplative dimension of the gospel. This commitment addresses the whole of our being and all our activity, whatever our states of life may be. A total surrender of ourselves to the spiritual journey is required, not just a patchwork of exercises that are part of daily life but do not affect the whole of it or penetrate the various aspects of our lives. When we begin the spiritual journey in earnest with a program of Centering Prayer as a path to contemplation, we are initiating a dynamic that involves our personal responses to Christ and affects our whole lives. These practices, along with our prayer, are a holistic response to Christ's invitation, "Come follow me."

The commitment of lay people and those in active ministries to contemplation is a new way of following Christ in our time. Just as the Spirit created a new way of following Christ at the close of the age of martyrdom by inspiring Anthony with his vision of the monastic lifestyle, so now the Holy Spirit is inviting lay persons and those in active ministries to become contemplatives where they are, to move beyond the restricted world of selfishness into service of their communities, and to join all others of goodwill in addressing the global problems of our time: poverty, hunger, oppression, violence, and above all, the refusal to love.

APPENDIX I

■

(See chapters 1–3)
THE FALSE SELF IN ACTION

WAYS OF REACTING TO
FRUSTRATIONS OF
EMOTIONAL CENTERS

Grief (refusal to let go of
loved possession)
   Self-pity
   Discouragement

Apathy (withdrawal from
life)
   Boredom
   Bitterness
   Aversion for others
   Sloth
   Despair

Lust (greed)
   Overweening desire for
   bodily, mental, or spiritual
   satisfactions
   Compulsive acting out

Pride
   Overweening desire for
   fame, wealth, or power
   Desire for vindictive
   triumph
   Vanity
   Self-hatred in face of
   failure

Anger
   Hostility
   Desire for revenge

Envy/Jealousy (sadness at
another's good)
   Competitiveness
   Loneliness

WAYS OF REACTING
ACCORDING TO
TEMPERAMENT

Withdrawal
   Tendency to passivity and
   to swallow the hurt

Aggression
   Tendency to fight back

Dependency
   Tendency to rely on
   strong figure in
   environment

WAYS OF EXPRESSING ONE'S
EMOTIONAL PROGRAMMING

Materialistic
   Workaholism
   Possessiveness
   Wealth, money, property
   Luxurious food and drink
   Sports

Emotional
   People pleasing
   Satisfying relationships
   Emotional exchange
   Sexual misconduct
   Certain kinds of music

Intellectual
   Academic excellence
   Need to be always right

Social
   Status
   Prestige
   Racism
   Nationalism
   Forms of domination
   Authoritarianism

Religious
   Legalism
   Pharisaism
   Hypocrisy
   Prejudice/bigotry
   Cults

Spiritual
   Attachment to psychic
   powers
   Attachment to spiritual
   consolation

APPENDIX II

■

(See chapters 4−6)
THE HUMAN CONDITION

LEVELS OF CONSCIOUSNESS	CULTURAL EVOLUTION	INDIVIDUAL EVOLUTION
Mental Egoic★ (Zeus, symbol of reason, slaying the dragon, symbol of primitive instinct and emotion)	3000 B.C.E. to present	8 years to adulthood
Mythic Membership (King as embodiment of city state or nation)	12,000 B.C.E.	4 to 8 years old
Typhonic (half-human, half-animal)	200,000 B.C.E.	2 to 4 years old
Reptilian (serpent eating its tail)	5 million years B.C.E.	0 to 2 years old

★Emergence of mental egoic powers prepares way for higher levels of consciousness (see p. 142). But unless the emotional programs for happiness are directly confronted, reason is co-opted to rationalize, justify, and glorify the values they represent.

SOCIETAL CHARACTERISTICS	PRIMARY DEVELOPMENTAL CHARACTERISTICS
Industrial/technological society	Full reflective self-consciousness
Participational government	Emergence of reason
	Personal responsibility
Stratification of society	Overidentification with group affiliation
Verbalization	
Socialization	Conformity to group values
Farming society	
Authoritarian government	Fear of death
Wars	Full formation of false self
Magical	Formation of body-self
Hunting society	Formation of power/ control center
Living from day to day	Formation of affection/ esteem center
Immersed in nature	No consciousness of a self
	Dependence on mother
	Prompt fulfillment of instinctual needs
	Formation of security/ survival center

APPENDIX III

■

(See chapters 8–22)
COMPARISON OF CHRISTIAN SPIRITUAL JOURNEY AND EVOLUTIONARY MODEL

EVOLUTIONARY MODEL (Chain of being)	CHRISTIAN SPIRITUAL JOURNEY
Levels of Consciousness	**Levels of Relating to God**
7. Unity (wisdom)	Unity
6. Unitive (holiness)	Transforming Union
	Night of Spirit
5. Intuitive	States of Prayer (Teresa of Avila)
	prayer of full union
	prayer of union
	prayer of quiet
	infused recollection
	Night of Sense
4. Mental Egoic (full reflective self-consciousness)	*Lectio Divina*
	contemplative prayer
	affective prayer
	discursive meditation
	reading of scripture
3. Mythic Membership (group overidentification)	
2. Typhonic	
1. Reptilian	

NOTES

■

CHAPTER FOUR. *The Human Condition*
1. Ken Wilber, *Up From Eden* (Boulder, Colo.: Shambhala Publications, 1983).
2. See, for example, Ernest Becker, *The Denial of Death* (New York: Free Press, 1973) and Norman O. Brown, *Life Against Death* (Middletown, Conn.: Wesleyan Univ. Press, 1959).

CHAPTER SIX. *Mental Egoic Consciousness*
1. P. Campbell and E. McMahon, *Bio-Spirituality* (Chicago: Loyola Univ. Press, 1985), ch. 6.

CHAPTER SEVEN. *The Four Consents*
1. John S. Dunne, *Time and Myth* (Garden City, N.Y.: Doubleday, 1973).

CHAPTER NINE. *Anthony as a Paradigm of the Spiritual Journey*
1. Athanasius, *The Life of Saint Anthony,* trans. Robert T. Meyer (Westminster: Newman Press, 1950).

CHAPTER ELEVEN. *Special Trials in the Night of Sense*
1. Saint John of the Cross, *Dark Night of the Soul,* trans. and ed. E. Allison Peers (Garden City, N.Y.: Image Books, 1959), bk. I, ch. XIV, no. 1.

CHAPTER TWELVE. *Anthony in the Tombs*
1. Athanasius, *The Life of Saint Anthony,* trans. Robert T. Meyer (Westminster: Newman Press, 1950).
2. In Christopher Isherwood, ed., *Vedanta and the Western World* (London: George Allen & Unwin, 1961).

CHAPTER NINETEEN. *The Essence of Contemplative Prayer*
1. Ruth Burrows, *Guidelines for Mystical Prayer* (Denville, N.J.: Dimension Books, 1980).

GLOSSARY OF TERMS

■

Afflictive Emotions   chiefly anger, fear, and discouragement, which are the spontaneous feeling reactions to the failure to acquire things perceived to be good and difficult to attain, or to the failure to avoid things perceived to be evil and difficult to avoid. Afflictive emotions include the capital sins enumerated by Evagrius, the Desert Father of the fourth century, which are a combination of several emotions: pride, vanity, envy, gluttony, greed, lust, anger, and apathy.

Centering Prayer   a contemporary form of prayer of the heart, prayer of simplicity, or prayer of faith; a method of reducing obstacles to the gift of contemplative prayer and of developing habits conducive to responding to the inspirations of the Spirit.

Consent   an act of the will expressing acceptance of someone, something, or some course of action; the manifestation of one's intention.

Consolations   among spiritual writers, this term generally refers to the sensible pleasure derived from devotional practices such as *lectio divina,* discursive meditation, prayer, liturgy, and good works. Such consolations may arise from sensible stimuli, imagination, memory, and reflection, or from purely spiritual sources such as the fruits of the spirit and the beatitudes.

Contemplation   a synonym for contemplative prayer.

Contemplative Living   activity in daily life promoted by the gifts of the Spirit; the fruit of a contemplative attitude.

Contemplative Prayer   the development of one's relationship with Christ to the point of communing beyond words, thoughts, and feelings; a process moving from the simplified activity of waiting upon God to the ever-increasing predominance of the gifts of the Spirit as the source of one's prayer.

Divine Therapy   a paradigm in which the spiritual journey is presented as a form of psychotherapy designed to heal the emotional wounds of early childhood and our mechanisms for coping with them.

Divine Union   a term describing either a single experience of the union of all the faculties in God, or the permanent state of union called transforming union (see transforming union).

Ecstasy the temporary suspension by the divine action of the thinking and feeling faculties, including at times the external senses, which facilitates the experience of the prayer of full union.

Emotional Programs for Happiness the growth of the instinctual needs of survival/security, affection/esteem, and power/control into centers of motivation, around which our thoughts, feelings, and behavior gravitate.

False Self the self developed in our own likeness rather than in the likeness of God; the self-image developed to cope with the emotional trauma of early childhood. It seeks happiness in satisfying the instinctual needs of survival/security, affection/esteem, and power/control, and bases its self-worth on cultural or group identification.

Human Condition a way of describing the consequences of original sin which are: illusion (not knowing how to find the happiness for which we are inherently programmed); concupiscence (the pursuit of happiness where it cannot be found); weakness of will (the inability to pursue happiness where it is to be found, unaided by grace).

Intuitive Consciousness the level of consciousness beyond rational thinking (not to be identified with bodily intuition), characterized by harmony, cooperation, forgiveness, negotiation to resolve differences, mutuality rather than competitiveness; a sense of oneness with others and of belonging to the universe.

Mental Egoic Consciousness the development of full reflective self-consciousness, beginning with the capacity for logical reasoning at about eight years of age and arriving at abstract thinking around twelve or thirteen; characterized by the sense of personal responsibility and guilt feelings regarding one's attitudes and behavior.

Mystical Prayer in the terminology of this book, a synonym for contemplative prayer.

Mythic Membership Consciousness the unquestioned assimilation of the values and ideas of one's social group; overidentification with one's family, ethnic, or religious community from which one draws one's identity and self-worth, and conformity to the group's value systems. It is characterized socially by the stratification of society into hierarchical forms.

Original Sin a way of explaining the universal experience of coming to full reflective self-consciousness without the inner conviction or experience of union with God.

Purification an essential part of the process of contemplation through which the dark side of one's personality, mixed motivation, and the emotional pain of a lifetime, stored in the unconscious, are gradually evacuated; the necessary preparation for transforming union.

Reptilian Consciousness the level of consciousness characterized by immersion in nature, prompt fulfillment of instinctual needs, and no consciousness of a self.

Spiritual Attentiveness the general loving attention to the presence of God in pure faith, characterized either by an undifferentiated sense of unity or by a more personal attention to one or other of the Divine Persons.

Spiritual Senses a teaching common among the Fathers of the Church to describe the stages of contemplative prayer through the analogy of the external senses of smell, touch, and taste. The point of the comparison is the immediacy of the experience.

Spirituality a life of faith in interior submission to God and pervading all one's motivation and behavior; a life of prayer and action prompted by the inspirations of the Holy Spirit; a disposition not limited to devotional practices, rituals, liturgy, or other particular acts of piety or service to others, but rather the catalyst that integrates, unifies, and directs all one's activity.

Transformation (Transforming Union) the stable sharing by all dimensions of the human person in God's life and loving presence, rather than a particular experience or set of experiences; a restructuring of consciousness in which the divine reality is perceived to be present in oneself and in all that is.

True Self the image of God in which every human being is created; our participation in the divine life manifested in our uniqueness.

Typhonic Consciousness the level of consciousness characterized by development of a body-self distinct from other objects. It is characterized by the inability to distinguish the part from the whole, and images in the imagination from external reality.

Ultimate Mystery/Ultimate Reality the ground of infinite potentiality and actualization; a term emphasizing the divine transcendence.

Unitive Consciousness the experience of transforming union together with the process of working the experience of divine love into all one's faculties and relationships.

Unloading the Unconscious the spontaneous release of previously unconscious emotional material from early childhood in the form of primitive feelings or a barrage of images or commentaries; it may occur both during the time of contemplative prayer and outside the time of prayer.

THE MYSTERY OF CHRIST

■

The Liturgy as Spiritual Experience

CONTENTS

■

PREFACE

■

CHRISTIAN SPIRITUALITY AND THEOLOGY cannot be separated. God has joined them together in an indissoluble bond. The liturgy enshrines and manifests this vital unity. It is designed above all to transmit "the mind of Christ"[1], the consciousness that Jesus manifested of the Ultimate Reality as "Abba," the God of infinite compassion. "Abba" is, at one and the same time, totally transcendent and totally concerned about the human condition. When those who participate in the liturgy are disposed by adequate preparation and understanding, this experience of God, in ever-increasing degrees, is transmitted.

This transmission may take place by way of insight into the Mystery of Christ, of an infusion of divine love, or of both at once. It can also take place beyond any psychological perception in the darkness and immediacy of pure faith. In the latter case, it is known only by its fruits in our lives. In whatever way the transmission of the Mystery of Christ takes place, it is always recognized as sheer gift or grace. In the context of the Mystery of Christ and our participation in it, grace is the presence and action of Christ not only in the sacraments of the church and in prayer, but also in everyday life.

Contemplative prayer is the ideal preparation for liturgy. Liturgy, in turn, when properly executed, fosters contemplative prayer. Together they further the ongoing process of conversion to which the Gospel calls us. They awaken us to the realization that we ourselves, as members of Christ's Body, are the cutting edge of the New Creation inaugurated by Christ's resurrection and ascension.

In the retreats of which these conferences were a part, four to five hours each day were devoted in common to contemplative prayer following the Centering Prayer method. Contemplative prayer in common is a powerful bonding experience as well as a profound form of liturgy. The daily practice of contemplative prayer, whether in common or in private, refines the capacity to listen to the word of God at ever deeper and more receptive levels of attentiveness. When the word of God in scripture and the sacramental rites have worked their way through our senses and reflective apparatus and penetrated to the intuitive level of our being, the immense energies of the Spirit are released, and our consciousness is gradually transformed into the mind of Christ.

The meaning of the terms in the title of this book may need explanation. The Greek word "mysterion," translated into Latin as "sacramentum," is translated in English as either "mystery" or "sacrament." In the context of the liturgy, these two words are synonymous and refer to a sacred sign or symbol—person, place, or thing—of a spiritual reality that transcends both the senses and the rational concepts that depend on them.

For example, the historical life and activity of Jesus are signs of the presence of the Eternal Word of God with whom his humanity was indissolubly united. That this union actually took place is the primary content of the Christian faith. How it took place is the Mystery of the Incarnation. When we speak of the "Mysteries" of Christ, we refer to his redeeming activities, especially his passion, death and resurrection, and the sacraments which prolong his activities in time through the ministry of the church. These visible, verifiable actions are signs that contain his presence and action here and now. Whenever and wherever the action of Jesus takes place, the life of God is transmitted.

The Power of Ritual

A large crowd followed, pushing against Jesus. There was a woman in the area who had been afflicted with a hemorrhage for twelve years. She had received treatment at the hands of doctors of every sort and exhausted her savings in the process. She got no relief; on the contrary, she only grew worse. She had heard about Jesus and came up behind him in the crowd and put her hand to his cloak. "If I just touch his clothing," she thought, "I shall get well." Immediately her flow of blood dried up and the feeling that she was cured of her affliction ran through her whole body.

Jesus was immediately conscious that healing power had gone out from him. Wheeling about in the crowd, he began to ask, "Who touched my clothing?"

His disciples said to him, "You can see how this crowd hems you in, yet you ask, who touched me?" Despite this, he kept looking around to see the woman who had done it.

Fearful and beginning to tremble now as she realized what had happened, the woman came and fell in front of him and told him the whole truth. He said to her, "Daughter, it is your faith that has cured you. Go in peace and be free of this illness." [Mark 5:28–35]

The woman afflicted with a hemorrhage was part of an immense crowd pushing against Jesus as he tried to make his way. This incident points to the meaning of ritual. Rituals are symbols, gestures, words, places and things that have a sacred meaning. They are the clothing of God, so to speak, and are saturated with the healing power of God. God, of course, does not wear clothes. Jesus, the Son of God made human, did wear clothes. And so, by touching the tassels of his cloak, this long-suffering woman was cured.

There is an intriguing analogy between her humble faith and what we do when we celebrate the liturgy. Notice that when the woman touched the clothing of Jesus, healing power went out from him. Healing power is going out from Christ when one approaches sacred rituals with faith; one is knocking at the door of his healing power and manifesting the measure of one's faith. Of course, ritual can become mere routine. Then it is an effort to renew one's faith in its healing power.

It is also possible to overdo ritual by the excessive multiplication of rites. Too many tassels or too few hinder the transmission of the healing power inherent in the discreet use of ritual. The sacred rites, like the garments of Jesus, do not have power of themselves. They merely clothe the reality concealed in them. To touch Jesus, we must not avoid the rituals or try to circumvent them, but go through them to the reality of his Presence. Ritual as a discipline is meant to sensitize our faculties to the sacredness of all reality.

There is an immense variety of ritual in the official worship of the church. The Liturgical Year is the most comprehensive and profound of them all.

The Liturgical Year focuses on the three great theological ideas that form the heart of Christian revelation: divine light, life and love. They constitute the gradual unfolding of what we mean by grace, God's gratuitous sharing of his nature with us. As the primary focus of divine activity, each emphasizes a special stage or aspect of God's self-communication. These theological ideas are all contained in condensed form in each celebration of the Eucharist. In the Liturgical Year they are expanded in order to be studied and savored one by one, the better to search out and assimilate the divine riches contained in each of them. This marvelous arrangement enhances the power of the Eucharist to transmit them. Divine light is then experienced as wisdom, divine life as empowering and divine love as transforming.

Transmitting the Mystery of Christ

When time began, the Word was there and the Word was face to face with God, and the Word was God. This Word when time began was face to face with God. All things came into being through Him and without Him there came to be not one thing that has come to be. In Him was life and the life was the light of humankind. The light shines in the darkness and the darkness did not lay hold of it.

There came upon the scene a man, a messenger from God whose name was John. This man came to give testimony on behalf of the light that all might believe through him. He was not himself the light; he was only to testify on behalf of the light.

Meanwhile, the true light which illumines everyone was making its entrance into the world. He was in the world and the world came to be through Him, and the world did not acknowledge Him. He came into his home and his own people did not welcome Him. But to as many as welcomed Him, he gave the power to become children of God. These are they who believe in his name, who are born not of blood or of carnal desire or of man's will. No, they are born of God. And the Word became a human being and lived among us, and we have looked upon His glory, such a glory as befits the Father's only-begotten Son, full of grace and truth. [John 1:1–14]

The prologue of John introduces us to the eternal plan of God in which Christ has the central position. The Eternal Word, the silence of the Father coming to full expression, has entered the world and manifested as a human being. Because of his infinite power, the Eternal Word has taken the entire human family into his divine relationship with the Father.

We who are incomplete, confused and riddled with the consequences of original sin constitute the human family that the Son of God took upon himself. The basic thrust of Jesus' message is to invite us into divine union, which is the sole remedy for the human predicament. Lacking the experience of divine union, we feel alienated from ourselves, God, other people and the cosmos. Hence, we seek substitutes for the happiness for which we are predestined but which we do not know how to find.

This misguided search for happiness is the human predicament that the Gospel addresses. The first word that Jesus speaks as he enters upon his ministry is "repent", which means, "change the direction in which you are looking for happiness." Happiness cannot be found in the programs fashioned in early childhood and based on instinctual needs for survival and security, affection and esteem, and power and control over as much of life as possible. These programs cannot possibly work in adult life, although everyone tries hard to make them workable. Happiness can be found only in the experience of union with God, the experience that also unites us to everyone else in the human family and to all reality.

This return to unity is the good news that the liturgy proclaims. It approaches us where we are. It engages our being with all its faculties and potentialities in a commitment to personal development and to the corporate development of the human family leading to the higher states of consciousness. The ripe fullness of this developmental process is what Paul calls the *pleroma*. The liturgy is the supreme vehicle for transmitting the divine life manifested in Jesus Christ, the divine-human being. When Jesus through his resurrection and ascension entered into his trans-historical life, the liturgy became the extension of his humanity in time. The feasts of the Liturgical Year are the clothes, so to speak, that make visible the Reality hidden but transmitted in sacramental rites.

The Liturgical Year was developed in the course of the first four centuries under the influence of the contemplative vision of the Gospel enjoyed by the Fathers of the church. It is a comprehensive program designed to enable the Christian people to assimilate the special graces attached to the principal events of Jesus' life. The divine plan according to Paul is to share with us the knowledge of the Father that belongs to the Word of God by nature and to the man Christ Jesus who was united to that Word. This consciousness is crystallized in Jesus' remarkable expression "Abba," translated "Father." "Abba" implies a relationship of awe, affection and intimacy. Jesus' personal experience of God as Abba is the heart of the Mystery that is being transmitted through the liturgy. The Liturgical Year provides the maximum communication of this consciousness. Each year it presents, relives and transmits the entire scope of the Mystery of Christ. As the process continues year after year, like a tree adding new rings to its growth, we grow toward maturity in Christ. And the expansion of our individual faith experience manifests the developing corporate personality of the New Creation called by Paul the "Body of Christ." The "Body of Christ," or simply "the Christ," is the symbol for Paul of the unfolding of the human family into Christ-consciousness, that is, into Christ's experience of the Ultimate Reality as *Abba*. Each of us, as living cells in the body of Christ, contributes to this cosmic plan through our own growth in faith and love and by supporting the same growth in others. Hence, the immense value of corporate worship and of sharing and celebrating the experience of the Mystery of Christ in a faith community.

The whole panorama of the mysteries of Jesus' life is condensed in a single Eucharistic celebration. The Liturgical Year divides up all that is contained in that single explosion of divine light, life and love so that we can more easily assimilate the significance of these theological ideas by experiencing them one by one. In the Christmas-Epiphany season, the focus is on the theological idea of light. In the Easter season, the focus is on the theological idea of life. In the Pentecost season, the focus is on the theological idea of love. Each of these theological ideas is communicated by means of a prolonged period of preparation leading up to the celebration of the principal feast. Each great theme is developed further in the feasts that follow, culminating in the celebration of the crowning feast of the season. We perceive the power of divine light, life and love when these great themes cease to be merely theological ideas and become our personal experience. This is the ultimate purpose of liturgy. Unlike other teachers, it transmits the knowledge that it expounds. Each year the Liturgical Year provides a complete course in moral, dogmatic, ascetical and mystical theology. More importantly, it empowers us to live the contemplative dimension of the Gospel—the stable and mature relationship with the Spirit of God that enables us to act habitually under the inspiration of the gifts of the Spirit both in prayer and action.

The Liturgical Year is an extraordinary production, addressing every level of our being at once and prodding our response. The liturgical texts for the various feasts and seasons are juxtaposed to bring out the spiritual significance of Jesus' life, death and resurrection. Insofar as the Liturgical Year is a course of Christian instruction, it might best be called "applied Scripture" because of its eminently practical character.

The Liturgical Year presents the events of Jesus' life in dramatic fashion. It commemorates them in a way similar to a documentary film. A documentary portrays real situations and thus engages us even more than drama.

Television offers an intriguing analogy to the way the liturgy commemorates the unfolding of Jesus' life as events that are happening here and now. For example, TV presents news or sports events live. Events that are happening on the other side of the world become present in one's living room. A liturgical celebration is not a live event in the ordinary sense since Jesus is no longer with us; rather, it makes the events of his life present spiritually through the communication of the grace attached to each of them and celebrated sacramentally. What happened twenty centuries ago is made present in our hearts. This television cannot do.

To continue this analogy, television coverage alternates close-up and long-distance shots. For example, in covering a sports event, the camera usually gives a panoramic view of the ball park and then a close-up, focusing on the action of a single player's performance. Then it returns to a long-distance shot and we see the crowd waving and cheering. This alternation of close-up and distance shots is precisely how the liturgy focuses our attention on the principal theological idea of each liturgical season. Each season presents us with an overview of the current theological idea, while the particular feasts within the season present close-ups of the action of Jesus in us and in the world.

For example, the Christmas-Epiphany Mystery begins with the season of Advent, an extended period of preparation that culminates in the climactic feast of Christmas. On the first Sunday of Advent, the liturgical camera gives us a broad view of the three-fold coming of Christ. On the following Sundays we are introduced to the three central figures of Advent: Mary, the Virgin Mother of the Savior; John the Baptist, who introduced Jesus to those who first heard his message; and Isaiah, who prophesied Christ's coming with extraordinary accuracy seven hundred years before the event. The dispositions and behavior of these principals become living models for us to imitate. In this way, the liturgy awakens in us longings similar to those of the prophets who yearned for the coming of the Messiah. We are thus prepared for the spiritual birth of Jesus in us through our participation in the unfolding of the Christmas-Epiphany Mystery.

The series of feasts that follow the celebration of Christmas flesh out its profound significance. The grace of Christmas is of such magnitude that it cannot be grasped in one burst of light. Only with the celebration of the crowning feast of Epiphany is all that is contained in the theological idea of divine light fully revealed.

The entire scope of the mystery of Christ is experienced at ever-deepening levels of assimilation as we celebrate the liturgical seasons and their various feasts year by year. The liturgy does not offer us a mere seat in the bleachers, or even a ringside seat. We are invited to participate in the event itself, to absorb its meaning and to relate to Christ on every level of his being as well as our own. This developing relationship with Christ is the main thrust of the liturgical seasons and of their capacity to engage all our faculties: will, intellect, memory, imagination, senses and body. The transmission of this personal relationship with Christ—and through him with the Father—is what Paul calls the *Mysterion,* the Greek word for mystery or sacrament, an external sign that contains and communicates sacred Reality. The liturgy teaches and empowers us, as we celebrate the mysteries of Christ, to perceive them not only as historical events, but as manifestations of Christ here and now. Through this living contact with Christ, we become icons of Christ, that is, manifestations of the Gospel in the shifting shapes, forms and colors of daily life.

The consciousness of Christ is transmitted to us in the liturgy according to our preparation. The best preparation for receiving this transmission is the regular practice of contemplative prayer, which refines and enhances our capacity to listen and to respond to the word of God in scripture and in the liturgy. The desire to assimilate and to be assimilated into Christ's inner experience of the Ultimate Reality as Abba also characterizes contemplative prayer.

The liturgy is God's way par excellence of transmitting Christ-consciousness. It is the chief place where it happens. It makes use of ritual to prepare the minds and hearts of the worshipers. When we are properly prepared, it grasps our attention at every level of our being and the special grace of the feast is, in fact, communicated.

The Five Presences of Christ in the Liturgy

The eleven disciples betook themselves to the mountain in Galilee to which Jesus had ordered them. When they saw him, they adored him, although at first they had doubts.

Jesus then came closer and spoke to them the following words, "Absolute authority in heaven and on earth has been conferred upon me. Go therefore and make all nations your disciples, baptizing them in the name of the Father and of the Son and of the Holy Spirit. Teach them to observe all the commandments I have given you. And mark: I am with you at all times, as long as the world will last." [Matt. 28:16–20]

This passage is the commission Jesus gave to the apostles to extend his teaching and experience of the Father throughout the world and throughout all time.

As has been noted, the liturgy expresses the whole of the Mystery of Christ in the celebration of a single Eucharist. In the Liturgical Year the treasures that are contained in a single Eucharist are separated from this profound unity and celebrated individually in the course of a yearly cycle. In the liturgy, eternal time penetrates each moment of chronological time. Eternal values breaking into chronological time are made available to us in the present moment. It is in this sense that Christ is present throughout all of time—past, present and to come. He is present to us insofar as we are present to the present moment. The present moment transcends all time and simultaneously manifests eternity in chronological time. The *kairos* is the moment in which eternity and our temporal lives intersect. In the perspective of the *kairos,* time is time to grow and to be transformed, time also for the Christian community to spread throughout the world and to become the *pleroma,* the fullness of time when Christ will be all in all.[2]

The present moment as an encounter with Christ is celebrated in a special way in each Eucharist. Each Eucharist gathers together all the different ways in which Christ is present to us throughout our evolving chronological lives. The Eucharist is the celebration of the unfolding of our chronological lifetimes into the fullness of the Christ-life within us and of our transcendent potential to become divine.

Every time we celebrate the Eucharist four distinct presences of Christ are available, according to the Constitution on the Sacred Liturgy approved by the Second Vatican Council.

The first presence of Christ occurs when we gather together in his name to worship him and the Father whom he manifests. Just by gathering together to acknowledge or worship Christ, the Christian community makes Christ present. Any group gathered together in his name becomes itself a center of Christ's presence: "Where two or three are gathered together in my name, there I am among them." This truth is manifested in several of the appearances of Jesus after his resurrection. On one occasion while the disciples were gathered together for fear of the authorities, with the doors locked and barred, Jesus suddenly appeared in their midst. Where did he come from? Perhaps he came right out of the center of their hearts and materialized in bodily form. At first they thought he was a ghost and were afraid. Perhaps they were even more afraid that if he could get in, so could the authorities. In any case, when we gather together for prayer and enter the place of worship, Jesus enters with us in his glorified body, ready to flood each of us, according to our openness to his coming, with the riches of divine light, life and love.

The second way that Christ is present in the Eucharist is during the proclamation of the Gospel. Lectors are not only communicators of the sacred texts, but of Christ himself. This fact is strikingly exemplified in Christian history. Many persons have experienced a direct call from Christ to total commitment upon hearing a particular Gospel text proclaimed in the liturgy. The words of the Gospel have power to reach hearts. Each time the Gospel is proclaimed, the text has the potential to communicate what the Spirit is trying to say to us at this moment in our lives. When we connect with that message, we experience what Paul calls "a word of wisdom." A word of wisdom is not just a wise saying. It is a word that penetrates our hearts in such a way that we are inwardly aware that God is addressing us. Whether we like it or not, we know that the word of God, like a sword, has pierced our inmost being. It fills us with delight or profoundly challenges us, as the case may be. The power of the proclamation of the Gospel to communicate the presence and action of Christ requires that it be surrounded by rituals of special honor.

The third presence of Christ takes place during the Eucharistic prayer in which the passion, death and resurrection of Christ become present. The elements of bread and wine also represent the gift of ourselves. The consecration of these gifts into the body and blood of Christ signifies our incorporation as individual cells into the body of Christ, the New Creation of redeemed humanity that is gradually maturing over time into the fullness of Christ, the *pleroma*.

The fourth presence of Christ takes place in the communion service. At this moment the consecrated elements of bread and wine are presented to each of us to consume, in order that we, in turn, may be transformed into the larger organism of the body of Christ. The Spirit assimilates us into the body of Christ just as we assimilate the elements of bread and wine into our material bodies. The reception of the Eucharist is thus a commitment to open ourselves to the process of transformation into Christ. Christ in his human and divine nature comes to us in the Eucharist in Holy Communion not just for a few passing instants—for as long as the sacred species may remain undissolved in our digestive system—but forever. Moreover, each reception of the Eucharist sustains and increases the Presence that is already there from previous receptions. The presence of Christ that emerged from the community, that was proclaimed in the Gospel and that was made present in the Eucharistic prayer, now enters our bodies, minds and inmost being as we assimilate the Mystery of Faith.

Notice the ascending structure of these presences. Each one is more sublime than the previous one.

As marvelous as these gifts of Christ's presence are, they serve only to awaken us to the supreme Presence, the Presence that is already present. Although this Presence is not mentioned specifically in the *Constitution on the Sacred Liturgy,* it seems to be presupposed. All the sacraments, all prayer, all ritual are designed to awaken us to our Christ nature, out of which we and all our faculties are emerging at every microcosmic moment. Jesus, in commissioning the apostles, seems to speak to this experience: "Go and make all nations your disciples!" The Gospel of Mark expresses it more clearly: "Go into the whole world and preach the Gospel to all creation!"

Does this text refer only to the geographical world? This is the usual interpretation, but it does not exhaust the profound meaning of the text. We are invited, or more exactly commanded, to go into the expanding worlds that open to us as we move from one level of faith to the next. It is as if Jesus were to say, "Go forth from the narrow limits of your preconceived ideas and prepackaged value systems! Penetrate every possible level of human consciousness! Enter into the fullness of divine union and then, out of that experience, preach the Gospel to all creation and transform it through the empowerment which union and unity with me will instill in you."

Divine love makes us apostles in our inmost being. From *there* comes the irresistible presence and example that can transform the world.

1

THE CHRISTMAS-EPIPHANY
MYSTERY

■

Zachary, the father of John, filled with the Holy Spirit, uttered this prophecy:
"Blessed be the Lord the God of Israel, because he has visited and ransomed
his people . . ."; [Luke 1:67–68]

The "Visitation" of God is the experience of God's presence, the Ultimate
Mystery making Itself known in the Word made flesh. This is the meaning
of the Christmas-Epiphany celebration.

Introduction

The Christmas-Epiphany Mystery is the celebration of the transmission of divine
light. The liturgical season begins with Advent, a period of intense preparation to
understand and accept the three comings of Christ. The first is his historical coming
in human weakness and the manifestation of his divinity to the world; the second
is his spiritual coming in our inmost being through the liturgical celebration of the
Christmas-Epiphany Mystery; the third is his final coming at the end of time in his
glorified humanity.

On the feast of Christmas, the joyful expectancy exemplified by the Virgin Mary,
John the Baptist and Isaiah—and shared by us in the Advent liturgy—comes to
fulfillment. Christ is born anew in our hearts through the increase of his light within
us, and the consequences of our union with him begin to unfold.

In the feasts that follow, all that is contained in the explosion of divine light at
Christmas is gradually revealed, culminating in the feast of Epiphany which is the
fullness and crowning feast of the Christmas-Epiphany Mystery. In the clear light
of Epiphany, faith in the divinity of Jesus and in our incorporation in him as members of his mystical body is the light (our guiding star) that empowers us to follow
him and to be transformed into him.

While the theological idea of light still predominates on the feast of Epiphany,
the theological ideas of divine life and love also appear, pointing to the great myster-

ies of Easter and Pentecost yet to come. We experience by anticipation the life-giving grace of Easter and the transforming graces of Pentecost. The liturgy commemorates, along with the coming of the Magi, two other events which symbolize the graces of Easter and Pentecost: the Baptism of Jesus in the Jordan and the changing of water into wine at the Marriage Feast of Cana.

Jesus sought baptism at the hands of John not for himself, but for us, the members of his mystical body. His descent into the waters of the Jordan prefigures his passion and death and his rising out of the Jordan and the descent of the Spirit prefigure his resurrection and his gift of the Spirit at Pentecost. Thus, in the Baptism of Jesus the sacraments of Baptism and Confirmation are prefigured and bestowed in advance. He purifies his people and prepares them for union with himself.

The union established between Christ and us in Baptism and deepened by Confirmation is consummated in the Eucharist, the sacrament of divine union. The Eucharist and its transforming effects are prefigured by Jesus' changing water into wine at the Marriage Feast of Cana, while the wedding party symbolizes the joys of divine union, the ripe fruit of the transforming graces of Pentecost.

Here is a summary of the teaching of the liturgy in the Christmas-Epiphany Mystery:

1. Human nature is united to the Eternal Word, the Son of God, in the womb of the Virgin Mary: Advent.
2. The Eternal Word appears in human form as the light of the world: Christmas.
3. He manifests his divinity through his humanity: Epiphany.
4. By his baptism in the Jordan, he purifies the church, the extension of his body in time, and sanctifies the waters of baptism: Epiphany and the Sunday following.
5. He takes his people to himself in spiritual marriage, transforming them into himself: Epiphany and the second Sunday following.
6. We are taught the practical consequences of being members of Christ's mystical body: the Second Reading for the Sundays in Ordinary Time following Epiphany.

The Christmas-Epiphany Mystery

The word of God was spoken to John, son of Zachariah, in the desert. He went about the entire region of the Jordan proclaiming the baptism of repentance which led to the forgiveness of sins, as is written in the book of the words of Isaiah the Prophet: "A herald's voice in the desert, crying, 'make ready the way of the Lord, clear him a straight path.' " [Luke 3:2–4][1]

Advent is the celebration of the three comings of Christ: his coming in the flesh, which is the primary focus of the feast of Christmas; his coming at the end of time, which is one of the underlying themes of Advent; and his coming in grace, which is his spiritual coming in our hearts through the Eucharistic celebration of the Christmas-Epiphany mystery.

His coming in grace is his birth within us. This coming emphasizes the primary thrust of the liturgy, which is the transmission of grace, not just the commemoration of an historical event. Thus, the liturgy communicates the graces commemorated in the liturgical seasons and feasts. These center around the three great theological ideas contained in the revelation of Jesus: divine light, life and love. Each season of the liturgical year—Christmas-Epiphany, Easter-Ascension, Pentecost—emphasizes a particular aspect of the mystery of salvation, God's gratuitous self-communication. The rest of the Liturgical Year flows from these major themes and investigates their practical implications.

The Liturgical Year begins with the theological idea of divine light. And what is this light? You find out by attending the liturgy, provided you are properly prepared and provided that the liturgy is sensitively and reverently executed.

Each liturgical season has a period of preparation that readies us for the celebration of the climactic feast. The feast of Christmas is the first burst of light in the unfolding of the Christmas-Epiphany Mystery. Theologically, Christmas is the revelation of the Eternal Word made flesh. But it takes time to celebrate and penetrate all that this event actually contains and involves. The most we can do on Christmas night is gasp in wonderment and rejoice with the angels and the shepherds who first experienced it. The various aspects of the Mystery of divine light are examined one by one in the days following Christmas. The liturgy carefully unpacks the marvelous treasures that are contained in the initial burst of light. Actually, we do not grasp the full import of the Mystery until we move through the other two cycles. As the divine light grows brighter, it reveals what it contains, that is, divine life; and divine life reveals that the Ultimate Reality is love.

Epiphany is the crowning feast of Christmas. We tend to think of Christmas as the greater feast, but in actual fact, it is only the beginning. It whets our appetite for the treasures to be revealed in the feasts to come. The great enlightenment of the Christmas-Epiphany Mystery is when we perceive that the divine light manifests not only that the Son of God has become a human being, but that we are incorporated as living members into his body. This is the special grace of Epiphany. In view of his divine dignity and power, the Son of God gathers into himself the entire human family past, present and future. The moment that the Eternal Word is uttered outside the bosom of the Trinity and steps forth into the human condition, the Word gives himself to all creatures. In the act of creating, God, in a sense, dies. He ceases to be alone and becomes, by virtue of his creative activity, totally involved in the human adventure. He cannot be indifferent. Any theology that suggests that he is unconcerned is not the revelation of Jesus. On the contrary, the meaning of the life and message of Jesus is that the reign of God is "close at hand": the whole of God is now available for every human being who wants him.

Epiphany, then, is the manifestation of all that is contained in the light of Christmas; it is the invitation to become divine. Epiphany reveals the marriage between the divine and human natures of Jesus Christ. It also reveals God's call to the church (meaning us, of course) to be transformed by entering into spiritual marriage with Christ and to become fully human.

The coming of Christ into our conscious lives is the ripe fruit of the Christmas-Epiphany Mystery. It presupposes a presence of Christ that is already within us waiting to be awakened. This might be called the fourth coming of Christ, except that it is not a coming in the strict sense since it is already here. The Christmas-Epiphany Mystery invites us to take possession of what is already ours. As Thomas Merton put it, we are "to become what we already are." The Christmas-Epiphany Mystery, as the coming of Christ into our lives, makes us aware of the fact that he is already here as our true self—the deepest reality in us and in everyone else. Once God takes upon himself the human condition, everyone is potentially divine. Through the Incarnation of his Son, God floods the whole human family—past, present and to come—with his majesty, dignity and grace. Christ dwells in us in a mysterious but real way. The principal purpose of all liturgy, prayer and ritual is to bring us to the awareness of his interior Presence and union with us. The potentiality for this awareness is innate in us by virtue of being human, but we have not yet realized it. All three comings of Christ are built on the fact that we are in God and that God is in us; they invite us to evolve out of our human limitations into the life of Christ. Christ has come, but not fully: this is the human predicament. The completion of the reign of God (the *pleroma*) will take place through the gradual evolution of Christians into the mature age of Christ. Meanwhile, every human being and every human institution, however holy, is incomplete.

In the light of the Christmas-Epiphany Mystery, we perceive that union with Christ is not some kind of spiritual happy hour. It is a war with the powers of evil that killed Jesus and that might kill us, too, if we get in their way. Because we live in the human condition, the divine light is constantly being challenged by the repressive and regressive forces within us as individuals and within society, neither of which wants to hear about love, certainly not about self-giving love. The Gospel message of service is not one that is easily heard. Hence, we need to deepen and nourish our faith through a liturgy that empowers us with the energy to go on showing love no matter what happens. This power is communicated to us in the Christmas-Epiphany Mystery according to our present receptive capacity.

The Annunciation

The angel Gabriel was sent from God to a town of Galilee named Nazareth, to a virgin betrothed to a man named Joseph, of the House of David. The virgin's name was Mary. Upon arriving, the angel said to her, "Rejoice, O highly favored daughter! The Lord is with you. Blessed are you among women."

She was deeply troubled by his words and wondered what his greeting meant. The angel went on to say to her, "Do not fear, Mary. You have found favor with God. You shall conceive and bear a son and give him the name Jesus. Great will be his dignity and he will be called Son of the Most High. The Lord God will give him the throne of David his father. He will rule over the House of Jacob forever and his reign will be without end."

Mary said to the angel, "How can this be since I do not know man?"

The angel answered her, "The Holy Spirit will come upon you and the power of the Most High will overshadow you; hence, the holy offspring to be born will be called Son of God. Know that Elizabeth your kinswoman has conceived a son in her old age; she who was thought to be sterile is now in her sixth month, for nothing is impossible with God."

Mary said, "I am the maid-servant of the Lord. Let it be done to me as you say." [Luke 1:26–38]²

Advent is like the time of pregnancy when a new life begins to make itself known. The light of Christmas grows in each of us as the Advent season progresses, manifesting itself through flashes of insight that bring intimations of the dazzling light of the Christmas-Epiphany Mystery.

Mary is the key figure in Advent. In this text we hear the Angel Gabriel's announcement of her future motherhood. As far as we know, Mary was a girl of fourteen or fifteen, living in a backwater town. Nazareth did not have a good reputation judging by what Nathaniel had to say of it later: "Can anything good come out of that place?"³

It seems that Mary have been called by God to dedicate herself to him by a celibate commitment. At the same time, she was in the ambiguous position of being "engaged to a man named Joseph." We do not know the details of this relationship or what their agreement was. Celibacy was a rare choice in those days, especially for a woman. The fact that Mary was free to be innovative and flexible with respect to the popular expectations of her time and milieu is an indication of her spiritual maturity. Her choice of virginity presupposes a conviction about what God wanted her to do. She apparently persuaded Joseph to go along with this idea. In the Jewish customs of the time, she was already committed to be his wife by virtue of their engagement.

Then comes the surprise visit of the messenger of God. As many of the parables will later point out, God's action is unexpected. Sometimes the surprise is delightful, as when one finds a treasure hidden in a field. At other times, if God makes known some demand or challenge, the surprise is experienced as the end of one's world; one's little nest is shattered. Such events occur regularly in the lives of Mary and Joseph. This is only the first time that God, without being invited, intrudes into their lives and turns them upside down. The acceptance of what Jesus later preaches as the reign (or kingdom) of God involves the willingness to allow God to enter our lives in any way he pleases and at any moment—including now. Not tomorrow, but now! The reign of God is what happens; to be open to that reign is to be prepared to accept what happens. That does not mean that we understand what is happening. Most trials consist of not knowing what is happening. If we knew we were doing the will of God, trials would not bother us so much.

Here Mary is faced with one of God's favorite scenarios; it might be called the *double-bind*. The double-bind does not consist in the choice between what is obviously good and obviously evil—that is a temptation—but of not knowing which is good and which is evil. The dilemma may arise in another form: one cannot decide which of two apparent goods is God's will. For a delicate conscience, this causes deep trouble. The turmoil comes from wanting to do God's will and not knowing what it is. As a consequence, one feels torn in two directions at once. Two apparent but opposing goods demand one's total adherence, and both seem to be God's will. People on the spiritual journey regularly find themselves in such double-binds, which may even become more searching as the journey proceeds. This is the kind of dilemma that occurs in a vocational crisis such as, "Shall I enter a contemplative order? I have duties to others that seem to be important, and yet I feel a consistent call to solitude." The attraction to solitude in an active ministry is one of the classical double-binds in which those in active ministries often find themselves. Persons in cloistered communities experience the reverse.

Here is another scriptural example that shows how searching this trial may become.

John the Baptist had staked his integrity as a prophet on pointing to Jesus as the Messiah, the one who was to save his people from their sins. After John's confrontation with Herod, he was thrown into prison. He stands for everyone who suffers for the cause of justice and truth. In solitary confinement, separated from his disciples, he may have fallen into a depression. He began to have doubts about whether he had pointed out the right man. Jesus ate and drank with public sinners. Both he and his disciples did not observe the customary fasts. Could Jesus, who made friends with prostitutes and tax collectors and who encouraged the free and easy lifestyle of his disciples, really be the Messiah? Was John tempted to think, "Have I made a terrible mistake?" Here was a holy man nearing the end of his life, yet undergoing the worst crisis he had ever had to face.

Notice the agonizing double-bind. John had pointed to Jesus as the Messiah, but Jesus was not acting as the Messiah was expected to act. Accordingly, John sent his disciples to Jesus to ask, "Are you the Messiah or do we look for another?" The question suggests the full extent of the problem of conscience that he was enduring. Should he now disclaim the one he had previously proclaimed to be the Messiah? That was his great doubt. He could not decide which course to follow. So he sent his disciples to question the very person upon whose identity he had staked his own prophetic mission—the one, to use this own words, "whose sandals I am not worthy to loose."

In the presence of John's disciples, Jesus worked a series of miracles that he knew would reassure John, fulfilling the prophesy of Isaiah which speaks of the blind receiving their sight and the poor having the Gospel preached to them. That was the resolution of John's double-bind.

Why did John suffer so terrible a trial right at the end of his life? The double-bind is sometimes designed to free us from the last vestiges of cultural conditioning, including our religious cultural conditioning. The means that we needed in the early part of our spiritual journey (but which we may have come to depend on too much) are gradually removed. One of the classical ways of removing them is a double-bind that forces one to grow beyond the limitations of one's culture, the influences of early childhood and one's early religious background. Family, ethnic and religious values are important and may support us for a certain time and to a certain place in the spiritual journey, but not to the place to total freedom that is God's ambition for each of us. Perhaps it was John's preconceived ideas about asceticism that God wanted to demolish in order to free him in the last days of his life to accept God's coming in any way at all, including through the eating and drinking and compassion of the actual Messiah.

Jesus, by the miracles he worked in the presence of John's disciples, thus said to John in answer to his question, "My friend, you did not make a mistake. I am the Messiah. But the Messiah is not limited to your ideas of what he should do and how he should behave."

That solved John's double-bind. Even holy people can be stuck in preconceived ideas or prepackaged value systems that are hard to let go. They may have strong expectations regarding how God should act or about how the spiritual journey and prayer should develop. War, persecution, bankruptcy, loss of a loved one, divorce, change of vocation, illness and death are all experiences that God uses to shatter their ideas or expectations.

When you are absolutely certain God wants two things that seem to be completely opposed, you are in a classical double-bind. Jesus himself endured the greatest double-bind there ever was in the Garden of Gethsemani. He, the innocent one, was asked to become sin for our sake; he who knew the goodness of God as no other human being has ever known or can know it, was asked to accept the inevitable result of identifying with our sins, namely, the sense of total alienation from God.

The experience of the double-bind hit Mary, as we saw, at the age of fourteen or fifteen. She had set up a plan for her life according to what she firmly believed was God's will. Along comes the Angel Gabriel and says, "God wants you to be the mother of the Messiah."

Mary was greatly troubled by the message of the angel. The underpinnings of her whole spiritual journey were shaken. She could not understand how God could have led her to believe that he wanted her to be a virgin and then be told by his messenger, "I want you to be a mother."

"How is this to be since I do not know man?" was Mary's response.

Notice the discretion of these words. She does not say she won't do it, but she delicately raises the problem of how it can be done since "I do not (and will not) know man." In other words, she takes her dilemma and respectfully places it in God's lap. "You created the problem," she seems to say, "Please solve it. I'm not saying yes. And, I'm not saying no. Please tell me how this problem is to be resolved."

The angel then goes on to explain, "The Holy Spirit will overshadow you." Her motherhood, in other words, is going to be outside the normal course of procreation. She will be able to consent to it because God is creating something absolutely unheard-of in human experience: a Virgin Mother.

The news the angel brought and its consequences completely disrupted Mary's plans for her life. Her mother soon became aware of her mysterious pregnancy. Joseph was so upset over it that he thought about giving her up. In other words, this pregnancy turned her life upside-down. Instead of being a respectable young woman engaged to Joseph, she now appeared to be someone who had engaged in premarital relations. She became one of the many disreputable people in her disreputable town. The same God who had inspired her to choose a celibate life made her the mother of the Messiah.

As human beings, we cannot presume that God will do something that has never been done before (although the angel said, "Nothing is impossible with God.") But we can be sure of that if we allow the creative energies of the double-bind to do their work, at some moment we will find ourselves in a higher state of consciousness. Suddenly we will perceive a new way of seeing all reality. Our old world view will end. A new relationship with God, ourselves and other people will emerge based on the new level of understanding, perception and union with God we have been given. The double-bind frees us to grow into an expanded relationship with all reality beginning with God. During Advent, as we celebrate the renewed coming of divine light, we receive encouragement to open to God's coming in any way that he may choose. This is the disposition that opens us completely to the light.

The Visitation

Mary set out, proceeding in haste into the hill country to a town of Judah, where she entered Zechariah's house and greeted Elizabeth. When Elizabeth heard Mary's greeting, the baby stirred in her womb. Elizabeth was filled with the Holy Spirit and cried out in a loud voice: "Blessed are you among women and blessed is the fruit of your womb. But who am I that the mother of my Lord should come to me? The moment your greeting sounded in my ears, the baby stirred in my womb for joy. Blessed is she who trusted that the Lord's words to her would be fulfilled." [Luke 1:39–45][4]

We observed that Mary, after questioning the angel carefully, surmounted her double-bind by a leap of confidence. Her dilemma was resolved in an absolutely unexpected way by her becoming simultaneously Virgin and Mother, demonstrating that there is no double-bind impossible for God to resolve. Even John the Baptist and Mary could not escape from God's enthusiasm to make them holier still. Difficulties give God the opportunity to refine and purify our motivation. They give us an opportunity to make a greater surrender.

God prepares us for the reception of his word the way a farmer tills a field in order to prepare it for the seed. God's preparation is like a tractor harrowing the field. Going one way, it tears up the soil and turns it over; going the other way it does the same as it criss-crosses the field. But everywhere it goes, it turns up new rocks buried unnoticed in the soil, each a possible destroyer of forthcoming seed.

Advent is a time of preparation. God prepared the soil of Mary's heart with incredible graces, culminating in the double-bind that enabled her to attain a new level of self-surrender. In order to bring forth in her body the Word of God, she first had to conceive and bring him forth spiritually. If you see somebody performing virtuous activity, this presupposes an enormous amount of preparation. He brought Mary to the point where he could fulfill his eternal plan. Paul says, "At that appointed time, God sent his Son, born of a woman."

Mary's union with God was so great that she was able to bring God physically into the world. All the images of the Old Testament referring to God's presence are crystallized in her. Having received the Word of God physically into her body, Mary contributed out of her human substance to the formation of the new divine-human person. The birth of Jesus was also the advent of a new aspect of time. The Greek word for "the appointed time" is *kairos*. The *kairos* is eternal time breaking into chronological time; it is vertical time cutting across horizontal time. As a result, the whole of the Mystery of Christ is totally available at every moment.

The liturgy celebrates certain special events in order to sensitize us to the fact that every moment is sacred. Time is time to grow, nothing else. Time is time to transform all the elements of life so that we can manifest Christ in our chronological lifetimes. The example of Mary is saturated with symbols of the most arresting kind to awaken us to the proper human response to the Eternal Word coming into chronological time and transforming it. The *pleroma* or "fullness of time" that Paul speaks of, when Christ will be "all in all," depends on our personal contribution as living cells in the body of Christ. The present moment is the moment in which eternity (vertical time) breaks into our lives. Thus, ordinary life, just as it is, contains the invitation to become divine.

Mary shows us, by the coming of the Eternal Word into her body, what to do with vertical time. Once we grasp the fact that the Word of God is living within us, we realize that we are not alone. We are lived in by God. God is living in us not as a statue or picture, but as energy ready to direct all our actions moment by moment. Hence, the necessity of a discipline of prayer and action to sensitize ourselves to the divine energy which Paul calls Spirit or the *pneuma* and which we translate as God.

What is Mary's first response to the gift of divine motherhood? She goes to see her cousin Elizabeth who happens to be having a baby and who needs help with whatever you do when you are getting ready for a baby: making diapers, preparing the bassinet, knitting little socks and bonnets. That is what she figured God wanted her to do. It never occurred to her to tell anyone about her incredible privilege. She simply did what she ordinarily did: she went to serve somebody in need. That is what the divine action is always suggesting: help someone at hand in some small but practical way. As you learn to love more, you can help more.

Mary did not go to counsel Elizabeth; she did not go to evangelize Elizabeth; she went to prepare the diapers. That is true religion: to manifest God in an appropriate way in the present moment. The angel had said that Elizabeth was soon to have a baby. Mary said, "Is that so? She must need help; I'll go at once." She went "in haste," manifesting her eagerness to be of service without any thought about her own condition, including, I presume, what Joseph or her mother were thinking about her unexpected pregnancy.

Mary entered the house of Elizabeth and said hello. The Presence that she carried within her was transmitted to Elizabeth by the sound of her voice. In response, the baby in Elizabeth's womb leapt for joy; he was sanctified by Mary's simple greeting. God's greatest works take place without our doing anything spectacular. They are almost side-effects of doing the ordinary things we are supposed to be doing. If you are transformed, everybody in your life will be changed too. There is a sense in which we create the world in which we live. If you are pouring out love everywhere you go, that love will start coming back; it cannot be otherwise. The more you give, the more you will receive.

Following Mary's example, the fundamental practice for healing the wounds of the false-self system is to fulfill the duties of our job in life. This includes helping people who are counting on us. If prayer gets in the way, there is some misunderstanding. Some devout persons think that if their activities at home or their job get in the way of praying, there is something wrong with their activities. On the contrary, there is something wrong with their prayer.

Contemplative prayer enables us to see the treasures of sanctification and the opportunities for spiritual growth that are present day by day in ordinary life. If one is truly transformed, one can walk down the street, drink a cup of tea or shake hands with somebody and be pouring divine life into the world. In Christianity motivation is everything. When the love of Christ is the principal motivation, ordinary actions transmit divine love. This is the fundamental Christian witness; this is evangelization in its primary form.

The early Christians seem to have taken evangelization in too literal a sense, preaching the word of God as if it were an end in itself. Because they were holy, their preaching had great effect, but not as great an effect as the witness of the martyrs of blood, and later, the martyrs of conscience. The essential thing, if one wishes to spread the Gospel, is the transformation of one's own consciousness. If that happens, and in the degree that it happens, one's ordinary actions become effective in communicating the Mystery of Christ to whoever comes into one's life.

A sanctified person is like a radio or TV station sending out signals. Whoever has the proper receptive apparatus can receive the transmission. What Mary teaches us by her visit to Elizabeth is that the sound of her voice awakened the transcendent potential in another person without her saying anything. She was simply Mary, the ark of the Covenant; that is, one in whom God was dwelling. Thus, when Mary said hello to Elizabeth, the child in her womb leapt for joy. His divine potentiality was fully awakened. So was Elizabeth's. She was filled with the Holy Spirit. This is the most sublime kind of communication. Transmission is not preaching as such. Transmission is the capacity to awaken in other people their own potentiality to become divine.

Christmas

In the beginning was the Word; the Word was in God's presence, and the Word was God. He was present to God in the beginning. Through him all things came into being, and apart from him nothing came to be. Whatever came to be in him, found life, life for the light of human beings. The light shines on in darkness, the darkness did not overcome it.

The real light which gives life to every person was coming into the world.

He was in the world, and through him the world was made, yet the world did not know who he was. To his own he came, yet his own did not accept him. Any who did accept him he empowered to become children of God.

These are they who believe in his name—who were begotten not by blood, nor by carnal desire, nor by anyone's willing it, but by God.

The Word became flesh and made his dwelling among us, and we have seen his glory, the glory of an only Son coming from the Father, filled with enduring love. [John 1:1–14]

The feast of Christmas is the celebration of divine light breaking into human consciousness. This light is so bright that it is impossible at first sight to grasp its full meaning. Only an intuitive realization such as that of the shepherds is able to enjoy it. Later, as our eyes adjust to the light, we perceive little by little all that is contained in this Mystery, culminating in the crowning feast of Epiphany, the manifestation of the divine in the Babe of Bethlehem.

Let us try to grasp the significance of the Word made flesh. The Greek New Testament word for flesh is *sarx*. *Sarx* means the human condition—the incomplete, unevolved, immature levels of human consciousness. It means human nature in its subjection to sinfulness. Jesus did not merely assume a human body and soul; he assumed the actual human condition in its entirety, including the instinctual needs of human nature and the cultural conditioning of his time.

Sarx refers to the human condition closed in on itself; fallen, and not interested in rising. It is the human condition committed to biological survival for its own sake or for the sake of the clan, tribe, nation or race.

The Greek word *soma* refers to the body insofar as it is open to further evolution: it is the human condition open to development. "The Word was made flesh" signifies that by taking the human condition upon himself with all its consequences, Jesus introduced into the entire human family the principle of transcendence, giving the evolutionary process a decisive thrust toward God-consciousness.

In the *Epistle to the Romans,* Adam is the symbol of solidarity in the flesh (*sarx*). Everybody shares the *sarx* of Adam and thus forms one corporate personality with him. Christ, assuming the human condition exactly as it is, penetrates it to its roots and becomes the source of a new corporate personality open to transcendence. The Spirit, the principle of transcendence, frees the human condition (*sarx*) for movement into the new corporate personality that Paul calls the Body of Christ. Our participation in the Body of Christ has a corporate and cosmic significance. To say "no" to that participation is the primary meaning of sin in the New Testament. It is the choice to remain just flesh (*sarx*), that is, to be dominated by the self-centered programs for happiness. It is to opt out of the divine plan for the transformation of human consciousness into Christ-consciousness. This transformation is what Christmas is all about. This is the growth process that the Gospel inaugurates and to which we are called. Self-centered human nature seeks out ever more and better ways to remain just as it is, because that seems to guarantee its survival. But to choose the status quo is to opt for solidarity with Adam and to reject "the Christ."

"To everyone who received him, he gave power to become the children of God," that is, to know their divine Source. This is the Mystery of the Word made flesh. *Flesh* does not merely mean skin and bones; it means the worldly *values* of the self-centered programs for happiness held firmly in place by conscious or unconscious habits or by overidentification with one's family, tribe or nation. Christ, by joining the human family, has subjected himself to the consequences of the flesh and at the same time introduced into it the principle of redemption from all pre-rational levels of consciousness. Our own development into higher states of consciousness is the cutting edge of the corporate personality of "the Christ," the gradual unfolding in time of the new Adam. Every act that is motivated by that vision—every healing of body, soul or social ill—is contributing to the growth of the Body of Christ and hence to the *pleroma*. This will occur when enough individuals have entered into Christ-consciousness and made it their own.

The joy of Christmas is the intuition that all limitations to growth into higher states of consciousness have been overcome. The divine light cuts across all darkness, prejudice, preconceived ideas, prepackaged values, false expectations, phonyness and hypocrisy. It presents us with the truth. To act out of the truth is to make Christ grow not only in ourselves, but in others. Thus, the humdrum duties and events of daily life become sacramental, shot through with eternal implications. This is what we celebrate in the liturgy. The *kairos,* "the appointed time," is *now.* According to Paul, "Now is the time of salvation," that is, now is the time when the whole of the divine mercy is available. Now is the time to risk further growth. To go on growing is to be at the cutting edge of human evolution and of the spiritual journey. The divine action may turn our lives upside-down; it may call us into various forms of service. Readiness for any eventuality is the attitude of one who has entered into the freedom of the Gospel. Commitment to the new world that Christ is creating—the new corporate personality of redeemed humanity— requires flexibility and detachment: the readiness to go anywhere or nowhere, to live or to die, to rest or to work, to be sick or to be well, to take up one service and to put down another. Everything is important when one is opening to Christ-consciousness. This awareness transforms our worldly concepts of security into the security of accepting, for love of God, an unknown future. The greatest safety is to take that risk. Everything else is dangerous.

The light of Christmas is an explosion of insight changing our whole idea of God. Our childish ways of thinking of God are left behind. As we turn our enchanted gaze toward the Babe in the crib, our inmost being opens to the new consciousness that the Babe has brought into the world.

Epiphany

The first text recalls the manifestation of Jesus in his divine Person to the Gentiles.

> After their audience with the king, they set out. The star which they had observed at its rising went ahead of them until it came to a stand still over the place where the child was. They were overjoyed at seeing the star, and on entering the house, found the child with Mary, his Mother. They prostrated themselves and did him homage. Then they opened their coffers and presented him with gifts of gold, frankincense, and myrrh. [Matt. 2:9–12]

The second text recalls the manifestation of Jesus in his divine Person to the Jews at the river Jordan.

> During that time Jesus came from Nazareth in Galilee and was baptized in the Jordan by John. Immediately, coming out of the water, he saw the sky rent in two and the Spirit descending on him like a dove. Then a voice came from the heavens: "You are my beloved Son. On you my favor rests." [Mark 1:9–11]

The third text recalls the manifestation of Jesus in his divine Person to his disciples at the wedding feast of Cana.

> There was a wedding at Cana in Galilee, and the mother of Jesus was there. Jesus and his disciples had likewise been invited to the celebration. At a certain point the wine ran out and Jesus' mother told him, "They have no more wine."
>
> Jesus replied, "Woman, how does this concern of yours involve me? My hour has not yet come."
>
> His mother said to the waiters, "Do whatever he tells you."
>
> As prescribed for Jewish ceremonial washings, there were at hand six stone water jars, each one holding twenty to thirty gallons.
>
> "Fill the jars with water," Jesus ordered, at which they filled them to the brim. "Now," he said, "draw some out and take it to the waiter in charge." They did as he instructed them. The waiter in charge tasted the water made wine, without knowing where it had come from; only the waiters knew, since they had drawn the water. The waiter in charge called the groom over and remarked to him: "Most people usually serve the choice wine first; then

when the guests have been drinking awhile, a lesser vintage. What you have done is to keep the choice wine until now." Jesus performed this first of his signs at Cana in Galilee. Thus did he reveal his glory, and the disciples believed in him. [John 2:1–12]

These three readings are an integral part of the celebration of Epiphany, the crowning feast of the Christmas-Epiphany Mystery and the full revelation of all that the light of Christmas contains. The manifestation of Jesus in his divinity to the Gentiles in the persons of the Magi is supplemented by two other events that are manifestations of Jesus' divine nature from a later period in his life. The liturgy is primarily a parable of what grace is doing now; it disregards historical considerations and juxtaposes texts in order to bring out the sublime significance of what is being transmitted in an invisible way through the visible signs.

The first text describes the manifestation of Jesus' divinity to the Magi. They came from the ends of the earth and thus are symbols for all time of genuine seekers of the truth.

Jesus' Baptism in the Jordan and the Marriage Feast of Cana are integrated into the celebration in order to enlarge the perspective from which we perceive the divinity of Jesus. Jesus' baptism by John represents the manifestation of Jesus' divinity to the Jews, the moment when Jesus entered fully into his mission for the salvation of the human family. His baptism in the Jordan is a preview of the graces of Easter and Pentecost, in which we celebrate the Mysteries of divine life and love. Jesus' descent into the waters of the Jordan anticipates his descent into the sufferings of his passion and death; his emergence from the Jordan symbolizes his resurrection; and the Dove's descent prefigures the outpouring of the Holy Spirit at Pentecost.

All water has been sanctified by its contact with the body of Jesus in the Jordan. Moreover, every drop of water in the universe, in virtue of the baptism of Jesus, has become a vehicle of grace. Every kind of affliction, symbolized by the waters of the Jordan, has become a vehicle of grace. Even suffering that is the direct consequence of sin has become an inexhaustible source of grace. This does not mean that suffering is an end in itself, but that it has to be accepted, passed through and transcended. It is the touch—the presence—of Jesus which transforms suffering into a vehicle of sanctification.

The third text describes the Marriage Feast at Cana where Jesus manifested his divinity to his disciples.

Epiphany celebrates the marriage, so to speak, between the church and Christ; we, of course, are the church. Hence, the wedding feast is a symbol of the celebration of the divine nuptials in the souls of those who have experienced the divine light, and the divine life and love which that light contains. The new wine is the transcendent principle that Christ has brought into the world by taking human nature into himself. The whole human family is taken up into this new life, which has been inserted once and for all into the heart of God by the Incarnation and the redemptive work of Jesus. The new wine is the message of the Gospel, a message that announces that this process is happening. This is the greatest news there ever was! The human family has become divine! Through baptism we accept our personal invitation and, by struggling with the false-self system, gradually enter into the marriage chamber—the permanent awareness, through faith, of our union with Christ who takes us into the bosom of the Trinity. Since human beings were formed from the earth, the earth itself, represented by us and in us, is taken up into the Eternal Word. In human beings, God reaches the highest conceivable level of self-communication and gathers all that he has created into oneness with himself.

The final consummation, when "God will be all in all," takes place when the new wine has been served to everyone. The head waiter said to the young man, "You have saved the good wine until now." This is the wine of the Spirit that rejoices the hearts of all who drink it.

The Significance of the Wedding Feast at Cana

There was a wedding at Cana in Galilee. The mother of Jesus was present. Jesus and his disciples had also been invited. When they ran out of wine, since the wine provided for the wedding was all finished, the Mother of Jesus said to him, "They have no wine." Jesus said, "Woman, why turn to me? My hour has not come yet." His Mother said to the servants, "do whatever he tells you."

There were six stone water jars standing there, meant for the purifications that are customary among the Jews. Each one held twenty or thirty gallons. Jesus said to the servants, "Fill the jars with water," and they filled them to the brim. "Draw some out now," he told them, "and take it to the chief steward." They did so. The chief steward tasted the water and it had turned into wine. Having no idea where it had come from (only the servants who had drawn the water knew), the chief steward called the bridegroom and said, "Most people serve the best wine first and keep the cheaper wine until the guests have had plenty to drink, but you have kept the best wine until now!"

This was the first of the signs given by Jesus. It was given at Cana in Galilee. He let his glory be seen and his disciples believed in him. [John 2:1–12][4]

Epiphany, as the celebration of the marriage of the Son of God with human nature, reveals the deepest significance of the Eternal Word becoming a human being. Furthermore, it is our personal call not only to the surrender of faith, but to transformation into divine life and love. The marriage feast, taking place in a tiny out-of-the-way town, becomes the symbol of the most fantastic event in human history, the most striking example of how eternal time enters into chronological time and transforms it. What happens when the wine begins to run out and the bridal couple are in danger of embarrassment, becomes a cosmic event. What Jesus does at the marriage feast is the symbol of what he will later accomplish through his passion, death and resurrection. The water stored in the jars is the symbol of the old Adam, of solidarity in human incompletion and sin. Jesus takes this water and transforms it into wine—not just into new water, but into something totally new! The sparkling, heady character of wine is the symbol of the experience of refreshment, enthusiasm and exhilaration that characterize the fruits of the Spirit.

The jars of water were required for purification according to Jewish custom, before, during and after the meal. Notice that each jar contained twenty to thirty gallons when filled to the brim. That is about a thousand quarts. After the miracle, there was wine enough to satisfy an army! The implication is that there is no limit to the new wine of the Gospel.

Who are the guests? You and I, of course. We see in this miracle the revelation of Christ's union with the human family, a marriage that is consummated in the Eucharist and that transports the guests into the New Creation. The corporate personality of the new humanity is called the Body of Christ. The Body of Christ grows through the process of our personal awakening to the divine life. Thus, everyone is invited to this wedding banquet. If we consent to participate, we receive the gift of the Spirit without measure, like the enormous superfluity of wine that Jesus provided for the embarrassed couple.

The three historical events singled out by the liturgy of Epiphany express this movement of incorporation into Christ and of transformation of consciousness.

1) The manifestation of the Babe's divine nature to the Magi signifies the call to divine union extended to every person—past, present and to come—in virtue of Christ's becoming a member of our race.

2) The manifestation of Jesus' divine nature to the Jews by the voice from heaven after his baptism in the Jordan signifies our proximate call to divine union. The human family and each of us is purified by the waters of baptism and prepared for spiritual marriage with the Son of God.

3) Finally, the manifestation of Jesus' divine nature to the apostles through the transformation of water into wine at the marriage feast of Cana signifies the consummation of the spiritual marriage of Christ with human nature and with each of us in particular.

Each of these three ascending invitations depends, of course, on our consent. As living cells in the Body of Christ, we are caught up in the process that is moving toward the *pleroma*. This term describes the ripening development of Christ-consciousness shared by each of the individual cells in the corporate Body of Christ. This transcendent movement is like leaven in the dough, raising us out of our separate-self sense into the life of the Spirit, symbolized by the new wine.

We can cling to the old Adam and solidarity with him, or we can accept the Spirit inviting us to unlimited personal and corporate growth in Christ, the new Adam. This incredible invitation is signified by a joke.

Mary, the Mother of Jesus, takes note of the impending embarrassment of the couple and says to him, "They have no wine." Jesus replies, "My hour (*kairos*) has not yet come." As if to say, "My self-awareness as the Son of God has not yet come to term, and this act would anticipate it."

She says to the waiters, "Do whatever he tells you." Jesus acquiesces and tells the waiters to fill the jars with water and then to take some of it to the chief steward to taste. When the steward tasted the water now become wine, he was astonished. It was by far the best wine yet. He was so impressed that he went to the bridal couple and said, "Everybody serves the good wine first and then, when the guests are well satisfied, serves the wine they would like to get rid of. But you have saved the best wine until now!"

The joke is more than funny. It should keep us in joyful laughter for the rest of our lives and indeed, for all eternity. We should be doing cartwheels, jumping up and down, standing on our heads! Not even a liturgical dance meets the requirements of this feast. Divine Love is ours in superabundance. This is the light that is revealed as the gifts of the Magi, symbolizing the inner treasures of the Christ, are opened up. All these gifts are ours, right now, in the Eucharistic liturgy. The new wine of the Spirit is being served.

2

THE EASTER-ASCENSION
MYSTERY

■

On that day you will know that I am in my Father, and you in me, and I in
you. The one who obeys the commandments one has from me is the one
who loves me; and the one who loves me will be loved by my Father. I too
will love that person and reveal myself to that person [John 14:20–21].

Introduction

The theological ideas of divine life and love, anticipated in Epiphany, the crowning
feast of the Christmas-Epiphany Mystery, now come into clear focus. Once again,
there is a prolonged period of preparation (Lent) for the principal feast which is
Easter. The Sundays after Easter develop the significance and fruits of Christ's resurrection, culminating in the crowning feast of the season, which is the Ascension.

Lent and the Human Condition

The Spirit sent Jesus out toward the desert. He stayed in the wasteland forty
days, put to the test there by Satan. He was with the wild beasts, and angels
waited on him.

After John's arrest, Jesus appeared in Galilee proclaiming God's good
news: "This is the time of fulfillment. The reign of God is at hand! Reform
your lives and believe in the good news!" [Mark 1:2–15][1]

Easter, with its grace of interior resurrection, is the radical healing of the human
condition. Lent, which prepares us for this grace, is about what needs to be healed.

According to the evidence of developmental psychology, each human being re-
capitulates the pre-rational stages of development toward full reflective self-consciousness that the human family as a whole has undergone in its evolutionary
ascent. In the first six months of life, the infant is immersed in nature and has no

awareness of a separate identity. As the infant begins to differentiate a body-self, its emotional life clusters around its instinctual drives for survival/security, affection/esteem, and power/control. Image patterns, emotional reactions and behavior gravitate around these instinctual needs and create elaborate and well-defended programs for happiness (or programs to avoid unhappiness) that might be called "energy centers". With the gift of language, the child begins to internalize the values of parents, peers and the prevailing culture, drawing its self-image, self-worth and value system from the values and expectations of the group. This process of socialization compounds the complex networking of the energy centers.

The greater the extent to which the infant or child feels deprived of instinctual needs, the more its energies are invested in emotional programs designed to satisfy one or all of these needs. When these programs for happiness are frustrated, upsetting emotions such as grief, apathy, greed, lust, pride or anger instantly arise. If these emotions are painful enough, one is prepared to trample on the rights and needs of others, as well as on our own true good, in order to escape the pain. This leads to the behavior that we call personal sin. Personal sin is the symptom of a disease. The disease is the false-self system: the gradual building up of the emotional programs for happiness initiated in early childhood and expanded into energy centers around which one's thoughts, feelings, reactions, mindsets, motivation and behavior gravitate. As each new stage of developing human consciousness unfolds, an increasing sense of separation emerges, along with the corresponding feelings of fear and guilt. We come to full reflective self-consciousness with the pervasive sense of alienation from ourselves, other people, and God. We feel more or less alone in a potentially hostile universe. We may even look back with longing to more primitive levels of awareness when we were able to enjoy life without self-reflection and hence without guilt feelings.

As we approach the age of reason, our developing self-consciousness finds itself at a crossroad: on one hand, the urge toward personhood and consequent responsibility; on the other, fear of increasing responsibility and the guilt feelings associated with it. But instead of evaluating our emotional programs for happiness, our rational faculties justify, rationalize and even glorify them. Into the human predicament—and the liturgical season of Lent—Jesus comes proclaiming, "Repent, for the reign of God is at hand".

"Repent" means "change the direction in which you are looking for happiness." The call to repentance is the invitation to take stock of our emotional programs for happiness based on instinctual needs and to change them. This is the fundamental program of Lent. Year by year, as the spiritual journey evolves, the destructive influences of these unevaluated program for happiness become more obvious and, in proportionate manner, the urgency to change them increases. Thus the process of conversion is initiated and carried on. The term of this process if the experience of inner resurrection celebrated in the Easter-Ascension Mystery.

The Lenten liturgy begins with the temptations of Jesus in the desert, which deal with the three areas of instinctual need that every human being experiences in growing up. Jesus was tempted to satisfy his bodily hunger by seeking security in magic rather than in God; to jump off the pinnacle of the temple in order to make a name for himself as a wonder-worker; and to fall down and worship Satan in order to receive in exchange absolute power over the nations of the world. Security, esteem, power—these are three classic areas where temptation works on our false programs for happiness.

Genuine human growth incorporates all that is good on the more primitive levels of consciousness as one ascends to higher levels. Only the limitations of the earlier levels are left behind. For example, the need for security and survival, a biological necessity for the infant, has to be integrated with other values as the organism experiences the unfolding of its human potentialities. For a human being in whom the desire for security has never been moderated by reason, there is never enough security no matter how much wealth or power is accumulated. Similarly, one who has not integrated the desire for affection and esteem, in the face of one critical remark, may require a week's vacation with tranquilizers to recover from the blow.

Here is a parable from another tradition that might throw light on the meaning of repentance in the Christian perspective.

A Sufi master had lost the key to his house and was looking for it on the lawn outside, running his fingers through each blade of grass. His disciples came along and asked the master what had happened. "I have lost the key to my house," he said. "Can we help you find it?" they asked. "I'd be delighted!" he replied. With that the disciples got down on their hands and knees beside him and started running their fingers through the grass, too. After some hours, one of them asked, "Master, have you any idea where you might have lost the key?" He answered, "Yes, of course. I lost it in the house." The disciples looked at one another in astonishment. "Then why are we looking for it out here?" they exclaimed. The master replied, "Because there is more light here!"

This parable speaks to the human condition. We have all lost the key to happiness and are looking for it outside ourselves where it cannot possibly be found. We search outside because it is easier or more pleasant; there is more light there. There is also more company. If we look for happiness in emotional programs that promise happiness through symbols of security/ survival, affection/ esteem, or power/control, we can find plenty of help, because everyone else is trying to do the same thing. When we look for the key where it can be found, we may find ourselves alone, abandoned by friends and relatives who feel threatened by our search. Lack of support for the spiritual journey, not to mention positive opposition, is one of its heaviest trials.

When we decide to follow the call of Christ, we soon find our emotional programs for happiness in opposition to the value system of the Gospel which we have embraced. The false-self system, firmly in place from early childhood, does not drop dead upon request. Paul describes this experience poignantly when he writes,

> No matter which way I turn, I can't make myself do right. I want to, but I can't. When I want to do good, I don't; and when I try not to do wrong, I do it anyway. Now if I am doing what I don't want to, it is plain where the trouble is: sin still has me in its evil grasp. It seems to be a fact of life that when I want to do what is right, I inevitably do what is wrong. I love to do God's will, so far as my new nature is concerned; but there is something else deep within me, in my lower nature, that is at war with my mind and wins the fight, and makes me a slave to the sin that is still within me. In my mind I want to be God's willing servant, but instead I find myself still enslaved to sin. My new life tells me to do right, but the old nature that is still inside me loves to sin. Oh, what a terrible predicament I am in! Who will free me from my slavery to this deadly lower nature? Thank God! It has been done by Jesus Christ the Lord. He has set me free.[2]

The struggle between the old and the new self is a constant theme in the New Testament. The false self easily adjusts to the circumstances of the spiritual journey as long as it does not have to change itself. Thus, it manifests its radical self-centeredness in various expressions of human activity: in material pursuits such as wealth and power; in emotional satisfactions such as relationships; in intellectual goals such as Ph.D.'s; in social goals such as status and prestige; in religious aspirations such as fasting and acts of piety; and even in spiritual commitments such as prayer, the practice of virtue and every form of ministry.

The Gospel calls us forth to full responsibility for our emotional life. We tend to blame other people or situations for the turmoil we experience. In actual fact, upsetting emotions prove beyond any doubt that the problem is in us. If we do not assume responsibility for our emotional programs on the unconscious level and take measure to change them, we will be influenced by them to the end of our lives. As long as these programs are in place, we cannot hear other people and their cries for help; their problems must first be filtered through our own emotional needs, reactions and prepackaged values. No amount of theological, scriptural or liturgical study can heal the false-self system, because as long as our emotional programs for happiness are firmly in place, such studies are easily co-opted by them.

The heart of the Christian ascesis—and the work of Lent—is to face the unconscious values that underlie the emotional programs for happiness and *to change them.* Hence the need of a discipline of contemplative prayer and action.

The Temptations in the Desert

Jesus was led into the desert by the Spirit to be tempted by the devil. He fasted forty days and forty nights, and afterward was hungry. The tempter approached and said to him: "If you are the Son of God, command these stones to turn into bread."

Jesus replied, "Scripture has it, 'Not on bread alone is man to live, but on every utterance that comes from the mouth of God.'"

Next the devil took him to the holy city, set him upon the parapet of the temple, and said, "If you are the Son of God, throw yourself down. Scripture has it, 'He will bid his angels take care of you; with their hands they will support you that you may never stumble on a stone.'"

Jesus replied, "Scripture also has it, 'You shall not put the Lord your God to the test.'"

The devil then took him to a lofty mountain peak and displayed before him all the kingdoms of the world in their magnificence, promising, "All these will I bestow on you if you prostrate yourself in homage before me."

At this, Jesus said to him, "Away with you, Satan! Scripture says: 'You shall do homage to the Lord your God; him alone shall you adore.'"

At that the devil left him, and angels came and waited on him. [Matt. 4:1–11][3]

Lent is the season in which the church as a whole enters into an extended retreat. Jesus went into the desert for forty days and forty nights. The practice of Lent is a participation in Jesus' solitude, silence and privation.

The forty days of Lent bring into focus a long biblical tradition beginning with the Flood in the Book of Genesis, when rain fell upon the earth for forty days and forty nights. We read about Elijah walking forty days and forty nights to the mountain of God, Mt. Horeb. We read about the forty years that the Israelites wandered through the desert in order to reach the Promised Land. The biblical desert is primarily a place of purification, a place of passage. The biblical desert is not so much a geographical location—a place of sand, stones or sagebrush—as a process of interior purification leading to the complete liberation from the false-self system with its programs for happiness that cannot possibly work.

Jesus deliberately took upon himself the human condition—fragile, broken, alienated from God and other people. A whole program of self-centered concerns has been built up around our instinctual needs and have become energy centers—sources of motivation around which our emotions, thoughts and behavior patterns circulate like planets around the sun. Whether consciously or unconsciously, these programs for happiness influence our view of the world and our relationship with God, nature, other people and ourselves. This is the situation that Jesus went into the desert to heal. During Lent our work is to confront these programs for happiness and to detach ourselves from them. The scripture readings chosen for Lent and the example of Jesus encourage us in this struggle for inner freedom and conversion.

Jesus redeemed us from the consequences of our emotional programs for happiness by experiencing them himself. As a human being, he passed through the pre-rational stages of developing human consciousness: immersion in matter; the emergence of a body-self; and the development of conformity consciousness—over-identification with one's family, nation, ethnic group and religion. He had to deal with the particular but limited values of each level of human development from infancy to the age of reason, without, of course, ever ratifying with his will their illusory projects for happiness.

Jesus appears in the desert as the representative of the human race. He bears within himself the experience of the human predicament in its raw intensity. Hence, he is vulnerable to the temptations of Satan. Satan in the New Testament means the Enemy or the Adversary, a mysterious and malicious spirit that seems to be more than a mere personification of our unconscious evil tendencies. The temptations of Satan are allowed by God to help us confront our own evil tendencies. If relatives and friends fail to bring out the worst in us, Satan is always around to finish the job. Self-knowledge is experiential; it tastes the full depths of human weakness.

In the desert Jesus is tempted by the primitive instincts of human nature. Satan first addresses Jesus' security/survival needs, which constitute the first energy center: "If you are the Son of God, command these stones to become bread."

After fasting forty days and forty nights, Jesus must have been desperately hungry. His reply to Satan's suggestion is that it is not up to him to protect or to save himself; it is up to the Father to provide for him. "Not on bread alone does one live, but on every word that comes from the mouth of God." God has promised to provide for everyone who trusts in him. Jesus refuses to take his own salvation in hand and waits for God to rescue him.

The devil then took Jesus to the holy city, set him on the parapet of the temple and suggested, "If you are the Son of God, throw yourself down. Scripture has it, 'He will bid his angels take care of you; with their hands they will support you, that you may not stumble upon a stone!'"

In other words, "If you are the Son of God, manifest your power as a wonder-worker. Jump off this skyscraper. When you stand up and walk, everybody will regard you as a bigshot and bow down before you." This is the temptation to love fame and public esteem.

Affection/esteem constitute the center of gravity of the second energy center. Everybody needs a measure of acceptance and affirmation. In the path from infancy to adulthood, if these needs are denied, one seeks compensation for the real or imagined deprivations of early childhood. The greater the deprivation, the greater the neurotic drive for compensation.

In the text, Satan subtly quotes Psalm 90, the great theme song of Lent, a psalm of boundless confidence in God under all circumstances. He suggests that if Jesus leaps off the temple parapet, God will have to protect him. Jesus responds, "You shall not put the Lord your God to the test." In other words, no matter how many proofs of God's special love we may have, we may not take our salvation into our own hands. Jesus rejects the happiness program that seeks the glorification of the self as a wonder-worker or spiritual luminary.

The third energy center is the desire to control events and to have power over others. Satan took Jesus to a lofty mountain and displayed before him all the king-doms of the world, promising, "All these I will bestow on you if you prostrate yourself in homage before me." The temptation to worship Satan in exchange for the symbols of unlimited power is the last-ditch effort of the false self to achieve its own invulnerability and immortality. Jesus replies, "Away with you, Satan. Scrip-ture say, 'You shall do homage to the Lord your God; him alone shall you adore.'" Adoration of God is the antidote to pride and the lust for power. Service of others and not domination is the path to true happiness.

Thus, out of love for us, Jesus experienced the temptations of the first three energy centers. Each Lent he invites us to join him in the desert and to share his trials. The Lenten observances are designed to facilitate the reduction of our emo-tional investment in the programs of early childhood. Liberation from the entire false-self system is the ultimate purpose of Lent. This process always has Easter as its goal. The primary observance of Lent is to confront the false-self. Fasting, prayer and almsgiving are in the service of this project. As we dismantle our emotional programs for happiness, the obstacles to the risen life of Jesus fall away, and our hearts are prepared for the infusion of divine life at Easter.

The Transfiguration

Jesus took Peter, James, and his brother John and led them up on a high mountain by themselves. He was transfigured before their eyes. His face became as dazzling as the sun, his clothes as radiant as light. Suddenly, Moses and Elijah appeared to them conversing with him. Upon this, Peter said, "Lord, how good it is for us to be here! With your permission, I will erect three booths here, one for you, one for Moses, and one for Elijah."

He was still speaking when suddenly a bright cloud overshadowed them. Out of the cloud came a voice which said, "This is my beloved Son on whom my favor rests. Listen to him."

When they heard this the disciples fell forward on the ground, overcome with fear. Jesus came toward them and laying his hand on them, said, "Get up! Do not be afraid." When they looked up they did not see anyone but Jesus. [Matt. 17:1–9][4]

On the first Sunday of Lent we were invited to accompany Jesus into the desert, there to confront the basic framework of the human condition: the emotional programs for happiness that develop around the instinctual needs of early childhood and eventually grow into energy centers. We continue to react, think, feel and act out of these centers of motivation unless we take ourselves in hand and try to change them. Jesus, being fully human, had the roots of these emotional programs in himself as he grew from infancy to manhood.

This text is the continuation of the invitation of Lent to undertake the inner purification that is required for divine union. On the mountain Jesus was "transfigured", that is to say, the divine Source of his human personality poured out through every pore of his body in the form of light. His face became dazzling as the sun. Even his clothes shared in the radiance of the inner glory that was flowing out through his body. By choosing this text for the second Sunday of Lent, the liturgy points to the fruit of struggling with the temptations arising from our conscious or unconscious emotional programming and of dying to the false-self system. Repentance leads to contemplation.

The Transfiguration manifests the kind of consciousness that Jesus enjoyed, which was not bound by the three-dimensional world. The spacious world of unity with the Ultimate Reality enabled him to be in direct contact with all creation, past, present and future.

The Transfiguration also reveals the state of mind and dispositions of the apostles who are paradigms of the developing consciousness of those who are growing in faith. In this experience, they are given a significant glimpse of the world beyond the limitations of space and time. At first they are overjoyed by the sensible consolation that floods their bodies and minds in the presence of the vision of Christ's glory. Then the implications of this new world with its demands dawns upon them, and they are terrified. At the end of the vision, they experienced the reassurance of Jesus' presence and touch. This presence vastly surpassed the ephemeral sweetness of their initial taste of sensible consolation. Their exterior and interior senses were quieted by the awesomeness of the Mystery manifested by the voice out of the cloud. Once their senses had been calmed and integrated into the spiritual experience which their intuitive faculties had perceived, peace was established throughout their whole being, and they were prepared to respond to the guidance of the Spirit.

Notice the influence of the false-self system at work in Peter. He was overwhelmed by the light emerging from the presence of Jesus. Like the other apostles, his senses were delighted. He saw the wonder of Moses and Elijah appearing and talking with Jesus. Both prophets had experienced forty days of purification, one on Mt. Sinai, the other on his long trek to Mt. Horeb. In the spiritual world there are no barriers of time or space; everyone is interrelated.

Peter's reaction to the vision was, "This is great! Let's make it permanent. Let us make three booths: one for Jesus, one for Moses and one for Elijah." Although this suggestion was very hospitable, it was singularly inappropriate. As was his custom, Peter moves to center-stage. Without being invited, he takes charge of the situation: "Let's build three booths."

Suddenly a cloud overshadowed Jesus, the prophets and the three apostles. It silenced Peter. A voice said, "This is my beloved. Listen to him." The apostles fell forward on their faces in an attitude of awe, praise, gratitude and love, all rolled into one.

The apostles remained in this position until Jesus touched them. "Don't be afraid," he said. They looked up and saw no one but Jesus. The experience of God may be scary at first but quickly becomes reassuring. Actually, there is nothing to be afraid of because we were made for divine union.

Here we find the basic pattern of the Christian path. Jesus, by his example and teaching, approaches us from without in order to awaken us to his divine Presence within. The Eternal Word of God has always been speaking to us interiorly, but we have not been able to hear his voice. When we are adequately prepared, the interior Word begins to be heard. The external word of scripture and the interior Word arising from the depths of our being become one. Our inner experience is confirmed by what we hear in the liturgy and read in scripture.

The ideal disposition for the divine encounter is the gathering together of one's whole being in silence and alert attentiveness. The practice of interior silence produces gradually what the voice in the vision produced instantly: the capacity to listen. It withdraws the false self from its self-centeredness and allows the true self to emerge into our awareness.

Revelation, in the fullest sense of the term, is our personal awakening to Christ. The external word of God and the liturgy dispose us for the experience of Christ's risen life within us. It is to this that the spiritual exercises of Lent are ordered. The awakening to the divine Presence emerges from what Meister Eckhardt called "the ground of being"—that level of being which in Christ is divine by nature and which in us is divine by participation.

The Prodigal Son

The tax collectors and the sinners were all gathering around Jesus to hear him, at which the Pharisees and the scribes murmured, "This man welcomes sinners and eats with them." Then he addressed this parable to them:

A man had two sons. The younger of them said to his father, "Father, give me the share of the estate that is coming to me." So the father divided up the property. Some days later this younger son collected all his belongings and went off to a distant land, where he squandered his money on dissolute living. After he had spent everything, a great famine broke out in that country and he was in dire need. So he attached himself to one of the propertied class of the place, who sent him to his farm to take care of the pigs. He longed to fill his belly with the husks that were fodder for the pigs, but no one made a move to give him anything.

Coming to his senses at last, he said: "How many hired hands at my father's place have more than enough to eat, while here I am starving! I will break away and return to my father, and say to him, 'Father, I have sinned against God and against you; I no longer deserve to be called your son. Treat me like one of your hired hands.'" With that he set off for his father's house.

While he was still a long way off, his father caught sight of him and was deeply moved. He ran out to meet him, threw his arms around his neck, and kissed him. The son said to him, "Father, I have sinned against God and against you; I no longer deserve to be called your son."

The father said to his servants: "Quick, bring out the finest robe and put it on him; put a ring on his finger and shoes on his feet. Take the fatted calf and kill it. Let us eat and celebrate because this son of mine was dead and has come back to life. He was lost and is found." Then the celebration began.

Meanwhile, the elder son was out on the land. As he neared the house on his way home, he heard the sound of music and dancing. He called one of the servants and asked him the reason for the dancing and the music. The servant answered, "Your brother is home, and your father has killed the fatted calf because he has him back in good health." The son grew angry at this and would not go in; but his father came out and began to plead with him.

He said in reply to his father: "For years now I have slaved for you. I never disobeyed one of our orders, yet you never gave me so much as a kid goat to celebrate with my friends. Then, when this son of yours returns after having gone through your property with loose women, you kill the fatted calf for him."

"My son," replied the father, "you are with me always, and everything I have is yours. But we had to celebrate and rejoice! This brother of yours was dead, and has come to life. He was lost, and is found." [Luke 15:1–32][5]

To understand the main thrust of this remarkable parable, it is good to remember to whom it was addressed. The public sinners had gathered to listen to Jesus to see what he might have to day, to check him out. Some of the scribes and pharisees were also present. They complained that he hobnobbed and hung out with tax collectors and prostitutes. Tax collecting was considered the lowest form of earning a living at that time. Jesus presents us with an image of God that must have come as quite a shock to everybody. Jesus spoke of Yahweh as *"Abba"*, Father, the God of infinite compassion. This was a revolutionary way of speaking of God compared to the popular concept of Yahweh as the God of armies.

The father in this parable was well-to-do and had two sons. The younger one seems to have had no sense at all. He was interested in his share of the inheritance because he wanted to live it up before he got too old, and this would cost money. So he negotiated with his father to hand over whatever was coming to him. He did not say what he was going to do with the money and his father did not inquire; he preferred to trust his son who was now a man. It only took the young man about three days after he got his hands on the money to pack his belongings and to take off to see the world. He went into a far country where nobody could check up on him and where he could have the maximum freedom to do what he liked. His luxurious living quickly consumed the fortune. The inheritance, of course, was not something that was owed to him, but something someone else had worked for; he just happened to be the heir.

The younger son was not a good manager. He drank a lot, caroused and squandered the money. Then what happened? As generally happens with projects for sheer pleasure, his plans did not work out as expected. He got clobbered by circumstances. This is the only way for some people to learn that their emotional projects for happiness are, in fact, programs for human misery. They go bankrupt, suffer a painful divorce, lose a child in an accident, are rejected by the people they most love, become alcoholics or drug addicts, and wind up on skid row or in a mental hospital. There it finally dawns on them that their happiness projects are not working out as well as expected.

In similar fashion, the only way that this young man discovered his mistake was to encounter disaster. A famine broke out in the country where he was living. Soon he was starving and the only job he could get was tending a herd of swine. But no one even offered him the husks that the swine were eating to assuage his hunger. In the popular opinion of his milieu, nothing could be worse than taking care of pigs. The young man had hit bottom. He began to reflect on the situation of the hired hands at home. Even if they did not have a share in the inheritance, they were well-fed. It was hard to leave the land of his cherished dreams of unlimited pleasure, but now all his fantasies had been shattered by the famine, his shameful occupation and his aching hunger. Reality, as it always does, had significantly insinuated itself into his emotional projects for happiness.

He decided to return to his father and began the long journey home. As he went, he prepared a speech to present to his father. "Father, I have sinned against God and against you; I no longer deserve to be called your son. Treat me as one of your hired hands."

As he neared the paternal estate, his father caught sight of him a long way off. The bereaved father had evidently been on the lookout for his long-lost son. As soon as he spotted him, he ran down the road to greet him, threw his arms around him and kissed him. The young man started to recite the speech he had so carefully prepared, but his father did not wait for him to finish. The Prodigal only got as far as to say that he was unworthy to be called his son. He never got the chance to say, "Treat me as one of your hired hands," because his father was too busy kissing and embracing him.

The father immediately calls his servants to bring out the finest robe, a precious ring, sandals for his son's bleeding feet, and to prepare the fatted calf, symbol of the epitome of celebration. The party begins. There is dancing, music, and everybody is having a bash. The father is aglow with happiness and the Prodigal is beginning to regain a glimmer of renewed self-respect. Everything is as it was before his departure, only more so.

This first part of the story is clearly addressed to the tax collectors, public sinners and prostitutes who happened to be listening. We next hear about the Elder Son who was working in the fields. He hears the celebration going on and asks one of the servants, "What is this rejoicing all about?" When he learns that his ne'er-do-well brother, who went off with half of the inheritance and squandered it, is the cause of the celebration, he is fit to be tied. He stoutly refuses to go in to the party. His father hears about this and comes out to remonstrate with him. The Elder Son refuses to listen and blasts the old man with an outburst marked by harshness toward his brother and bitterness toward his father. "This is unjust," he complains. "This guy wasted the inheritance you worked so hard to acquire. I have slaved for you all my life, and you never gave me so much as a kid goat to celebrate with my friends!"

His father replies, "Son, everything I have is yours. But we had to celebrate and rejoice. This brother of yours was dead, and has come back to life."

The story ends without our knowing whether the Elder Son came in and joined the celebration. But this much is certain. The parable is not just about the Prodigal Son. It is about two prodigal sons. The elder brother turns out to be a bigger sinner than the younger. He is the chief prodigal because he refuses to forgive. He is just as interested in the inheritance, or more so, than the younger son who squandered it on a good time. The inheritance was a symbol for him of prestige, security and power. He thought that he could guarantee his share by earning it. But salvation, the sublime inheritance that is the central point of this parable, cannot be earned; it can only be received. The divine inheritance is the banquet of the Father's love. The Prodigal Son accepted the invitation to the banquet. The Elder Son refused. He did not understand that the divine inheritance consists in participating in the Father's love, a love whose only condition is that we accept it as a gift. The younger son came to understand the futility of his self-centered projects for happiness through disaster. The elder was favored by the quiet call to growth contained in the faithful fulfillment of his duties as eldest son. Unfortunately, his self-centered projects for happiness prevented him from recognizing the precious gift he was being offered. Thus he squandered his inheritance just as much as his younger brother.

This parable does not stop at upsetting the prevailing value systems of the time. The self-righteous pharisees felt that the special favor of God belonged to them in view of their good works. From that vantage point, it was easy to despise those who indulged in the weaknesses of human nature. This is the typical attitude of people who serve God for the sake of reward. As a result of their service, they feel that they have a strict right to suitable remuneration. The pharisees complained when Jesus offered God's forgiveness to publicans and sinners. The parable, as Jesus' response to their complaints, implies that sinners rejected by society are more apt than they are to receive the reign of God. Unlike the pharisees, public sinners do not have the attitude that God owes them something. The scribes and pharisees had kept all the commandments except the most important one, which was to show love.

The parable invites us to consider our own value system. Lent is about repentance, about letting go of our false value system in order to open to the values of the Gospel. The chief point of this parable is the invitation to each of us (whichever son you wish to identify with) to recognize that the reign of God is sheer gift. The divine inheritance does not belong to us or anyone else. It is the result of the sheer goodness of our Father. The father in this parable is characterized by unconditional love toward both his sons, each of whom abused the inheritance by wanting to take possession of it in his own way. Each is equally guilty of rejecting the goodness and love of this extraordinary father who is not put off by either of them; neither by the wild dissipation of the younger son, nor by the bitter self-righteousness of the elder. The Elder Son is offered just as much mercy as the younger, but because of his self-righteousness, it is harder for him to receive it. His pride will not allow him to accept the inheritance as sheer gift.

Actually, there is no inheritance; there is only stewardship for what has been freely given. As stewards, we have an obligation to share with others the mercy we have freely received. This is the value system that shook the conventional piety of the people of Jesus' time to its roots.

Martha and Mary

Now as they went on their way, he entered a village; and a woman named Martha received him into her house. And she had a sister called Mary who sat at the Lord's feet and listened to his teaching. But Martha was distracted with much serving; and she went to him and said, "Lord, do you not care that my sister has left me to serve alone? Tell her then to help me." But the Lord answered her, "Martha, Martha, you are anxious and troubled about many things; one thing is needful. Mary has chosen the good portion, which shall not be taken away from her." [Luke 10:38–42]

This text is one that has exercised exegetes down through the ages and has been the basis for distinguishing two evangelical lifestyles, the contemplative and the active. On closer look, however, the point of this story is not about which lifestyle is more perfect, but about the quality of Christian life. What Jesus disapproves of in Martha's behavior is not her good works, of which he was about to be the beneficiary, but her motive in doing them. The quality of one's service does not come from the activity itself, but from the purity of one's intention. The single eye of the Gospel is the eye of love, which is the desire to please God in all our actions, whatever these may be. Jesus' defense of Mary, who was sitting at his feet, is not an excuse for lazy folks to avoid the chores. But neither is it a motive for those who are working hard to get annoyed if those engaged in a contemplative lifestyle do not come forth to help them.

The story is a parable about the quality of Christian life, about growing in it, and about the necessity of the contemplative dimension of the Gospel as the means of doing so. When Jesus tells Martha that Mary had chosen the good portion, he is telling Martha that she needs to find a place in her life for this contemplative quality, and that this perspective would make her good actions better. He is also warning Mary that there is something even better than the good portion. This is the union of contemplation and action.

Purity of intention developed through contemplation brings to action the quality of love. Without contemplative prayer, action easily becomes mechanical, routine, draining, and may lead to burnout. At the very least, it fails to perceive the goldmine that ordinary life contains. Daily life is practice number-one for a Christian, but it can cease to be a practice without the discipline of contemplative prayer. The contemplative dimension of the Gospel perceives in daily life the treasures of holiness hidden in the most trivial and mundane events.

Jesus' statement is a call to Mary and Martha, not just to Martha. Martha's activity was good, Mary's was better, but neither was good enough. Both needed to move into the union and harmony of the two, which is the contemplative dimension of the Gospel. Through contemplative prayer we come under the influence of the Spirit both in prayer and action. Then action is truly prayer. Prayer is relationship, and hence capable of almost infinite growth. Relationship can go on growing forever, especially relationship with the infinite God. Prayer is the relationship in which purity of heart, reached through the unloading of the unconscious and the dismantling of the false-self system, opens us to the will of God in everything and enables us to respond out of divine love to the events of everyday life.

Jesus said to Martha, "You are agitated and upset by many things." "Agitated" is the key word; it means that she was attached to her activity, or possibly to Mary's inactivity. She was serving the Lord to please herself, not with purity of heart, which seeks to please God and to do what divine love would do in each situation. Her agitation pointed to the fact that one of her emotional programs for happiness had been frustrated. There was nothing wrong with her activity, but to be agitated or upset indicated that she was under the influence of the false self and withdrawn from the purity of divine inspiration.

This parable encourages us to seek the integration of action and prayer. The time of contemplative prayer is the place of encounter between the creative vision of union with Christ and its incarnation in daily life. Without this daily confrontation, the contemplative vision can stagnate into a privatized game of perfectionism or succumb to the subtle poison of seeking one's own satisfaction in prayer. On the other hand, without the contemplative vision, daily renewed in contemplative prayer, action can become self-centered and forgetful of God. The contemplative dimension guarantees the union of Martha and Mary. This union is symbolized by Lazarus, who was the third member of the household. He is the symbol of the union of the active and contemplative lives. The mysterious illness that led to his death was self-knowledge, the awareness of his false-self system. As the risen life of Christ emerges from the ashes of his false-self system, he enters into the freedom and joy of divine life.

Teresa of Avila says that transforming union might be likened to the transformation of a worm into a butterfly. The life of a butterfly totally transcends that of a worm, but the worm contributes to the process by weaving its own cocoon. By the regular practice of contemplative prayer and by dismantling the emotional programs for happiness, we too weave our cocoon, die to the false-self system, and await the moment of resurrection.

The Anointing at Bethany

Six days before the Passover Jesus was in the home of Simon the leper at Bethany. While he reclined at table, a woman with an alabaster flask of pure and very costly nard perfume entered the room. She broke the alabaster flask and emptied it over his head.

Now some were indignant, saying to one another: "What good is the waste of this perfume: Why, this perfume could have been sold for upwards of three-hundred denarii and the money given to the poor!" So they gave way to bitter feelings toward her.

But Jesus said, "Let her have her way. Why do you molest her? She has given beautiful expression of her devotion to me. After all, you always have the poor with you, but you do not always have me. She did what she could: by anointing my body, she prepared it for burial just in time! I assure you, wherever the Gospel is preached, in any part of the world, what this woman has done will likewise be proclaimed to perpetuate her memory." [Mark 14:3–9][6]

This Gospel must be of great importance. Wherever the good news is preached, this event is to be repeated, so that everyone will know of this woman's devotion to Jesus. She is identified in John's Gospel as Mary of Bethany. John records the setting of this event in the following words: "Six days before the Passover Jesus came to Bethany." The home of Lazarus, Martha and Mary was a favorite stopping-off place for Jesus on his trips to Jerusalem.

Mary of Bethany is one of the few persons in the Gospel who are clearly delineated. As we saw in the last chapter, she was a contemplative. She is depicted as sitting at the feet of Jesus and listening to him—the principal practice of contemplative prayer. The Gospel says she was listening to his word, not his words. She was not following his teaching at this point. She was listening to him, that is, to the Speaker. She was identifying with the divine Person of the Word beyond his human words. She was moving to deeper levels of identification with him, beyond thinking, feeling and particular acts. She magnificently exemplifies what contemplative prayer is: the interiorization of the *person* of Jesus Christ, not just his words and teaching.

Evidently this meant a lot to Jesus because he would not allow her to be disturbed by her sister's importunities. Few people have ever been defended in this manner by divine Wisdom itself. It was in answer to her prayer that Jesus had raised Lazarus from the dead a few days before.

The dinner at Bethany was given in honor of Jesus six days before his passion and death. The Jewish authorities were now plotting vigorously for his destruction. Judas had already decided to betray him into the hands of his enemies. Simon the leper was the host at the dinner. Martha was fulfilling her customary role as perfect hostess, and Lazarus was one of the guests at table. It was an interesting group of people: Jesus the Messiah, Mary the contemplative, Martha the activist, Simon the leper, Judas the thief, and Lazarus the corpse—a fairly motley crew—what we might call a typical Sunday congregation. Jesus does not always choose the most respectable people to be his guests.

Everyone was reclining at table except Mary. When she walked in, all eyes turned toward her. Everybody knew she had a deep love for Jesus. She was carrying an alabaster jar in which there was a pound of nard perfume. A pound of nard perfume was extremely expensive. Later we learn that it was worth three hundred denarii, an amount that represented the ordinary workingman's wages for an entire year.

She entered the room carrying the alabaster jar filled to the brim with the precious nard perfume and came to where Jesus was reclining. Suddenly, without a word, she smashed the bottle and poured the entire contents over his head. Out poured a pound of the incredibly costly perfume. The delicious odor billowed forth, filling the whole house with its fragrance. John adds that Mary also anointed the feet of Jesus and wiped them with her hair.

The guests were flabbergasted. No one had ever done anything like this. Was the woman crazy? Gradually, the disciples regained their composure and started grumbling. They said to one another, "Why wasn't this costly perfume sold and the proceeds given to the poor? What a waste!"

John identifies Judas as the ringleader of these remarks and comments sardonically, "It was not because he loved the poor that he said this, but because he was a thief and used to take what was put in the common purse and put it in his own pocket." The other disciples, however, also gave way to bitter feelings against her.

Jesus then intervened with the words, "Let her have her way." He was dripping with perfume from head to foot, saturated with the stuff, a whole pound of it!

When a well-to-do lady is invited to an important dinner and wants to put her best foot forward, she may dab a little perfume on her hair. But how much would she use? Probably just a tiny bit. What would she think if her husband came in and said, "Darling, I want you to smell nice," and poured a pound of the most expensive perfume on the market over her head?

The house was now filled with a dense cloud of delicious perfume billowing through every room. The scent was overpowering. The disciples continued to complain. Nobody could eat; the meal had come to an end. Mary's astonishing action had completely shattered the festive atmosphere. Everyone was upset except Jesus.

"Why do you bother her?" he continued. "She has given a beautiful expression of her devotion to me." The Master had perceived the meaning of Mary's symbolic gesture. She had penetrated the Mystery of Jesus' true identity far in advance of the disciples.

In the cultural context of the time, courtesy required anointing the head of an honored guest with oil, washing his feet and giving him a kiss. These were the ordinary courtesies extended to everyone invited to an important dinner. The crucial point that Mary was trying to express by means of her symbolic gesture was, "This is no ordinary guest! The ordinary courtesies are not enough!"

Mary was aware of what was being plotted by the authorities and wanted to affirm the depth of her faith in Jesus in a way that could not possibly be misunderstood. Some gesture had to be made before it was too late. Everyone recognized that by anointing him with expensive perfume, the symbol of her love, she was expressing her devotion to him and manifesting the gift of herself. But the deepest meaning of her symbolic gesture was not simply the gift of herself, but the *totality* of that gift. Not only did she anoint him with the costly perfume; she smashed the bottle and emptied its entire contents over his head! She threw herself away, so to speak, emptying every last drop of the perfume in superabundant expression of the *total* gift of herself. This is the meaning of her extraordinary gesture as Jesus perceived it and which so moved him. "You always have the poor with you," he said, "but you do not always have me. She did what she could: by anointing my body, she prepared it for burial just in time."

Anointing the bodies of the dead was one of the burial rites of the Jews at the time of Jesus. By referring to this practice, Jesus introduces a further element in her extraordinary gesture. The smashing of the jar filled with precious perfume represents not only Mary's total gift of herself to Christ; it also represents the totality of the Father's gift to us in Christ. Her action prefigures the smashing of Jesus' body on the cross. His body is the alabaster jar filled with the perfume of infinite value, that is, the Spirit of God. It was to be broken to pieces in order that the divine Spirit dwelling in it might be poured out over the world without any limit and fill the entire human family with divine love.

Mary's prophetic action points to the crushing of Jesus' body on the cross as the symbol of the Father's infinite mercy, the visible sign of God's fundamental attitude toward the human family: unconditional love. In the passion of Jesus, God throws himself away, so to speak, and dies for us.

In this remarkable incident, Mary manifests her intuition into what Jesus is about to do. Moreover, she identifies with him to such an intimate degree that she manifests the same disposition of total self-giving that he is about to manifest on the cross. She had learned from Jesus how to throw herself away and become like God. That is why this story must be proclaimed wherever the Gospel is preached. "To perpetuate Mary's memory" is to fill the whole world with the perfume of God's love, the love that is totally self-giving. In the concrete, it is to anoint the poor and the afflicted, the favored members of Christ's Body, with this love.

The Father and I Are One

Jesus said to his disciples: "Do not let your hearts be troubled. Have faith in God and faith in me. In my Father's house there are many dwelling places;

otherwise, how could I have told you that I was going to prepare a place for you? I am indeed going to prepare a place for you, and then I shall come back to take you with me, that where I am you also may be. You know the way that leads where I go."

"Lord," said Thomas, "we do not know where you are going. How can we know the way?" Jesus told him: "I am the way, and the truth, and the life; no one comes to the Father but through me. If you really knew me, you would know my Father also. From this point on you know him; you have seen him."

"Lord," Philip said to him, "show us the Father and that will be enough for us." "Philip," Jesus replied, "after I have been with you all this time, you still do not know me?"

"Whoever has seen me has seen the Father. How can you say, 'Show us the Father'? Do you not believe that I am in the Father and the Father is in me? The words I speak are not spoken of myself; it is the Father who lives in me accomplishing his works. Believe me that I am in the Father and the Father is in me, or else, believe because of the works I do. I solemnly assure you, the one who has faith in me will do the works I do, and greater far than these. Why? Because I go to the Father." [John 14:1–12][7]

The basic text for Christian practice is "the Father and I are one."[8] Christ came to save us from our sins, but only as the essential preliminary to our ultimate destiny. The source of all sin is the sense of a separate self. The separate-self sense is, of course, the false self, but not only the false-self, as we shall see. The false self is to be surrendered to Christ through the love of his sacred humanity and the divine Person who possesses it. Christ is the way to the Father. His human nature and personality is the door to his divinity. By identification with him as a human being, we find our true-self—the divine life within us—and begin the process of integration into the life of the Father, Son and Holy Spirit.

Christ came to communicate to each of us his own personal experience of the Father. However, even when the separate self has been joined to Christ, it is still a self. The ultimate state to which we are called is beyond any fixed point of reference such as a self. It transcends the personal union with Christ to which Paul referred when he said, "It is no longer I who live, but Christ lives in me."[9]

The death of Jesus on the cross was the death of his personal self, which in his case was a deified self. Christ's resurrection and ascension is his passage into the Ultimate Reality: the sacrifice and loss of his deified self to become one with the Godhead. Since all reality is the manifestation of the Godhead and Christ has passed into identification with It, Christ is present everywhere and in everything. The cosmos is now the Body of the glorified Christ who dwells in every part of it.

Union with Christ on the cross—our entrance into his experience—leads to the death of our separate-self sense. To embrace the cross of Christ is to be willing to leave behind the self as a fixed point of reference. It is to die to all separation, even to a self that has been transformed. It is to be one with God, not just to experience it.

Jesus' invitation to "take up your cross every day and follow me" is a call to do what he actually did. As the Way, Jesus invites us to follow his example step-by-step into the bosom of the Father. As the Truth, he shares with us, through participation in his death on the cross, the experience of the transpersonal aspect of the Father. As the Life, he leads us to unity with the Godhead beyond personal and impersonal relationships. On the Christian path, God is known first as the personal God, then as the transpersonal God, and finally as the Ultimate Reality beyond all personal and impersonal categories. Since God's existence, knowledge and activity are one, Ultimate Reality is discovered to be *That-which-is.*

The Passion

When they brought Jesus to Golgotha (which means the place of the skull), they tried to give him wine drugged with myrrh, but he would not take it. Then they crucified him and divided up his garments by rolling dice for them to see what each should take. It was about nine in the morning when they crucified him. . . .

With him they crucified two insurgents, one at his right and one at his left. People going by kept insulting him, tossing their heads and saying, "Ha, ha! So you were going to destroy the temple and rebuild it in three days! Save yourself now by coming down from that cross!"

The chief priests and the scribes also joined in and jeered, "He saved others, but he cannot save himself! Let the 'Messiah', the king of Israel, come down from the cross here and now so that we can see it and believe in him!" The men who had been crucified with him likewise kept taunting him.

When noon came, darkness fell on the whole countryside and lasted until midafternoon. At that time Jesus cried out in a loud voice, "Eloi, Eloi, lama sabachthani?" which means, "My God, my God, why have you forsaken me?"

A few of the bystanders who heard it remarked: "Listen! He is calling on Elijah." Someone ran, and soaking a sponge in sour wine, stuck it on a reed to try to make him drink. The man said, "Now let's see whether Elijah comes to take him down."

Then Jesus, uttering a loud cry, breathed his last. [Mark 15:22–38][10]

The double-bind is one of the crucial experiences of the spiritual journey. No one ever experienced it to the degree that Jesus did. By "double-bind" I mean a crisis of principle that brings about an overwhelming problem of conscience. Two apparent duties that call out for total adherence seem to be in complete opposition to each other. This is not the same as hitting bottom where there is no place to go but up. It is the agonizing problem of facing two opposing goods that cannot be integrated or resolved. Our dilemma is not a choice between good or evil, which would be a temptation. It is usually a choice between two apparent goods. Or again, an event may arise in our life that is absolutely contrary to our deepest loyalties, to our spiritual tradition, religious education or cultural conditioning. Such a choice or event causes incredible suffering, especially to those who are most advanced in purity of conscience. For a crisis of this kind there is no solution on the rational level. The double bind can only be resolved by moving to a higher level of conscious-ness, where the two opposites that seem irreconcilable on the level of reason are resolved, not by rational explanation, but in the light of the new perspective that sees the opposites as complementary rather than contradictory.

One of the classical examples of this kind of crisis appears in the book of Job, one of the great wisdom books of the Old Testament. Through most of the book, Job is struggling with the problem of innocent suffering. He knows himself to be innocent and yet he is experiencing tremendous suffering on every level of his being. He ends up sitting on a dunghill, covered with sores from head to foot. All his possessions, his family and friends have been taken from him, and he is over-whelmed by physical infirmities. Yet he had never offended God in any way. Prior to his misfortunes, he was recognized by everyone as a just man. His comforters, representing the cultural preconceptions of the time, kept telling him, "If only you will admit that you have sinned, God will forgive you and your suffering will be taken away."

In Job's day misfortune was considered a sign of personal sin; either one had done something wrong in early life, or one had committed a hidden sin. Job was confronted with the dilemma of being faithful to his own integrity (He knew he had not done anything wrong.) or of accusing God of injustice for allowing him to suffer as if he had committed some secret crime. Job maintains his innocence throughout the book. His double-bind consisted of trying to avoid accusing God of injustice and at the same time, of remaining faithful to his conscience which told him that he had done nothing wrong.

The resolution of Job's double-bind comes in the last chapter of the book, when God reveals to him a higher view of reality without explaining the mystery of innocent suffering. God seems to say that suffering is one of the impenetrables of life while remaining an inescapable part of it.

Job's suffering helps us understand what the passion of Jesus involved as a double-bind. In the desert Jesus experienced the human condition with the same concrete-ness with which we experience it, namely, in the form of the emotional programming of early childhood. As Jesus' life unfolded, his awareness of his personal union with the Father constantly increased. As he approached the end of his life, he revealed the God of Israel, not as a God of armies, of fear or of sheer transcendence, but as the God of compassion, a Presence that bends over creatures with incredible tenderness, care and affection. At the same time, God is firm in training his children so that they may grow into the transcendent destiny that he has planned for them.

No one ever knew God the way that Jesus knew him. He penetrated the depths of the Ultimate Reality and revealed that the interior life of Limitless Being is relationship: a community of persons sharing infinite life and love. Jesus entered into that relationship, made it his own, and tried to transmit it to his disciples. For him, the Father, *Abba,* was absolutely everything. In coming to the age of reason and to full reflective self-consciousness, Jesus never suffered from the feeling of separation from God that is our experience as we come to rational consciousness. This feeling of separation is the source of our deep sense of incompletion, guilt and alienation.

Jesus took upon himself the human condition more and more concretely as his life progressed. In the Garden of Gethsemani, he took upon himself the sin of the world with all its consequences. He experienced every level of loneliness, guilt and anguish that you or I or any human being has ever felt. The ghastly sum of accumulated human misery, sin and guilt descended upon him. He felt himself being asked by his Father to identify with this misery in all its immensity and horror. This was the double-bind Jesus articulated so graphically in the Garden of Gethsemani. After pleading in vain to the apostles to watch one hour with him, he withdrew a little way from them and fell on his face crying out, "Abba, if it be possible, let this chalice pass from me!" The clear realization that he was being asked by the Father to thrust himself as far from him as anyone has ever experienced, caused him unimaginable agony. By absorbing the separate-self sense into his inmost being, Jesus *became* sin. As Paul writes, "He who knew not sin was made sin for our salvation."

Jesus was torn between the choices presented by the double-bind: "Am I to become sin and thus renounce my personal relationship with Abba?" Or again, "Am I to become sin and thus experience separation from the One who is my whole life?"

His prayer continues, "Nevertheless, Father, not my will, but thine be done."

Jesus made this petition three times over and as he prayed, he sweat drops of blood, manifesting the incredible agony of his double-bind. The source of Jesus' dread was not so much the prospect of physical suffering, but the impending loss of his personal relationship with the One who meant everything to him.

"Father, how can I, your *Son,* become sin?" That is the cup of bitterness that Jesus desperately wanted to avoid. And yet, because of his boundless love for the

Father and for us, he kept repeating with ever-increasing desperation, "Not my will, but Thine be done!"

"My Father, if it is possible, let this cup pass from me."[11] That is the voice of human weakness reaching to infinity, the voice of human sinfulness that Jesus took upon himself and identified with in the Garden.

"Not my will, but Thine be done." That is the voice of God's infinite love for us, throbbing in the heart of Christ, forgiving everything and everyone. Infinite weakness and infinite love have met in the passion and death of Jesus. Our anguish has become his anguish.

Jesus rose from his prayer and returned to the disciples only to find them asleep. There was to be no human support for him in his supreme moment of isolation and need. Soon all but one of the apostles would run away. Soon he was to be rejected by his own people, condemned by the civil and religious authorities, subjected to insult and mockery, and crucified between two murderers. In his last moments he would watch his life's work disintegrate before his eyes.

As Jesus approached the end of his physical endurance on the cross, he cried out, "My God, my God, why have you forsaken me?" With these words, he revealed the fact that the act of taking upon himself the entire weight of human sinfulness had cost him the loss of his personal union with the Father. It is the final stage of Jesus' spiritual journey. This double-bind, when it was resolved at the moment of his resurrection, catapulted him into a state of being beyond the personal union with the Father which had been his whole life until then. While his sacrifice opened up for the whole human family the possibility of sharing in his experience of personal union with the Father, it opened up for him a totally new level of being. His humanity was glorified to such a degree that he could enter the heart of all creation as its Source. Now he is present everywhere, in the inmost being of all creation, transcending time and space and bringing the transmission of divine life to its ultimate fulfillment.

Unity with the Godhead was the resolution of Jesus' double-bind. There is a resolution for every double-bind. It remains, however, a terrible crisis. In the face of such a crisis, one may regress to a lower level of consciousness. But one who seeks God will not give in to this temptation. The energy built up by living with the seemingly impossible situation will eventually give birth to the resolution that only God knows and that only God can give.

Father, How Can I, Your Son, Become Sin?

> Your attitude must be Christ's:
> though he was in the form of God
> he did not deem equality with God

> something to be grasped at.
> Rather, he emptied himself
> and took the form of a slave,
> being born in the likeness of men.
> He was known to be of human estate,
> and it was thus he humbled himself,
> obediently accepting even death,
> death on a cross! [Phil. 2:6–9]

To become sin is to cease to be God's son—or at least to cease to be conscious of being God's son. To cease to be conscious of being God's son is to cease to experience God as Father. The cross of Jesus represents the ultimate death-of-God experience: "My God, my God, why have You forsaken me?" The crucifixion is much more than the physical death of Jesus and the emotional and mental anguish that accompanied it. It is the death of his relationship with the Father. The crucifixion was not the death of his false self because he never had one. It was the death of his deified self and the annihilation of the ineffable union which he enjoyed with the Father in his human faculties. This was more than spiritual death; it was dying to being God and hence the dying *of* God: "He emptied himself, and took the form of a slave . . . accepting even death, death on a cross!" The loss of personal identity is the ultimate kenosis.

In the crucifixion, his relationship with the Father disappeared and with it the loss of his experience of *who* the Father is. In his resurrection and ascension, Jesus discovered all that the Father is, and in doing so, became one with the Ultimate Reality: *all that God is* emerging eternally from *all that God is.*

This passing of Jesus from human to divine subjectivity is called in Christian tradition the Paschal Mystery. Our participation in this Mystery is the passing over of the transformed self into the loss of self as a fixed point of reference[12]; of *who* God is into *all that* God is. The dismantling of the false self and the inward journey to the true self is the first phase of this transition or passing over. The loss of the true self as a fixed point of reference is the second phase. The first phase results in the consciousness of personal union with the Trinity. The second phase consists in being emptied of this union and identifying with the absolute nothingness from which all things emerge, to which all things return, and which manifests Itself as *That-Which-Is.*

The Burial

It was now around midday, and darkness came over the whole land until midafternoon . . . Jesus uttered a loud cry and said, "Father, into your hands I commend my spirit." After he said this, he expired.

The centurion, upon seeing what had happened, gave glory to God by saying, "Surely this was an innocent man." After the crowd assembled for this spectacle witnessed what had happened, they returned beating their breasts. All his friends and the women who had accompanied him from Galilee were standing at a distance watching everything.

There was a man named Joseph . . . from Arimathea . . . and he looked expectantly for the reign of God. This man approached Pilate with a request for Jesus' body. He took it down, wrapped it in fine linen, and laid it in a tomb hewn out of rock, in which no one had yet been buried.

That was the day of Preparation, and the Sabbath was about to begin. The women who had come with him from Galilee followed along behind. They saw the tomb and how his body was buried. Then they went back home to prepare spices and perfumes. They observed the Sabbath as a day of rest, in accordance with the Law. [Luke 23:44–56][13]

Jesus died on the day before the Sabbath. His body was taken down in a hurry and laid in the tomb. The Sabbath commemorates the seventh day of creation, the day God rested from all his works. In honor of creation and at God's express command, the Jewish people observed the Sabbath as a day of complete rest. But its most profound meaning is contained in this particular Sabbath in which, having laid down his life for the human family, Jesus, the Son of God, rested.

Out of respect for the death of the Redeemer, there is no liturgical celebration on Holy Saturday. In honor of Jesus' body resting in the tomb, the church also rests. There is nothing more to be said, nothing more to be done. On this day everything rests.

In the Hebrew cosmology of the time, the souls of the just after death were thought to descend through the waters of the Great Abyss to a place of rest called Sheol, where they awaited their deliverance at the time of the Messiah. Accordingly, when Jesus died on Good Friday, his soul was believed by the first Christians to have passed through the waters of the Great Abyss to the place of Sheol, where he released the souls of the just. In Matthew's Gospel it is recorded that "After Jesus' resurrection they came forth from their tombs and entered the holy city and appeared to many."[14]

In the Old Testament, water is often the symbol of destruction. Water destroyed the wicked at the time of Noah. Water destroyed the Egyptians in the Red Sea when they tried to pursue the Israelites. At the same time, water also appears in the Old Testament as the symbol of life. In the Book of Genesis we read that the Spirit breathed over the waters of primeval chaos and they brought forth living creatures.

As Jesus' soul descended through the waters of the Great Abyss, the sins of the world which he was bearing were completely destroyed. In the ceremonies of baptism, we ritually descend into the waters of the Great Abyss together with Jesus, identifying with his holiness as he identified with our sinfulness. All our sins are destroyed in the waters of baptism. The one who emerges from the baptismal pool after being submerged in it joins Jesus in his ascent out of Sheol into the New Creation. The resurrection of Jesus is not the resuscitation of a corpse or the mere vindication of a just man. It is totally a new way of being. As Jesus' soul is reunited with his glorified body—baked, so to speak, in the limitless energy of the Spirit—he moves triumphantly into the heart of all creation. God's answer to Jesus' double-bind is to bestow upon him complete and unlimited participation in the Father's glory.

Creation is totally new in the light of the resurrection. The Sabbath belongs to the old world of sin that has passed away in the destruction of Christ's body on the cross. The New Creation, the eighth day, the day after the Sabbath, is the first day of eternal life in union with Christ, a day that will never end.

This new life is the significance of Jesus' death, his descent into Sheol and his resting in the tomb. The revelation of the enormous energy of the New Creation awaits the moment of his resurrection. God's first creative word, "Let there be light!"[15] becomes "Let there be life!"

The Anointing of the Body of Jesus

Afterward, Joseph of Arimathea asked Pilate's permission to remove the body of Jesus. Pilot granted it, so they came and took the body away. Nicodemus (the man who had first come to Jesus at night) likewise came bringing a mixture of myrrh and aloes which weighed about a hundred pounds. They took Jesus' body, and in accordance with Jewish burial custom, bound it up in wrappings of cloth with perfumed oils.

In the place where he had been crucified there was a garden, and in the garden a new tomb in which no one had ever been laid. Because it was the Jewish Preparation Day, they laid Jesus there, for the tomb was close at hand. [John 19:38–42][16]

The text describes Nicodemus and the holy women anointing Christ's body with a generous portion of myrrh, aloes and perfumed oils in accordance with the Jewish custom.

We have already become acquainted with the symbolism of perfumed oil through the story of Mary of Bethany and her anointing of Jesus six days before his death. Oil is one of the symbols that appears frequently in the Old Testament as well as in the Gospel of John. In the Old Testament, the sick were anointed with oil, and kings and prophets were anointed with chrism (perfumed oil). In the sacrament of baptism, the catechumen is anointed with oil; in the sacrament of confirmation, the anointing is conferred with chrism (perfumed oil). The latter implies not only the bestowal of the Holy Spirit, symbolized by the anointing with oil, but also the *perception* of the presence and action of the Spirit, symbolized by the delicious odor of the perfume.

When Mary of Bethany anointed Jesus with the perfume of great price—smashing the bottle and emptying the entire contents over him—she was affirming that he was no ordinary guest. She manifested her awareness that the Spirit had been imparted to Jesus not just in part, as was the case of the kings and prophets, but completely. She perceived that Jesus' sacred body was filled with the most costly perfume that ever existed, the Holy Spirit. Like the alabaster jar that she broke and emptied over his head, his body, too, was about to be broken and its sacred contents were to be poured out over the whole human family for its salvation.

Thus the outpouring of the Spirit as the fruit of Christ's sacrifice on the cross is magnificently expressed by Mary's lavish gesture. The text states that Jesus' body was anointed with a hundred pounds of myrrh, aloes and perfumed oils. Jesus' prophetic praise of Mary's action was thus thoroughly fulfilled: "What she has done is in anticipation of my burial."

In Christ, matter itself has become divine. At the moment of Christ's rising from the dead, the Holy Spirit rushed upon his body, anointing it with the fire of divine love, penetrating his sacred flesh until it was totally transformed not only into pure spirit, but into the divine nature itself. The entire material creation is now Christ's body. When we celebrate the Eucharist, we are celebrating the glorification of the entire cosmos, present in some mysterious manner in the glorification of Christ's body. It is only a question of time until the fullness of that revelation becomes manifest.

In the Paschal Vigil, the liturgy makes extensive use of fire, which is a source of light, heat, and energy. The New Fire, symbolizing the Holy Spirit poured out over the world in the outpouring of Christ's blood, is blessed at the beginning of the Paschal Vigil. From that fire, the Paschal Candle, symbol of Christ's body waiting to be raised from the dead, is lit. When the celebrant touches the flame taken from the New Fire to the Paschal Candle, symbol of the glorified Christ, the eternal event of Jesus' resurrection becomes our own inner experience.

The assembly gathered for the Vigil walks in the darkness as the Paschal Candle leads the way to the sanctuary. This procession reenacts the deliverance of God's people from its oppressors in the Red Sea. Moses was sent to save his people from the bondage of Egypt. God said to him, "I have witnessed the affliction of my people in Egypt and have heard their cry . . . therefore I have come down to rescue them."[17]

In his passion Jesus equivalently says to us, "I have seen the affliction of the human family, and I have come down to free you for the full reception of the Spirit and the complete transformation of your nature into the divine—body, soul, and spirit."

In that sacred procession, reliving by faith the passage of the Israelites through the Red Sea and identifying with Christ's descent into Sheol through the waters of the Great Abyss, all our sins are once again utterly destroyed. As we enter the church, we receive a parted tongue of flame from the Paschal Candle, symbolizing a share of the Spirit. As we listen to the *Exultet,* the ancient hymn of thanksgiving chanted by a representative of the community, the candle we hold in our hands represents the light of faith in Christ's resurrection rising as an invincible conviction in our hearts. It is at that moment that the *Alleluia* is intoned.

The *Alleluia* is the song of ecstatic love, joy, praise, adoration and gratitude all rolled into one. It proclaims the triumph of God over death in every form. It is our response to the resolution of Christ's double-bind. As he passes into his glorification, he incorporates us into his own glorified body and shares with us his own happiness, the joy of eternal life. The *Alleluia* is the song of resurrection. It is the cry of those in whom the inner resurrection is taking place. Faith and confidence in Christ explode into the experience of divine union.

The Women Visit the Tomb

When the Sabbath was over, Mary Magdalene, Mary the Mother of James, and Salome brought perfumed oils with which they intended to anoint the body of Jesus. Very early, just after sunrise, on the first day of the week they came to the tomb. They were saying to one another, "Who will roll back the stone from the entrance to the tomb for us?" When they looked, they found that the stone had been rolled back. (It was a huge one.) On entering the tomb, they saw a young man sitting at the right, dressed in a white robe. This frightened them thoroughly, but he reassured them: "You need not be amazed. You are looking for Jesus of Nazareth, the one who was crucified. He has been raised up; he is not here. See the place where they laid him. Go and tell his disciples and Peter, 'He is going ahead of you to Galilee where you will see him, just as he told you.' "

They made their way out and fled from the tomb, bewildered and trembling; and because of their great fear, they said nothing to anyone. [Mark 16:1–8][18]

In his last moments on the cross Jesus was called upon by the Father to identify himself with the human family in all the consequences of sin. In doing so, Jesus experienced to the utmost degree the sense of alienation from God that is the result of coming to full reflective self-consciousness without the experience of divine union. This process happens to every human being; in the Christian tradition, it is called original sin.

The alienation that Jesus experienced in his passion caused him to die without the experience of the personal union with the Father that he had enjoyed throughout his earthly life. His holy soul, bearing our sins, descended into the destructive waters of the Great Abyss in order that our sinfulness might be utterly destroyed. Because of Christ's divine power, at the moment that sin was destroyed in the waters of the Great Abyss, these same waters instantly became the waters of eternal life. Christ gave to water the capacity to flow forever in superabundant mercy and to bring forth creatures capable of sharing his divine light, life and love.

As Christ's soul emerged from the waters made life-giving by the touch of his sacred humanity and re-entered his body, the sacrifice he had offered released within the bosom of the Father an incredible outpouring of divine light, life and love. The fire of the Holy Spirit, bursting with the fullness of divine energy, rushed upon his sacred remains. The perfumed oil of immense weight and value, symbolizing the Spirit, suggests the immense power that the Spirit exerted when the soul of Christ re-entered his body. In this reunion, the Father poured into the risen Jesus the whole of the divine essence—the utter riches, glory, and prerogatives of the divine nature—in a way that is utterly inconceivable to us.

In the Book of Revelation John tells of his vision of Christ as Lord of the universe: "His feet gleamed like polished brass refined in a furnace."[19] These words suggest that the Spirit glorified the flesh of Jesus until it was melted, so to speak, into divinity. It is this glorified flesh, united to the Eternal Word of God, that has entered into the heart of all creation and become one with all reality.

The reunion of the body and soul of Jesus took place in the secret of the night just before dawn, a moment that no one saw or witnessed. This is the event that is celebrated during the Paschal Vigil. The first rite of that sacred ceremony, as we saw, is the blessing of the New Fire, the symbol of the Spirit descending upon the precious blood of Christ poured out upon the ground. A spark is taken from the New Fire to light the Paschal Candle, celebrating the moment that Christ rose from the dead in glory. The Paschal Candle is the symbol of the pillar of fire by which God led the Israelites out of the slavery of Egypt into the Promised Land. The same presence and action is now leading us from sin and disbelief to higher levels of faith and consciousness. The passage of the Israelites through the Red Sea is reenacted by the assembly as they walk through the darkened cloister or church into the sanctuary. The Paschal Candle symbolizes the risen Christ leading his people to the promised land of divine transformation. As the single flame atop the Paschal Candle is shared and becomes the possession of each member of the assembly, the whole church is gradually illumined without the original flame being diminished. Divine charity, the ripe fruit of Christ's resurrection, never diminishes; it is increased by being shared. Because of the intrinsic power of the Easter mystery, the Paschal Vigil is not a mere commemoration of Christ's resurrection; it awakens the experience of Christ rising in our inmost being and spreading the fire of his love throughout all our faculties.

At this point in the celebration of the Paschal Vigil, the great hymn of Easter is sung by the deacon. In this magnificent hymn in honor of the resurrection, we can feel welling up inside of us the enthusiasm of the Christian people of all time.

> Rejoice, heavenly powers! Sing, choirs of angels!
> Exult, all creation around God's throne!
> Jesus Christ, our King, is risen!
> Sound the trumpet of salvation!
>
> Rejoice, O earth, in shining splendor,
> radiant in the brightness of your King!
> Christ has conquered! Glory fills you!
> Darkness vanishes forever! . . .
>
> This is our passover feast, when Christ,
> the true Lamb, is slain . . .
>
> This is the night when first you saved our fathers:
> You freed the people of Israel from their slavery
> And led them dry-shod through the sea.
>
> This is the night when Christians everywhere,
> washed clean of sin, and freed from all defilement,
> are restored to grace and grow together in holiness.
>
> This is the night when Jesus Christ broke the chains
> of death and rose triumphant from the grave.
> What good, indeed, would life have been to us,
> had Christ not come as our Redeemer?
>
> Father, how wonderful your care for us! How boundless
> your merciful love! To ransom a slave, you gave away
> your Son!
>
> O happy fault! O necessary sin of Adam which gained
> for us so great a Redeemer! . . .
>
> The power of this night dispels all evil, washes guilt
> away, and restores lost innocence . . .

O night truly blessed, when heaven is wedded to earth,
and man is reconciled with God!

After the chanting of the *Exultet,* everyone is seated and the lessons containing the biblical symbols highlighted by the hymn are explained. Then the *Alleluia* is sung and the saving presence and power of Christ is applied concretely to the community in the baptism of its catechumens.

Notice in the hymn there is the statement that this sacred night "restores lost innocence". This phrase, of course, refers to the Garden of Eden and the story of Adam and Eve. It recalls their loss of intimacy with God. The heart of the Easter mystery is our personal discovery of intimacy with God which scripture calls "innocence." It is the innocence arising from easy and continual exchange of the most delightful kind with God. This relationship casts out all fear.

In order to understand the meaning of scriptural innocence, we must distinguish it from the innocence of ignorance. The innocence of ignorance is the mindlessness that the animal world enjoys, the inability to reflect on oneself or to take responsibility for one's actions. The loss of that kind of innocence does not need to be regretted. Rather, rational consciousness is the greatest achievement of the evolutionary process to date.

At the same time, there is a sense in which we have known God before. This sense comes from the ontological unconscious, which is God remembering himself in us, so to speak. We have a deep-seated intuition that some indispensable relationship essential for our wellbeing and happiness is missing. The spiritual journey is a way of remembering our Source, what Meister Eckhart calls the "ground unconscious." The ground unconscious becoming conscious is our awakening to the Mystery of God's presence within us. This is the innocence to which scripture and the *Exultet* refer.

Easter is the awakening of divine life in us. "Christ is risen!" is not merely the cry of historical witnesses. It is the cry of all the people of God throughout the centuries who have realized Christ rising in them, not only in the form of emotional enthusiasm, but in the form of unshakable conviction. The light of Christ reveals the fact of our abiding union with him and its potential to transform every aspect of our lives.

Mary Magdalene Meets the Risen Christ

Mary Magdalene was lingering outside the tomb, weeping. As she was giving vent to her tears she stooped to look into the tomb, and she saw two angels in white seated where the body had lain, one at the head, the other at the feet. "Woman," they said to her, "why are you weeping?"

"Because," she replied, "they have taken away my master and I do not know where they laid him." With this she turned around to look behind and saw Jesus standing by, but did not know that it was Jesus.

"Woman," Jesus said to her, "why are you weeping? Who is it you are looking for?" Taking him to be the gardener, she replied, "Sir, if you carried him away, tell me where you laid him. I want to remove him."

Then Jesus said, "Mary!" Turning around she said to him in Hebrew, "Raboni!" (which means "Master").

"Stop clinging to me," Jesus said to her. "I am ascending to the Father. Go therefore to my brothers and say to them, 'I am ascending to my Father and to your Father, to my God and to your God.'" Mary Magdalene went to carry the message to the disciples [John 20:11–18][20]

The resurrection of Jesus is the first day of the New Creation. The events following the resurrection and the various appearances of Jesus to his disciples and friends are used in the liturgy to help us understand the significance of this central Mystery of our faith.

We have seen how Jesus died in the unresolved double-bind between identification with the human condition and the loss of personal union with the Father that is the inevitable result of this identification. The resurrection of Jesus is the resolution of that double-bind. It is the answer of the Father to the sacrifice of Jesus. It opened for us, as well as for him, a totally new life. It is the decisive moment in human history: as a result, divine union is now accessible to every human being.

The first resurrection scene is cast in a cosmic context. From the scriptural point of view, the garden in which the tomb of Jesus was situated reminds us of the garden of Eden. The two gardens are juxtaposed: in the first, the human family, in the persons of Adam and Eve, lost God's intimacy and friendship; in the second, Mary Magdalene (out of whom Jesus had cast seven devils) appears as the first recipient of the good news that intimacy and union with God are once again available.

She came to the tomb in great distress. The huge stone, symbol of the heavy weight of sin and the downward pull of the lower levels of consciousness, had been rolled away. When the women looked in, there was nothing in the tomb but the winding cloths with which Jesus had been buried. This caused Mary to think that his body had been stolen. In her great love for Jesus, she lingered outside the tomb after the other women had gone. She looked into the tomb again just to make sure, and now she saw two angels in white. They were surprised to see someone in tears on such a joyful occasion and said, "Woman, why are you weeping?"

She does not seem to have noticed that angels were speaking to her. She was totally absorbed in one thing only, and that was missing. She said to them, "If you have removed his body, tell me where you have put it and I will come and take it away." She was completely oblivious to the fact that Jesus' body would be too heavy for her to move. It had been anointed with a hundred pounds of myrrh, aloes and perfumed oil, so it was a hundred pounds heavier than before. But these considerations were obliterated by the intensity of her grief. Paying no further attention to these unusual personages, she started looking around in the garden. There she saw a man whom she presumed to be the gardener.

She was not mistaken. Jesus *is* the gardener in the garden of the New Creation. Because of her emotional turmoil, however, she does not recognize him. This is characteristic of the post-resurrection apparitions. It is only gradually that Jesus usually manifests himself. We can presume from this fact that he had acquired a new form. Apparently Jesus did not enter into his full glory right away; it was withheld so that he could spend time with his disciples. It is only at his ascension that he enters fully into the glory that the fire of the Holy Spirit initiated at the moment of his resurrection.

The "gardener" says with a certain irony, "Woman, whom are you looking for? Why are you weeping?" This question seems to have crystallized Mary's immense grief, and she poured out her heart in a jumble of words: "Tell me where you have laid him, sir, and I will remove him."

Jesus then spoke her name, "Mary!" Only he could say her name in that way. Instantly, with the whole of her being, she recognized him and in that moment *knew* that he had risen from the dead.

In the scripture, to be called by name has special significance. To call someone or something by name is to identify who or what it is. Adam, in paradise, named each beast and flower according to its essence. God often changed the names of prophets to fit their roles. By calling her by name, Jesus manifests his knowledge of everything in her life and his total acceptance of all that she is. This is the moment in which Mary realizes that Jesus loved her. This is the first step in her transformation.

In the Christian scheme of things, the movement from the human condition to divine transformation requires the mediation of a personal relationship with God. The personal love of Jesus facilitates the growth of this relationship. The experience of being loved by him draws the Christian out of all selfishness into deeper levels of self-surrender. How could this movement occur without the conviction of being personally loved by him? The simple utterance of one word, "Mary!" brought to focus all her longings. Her response was to throw herself into the arms of Jesus as she cried out in her joy, "Master!"

The realization of being loved by God characterizes the first stage of contemplative prayer. It enables us to see God in all things. Mary's acceptance of that grace leads to a further insight; she becomes aware that she loves Jesus in return. Accordingly, she throws herself into his arms and clings to him. We are not told how long this embrace lasted, but through that experience she was raised to the next level of contemplative prayer, which is the capacity to see all things in God.

In this conversation, Jesus is raising Mary step-by-step through the progressive stages of contemplative prayer to divine union. Finally, he says to her, "Stop clinging to me! I have not yet risen to my Father. But, go and tell my brothers that I ascend to my Father and to your Father."

Those words are the manifesto of the New Creation! God is now not only the Father of Jesus Christ, not just the "Abba" whom Jesus has revealed out of his own personal experience of divine union. The Abba has now been given to us! The experience that Christ has of the Father is completely ours! Thus, the same relationship with the Father that Christ enjoys is rising up in Mary Magdalene—and in each of us as we assimilate the grace of Easter.

With these words of Jesus, Mary is sent to be the apostle of the apostles. What makes an apostle is divine love, nothing else. Since she now had within herself the experience of intimacy with the Father, bestowed upon her by Jesus, she is the one who proclaims to the apostles the message of Easter. "You, my brothers," Jesus says through her, "have been initiated into the reign of God, into my experience of the Father as Abba, the God of infinite compassion."

Jesus, in the plan of God, has opened the way to the highest states of consciousness. The pain and agony of self-consciousness, with its guilt-ridden sense of responsibility, has been replaced by the invitation to enter into the human potential for unlimited growth. The Garden of Eden is both a memory of what could be and a preview of what is to come. In the Garden of the Resurrection the full revelation of the Mystery of Christ is unveiled. And with that knowledge and experience, Mary reaches the third level of contemplative prayer, the abiding *state* of divine union, which is to see God giving himself in everything. This is the transformed consciousness of inner resurrection. And this is the Good News she was sent to announce to the apostles.

Adam and Eve were thrown out of the first garden as a result of the emergence of their self-consciousness apart from divine union. Mary was so rooted in the experience of divine union that the Garden of Paradise was inside her and she could never leave it. The Garden of Eden stands for a state of consciousness, not a geographical location. She is sent out of the garden, but with the abiding interior state the garden represents: the certitude of being loved by God, of loving him in return, and of God giving himself in every event and at every moment, both within or without. In this state, outside and inside are in harmony; they have become one. In the course of this conversation, the Ultimate Mystery becomes for Mary the Ultimate Presence, and the Ultimate Presence becomes the Ultimate Reality.

The outpouring of grace that we see in this first appearance of Jesus after his resurrection is God's response to Christ's sacrifice; it is his glorification in response to his utter humiliation. Like Mary Magdalene, Christ is also calling us by name as we celebrate the feast of his resurrection.

On the Road to Emmaus

Two disciples of Jesus that same day (the first day of the Sabbath) were making their way to a village named Emmaus, seven miles distant from Jerusalem, discussing as they went all that had happened. In the course of their lively exchange, Jesus approached and began to walk along with them. However, they were restrained from recognizing him. He said to them, "What are you discussing as you go your way?"

They halted in distress, and one of them, Cleopas by name, asked him, "Are you the only resident of Jerusalem who does not know the things that went on there these past few days?"

He said to them, "What things?"

They said, "All those that had to do with Jesus of Nazareth, a prophet powerful in word and deed in the eyes of God and all the people; however, our chief priests and leaders delivered him up to be condemned to death, and crucified him. We were hoping that he was the one who would set Israel free. Besides all this, today, the third day since all these things happened, some women of our group just brought us some astounding news. They were there at the tomb before dawn and failed to find his body, but returned with the tale that they had seen a vision of angels who declared he was alive. Some of our number went to the tomb and found it just as the women had said; but him they did not see."

Then he said to them, "What little sense you have! How slow you are to believe all that the prophets have announced! Did not the Messiah have to undergo all this so as to enter into his glory?" Beginning, then, with Moses and all the prophets, he interpreted for them every passage of scripture which referred to him.

By now they were near the village to which they were going, and he acted as if he were going farther. But they pressed him: "Stay with us. It is nearly evening—the day is practically over." So he went in and stayed with them.

When he had seated himself with them to eat, he took bread, pronounced the blessing, and then broke the bread and distributed it to them. With that their eyes were opened and they recognized him; whereupon he vanished from their sight. They said to one another, "Were not our hearts burning inside us as he talked to us on the road and explained the scriptures to us?"

They got up immediately and returned to Jerusalem, where they found the Eleven and the rest of the company assembled. They were greeted with,

"The Lord has been raised! It is true! He has appeared to Simon." Then they recounted what had happened on the road and how they had come to know him in the breaking of the bread. [Luke 24:13–35][21]

This story shows us two of Jesus' disciples who represent the basic state of mind in which most of the disciples found themselves on the day of the resurrection. They were utterly discouraged. No one's career and message had ever been so thoroughly defeated and discredited in the public eye as had that of Jesus. Even his disciples and closest friends had left him and fled; indeed, he had been betrayed into the hands of the ecclesiastical and civil officials by one of his closest friends. The hopes of his disciples were in shreds.

It is clear from this text that the hopes of these two disciples were not in accord with the message that Jesus had been trying to communicate during his lifetime. One of the things they said when he asked for an explanation of their sadness was, "We were hoping that he was the one who would set Israel free." In other words, these disciples—and this may have been Judas' problem as well—had preconceived ideas about who the Messiah was to be and what he was to do. One of their expectations was that he would deliver Israel from the domination of the Roman Empire. In other words, they wanted a Messiah who would fit into the nationalistic aspirations of the Jewish people of that time. Although Jesus had made it clear that he would have nothing to do with political programs, he could not get this idea out of the heads of his disciples. Consequently, when he predicted well in advance that he would be delivered into the hands of the Gentiles and put to death, they did not hear what he said.

Our emotional programming is such that we rarely hear what we do not wish to hear. The disciples envisaged the reign of God as a political triumph, not as the mystery of God's intervention in their personal lives.

The two disciples had heard reports about women going to the tomb and not finding the body of Jesus. It does not seem to have occurred to them that if the women's report about the empty tomb were true, their report that Jesus had risen from the dead might also be true. The confused and disgruntled disciples were paralyzed by disappointment and grief.

Hiding his identity, Jesus appeared as a stranger, a fellow-traveler along the road, and asked, "Friends, what are you talking about, and why do you look so sad?" His friendly and courteous manner opened them up to dialogue, and they poured out the reasons for their distress.

Notice that the disciples were heading away from Jerusalem. They had evidently decided, despite what the women were reported to have said, that their part in the community of Jesus' disciples was over.

Jesus' response to their sad tale was, "How little sense you have! How slow you are to believe all that the prophets have announced!" Then, opening the scriptures to them, he began to put into perspective the true meaning of the Messiah. As they approached the outskirts of Emmaus, Jesus indicated that he was going further; he probably would have gone on unless they had urged him to stay with them.

He went in to the inn with them and sat down at the table. It was now evening, the time of the evening sacrifice and the time that the Last Supper had been eaten. He took bread, pronounced the blessing and broke the bread. Then he distributed it to them just as they had seen him do many times before at common meals.

Later the disciples acknowledged to each other that their hearts were burning as Jesus explained the scriptures to them. This "burning" brought them to a high level of concentration and attentiveness. Suddenly, as Jesus broke the bread, the data of their external senses and their interior alertness connected. The intuition of faith saw through the outward appearance of the stranger to the Reality. In front of them was the risen Christ! As soon as they recognized him, he vanished from their eyes.

"They immediately turned around and went back to Jerusalem." There they learned that Jesus had also appeared to Peter. During the course of the day, the apostles had come to accept the fact of the resurrection, either because they had been to the empty tomb or because Peter had seen the Lord. More importantly, they were beginning to experience interiorly the grace of the resurrection. The risen Christ was awakening within them, enabling them to see the events of the past few days with the x-ray eyes of faith.

Like the disciples of Emmaus, we, too, have our own ideas of Jesus Christ, his message and his church. We, too, are conditioned by our upbringing, early education, culture and life experience. The disciples could not recognize Jesus as long as their mindsets about who he was and what he was to do were in place. When Jesus demolished their blindness with his explanation of the scriptures, their vision of him began to assume a more realistic tone. The price of recognizing Jesus is always the same: our idea of him, of the church, of the spiritual journey, of God himself has to be shattered. To see with the eyes of faith we must be free of our culturally conditioned mindsets. When we let go of our private and limited vision, he who has been hidden from us by our pre-packaged values and preconceived ideas causes the scales to fall from our eyes. He was there all the time. Now at last we perceive his Presence. With the transformed vision of faith, we return to the humdrum routines and duties of daily life, but now, like Mary Magdalene, we recognize God giving himself to us in everyone and in everything.

The Appearance in the Upper Room

Late in the evening of that same day, the first day of the week, although the doors of the place where the disciples had gathered were bolted for fear of the authorities, Jesus came and stood before them. "Peace be to you," he said. [John 20:19]

They were in a complete panic, fancying they were seeing a ghost. "Why are you disturbed?" he said to them, "and why do you let doubts come into your minds? Look at my hands and my feet. Surely it is my very self! Feel me, and convince yourselves; no ghost has flesh and bones such as you see I have!" With that, he showed them his hands and his feet.

But they still refused to believe; it was too good to be true, and continued in their perplexity. So he said to them, "Have you something here to eat?" Then they offered him a piece of broiled fish which he accepted and ate before their eyes.

He said to them, "These events are the fulfillment of what I predicted to you when I was still with you, namely that anything ever written concerning me—in the Law of Moses, in the prophets, or in the psalms—must be fulfilled." He then gave them the key to the understanding of the scriptures. "This," he said to them, "is the gist of the scripture: The messiah must suffer, and on the third day rise from the dead. Furthermore: In his name the need of a change of heart and the forgiveness of sins must be preached to all the nations." [Luke 24:37–47][22]

This appearance of Jesus took place after the two disciples had returned to Jerusalem and heard the other disciples joyfully announce, "It is true! The Lord is risen! He has appeared to Simon!"

In the midst of their conversation, Jesus suddenly appeared, throwing the group into a state of panic. They thought he was a ghost, even though they had just been talking about his appearance to Peter. Jesus' words to them are fraught with significance: "Peace be to you!" Peace is the tranquility of order. It is true security. True security is the direct consequence of divine union. There is nothing wrong with desiring security. Everybody wants it and needs it. The problem is that we look for it in the wrong places. Peace is the result of the principal benefit of Christ's resurrection—the experience of the divine Presence as permanent. Peace is the treasure that Jesus triumphantly and joyfully bestows, or tried to bestow, on his crushed and demoralized apostles.

"Peace be with you!" he said again. But these words made no impression on them because they were preoccupied with the fear that they might be seized and put in jail as his disciples. They were a little band of frightened people just beginning to revive from their crushing bereavement. Suddenly, Jesus is visibly in their midst. Their first thought probably was, "I thought we bolted the door!"

Jesus had now passed beyond spatial limitations. He came in through the bolted door. Or maybe he was already present on another level of reality, invisible to the disciples. He had previously said to them, "Wherever two or three are gathered in my name, I am there with you." In any case, to the disciples' great astonishment he was there in their midst, and their first reaction was, "It's a ghost!"

He said to them, "Why are you disturbed?" As usual, Jesus goes to the heart of their motivation. At this point, their emotional programs and their imaginations were working overtime: they were projecting a ghost where there was obviously a person of flesh and blood. They did not even have the courtesy to invite him to sit down.

Jesus, perhaps with a certain amusement, asked them again, "Who do you let doubts arise in your minds?" He was trying to reassure them.

Failing in that approach, he tried to calm them by engaging their external senses. "Look at my hands and my feet. Isn't it I?" Holding out his hands to them to satisfy their curiosity, he said, "Feel me and convince yourselves." "No ghost has flesh and bones such as I have!"

Yet still they could not accept the plain fact of his visible presence among them. It was too good to be true! As they lingered in their perplexity, he continued to try to put them at ease.

"Have you something to eat?" he asked. Nothing could convince us more quickly that an apparent ghost is a real human being than a request for something to eat. The disciples frantically looked around and came up with a piece of broiled fish.

This detail is not without significance. Everything in the Gospel narratives of the resurrection has symbolic overtones. Fish, at the time these Gospels were written, had already become the symbol of Christ or one of his followers. In Greek the first two letters for *Christ* are also the first two letters for the word "fish". If a fish is the symbol of Christ, a broiled fish is the symbol of his transformed humanity. Jesus is standing before them, but in a transfigured humanity.

After he had consumed the broiled fish, the disciples began to calm down. At last they were ready to receive his instructions. "These events," he said, "are the fulfillment of what I told you would happen." He had predicted on numerous occasions that he would be handed over to the authorities, put to death and rise on the third day, but the disciples' emotional blocks has not allowed them to hear what he was saying.

"Everything written about me in the Law of Moses, in the prophets and in the psalms must be fulfilled," Jesus continued. Then he gave them the key to *understanding* the scriptures. The key to understanding the scriptures enables one to perceive the spiritual meaning contained in the text. Jesus showed the disciples that the meaning of certain prophetic texts was fulfilled in the events that had just taken place: "The Messiah must suffer and on the third day rise from the dead, and that in his name the need for a change of heart and the forgiveness of sins must be preached to all the nations."

The need for a change of heart is the need to change the direction in which we are looking for happiness. The same key that opens the scriptures opens the door to happiness.

The forgiveness of sins and the consequent restoration of friendship with God is the great triumph of Jesus' sacrifice. This is the true security that every human heart yearns for. Jesus' sacrifice frees us from the separate-self sense and from the alienation that flows from it. This is the peace which the world cannot give. The peace of Christ comes from the inner experience of his resurrection, the realization of the union of our true self with the Ultimate Reality.

Christ Satisfies Thomas' Doubts

Late in the evening of that day, the first day of the week, although the doors of the place where the disciples were gathered were bolted for fear of the authorities, Jesus came and stood before them and said, "Peace be with you!" With that, he let them see his hands and his side. The disciples were delighted to see the Lord.

Then Jesus said to them again, "Peace be with you! As the Father has sent me, so also I am sending you." With this, he breathed on them and said: "Receive the Holy Spirit. Whenever you remit anyone's sins, they are remitted; when you retain anyone's sins, they are retained."

Thomas, one of the twelve, was not with the group when Jesus came, so the other disciples said to him, "We have seen the Master!" But he replied, "Unless I see in his hands the print of the nails, and put my finger into the place where the nails were, and lay my hand into his side, I am not going to believe!"

Eight days later, his disciples were again in the room and Thomas was with them. Jesus came, though the doors were bolted, and standing before them said, "Peace be to you!" He then addressed Thomas: "Let me have your finger; put it here, and look at my hands. Now let me have your hand, and lay it into my side. And do not be incredulous, but believe."

Then Thomas burst out into the words, "My Master and my God!"

Because you have seen me," Jesus said to him, "is that why you believed? Blessed are those that have not seen and yet believe." [John 20:19–31][23]

The two great gifts of Jesus to his disciples on the day of his resurrection, the first day of the New Creation, were the forgiveness of sin and the restoration of divine union. But a still greater gift is implied: he gave them the Holy Spirit, the Source of the forgiveness of sin and of divine union.

The events of the resurrection place before us various aspects of the Paschal Mystery including the meaning of the New Creation. Let us take a look at the intriguing narrative of the apostle Thomas and his particular response to the news of the resurrection.

Thomas was not present when the disciples had their first meeting with the risen Christ. His story is regarding the caliber of the disciples whom Jesus chose. Here is an apostle who had spent three years in the intimate company of Jesus undergoing intensive spiritual training, listening daily to his teaching, and witnessing many of his miracles. Yet it is obvious from this event that Thomas was still heavily under the influence of his emotional programs for happiness. Because Jesus chose to visit the apostles at a time when Thomas was absent, his reaction was, "How come I was left out? What's wrong with me? How do these other guys rate?"

As Thomas thought about the situation, his indignation continued to increase. The other apostles kept telling him, "We have seen the Lord!" Deep down inside, his response was resentment rather than joy. He felt neglected, rejected, frustrated, and, finally, enraged.

What was Thomas thinking? "If Jesus is not going to include me, I'm not going to include him. If he doesn't want me, I don't want him either." It was the childish reaction of withdrawal. He would price himself out of the market, so to speak. Have there ever been more outrageous conditions that a little clay man demanded of the Almighty in exchange for his faith? "Unless I see in his hands the print of the nails, *and* unless I put my finger into the place where the nails were; *and* lay my hand into his side, I am not going to believe!"

This was the equivalent of saying, "Goodbye! I am through with you guys. I am through with Jesus."

We do not know how long Thomas nursed his bitterness, hurt feelings and sense of rejection. It did not make matters any better to observe the other apostles ecstatic with joy. Somehow they persuaded him to join them a week later for supper. We are not told why Thomas condescended to join them but we read: "Eight days later his disciples were once again in the room and Thomas with them. Jesus came, though the doors were bolted, and standing before them said, 'Peace be with you.'"

Jesus looked around the room until his eyes rested on Thomas. Thomas, at this point, was looking for a hole in the floor into which he could crawl. "My God! What have I said?" The outrageous conditions he had laid down in exchange for his faith struck home in their full clarity. Jesus looked straight at him. Maybe Jesus was smiling. Thomas foresaw what was going to happen.

Jesus said, "Thomas, let me have your finger. Put it here in my hands! And now let me have your hand. Place it here in my side!" Notice the detail with which Jesus meets his outrageous demands: point-by-point and word-for-word. "And do not be incredulous but believe!"

That final remark pierced Thomas to the heart. He recognized the incredible goodness of Jesus in submitting himself to his demands. This loving acquiescence to every detail of his ridiculous demands placed Thomas in a state of complete vulnerability. Like Adam and Eve, he was being called out of the woods, out of the underbrush where his false self had been hiding from the truth, into the stark reality of Jesus' love. What could he say? His response was the total gift of himself: "My Master and my God!"

We do not know whether Thomas actually put his hand into Jesus' side. But we do know that he had all the evidence he needed. He put his faith in the risen Jesus, perhaps to a greater degree than the other disciples. One marvelous effect of divine mercy is that the harder you fall, the higher you rise, provided you accept the humiliation. "When I am weak," Paul confessed, "then I am strong."[24]

Jesus added one final remark: "Blest are those who have not seen and yet believe!" As if to say, "I am happy, Thomas, that you have found faith. But leaving you out of my first visit was not a rejection but an invitation to a greater grace. It was an invitation to put your faith in me on the basis of your own inner experience."

The resurrection of Jesus is not only an historical event. The words of Jesus to Thomas suggest something more. They might be paraphrased as follows: "You based your faith on seeing me, Thomas, but there is greater happiness—to believe in my resurrection because you experience its effects within yourself."

This, of course, is an important message for us. It tells us that it is far better to relate to the risen Christ on the basis of pure faith that rests not on appearances, feelings, external evidence, or what other people say, but on our personal experience of the Christ-life rising up and manifesting its fruits within us. This is the living faith that empowers us to act under the influence of the Spirit—the same Spirit that Jesus breathed upon the apostles on the evening of his resurrection.

Christ Appears to His Friends at the Sea of Galilee

On a later occasion Jesus showed himself again to the disciples, this time by the Lake of Tiberias. He did so under the following circumstances: Simon Peter, Thomas, Nathaniel, the sons of Zebedee, and two other of the disciples happened to be together. Peter said to them, "I am going fishing." "We will go with you," they replied.

So they set out and got into the boat and during the entire night they caught nothing. But just as day was breaking Jesus stood on the beach. The disciples did not know, however, that it was Jesus. "Well, lads," Jesus said, "have you any fish?"

"No," they replied.

"Cast your net to the right of the boat," he said to them, "and you will find something." They cast it and now they were not strong enough to haul it up into the boat because of the great number of fish in it.

Then the disciple whom Jesus loved said to Peter, "It is the Master!" As soon as Peter learned that it was the Master, he girt his upper garment about him and plunged into the lake. Meanwhile, the other disciples came in the boat—for they were not far from the shore, only about two hundred yards— dragging along the net full of fish.

When they had come ashore, they noticed hot embers on the ground, with fish lying on the fire, and bread. Jesus said to them, "Bring some of the fish you caught just now." So Peter boarded the boat and hauled the net up on the beach. It was full of fish, 153 in all, and in spite of the great number the net did not break. "Come now," Jesus said to them, "and have break-fast." Not one of his disciples could find it in his heart to ask him, "Who are you?" They knew it was the Master.

Then Jesus approached, took bread in his hands, and gave them of it. He did the same with the fish.

This was now the third time Jesus showed himself to the disciples after he had risen from the dead. [John 21:1–14][25]

This text has an unmistakable nostalgia about it. One senses the leisurely pace of this third appearance of Jesus to the apostles.

Some of the apostles had gathered together in their old home town. He had said to them, "I go before you into Galilee. There you will see me." So they went back home according to his instructions and were hanging around their old haunts by the Lake of Tiberias, where they had earned their living before Jesus had called them out of their respective businesses to join him in proclaiming the reign of God.

Jesus had said he would meet them there. But where was he? Peter said to the other disciples, "How about going for a catch?" The other disciples said, "Fine, we'll go with you."

So they got into a boat and rowed out into the middle of the lake. They fished all day without a nibble. Twilight came; no bites. Night fell, and they were still sitting in the middle of the lake waiting for a catch. They tried their nets first on one side and then on the other. They rowed up and down the lake. It got darker and darker. The moon rose and set, and still they remained out on the lake. It was a night full of effort but no fish.

As they waited for the dawn, they grew more and more disgruntled. They were tired, cold and irritable. They had long since given up talking and sat slumped in the boat, glowering at the lake. They were now only a few hundred yards offshore. All at once, on the beach, emerging slowly from the shadows, was the outline of a man. As the light increased, the stranger became more and more visible. After a long time he called out to them in a friendly manner, "Lads, did you catch anything?"

They exchanged a few knowing glances. Couldn't this man figure out that a boatload of fishermen would not be sitting there at that hour if they had caught anything?

So they shouted back, "Naw!" The stranger, not put off by their unfriendly response, called back, "Try casting your net to the right side of the boat. Then you will catch something."

They said to each other, "Who is this guy, trying to tell us what to do?" We've been here all night. We know there are no fish in this lake." But one of them said, "We have nothing to lose."

So for the umpteenth time they grabbed the net, pulled it in and lowered it on the right side of the boat. All of a sudden there was an immense tug. A huge school of fish had swum into the net. In a moment the men were hanging on to the net for dear life and the boat was tipping dangerously to the side. "It is the Lord!" John exclaimed. This is the second time the Gospel records a fishless night—a night full of effort and no result. It is a lively symbol of our experience interminable purification, giving way to the dawn of inner resurrection.

As soon as Peter heard that the stranger was Jesus, he jumped into the sea and swam ashore. The other disciples dragged the boat to shore and pulled the net onto the beach. There they noticed that Jesus had prepared a fire and a fish was broiling on top of it. Jesus, the breakfast cook, said to Peter, "Bring some of the fish that you have just caught."

While Peter went to look through the catch, the other apostles were in the process of counting them. It took awhile to count to a hundred and fifty-three fish, to select the best ones and to cook them. When everything was ready, Jesus said to them, "Come and have breakfast." Not one of the disciples could find it in his heart to ask, "Who are you?" They knew it was the Lord.

They all sat down. Jesus took the bread in his hands, said the blessing, broke it and gave it to them. He did the same with the fish. As they sat in silence consuming the meal, they recognized an unmistakable shift in their relationship with him. A meal together is a symbol of belonging. Before it had always meant conversation, laughter and singing. This was a new level of belonging. Their former relationship with Jesus was coming to an end and a new relationship was being communicated to them at a far deeper level. This sharing was not by word of mouth, nor by ideas or feelings, but by the Spirit dwelling in their inmost being, a far better form of communication than the one they had before. This is the relationship Jesus was referring to when he rebuked Thomas and pointed out to him that to believe on the basis of personal experience is a greater gift than to believe on the basis of external evidence.

The fifty days during which Jesus revealed himself to his disciples brought them out of their discouragement and into close relationship with the divine Spirit whom he had promised to send them. The disciples were brought from a merely human relationship with Jesus to the interior exchange that is proper to those who are advancing in faith and in sensitivity to the inspirations of the Spirit.

The Ascension

After speaking with them, the Lord Jesus was taken up into heaven and took his seat at God's right hand. The Eleven went forth and preached everywhere. [Mark 16:19–20]

By becoming a human being Christ annihilated the dichotomy between matter and spirit. In the Person of the Divine-human Being, a continuum between the divine and the human has been established. Thus, God's plan is not only to spiritualize the material universe, but to make matter itself divine. This he has already done in the glorified humanity of his Son. The grace bestowed on us by the Ascension of Jesus is the divinization of our humanity. Our individuality is permeated by the Spirit of God through the grace of the Ascension and more specifically through the grace of Pentecost. Thus we, in Christ, are also annihilating the dichotomy between matter and spirit. Our life is a mysterious interpenetration of material experience, spiritual reality and the divine Presence.

The key to being a Christian is to know Jesus Christ with the whole of our being. It is important to know his sacred humanity through our senses and to reflect upon it with our reason, to treasure his teaching and example in our imagination and memory, and to imitate him by a life of moral integrity. But this is only the beginning. It is to the transcendent potential in ourselves—to our mind which opens up to unlimited truth, and to our will which reaches out for unlimited love— that Christ addresses himself in the Gospel with particular urgency.

Not only is it important to know Jesus Christ with the whole of our being; it is also important to know Jesus Christ in the whole of *his* being. We must know Christ, first of all, in his sacred humanity and historical reality and, more precisely, in his passion, which was the culminating point of his life on earth. The essential note of his passion is the emptying of his divinity. We enter into his emptying by accepting the emptying process in our own life, by laying aside our false self and by living in the presence of God, the source of our being.

We must know Christ, however, not only in his human nature—his passion and emptying—but also in his divinity. This is the grace of the resurrection. It is the empowerment to live his risen life. It is the grace not to sin. It is the grace to express his risen life in the face of our inner poverty without at the same time ceasing to feel it.

The grace of the Ascension offers a still more incredible union, a more entrancing invitation to unbounded life and love. This is the invitation to enter into the cosmic Christ—into his divine person, the Word of God, who has always been present in the world. And he has always been present in a saving way because of God's foreknowledge of his incarnation, death, and resurrection. Christ is "the light that enlightens everyone" [John 1:9]—the God who is secretly at work in the most unexpected and hidden ways. This is the Christ who disappeared in his Ascension beyond the clouds, not into some geographical location, but into the heart of all creation. In particular, he has penetrated the very depths of our being, our separate-self sense has melted into his divine Person, and now we can act under the direct influence of his Spirit. Thus, even if we drink a cup of soup or walk down the street, it is Christ living and acting in us, transforming the world from within. This transformation appears in the guise of ordinary things—in the guise of our seemingly insignificant daily routine.

The Ascension is Christ's return to the heart of all creation where he dwells now in his glorified humanity. The mystery of his Presence is hidden throughout creation and in every part of it. At some moment of history, which prophecy calls the Last Day, our eyes will be opened and we will see reality as it is, which we know now only by faith. That faith reveals that Christ, dwelling at the center of all creation and of each individual member of it, is transforming it and bringing it back, in union with himself, into the bosom of the Father. Thus, the maximum glory of the Trinity is achieved through the maximum sharing of the divine life with every creature according to its capacity. This is "the mystery hidden for ages in God" [Eph. 3:9].

The grace of the Ascension is the triumphant faith that believes that God's will is being done no matter what happens. It believes that creation is already glorified, though in a hidden manner, as it awaits the full revelation of the children of God.

The grace of the Ascension enables us to perceive the irresistible power of the Spirit transforming everything into Christ despite any and all appearances to the contrary. In the misery of the ghetto, the battlefield, the concentration camp; in the family torn by dissension; in the loneliness of the orphanage, old-age home, or hospital ward—whatever we see that seems to be disintegrating into grosser forms of evil—the light of the Ascension is burning with irresistible power. This is one of the greatest intuitions of faith. This faith finds Christ not only in the beauty of nature, art, human friendship and the service of others, but also in the malice and injustice of people or institutions, and in the inexplicable suffering of the innocent. Even there it finds the same infinite love expressing the hunger of God for humanity, a hunger that he intends to satisfy.

Thus, in Colossians, Paul does not hesitate to cry out with his triumphant faith in the Ascension: "Christ is all and in all"[26]—meaning now, not just in the future. At this very moment we too have the grace to see Christ's light shining in our hearts, to feel his absorbing Presence within us, and to perceive in every created thing—even in the most disconcerting—the presence of his light, love and glory.

3

THE PENTECOST MYSTERY

∎

If you love me and obey the commands I give you, I will ask the Father and he will give you another Paraclete—to be with you always: the spirit of truth, whom the world cannot accept because it neither sees him nor recognizes him; but you can recognize him because he remains with you and will be within you. [John 14:15–17]

Introduction

The period of preparation for the feast of Pentecost is brief (just ten days) because the two previous seasons have served as a remote preparation and have thoroughly prepared us for it.

Pentecost is, at the same time, the principal and crowning feast of the theological idea of divine love. It is, in fact, the crowning feast of the whole liturgical year. The rest of the year examines the teaching and example of Jesus in the light of Pentecost, that is, from the perspective of divine love.

The Feast of Pentecost

On the last and great day of the feast, Jesus stood and cried out: "If any one is thirsty, let that person come to me and drink. The one who believes in me, as Scripture said: 'From his innermost being shall flow rivers of living water'" [John 7:37–39]

Each feast of the Liturgical Year is both an event to be celebrated and a grace to be received. The grace of Christmas is to know Christ in his humanity. The grace of Epiphany is to know him in his divinity. The grace of Holy Week is to know him in his emptying and dying. The grace of Easter is to know him in his triumph over sin and death. The grace of the Ascension is to know him as the cosmic Christ.

It is to know the glorified Christ, who has passed, not into some geographical location, but into the heart of all creation.

The cosmic Christ, revealed in the Mystery of the Ascension, manifests our true self and the inner nature of all reality. What is manifested is the living, vibrant Spirit, filling us and all things with boundless light, life and love. The Spirit is always present, yet always coming. That is because the Divine actuality becomes present in a new way each time we move to a new level of spiritual awareness. The Spirit has been given; yet he is always waiting to be received so that he can give himself again, and more completely. What then is the special grace of Pentecost?

On the day of his resurrection, Jesus breathed his Spirit upon his disciples, saying: "Receive the Holy Spirit."[1] On the day of the Ascension, forty days later, he "charged them not to depart from Jerusalem, but to wait for the promise of the Father . . . before many days, you shall be baptized with the Holy Spirit."[2]

The Spirit, then, is not given only once. He is an ongoing promise, an endless promise—a promise that is always fulfilled and always being fulfilled, because the Spirit is infinite and boundless and can never be fully plumbed.

The Spirit is the ultimate promise of the Father. A promise is a free gift. No one is bound to make a promise. Once a promise is made, however, one is bound. When God binds himself, it is with absolute freedom, absolute fidelity. The Spirit, as promise, is a gift, not a possession. He is a promise that has been communicated; hence never to be taken back, since God is infinitely faithful to his promises. Note that the communication is by way of gift, not possession. Like the air we breathe, we can have all that we wish to take into our lungs; but it does not belong to us. If we try to take possession of it—stuff it in a closet for safekeeping—our efforts will be in vain. Air is not made to be possessed, and neither is the Spirit.

The divine Spirit is all gift but will not acquiesce to a possessive attitude. He is all ours as long as we give him away. "The wind blows where it wills and you hear the sound of it, but you do not know when it comes or whither it goes; so it is with everyone who is born of the Spirit."[3] In these words, Jesus explained to Nicodemus and to us that we have no control over the Spirit. In fact, it is in giving him away that we manifest that we truly have received him. He is the supreme gift, but supremely himself, supremely free.

The Spirit of God, the promise of the Father, sums up in himself all the promises of Christ. For they all point to him. The Incarnation is a promise. The passion and death of Jesus are promises. His resurrection and Ascension are each a promise. Pentecost itself, the outpouring of the Spirit, is a promise. All are promises and pledges of the divine Spirit, present and to be received at every moment. He is the last, the greatest and the completion of all God's promises, the living summary of them all. Faith in him is faith in the whole of revelation. Openness and surrender to his guidance is the continuation of God's revelation in us and through us. It is to be involved in the redemption of the world and in the divinization of the cosmos. To know that Christ is all in all and to know his Spirit, the ongoing promise of the Father—this is the grace of Pentecost.

Between God and us, two extremes meet: He who is everything and we who are nothing at all. It is the Spirit who makes us one with God and in God, just as the Word is with God and is God—the Word by nature, we by participation and communication. Jesus prayed for this unity at the Last Supper. Many of his words on that occasion find their fulfillment and ultimate significance in the outpouring of the Spirit into our minds and hearts. Jesus said, "The glory you have given to me, I have given to them, that they may be one as we are one. I in them and you in me, that they may become perfectly one."[4]

The Spirit is the gift of God welling up in the Trinity from the common heart of the Father and the Son. He is the overflow of the divine life into the sacred humanity of Jesus, and then into the rest of us, his members.

"If anyone thirst, let him come to me and drink. He who believes in me, as the scripture has said, 'Out of his heart will flow rivers of living water.' "[5]John tells us that Jesus was speaking of the Spirit when he uttered these words. The Spirit is the stream of living water which wells up in those who believe. It is the same Spirit that causes our hearts to rejoice because of the confidence that he inspires in God as Father. Abba, the word that spontaneously wells up in us, sums up our intimacy with God and our awareness of being not only with God as friend to friend, but in God. We are penetrated by God and penetrating into God, through the mysterious, all-enveloping, all-absorbing and all-embracing Spirit.

Jesus in his priestly prayer for his disciples prayed "that they may all be one; as you, Father, are in me, and I in you, that they also may be in us."[6] It is the Spirit who causes us to be one in the Body of Christ. We have all received the same Spirit, enlivening us and causing us to be in Christ, in the Father, in the Spirit.

We are in God and God is in us, and the unifying force is the Spirit. To live in the Spirit is the fulfillment of every law and commandment, the sum of every duty to each other, and the joy of oneness with everything that is.

4

ORDINARY TIME

■

"I came that they may have life and have it to the full." [John 10:10]

INTRODUCTION

Ordinary Time is time from the perspective of the Pentecost; time that has been transformed by the eternal values introduced by Jesus through his entrance into the space-time continuum of human experience. Every moment of chronological time is now the precious present in which eternal values are being offered, communicated and transmitted. Chronological and eternal time intersect in the mystery of the present moment and become one: the stream of time and eternity are coterminus. The liturgy, under the influence of the Spirit, examines the teaching and example of Jesus from this contemplative perspective.

In this section examples from Jesus' teachings as expressed in the beatitudes and the parables along with several incidents of his ministry are presented to show how ordinary life is transformed through the liturgy. In this sense, Ordinary Time is in fact totally extraordinary—time that has been transformed or time to be transformed.

The Beatitudes

The ripe fruit of the grace of Pentecost is the practice of the beatitudes. The beatitudes are acts of virtue inspired by the Spirit and which manifest the risen life of Christ within us.

True Happiness

When he saw the crowds, Jesus went up on the mountainside. After he had sat down his disciples gathered around him, and he began to teach them:

"How blest are the poor in spirit: the reign of God is theirs.

Blest too are the sorrowing; they shall be consoled.

Blest are the lowly; they shall inherit the land.

Blest are they who hunger and thirst for holiness; they shall have their fill.

Blest are they who show mercy; mercy shall be theirs.

Blest are the single-hearted for they shall see God.

Blest too are the peacemakers; they shall be called sons of God.

Blest are those persecuted for holiness' sake; the reign of God is theirs.

Blest are you when they insult you and persecute you and utter every kind of slander against you because of me.

Be glad and rejoice, for your reward is great in heaven; they persecuted the prophets before you in the very same way." [Matt. 5:1–12][1]

The beginning of the Sermon on the Mount contains a number of affirmations called the beatitudes that summarize Jesus' teaching about the nature of true happiness. Each begins with the term "blest," which means, "Oh, how happy you would be!" The first three beatitudes are aimed at demolishing the values of the first three energy centers and the programs for happiness on which they are based. Those who are motivated by one of these three energy centers have designed for themselves a program for human misery.

The first three energy centers are elaborate programs for happiness that evolved at a pre-rational age and that are now heavily defended. Hence, the emphasis in Jesus' ministry on repentance, which means "change the direction in which you are looking for happiness." The beatitudes came out of the heart of Jesus when he looked at the multitudes that were following him and realized with infinite compassion that "they were like sheep without a shepherd," all going their own way—that is, nowhere at a great rate. "Jetting to nowhere" summarizes in modern language the projects of the first three energy centers. The beatitudes give us some insight into how to dismantle them and to move toward true happiness.

The first three beatitudes might be summed up by the commandment, "Love your neighbor as yourself." If that commandment were lived out, it would quickly dismantle the false-self system. We cannot possibly love our neighbor as ourself so long as we are acting out fantastic demands for security and survival, affection and esteem, and power and control.

The next four beatitudes are aimed at higher states of consciousness. Once love of neighbor has been established, divine love begins to unfold its secrets. The last four beatitudes might be summed up by Jesus' commandment, "love one another as I have loved you." This dimension of love is more profound and all-inclusive than the commandment to love your neighbor as yourself.

Let us consider the first beatitude, "How blest are the poor in spirit: the reign of God is theirs." What is the reign of God? It is what God does in us. It certainly is not a rule of life of our own making. It is the openness that allows God to enter our lives at any time. Hence, it presupposes a flexibility to adjust to events and circumstances and a willingness to let go of our own plans in favor of the inspirations that come from the Spirit.

Who are the poor in spirit? The poor in spirit are the oppressed, the downtrodden and the despised in a particular culture. They are the nobodies, the insignificant, the people who don't rate. The term embraces those who are not necessarily materially poor, although that can be one of the factors that makes the destitute objects of contempt for those who are better off. Evangelical poverty addresses itself to those who suffer any form of human privation. The additional words "in spirit" point to the fact that to experience this beatitude, it is not enough to be materially poor or to suffer affliction, it is necessary to accept whatever the painful condition is. The poor in spirit are those who are willing to endure affliction of whatever kind for God's sake.

The final beatitude declares those who are persecuted for justice or truth's sake to be especially happy because they have a special claim to the reign of God and to the fullness of happiness. One is not normally persecuted for inaction, but for trying to change unjust societal structures. This warns us that the poor in spirit are not simply passive in the face of the oppressive circumstances in which they find themselves. Their first movement or response, it is true, is to accept what is. But God's will may also suggest that we act to correct, improve, or change unjust structures or oppressive situations in ways that are in accord with God's will and as the Holy Spirit may inspire.

To accept everything passively could indicate a passive-dependent personality that leans too heavily on pleasing others, especially authority figures, in order to bolster up one's fragile sense of security. Passive acceptance could also result from years of suffering some form of physical, psychological, social, economic or religious oppression which has finally exhausted one's capacity to resist injustice anymore or to take any significant initiative to oppose it. Oppression of whatever kind, if it continues for a long period of time, crushes the potential of the will to act and relegates its victims to the enormous dump of human inertia and indifference.

The poor in spirit, then, are those who accept affliction actively, not passively. They willingly accept the situation for what it is—a fact of life—and then work to make it better. This is co-creating the world with God, and this is the basic vocation of human beings. It is the message of the Garden of Eden.[2]

Of all the people who have lived on earth, Jesus, the Son of God, was the most free to choose where to be born, where to live and where to die. His choices are striking, to say the least. They bear no resemblance to the programs of the first three energy centers that everyone else is plagued with.

First of all, he lived in a town that was regarded as totally insignificant. One text reads, "Can any good come out of Nazareth?"[3] Or again, Jesus insisted on being baptized by John the Baptist. When John objected, Jesus replied, "We must do this if we would fulfill all of God's demands."[4] The baptism of John was a call to repentance. Jesus wanted to reinforce that call by experiencing John's baptism himself. Baptism is a commitment to free oneself from excessive demands for security and survival, affection and esteem, and power and control. The beatitude of the poor in spirit focuses on the security center that constantly demands more and better of everything in order to feel secure.

Jesus could have been an austere ascetic like John the Baptist, but instead he chose a middle way. He ate with sinners and drank wine, two things that the disciples of John would not think of doing. He talked to women in public, something that a rabbi at that time was not supposed to do. Jesus was free from the conformity level of morality that his contemporaries were locked into. He would not conform to local custom merely for the sake of satisfying the religious sensibilities of the time.

In the end, Jesus died between two criminals, betrayed by a friend and abandoned by his disciples. No public benefactor was ever so thoroughly disgraced from every point of view and rejected by both the religious and civil authorities. In the example of Jesus' life, being is more important than doing; it is not how successful one is, but who one is that counts. As in the example of Jesus, one's lifework can be completely destroyed and still one's life can be an immense success. Indeed, the destruction of one's lifework is one of the classic ways through which God brings his servants to their final surrender. The spiritual journey becomes more demanding as it unfolds, but also more liberating.

All creation is ours on the condition that we do not try to possess it. The innate desire to feel secure is an obstacle to enjoying all that exists. This does not mean that we are not to have possessions at all, but that we need to be detached from whatever we have. Otherwise, we lose the true perspective and, with it, the joy of this beatitude. John of the Cross wrote, "If you want to possess everything, desire to possess nothing."[5] By cultivating a non-possessive attitude toward everything, including ourselves, everything is experienced as gift. Then one is truly poor in spirit and will find joy in everything.

A New Kind of Consciousness

Jesus then came down with his apostles and stopped on some level ground. A large group of his disciples, besides a great many people from all over the Jewish country, including Jerusalem and from the seacoast of Tyre and Sidon, had come to hear him and be cured of their diseases. Everybody in the crowd endeavored to come and touch him and power was going out from him and healing everyone. It was then that he raised his eyes and fixed them upon his disciples and spoke as follows: "How blest are the poor in spirit; the reign of God is theirs. Blest are the meek; they shall inherit the land. Blest are the sorrowing; they shall be consoled." [Luke 6:17–20; Matt. 5:3–5]

In this rendering of the Sermon on the Mount, we are told that a great crowd had gathered. Many of the people had come to be healed of their diseases and had no concern for spiritual instruction. Jesus simply presented his teaching to everyone who happened to be present. We can be sure, therefore, that his words were also intended for us.

We saw that the poor in spirit are those afflicted for God's sake. People who are cut off from the normal symbols of security in society have the ideal disposition for the reign of God because they have nothing to lose. One who has nothing to lose obviously is much more willing to allow God into one's life. Jesus in his teaching suggests that the healing of our security center comes when we trust God to take care of all our needs. In the Sermon on the Mount, Jesus elaborates on what he means by letting go of the anxious search for more and more possessions to assuage our feelings of insecurity:

> Do not fret about what to eat and what to drink or about what to wear on your bodies. Is not life more precious than clothing? Look at the birds. They don't sow or reap or store provisions in barns, yet your heavenly Father feeds them. Observe the lilies of the field, how they grow. They do not toil or spin, yet even Solomon in all his glory did not dress like one of these.[6]

"Blest are the sorrowing; they shall be consoled." Love distorted by selfishness wants to cling to ephemeral or illusory projects for happiness. When we let such things go, we are bound to feel loss and the corresponding emotion of sorrow. This sorrow is not the same as that which comes from the unwillingness to let go of what is being asked or taken from us and which may give rise to discouragement, depression and even despair. The willingness to let go and bear the loss of what we love gives rise to a new inner freedom that enables us to live without what we previously thought was so essential. That freedom with its accompanying peace is the consolation that is promised in this beatitude. We have to allow for the grieving period to run its course and not run away from it. Nor should we think there is something wrong if we sometimes cast a backward glance at something we left behind or are overtaken at times by a backlash of emotional turmoil. In actual fact, we never lose anything that truly deserves to be loved; we simply enter into a more mature relationship with it.

"Blest are the meek; they shall inherit the land." The meek are those who do not get angry in the face of insult or injury and who have begun to dismantle their need or demand to control other people, events, and their own lives. When they experience an insult or humiliation, they do not feel it as a loss of power. Hence, they are free to continue to show love. The meek refuse to injure others regardless of the provocation. They are not judgmental. They may not approve of someone's conduct or principles, but they refuse to make a moral judgment about the person in question. Rather, their freedom from their power/control center enables them to have great compassion for those who are still imprisoned in the straightjacket of power needs that never rest and that can never be fulfilled.

The teaching of Gandhi, who preached *abimsa* (usually translated as "the practice of nonviolence"), points to a new kind of consciousness in which, instead of returning an eye for an eye and a tooth for a tooth, one goes on showing love. *Abimsa* is not a passive attitude but one that actively shows love no matter what happens. The love is so delicate and sincere that it refuses to take advantage of one's persecutor when he is vulnerable.

The meekness proposed in this beatitude is not passivity but the firm determination to go on loving no matter what evil another person does to us. It believes that to show love is the true nature of being human. This behavior undercuts violence at its roots. Violence tends to beget violence. When people feel attacked, they defend themselves. There is no end to the chain of violence until one of the contenders refuses to respond in kind. The determination to go on loving in spite of immense provocation is the only way to achieve peace among families, communities and nations. It presupposes and manifests the inner freedom to which the Gospel invites us.

Outreach

Jesus now entered Jericho. As he made his way through the town, there was a stir. A man named Zacchaeus, a high official among the tax collectors and rich as well, was curious to find out who Jesus was, but owing to the press of people, had no chance to do so, for he was small of stature. In order, therefore, to get a glimpse of Jesus, he ran ahead and climbed a sycamore tree because Jesus was expected to pass that way.

When Jesus came to the spot, he looked up. "Zacchaeus," he said to him, "come down quickly. Today I must be your guest." Coming down quickly, he welcomed him joyfully. A murmur ran through the crowd of spectators. "He has turned in," they commented, "to accept the hospitality of a sinner." Then Zacchaeus drew himself up and addressed the Lord, "Upon my word, Lord, I give to the poor one-half of my possessions, and if I have obtained anything from anybody by extortion, I will refund four times as much."

Then in his presence Jesus said, "Today salvation has visited this household because he, too, is the son of Abraham. After all, it is the mission of the son of man to seek and to save what is lost." [Luke 19:1–10][7]

This Gospel about Zacchaeus is a practical example of two of the beatitudes. "How happy are they who hunger and thirst after holiness for they shall be fully satisfied" refers to life without the tyranny of the false-self system. It heralds graduation from the emotional programs of early childhood, whose force or cutting edge has been blunted by the discipline of contemplative prayer. The fruits of that discipline manifest themselves in the determination to practice what is characteristic of this level of human consciousness, which is to show love. Divine love is not mere feeling; it is the love that manifests itself by deeds.

The primary sacrament of Christianity is Jesus himself. A sacrament is a visible sign of the invisible presence of grace; it communicates and transmits what it signifies. Jesus transmitted what he signified, divine love, by his teaching and example. He manifested how the divine nature functions. He revealed that the inner life of God is sheer gift: surrender that tends to throw itself away. The humility of God is to cease to be God. Within the Trinity there is the total emptying of the Father into the Son and the Son into the Father. What binds them together is the Spirit, the mutual love of the Father and the Son. Each member of the Trinity lives in the others rather than in itself. This is what is meant by "Tri-Unity": one divine nature possessed by three different Relationships. Relationship is the only distinction in God, but it is infinite. Thus, in the Trinity there is infinite Unity and infinite diversity because of the unique relationship of each member to the divine nature. Jesus manifests this unity insofar as it can be manifested in a human being.

After Jesus, the greatest sacrament is another human being. We are made in the image and likeness of God. Moreover, those who have been taken up through faith and baptism into the Body of Christ are growing as a corporate personality into the fullness of Christ. Paul calls this the Mystery that has been hidden from the beginning of the world and which is now revealed in Jesus Christ. To hunger and thirst after justice is to manifest divine love under all circumstances. This is what human beings were created to do. It is our nature. Everything else is unnatural; any other disposition is abnormal.

The next beatitude, "Blessed are they who show mercy; mercy shall be theirs," describes the result of moving beyond selfishness into the love that is totally self-giving. It is the imitation of Christ and the fulfillment of the new commandment "to love one another as I have loved you." This means to love people not only in their hidden beauty as members of Christ, but in their concreteness and individuality; that is, in their personality traits, idiosyncrasies and opinions which we may find irritating or unbearable. Even in the face of persecution and injury, if one enjoys the inner freedom of this beatitude, one continues to show love.

How do we show love in the concrete? How do we build up society when we have our own problems that scarcely leave us enough time or resources to take care of our own family, business, or spiritual life? As the consciousness of the inequalities in the world increases, the question of personal responsibility emerges with ever-increasing urgency. The nations of the West use up most of the world's resources while the rest of the world has barely enough to subsist on. As individuals, we may feel overwhelmed by the injustice in the world. We are painfully aware that the greed of human beings is the cause of starvation. We realize that if the global community was ordered properly and technology were shared equally, no one would go hungry even for a day. We ask what it means to show love when we do not know how to team up with others to alter governments, institutions and economies that take no interest in the equitable distribution of the earth's goods. Our frustration level rises as we feel unable to effect any change.

The author of *Caring for Society*[8] tells the story of a young couple managing a catering service. While taking part in a prison ministry, they heard about an inmate who was about to be released and needed a job. They talked it over and decided to offer him a job in their business. They were uneasy about how he would work out, but felt inspired to offer him this opportunity, so they hired him to deliver food to their clients. When it became known that he was an ex-convict, a number of the customers became uneasy also and decided to make use of another catering service. The couple began to lose money and eventually had to close down. Instead of firing their employee, they started another catering business and integrated him into it. Their new business became a bigger success than the former one. Showing mercy is actually the best investment one can make. Failures and losses may be God's way of getting us into a better situation.

Zacchaeus was a representative of the despised profession of tax collectors, generally considered to be the worst of sinners. When Jesus came to Jericho, this little man climbed a sycamore tree to get a better view of him. Jesus looked up at Zacchaeus and said, "I want to stay at your house." Zacchaeus was delighted. He shinnied down the tree and welcomed Jesus into his home. Preparing a great feast, he invited all his disreputable friends and staged a party.

After a few cups of wine, the little man, pleased to have Jesus in his house, pulled himself up to his full height and announced, "I give half of my possessions to the poor. If I have extorted money from anyone, I pay back four times over." Thus he freely admitted the unethical character of some of his financial success. Jesus' reply was, "Today, salvation has visited this household." Because Zacchaeus had welcomed Jesus into his house and not just watched him pass by, he had been changed. Salvation had entered his house through the gift of hospitality.

This is exactly what the couple did in our story. They could have watched while other people tried to find a position for the ex-convict. They heard Jesus' request as he was passing by, "Will you invite me into your house?" And they invited him in.

The inner movement to reach out to someone in need is the inspiration of the Spirit. To respond, one has to take the first step and show love in some small but practical, concrete way. If you hunger and thirst for holiness, the opportunities for practicing this beatitude will multiply.

Jesus' encounter with Zacchaeus is a wisdom teaching meaning, "If you want to practice love, observe the opportunities that are right in front of your noses."

The Higher Degrees of Happiness

Blest are the single-hearted; for they shall see God. Blest are the peacemakers; they shall be called children of God. [Matt. 5:6–9]

The opportunities for satisfying the hunger for holiness are immediately at hand if we are sensitive to the needs of others. Every now and then we are prompted to offer some kind of assistance at considerable cost to ourselves. This offer has to be appropriate to our state of life; at the same time, it challenges us to go beyond our routines and preconceptions, and to reach out to someone needing special care. This is the inspiration that leads to the beatitude of the merciful, which is to put into practice our contemplative vision.

The dialogue between our contemplative vision and how we incarnate it is the subject of the next beatitude, "Blest are the single-hearted for they shall see God." The single-hearted see God in themselves, in others and in the ordinary events of life. Jesus said, "The Son cannot do anything by himself—he can only do what he sees the father doing."[9] Thus, he is always looking at the Father. What Jesus does is to translate his vision of the Father into his daily life and teaching and ultimately into his passion and death on the cross. This is an important point for our practice. Contemplative prayer is the place of encounter between the creative vision of transformation and the actual incarnation of that vision day by day. Practice is the translation of the creative vision into the concrete circumstances of each day.

It must be emphasized over and over that daily life is the fundamental practice. Hence, the incarnation of our vision—how we live it—is of supreme importance. If we are not available for daily encounter with God in contemplative prayer, the dynamic dialogue between the creative vision and its practical incarnation will be missing in our lives; or at least it will not pass through the intimate discerning experience of contemplative prayer. To bring both our activity and our vision together in vital dialogue is to perceive the right way of manifesting that vision *today*. Maybe it will be a little different tomorrow. We must not respond to Christ in a static way—with one set of resolutions or with the same set of tools all the time. Our practice has to be adjusted as we keep climbing the spiral ascent that the beatitudes describe. The eagle circles as it rises toward the sun. The same movement is present in the beatitudes. As we circle around the creative vision and see different aspects of it, our understanding is enhanced. In addition to circling on the horizontal plane as we negotiate the spiral ascent, we also perceive reality on the vertical plane from ever higher perspectives.

To emphasize only the contemplative vision is to risk stagnating in one's spiritual evolution. To emphasize only its incarnation is to risk becoming drained, or even to lose the vision itself. Hence, the necessity of bringing the two together every day in confrontation and dialogue. Every day is a new unfolding of our life in Christ. Surprises are always happening. God reserves the right to intrude into our lives at a moment's notice, sometimes turning them upside-down. It is essential to be flexible, adjustable, ready to tear up our plans and put them in the wastebasket at God's request. Hence, both the contemplative vision and its incarnation are essential, and the place where they meet is contemplative prayer. This is the key to the preservation and growth of the creative vision as well as its appropriate incarnation on a day-to-day basis. This is what leads to purity of heart, which is freedom from the false-self system and hence, freedom to be at the disposal of God and those we serve.

The beatitude of the peacemakers reveals that the peacemaker is one who has established peace within oneself. Peace is not a naive simplicity, but the perfect harmony of immense complexity. It is the delicate balance between all the faculties of human nature totally subject to God's will and transformed by divine love into a finely tuned instrument.

Peacemaking is the normal overflow of rootedness in Christ. Peacemakers are those who have the assurance of being the children of God. They are the ones who in a sense are God acting in the world. They pour into the world the being they have received from God, which is a share in his divine nature.

Today, God seems to be urging us to take more initiative in dealing with global problems and to take part in the transformation of society, beginning, of course, with what is closest to us. A creative vision releases an enormous amount of energy and can transform society beyond our wildest dreams. Divine empowerment is more present in those who climb the ladder of the beatitudes than anywhere else in creation. The power of the stars is nothing compared to the energy of a person whose will has been freed from the false-self system and who is thus enabled to co-create the cosmos together with God. God's top priority is the creation of a world in which the goods of the earth are equitably distributed, where no one is forgotten or left out, and where no one can rest until everyone has enough to eat, the oppressed have been liberated, and justice and peace are the norm among the nations and religions of the world. Until then, even the joy of transforming union is incomplete. The commitment to the spiritual journey is not a commitment to pure joy, but to taking responsibility for the whole human family, its needs and destiny. We are not our own; we belong to everyone else.

The Ultimate Beatitude

Jesus said to his disciples: To you who hear me, I say: Love your enemies, do good to those who hate you; bless those who curse you and pray for those who maltreat you. When someone slaps you on one cheek, turn and give him the other; when someone takes your coat, let him have your shirt as well. Give to all who beg from you. When a man takes what is yours, do not demand it back. Do to others what you would have them do to you.

If you love those who love you, what credit is that to you? Even sinners love those who love them. If you do good to those who do good to you, how can you claim any credit? Sinners do as much. If you lend to those from whom you expect repayment, what merit is there in it for you? Even sinners lend to sinners, expecting to be repaid in full.

Love your enemy and do good; lend without expecting repayment. Then will your recompense be great. You will rightly be called sons of the Most High, since He Himself is good to the ungrateful and the wicked.

Be compassionate, as your Father is compassionate. Do not judge, and you will not be judged. Do not condemn, and you will not be condemned. Pardon, and you shall be pardoned. Give, and it shall be given to you. Good measure pressed down, shaken together, running over, will they pour into the fold of your garment. For the measure you measure with will be measured back to you. [Luke 6:27–38][10]

Humility is a relationship of honesty to everything: to God, oneself, other people and all reality. God is selfless love, giving to the point of emptying himself and trying not to be God. It is a great gift to be detached from this world's goods; it is a still greater gift to be detached from all spiritual goods. This is the way that God relates to us: not interested in his own majesty or transcendence, but trying to be nobody—without, of course, much success. It must be fun when you are everything to be nothing. In any case, his disposition to give away everything that he has or is, seems to characterize the divine goodness and compassion.

This is the disposition that Jesus invites us to imitate on the mountainside in his seemingly casual sermon. Jesus urges us to have the freedom not to harbor a possessive attitude toward anything, including oneself; to be, without wanting to be anything special; and to be one with everything that is, in an all-inclusive attitude of belonging and sharing. One of the examples of this attitude is lending without hope of return. Actually, from the perspective of the beatitudes, one is only lending to oneself. Again, there is no sense in judging others because that would be judging oneself. This disposition of giving everything away—one's time, energy, space, virtues, spirituality, and finally oneself—is not really giving anything away because, in the truest sense, whatever we give away, we are giving to ourselves. The gesture of opening one's hand is the same gesture as receiving.

This emptying of ourselves for the good of others is a continuation of the same movement of emptying—*kenosis*—that goes on in the Trinity: giving away (or throwing away) all that the Father is to the Son and vice-versa, and each receiving everything back in and through the Person of infinite love, the Holy Spirit. As one manifests this love, one is giving everything away and receiving everything in return again and again, but each time with greater inclusiveness. The same love that one gives away keeps coming back, "Good measure pressed down, shaken together, running over."[11] In the same degree that love goes forth, it returns into our lap. This compassionate, non-judgmental, selfless love is the Source of all that is; the ultimate beatitude is to disappear into it.

The Parables

"It is one thing to communicate to others conclusions and admonitions based on one's profound spiritual experience . . . It is quite another thing to try to communicate that experience itself, or better, to assist people to find their own ultimate encounter. This is what the parables of Jesus seek to do: to help others into their own experience of the Reign of God and to draw from that experience *their own way of life*."[12]

The Reign of God

Jesus proposed to the crowd another parable: The reign of God may be likened to the man who sowed good seed in his field. While everyone else was asleep, his enemy came and sowed weeds among the wheat and then made off. When the crop began to mature and yield grain the weeds made their appearance as well. The owner's slaves came to him and said, "Sir, did you not sow good seed in your field? Where are the weeds coming from?" He answered, "I see an enemy's hand in this." The slave said to him, "Do you want us to go out and pull them up?" "No," he replied, "Pull up the weeds and you might take the wheat along with them. Let them grow together until harvest. Then at harvest time I will order the harvesters: 'First collect the weeds and bundle them to burn. Then gather the wheat into my barn.' "

He proposed still another parable: The reign of God is like a mustard seed which someone took and sowed in his field. It is the smallest seed of all, yet when full-grown it is the largest of plants. It becomes so big that the birds of the sky come and build their nests in its branches.

He offered them still another image: The reign of God is like yeast which a woman took and kneaded into three measures of flour. Eventually the whole mass of dough began to rise.

All these lessons Jesus taught to the crowd in the form of parables. He spoke to them in parables only to fulfill what had been said through the prophet: "I will open my mouth in parables; I will announce what has lain hidden since the creation of the world." [Matt. 13:24–35][13]

The parables reveal Jesus as a wisdom teacher of extraordinary qualities. In order to understand his teaching, we need to understand the nature of what he calls the reign (or kingdom) of God. The reign (or kingdom) of God does not consist of a place, a form of government, or even of the rule of God over our actions and interior life. It is not an organization into which we are supposed to fit. It generally introduces itself by an event (or a series of events) that changes our lives. Many of the parables describe situations in which someone's life is suddenly turned upside-down. In these parables Jesus seems to say that this intrusion into one's life is how the reign of God manifests itself. To allow one's life to be turned upside-down requires a change of heart. And a change of heart presupposes a certain disenchantment with what we have been considering happiness.

The parables were directed to people who were just coming out of their selfish programs for happiness and becoming aware that there is an alternative. It is not easy to let go of what we believe to be essential to our happiness even for the sake of participating in God's reign or kingdom.

At the beginning of our conversion most of us experience the gnawing sensation of wanting to move more deeply into the reign of God and to be able to find it in daily life. At the same time, we want to hang onto our emotional routines, fixations, ways of looking at things and our commentaries on people and events that exasperate us. These three parables offer encouragement to those who are beginning the path or struggling along it.

The reign of God is not so much what we do under God's inspiration as what the divine action does in us, with or without our cooperation. The reign of God often is disruptive, to judge by many of the parables. One day Jesus told a parable about a day laborer who was digging in a field and found hidden treasure.[14] With the endless movement of armies throughout the Holy Land during the pre-Gospel period, people often hid their valuables in open fields with the hope of coming back later and recovering them. So it was not extraordinary for someone digging in a field to come upon a hidden treasure. The parable concludes: "Immediately, he went and sold everything he had and bought that field." I suppose he built a mansion somewhere. His good luck changed his life. He was no longer a day laborer.

In another parable, Jesus recounted the story of a man who was in the jewelry business. One day he found a pearl of great price, so he sold everything he had and bought that pearl.[15] This purchase changed his life in much the same way that winning in the state lottery today completely changes a person's life-style. The reign of God breaks into the course of our ordinary occupations, business or family life and changes things around. It is what we do with that intrusion that determines whether we enter or belong to the reign of God or not. The willingness to allow God to walk into our lives, tear up our plans and throw them in the wastebasket is a good beginning.

These two parables emphasize the fact that the reign of God is what happens. It is not any one thing that happens. It is the fact of God's entering our lives at any moment and shifting things around, and our consenting to the break-in. Once we have found "the pearl of great price" or "the treasure hidden in a field", a conflict arises between our desire to be open to the continuing intrusions of the reign of God and our habitual unwillingness to change or be changed. What do we do with that? The three parables in the present text offer insight and encouragement.

A householder of apparent wealth sowed wheat in his field. Shortly there appeared a "weed." This weed was not just any kind of weed; it was darnel, which is the spitting image of wheat. It is very hard to distinguish the two. The zealous farmhands asked the householder how this mischance had come to be. He said, "An enemy has done this." They asked, "Shall we pull out the weeds?"

"No," he replied, "let them grow until the proper time. Then we will have the harvest and separate the two, lest in pulling up the weeds, we lose some of the wheat."

This parable is a warning to over-zealous reformers to go at a pace that will not destroy the good even if it is mixed up with a lot of evil. There will always be a mixture of good and evil in everything until the end of the world. The parable reminds us that we must put up with the evil in ourselves and have a friendly attitude toward our weaknesses. We feel the attraction of grace to move to an ever-deepening spiritual commitment to God, but our resolutions seem so tenuous at times that we fear we may lose them.

But Jesus seems to be saying, "Don't worry about it." God expects that we will experience confusion and weakness. We may at times be unable to discern where our attitudes and actions are coming from, but the parable implies that the wheat is more powerful than the weeds and will eventually win. At some point in our spiritual journey we will be ready for the separation of the wheat from the chaff. God wants us to give the crop time to mature and to leave the harvest to him.

The parable about the mustard seed suggests a positive view of the conflict. The mustard seed is one of the tiniest and most insignificant of all seeds, but when it is put into the ground and allowed to grow to maturity, it turns into the biggest of all shrubs. Birds come and build their nests in it. The message is that the reign of God, like the germinating mustard seed, is incredibly powerful even though its energy is out of reach of our faculties. Though it seems insignificant to us and we feel over-whelmed by the density of the weeds, we should have no fear. With time the seed time will grow in spite of the difficulties that seem to be overwhelming it.

The third parable is about the yeast in the dough. Yeast is a living organism and requires water to be activated. The activating principle in the reign of God is faith. The divine action is at first hidden from our psyche. So, too, yeast is hard to identify when it is hidden in the dough. But its inherent power, when activated, gradually causes the dough to rise. Similarly, the reign of God with the consent of faith has the power to transform; it changes us into something new.

Jesus lays out the principles, offers the invitation, gives encouragement and finally appeals to our freedom: "If you wish, the reign of God is yours. But you have to take the responsibility of deciding. If you choose to enter it, you have nothing to worry about. The evil in you will not overcome the good that has been sown. At some point, the life you now experience with so much conflict will be transformed, and all the evils that weigh you down will disappear."

The Talents

Jesus presented this parable to the crowd. Imagine a man who, before going abroad, sent for his officials and entrusted his money to them. Then he gave five talents to one, to another he gave two, and to a third, just one; to each the amount proportioned to his individual ability. He then went abroad. At once, the recipient of the five talents went to invest them in enterprise and made another five. In like manner, the recipient of the two talents made another two. But the recipient of the one talent went away to dig a hole in the ground and buried his master's money. After a long delay, the master of those officials returned and settled accounts with them. So the recipient of the five talents came forward and presented five additional talents. "Master," he said, "you entrusted me with five talents. Look, I made another five." "Well done, good and faithful servant," the master said to him. "You were faithful in managing something small. I will now put you in charge of some-thing great. Share to the full your master's happiness."

When the recipient of the two talents came, he said in turn, "Master, you entrusted me with two talents. Look, I made another two." "Well done, good and faithful servant," the master said to him. "You were faithful in managing something small. I will now put you in charge of something great. Share to the full your master's happiness."

Finally the recipient of the one talent came before him and said, "Master, I know you are a hard taskmaster. You reap where you have not sown and you store away what you have not winnowed. So I shrank from doing anything at all and went to bury your talent in the ground. Here, you have your capital back again."

But his master had an answer for him. "You lazy good-for-nothing fellow," he said to him, "you knew that I reap where I have not sown and store away what I have winnowed. Then you ought to have put my money in the bank and on my return I might have at least recovered my capital plus the interest. Therefore, take the talent away from him and give it to the one who has the ten talents. Everyone who already has will receive more yet till he abounds in wealth, while the one who does not have will lose even what he has." [Matt. 25:14–29][16]

According to contemporary exegetes, the parables are the most authentic part of the Gospel. Their repetitive quality helps the memory retain and repeat them with ease. Almost all the parables are designed to shake up the values of the people who are listening and to invite them to reflect on what their values actually are.

In the parable of the Good Samaritan, a priest and levite pass by a man who had been beaten up by robbers and left by the roadside. Both go to the other side of the road to avoid getting close to him. The Good Samaritan takes care of the victim, puts him in a hostel, pays for his food, binds up his wounds, and even leaves some money behind so that he can be properly cared for until the Samaritan can come back. In the minds of the people hearing this story, the Samaritans were the scum of the earth. The paradox of a Samaritan doing the right thing and two respectable religious figures doing the wrong thing forces the listeners to reflect. The reversal of their expectations invites them to raise questions about their own motivation and values.

We might think that the man who hid his talent in the ground was a smart fellow. After all, wouldn't we do the same thing if we felt we were not astute in business? Suppose the man had invested his only talent and lost it through a poor investment. He would have had nothing. He hid it in the ground so that he could at least return it to his master. As he later explained, "I was afraid that I wouldn't do a good job of investing your money. Knowing that you are a hard taskmaster, I hid it in the ground to be sure that I would have it to give back to you upon your return. Here it is."

The master, instead of being grateful, grabbed the money out of his hand, shouting, "You lousy good-for-nothing! Get out of my sight!" Then he gave the money to the one who already possessed ten talents. We are left wondering what the man did to deserve such wrath. Is it better to take a risk or to protect what we have received?

The Gospel invites us to holiness and higher states of consciousness. This invitation involves risk; it means growing beyond where we are. It asks us to invest our talents even when we feel they are inadequate to a particular situation, job or ministry. It means that God, when he calls us to ministry, does not promise success, especially immediate success.

The parable of the talents shows what happens to two people who accepted God's invitation. They worked hard and with God's help, doubled their investment. The man who hid his talent in the ground is like those who opt for the status quo because they know what it is; they are unwilling to open themselves to the risks of the spiritual journey. They refuse to work at the potential that God has given them and thus obstruct the upward evolution of the human family. Even if they do not regress to lower levels of consciousness, they fail to support the development of human consciousness into Christ-consciousness.

The man in the parable chose security as his happiness project and in so doing, closed himself off from the opportunity of further growth. Hence, the judgment: "Take away his talent and give it to those who are already advancing."

Notice that the parable of the talents is taken from the business world. All the parables are based upon ordinary events: some from business, for the sake of the urban population; some from farming or fishing, for the sake of the rural population. Cooking, sweeping, lighting lamps, sewing, harvesting, investing, going to the bank—these daily occurrences form the basis of the parables. This suggests that everyday life is the place where the reign of God takes place. We don't have to go to a monastery, convent, or hermitage. We do not have to go anywhere because the reign of God is right in front of our eyes. It is "close at hand." Divine union is available to everyone on the face of the earth. Our potential for divine union is the talent, above every other, that must not be hidden in the ground.

The experience of trying and failing is the way to learn to discard self-centered programs for happiness and to surrender to the movement of transformation. Sin is the refusal to continue to evolve. By clinging to mere survival and security, we withdraw ourselves and others from the opportunity and adventure of continuing to grow into the body of Christ.

Incidents from Jesus' Ministry

In the afterglow of Pentecost, we celebrate the historical life of Jesus in the light of our experience of the Spirit, who introduces us to the trans-historical life of Jesus. In this perspective, grace is the presence and action of Christ in our lives right now, and the Gospel texts are mirrors reflecting back to us the same presence and action of Christ in the lives of his disciples.

Peter at Capernaum

The disciples and Jesus now entered Capernaum whereon, the very next Sabbath, he went into the synagogue to teach. Immediately after that they went to the house of Simon and Andrew. Now Simon's mother-in-law lay in bed with a fever and they at once appealed to him on her behalf. He approached and taking her by the hand, raised her up and set her on her feet. The fever left her and she waited on them.

Late in the evening after the sun had set, all the sick as well as possessed persons were brought to him. Presently the whole town was assembled at the door. He cured many that were suffering from various diseases.

Very early the next morning, while it was still dark, he rose, left the house and went to an out-of-the-way place, and there he prayed. Simon and his companions went in pursuit of him and when they found him said to him, "Everyone is looking for you."

He replied, "Let us go elsewhere and visit the neighboring hamlets. I want to preach there too. That is the purpose of my mission." [Mark 1:21, 29–39][17]

The spiritual journey is God's idea. We did not invent it. Nor did we choose ourselves as candidates for it. God chose us. Of course, He doesn't call us on the phone and say, "I have made a reservation for you." Through the various circumstances in our lives, doors open and close. It is not we who are pursuing God, but God who is pursuing us. Every effort we make to go to God is a lowering of our defenses against the divine approach. God surrounds us with infinite mercy like sunshine. But we tend to keep the curtains at our windows closed, occasionally opening them ajar to let in just a tiny ray of light. If we chose to, we could yank open the heavy drapes, and find ourselves bathed in light!

Peter is presented in the Gospel as one of the more unreliable and unstable of Jesus' followers. Nobody but Jesus would have thought of making him an apostle. Peter wanted all the things that worldly people want, only transposed into a religious context.

One day Jesus entered Peter's hometown and walked down the main street. A man like Peter was impressed when Jesus stopped at his house and said, "We'll stay here." But then Peter discovered that his mother-in-law was sick with a fever. "My God," he thought, "of all the days for that woman to get sick, why does she have to choose this one?"

Jesus noticed Peter's discomfort, went upstairs, took the woman by the hand and set her on her feet. Whereupon she came down and prepared a meal that was a smashing success. Everyone was aglow with the festivities when the whole town started coming to Peter's doorstep, bringing the sick to be healed. Jesus went out and healed them all.

Everybody went to bed in high spirits. Jesus got up early in the morning and slipped away to pray in solitude. It did not take Peter long to realize that he had disappeared. The local equivalent of the rotary club noticed his disappearance too. They hastened to Peter and said, "What are we going to do? We can't lose this important man! Think what it would mean for our town if he makes this his head-quarters. He worked miracles at your doorstep; he healed your mother-in-law. You're the man to go and bring him back!"

Accordingly, a delegation with Peter at its head was sent in pursuit of Jesus. When they found him, Peter blurted out, "Everybody is looking for you!" He might have added, "If you come back, we'll build you a synagogue and a house! We'll set up concessions and you'll get a share of the revenues."

Jesus replied, "Let us go someplace else." Notice the word "us," that is, "you and me." It is as if Jesus was saying, "I don't care what other people think of me. What I'm interested in is, what do *you* think of me? Are you willing to go where I want to go rather than where you want me to go?"

Launching Out into Deep Waters

One day the crowd was surging up against Jesus and listening to the word of God. While he was standing on the beach of Lake Gennesaret, he saw two boats drawn up on the beach. The fishermen had disembarked and were washing their nets. After entering one of the boats, which belonged to Simon, he asked them to push out a little from the shore. He then sat down and taught the crowds from the boat.

When he had finished speaking, he said to Simon, "Launch out into the deep water and have your men lower the net for a haul."

"Master," Simon said, "we worked all night without catching a thing. However, since you tell us to do so, I will have the nets let down." When they had done this, they caught in a single haul an extraordinary number of fish. In fact their nets threatened to break. They beckoned to their partners in the other boat to come and lend them a hand. They came and both boats were filled so that they were on the point of sinking.

When Simon Peter saw what had happened, he threw himself down at the feet of Jesus and said, "Lord, leave my boat, for I am a sinful man." A feeling of awe had gripped him, as it had all his associates, because of the number of fish caught in the haul. So, too, it had seized James and John, the sons of Zebedee who were Simon's partners.

Jesus then said to Simon, "You have nothing to fear. Hereafter you will be a fisher of people."

When they had brought the boat to shore, they abandoned everything and became his followers. [Luke 5:1–11][18]

Peter was not ready to leave his hometown and returned to his fishing business. Jesus, however, continued to show interest in him. One day, Jesus was at the shore of the lake teaching a large crowd. He looked around and saw several boats along the shore. He could have gotten into one of several boats, but he chose to get into Peter's and to preach from there.

After preaching at length to the people, Jesus turned to Peter and said, "Launch out into the deep waters and ask your men to put down their nets for a catch." This was not a welcome suggestion. The little fishing company had been up all night and had caught nothing.

The fishermen took to their oars, rowed out into the middle of the lake and lowered their nets. Suddenly a school of fish swam into their nets. The boat started listing to one side, and they had to call to their companions in another boat for help. Both boats were filled with so many fish that they were at the point of sinking. When they finally got to shore and what had happened fully dawned on Peter, his eyes grew bigger and bigger. He threw himself at the feet of Jesus saying, "Leave my boat, for I am a sinful man." A feeling of awe had gripped him. Jesus said to him, "Don't be afraid. I will make you a fisher of people."

Notice that it was while plying his trade that Peter was finally converted. God generally approaches us where we are: with children who are unmanageable, with a spouse who is late for supper, or with relatives who are unbearable.

Peter at Lake Gennesaret

After the miraculous multiplication of the loaves and fishes, Jesus obliged the disciples to re-enter a boat and precede him to the other shore while he would dismiss the crowds. After dismissing them, he went up the mountainside alone to pray. Night fell and he was still there alone while the boat was far out at sea. It was hit hard by the waves since the wind was against them. During the last part of the night, however, he came toward them, walking over the sea. When they saw him walk upon the sea, they were perplexed. "It is a ghost!" they said, and from fright cried out. Jesus at once addressed them. "Take heart," he said, "it is I. Do not be afraid."

Thus reassured, Peter said to him, "Master, if it is you, tell me to come to you over the water."

"Come," he replied. So Peter climbed out and started in the direction of Jesus, walking over the water. But when he felt the stiff breeze, he took alarm, and when he began to sink, cried out, "Lord, save me!" Jesus immediately reached out his hand and took hold of him. "How little faith you have," he said to him. "What made you doubt?"

Then they climbed up into the boat and the wind subsided. The men in the boat prostrated themselves before him and said, "You are indeed the Son of God." [Matt. 14:22–33][19]

Having dismissed the crowd, Jesus went off to pray in solitude. While absorbed in God, he did not notice that a storm had arisen on the lake and that his disciples, whom he had sent off to the other shore, were being bounced around by the waves and the wind. The disciples were rowing with all their might but were not making any headway. Jesus started coming to them walking on the water. They thought he was a ghost! Jesus reassured them, "Don't be afraid. It is I."

The words, "Don't be afraid," seem to have served as a bugle call in Peter's ears, and he responded, "Master, if it is you, tell me to come to you over the water!"

Jesus could have said, "Stay in the boat. We don't want to have two ghosts walking on the water." Instead, Jesus called back, "Come!"

When Peter, after a few steps, began to sink, Jesus reached out and pulled him out of the water. As soon as they were back in the boat, Jesus said, "How little faith you have! What made you doubt?" There is nothing like humiliation and failure, especially when witnessed by our peers, to help us face up to our motivation and to ask important questions: Why did you do it? Excessive desires for security and survival, affection and esteem, and power and control are out-of-date motives as far as the Gospel is concerned. Since Peter was deeply enmeshed in them, this was a crucial experience for him. It challenged him to change the direction in which he was looking for happiness and in particular, to stop seeking the esteem of others.

The Mission of the Seventy-two

After these incident, the Lord appointed another group, seventy-two in all, and sent them out two-by-two to go ahead of him to every town and place where he intended to visit personally. He said to them, "The harvest is plentiful but the laborers are few. Pray the owner of the harvest, therefore, to send out laborers to do his harvesting. Go now, but mind you, I am sending you out like lambs among a pack of wolves. Do not burden yourselves with purse or bag or sandals and greet no one by the way. Whatever house you enter, the first thing you say must be a blessing on this house. Make your headquarters in just that house and eat and drink whatever they have to offer. Do not be constantly shifting from house to house. Whatever town you enter, if the people make you welcome, eat what is set before you, take care of the sick in the place and speak to the inhabitants on this theme: 'The Kingdom of God has finally come to you.'"

The seventy-two returned in high spirits. "Master," they said, "even the demons are subject to us because we use your name."

"Yes," he said to them, "I was watching Satan fall like lightning flashes from heaven. But, mind you, it is I that have given you the power to tread upon serpents and scorpions and break the dominion of the enemy everywhere. Just the same, do not rejoice in the fact that the spirits are subject to you, but rejoice in the fact that your names are engraved in Heaven." [Luke 10:1–9; 17–20][20]

The miraculous haul of fish prompted Peter and his companions to leave everything and to follow Jesus. Jesus then began to train the disciples for their future ministries. In our text Jesus called together a group of seventy-two and sent them out two-by-two, instructing them to preach the reign of God and giving them the power to cure the sick and to cast out demons. The actual exercise of these healing gifts must have been sensational. Perhaps you are familiar with the healing services currently taking place in the charismatic movement and are sometimes attended by thousands of people and often lasting up to five or six hours. Scores of people are often healed. Imagine the intense emotion and enthusiasm building up in such a service!

The disciples were evidently excited when, after a brief initiation into the reign of God, they were able to heal diseases and cast out demons. They came back in high spirits and poured out their success story to the Master: "The demons are subject to us in your name!" Jesus gently put the lid on their enthusiasm with these words: "It's good to work miracles, but don't get too excited about such things. If you want to know what to get excited about, it's that your names are written in heaven." With these words, he shifted the focus of their enthusiasm from the natural satisfaction of success to what apostolic ministry is actually based upon—the work of the Spirit within us. Apostolic virtues come not from our natural talents but from a mysterious emptying process in which our talents are put at the disposal of the Spirit rather than of pride.

The disciples did not know what to do with Jesus' remarks; they had to think them over. It is worth noting that Jesus sent these men out with a special ministry so early in their formation, their fishing nets scarcely out of their hands. In earlier times, it was generally believed that one should spend a long time in preparation for a special ministry, maybe even living an eremetical life for awhile. At the very least, it seemed necessary to go to a seminary or to join a monastery and subject oneself to an austere regime or to a highly disciplined lifestyle for a time. There is great merit in such a structured environment. Many famous missionaries enjoyed that kind of preparation for their ministries.

But here is the paradox. Whatever the value of such an approach to ministry, it is not the way that Jesus prepared his disciples. His method was similar to that of a swimming instructor who throws his students into the water. Jesus gave his disciples a ministry for which they were totally unprepared, knowing that they would enjoy a success for which they were even more unprepared.

In our day many ministries are emerging for lay folks that have not existed for centuries—counselors, administrators of parishes, liturgical ministers, justice and peace witnesses, social workers. These people often have to begin their ministries with little or no preparation. One wonders whether we should insist on adequate preparation or put more faith in the way that Jesus launched his disciples—jump in and see what happens. At least there was no danger of his disciples thinking that their success was due to their study of scripture, theology or the length of their preparation. The inexperienced disciples knew that their success could only have come from the empowerment that Jesus had given them.

In our day, there seems to be less and less time for a prolonged preparation for any ministry. The demands are great, the harvest is plentiful, and some ministries are so difficult that it would take a lifetime to prepare adequately for them. The only choice is to start ministering.

Thus the Gospel encourages the ministries of our time, but with this caution: *Don't expect success.* The seventy-two disciples had immediate success. Perhaps they were granted instant success because Jesus wanted them to realize their inability to handle it. In every ministry, success is normally accompanied sooner or later by trials, disappointments and failures.

In and through the ups and downs of ministry, God purifies the minister. Like the seventy-two disciples, he may throw us into a demanding form of service to let us find out right away that we can't do it on our own. A special mission is not a sign that we are holy; it is a challenge to become holy. The path to holiness is the experience of failure, and failure is certain if we are thrust into a form of ministry that we are not adequately prepared for. If we were fully prepared, it would be a lot easier on our families, friends, superiors and—above all—on our own self-image. As it is, people are bound to get upset with us—and we may become thoroughly discouraged with ourselves. We need to understand that we only grow in ministry through the experience of failure and humiliation. It is by becoming humble that one is able to practice ministry rightly, and humiliation is the path to humility.

In order to understand this teaching of Jesus more concretely, I offer the following tips. If you want to find out what a poor monk or nun you would make, join a monastery or convent. If you want to find out what a poor priest you would make, get yourself ordained. If you want to find out what a poor meditator you would make, start meditating. If you want to find out what a poor prayer you would make, try to pray. If you want to find out what a poor husband or wife you would make, find yourself a spouse.

When married couples experience marital difficulties, they think something is wrong with their spouse. When a priest experiences his inadequacies, he thinks the bishop is no good. When monks or nuns in a monastery enter the night of sense, they think something is wrong with the community: "If the rule was better ob-

served, I would be perfect," the say; or "If the superiors were reasonable, I would
be in the seventh mansion with Teresa of Avila."

Love makes us vulnerable. The love of another person (including God) reduces
our defense mechanisms. As soon as we trust somebody, we no longer have to be
self-protective in their presence, and our defenses diminish. Then the faults and limitations that we have never seen or always tried to hide begin to emerge as clear as
crystal for the benefit of our friends, relatives, colleagues and spouses. Such difficulties
generally indicate that our particular ministry or relationship is working well.

Once we learn to accept failure, love grows. We do not grow by thinking about
it or by wishing for it, but only through the experience of failure.

There are three stages of transformation that repeat themselves as we climb the
spiritual ladder. The first step is human effort—the willingness to accept the invitation to Christ to undertake a ministry or relationship. The second is the inevitable
result of doing something for which we are inadequate and unprepared—the experience of failure, which may be real or apparent, private or public. The final stage
is the triumph of grace. One cannot predict it; one cannot demand it. All of a
sudden, after one has persevered in the way of humiliation, the difficulties cease
and one finds oneself in a new place. The experiences of failure has taught us how
to live and how to minister, which is to act with complete dependence on God.

There is no reason to get excited because we have a special ministry; it could be
largely a question of natural endowment. We should rejoice, rather, because our
names are written in heaven. We are part of God's unfolding plan to transform
human consciousness. Our failures become the source of our strength according to
Paul's formula, "When I am weak, then I am strong."[21] Christ will then empower
us to minister to his people in ways that know no bounds.

On the other hand, if we make only a casual or an impermanent commitment to
a ministry or to a marriage partner, we do not give enough time for the dynamic of
self-knowledge to work. That dynamic gradually unveils the dark side of our personality and our false-self system with its self-centered programs for happiness that
cannot possibly work.

In every vocation, events and other people constantly reactivate our emotional
programs for happiness, along with the accompanying turmoil that occurs when
these programs are frustrated. Such self-knowledge is not a disaster but the necessary
condition for changing them. When these have been dismantled, our ministry starts
to work of itself because, once freed from the obstacles of pride and subtle forms of
selfishness that hold the false-self system in place, the Spirit of God can work in us.

The seventy-two disciples, flushed with success, came to the Lord expecting to
get a pat on the back, and all he said was, "Don't get excited about working
miracles. Anybody with a little psychic power can do that. What really counts is
that you are part of God's plan. The thing to rejoice in is that you are chosen to
become divine and to join me in raising the consciousness of the world."

APPENDIX I

■

The Rosary

The joyful, sorrowful and glorious mysteries of the rosary are the mysteries of divine light, life and love that the liturgy celebrates from Advent to Epiphany, from Lent to the Ascension, and from Pentecost throughout the Sundays of Ordinary Time. Christmas is the feast of divine light and Epiphany is the fullness of it. Easter is the feast of divine life and Ascension is the fullness of it. Pentecost is the feast of divine love and the rest of the year is the expression of it. The revelation of divine light, life and love grows in proportion to the growth of faith, hope and charity, and vice-versa.

The rosary is a school of contemplative prayer. As the lips and hands are saying the beads and the mind is reflecting on the mysteries, the presence of Christ in our inmost being awakens and we rest in his presence. Whether we focus on the words of the individual prayers or reflect on the unfolding mysteries, we may feel drawn into this rest. At that time we leave behind both the words and the reflections and enjoy the presence of Christ. When his presence begins to dissolve, we return to the prayers and reflections where we left off. In this way, we move up and down the ladder of interior prayer and allow the habit of contemplation to develop. Contemplation gradually overflows into daily life and extends the enjoyment of God's presence into the whole of life.

APPENDIX II

∎

Contemplative Liturgy

For members of contemplative communities, the celebration of the Eucharist in a contemplative setting and mode is extremely refreshing. Shared silence is genuine liturgy. The practice of exterior and interior silence as an integral part of liturgy needs to be restored. Just as the Word of God emerges from the silence of the Father, so the sacred texts of the liturgy should emerge from the silence of the community. It is then that they achieve their full effect.

To prepare the congregation to worship in this fashion, a vestibule to pass from our external activity and preoccupations into the inner sanctuary of our hearts may be helpful and even necessary. The community of Taize has developed a series of chants which are available in English.[1] If one of these is chanted by the congregation for five or ten minutes at the beginning of the liturgy, preferably in four parts, a suitable atmosphere of recollection and prayer can be created.

After each lesson or group of lessons, a period of ten minutes of silence might be introduced. After the reception of the Eucharist, a similar period of silence, up to twenty minutes, might also be shared, depending on the amount of time at the disposal of the assembly. Hymns and sung responses are omitted and movements are reduced to a minimum. If the group is small, sitting around the altar table may help to sustain the atmosphere of recollection and silence.

The texts are read slowly and deliberately. The gestures of the celebrant and the words of the Eucharistic prayer are done with the utmost reverence and simplicity. A brief homily could invite the people to identify and commune with the presence of the risen Christ among them and within them.

NOTES

■

PREFACE
1. 1 Cor. 2:16
2. 1 Col. 3:11

CHAPTER I
1. Gospel of Second Sunday of Advent
2. Gospel of Fourth Sunday of Advent
3. John 1:46
4. Gospel of Second Sunday in Ordinary Time

CHAPTER II
1. Gospel of the First Sunday of Lent
2. Romans 7:18–25 (*The Living New Testament,* Tyndale House Foundation, Wheaton, Ill.)
3. Gospel of the First Sunday of Lent
4. Gospel of the Second Sunday of Lent
5. Gospel of the Fourth Sunday of Lent
6. Gospel for Monday of Holy Week
7. From Jesus' final discourse at the Last Supper
8. John 10:30
9. Gal. 2:20
10. From the Gospel of Passion Sunday
11. Matt. 26:39
12. cf. Bernadette Roberts, *The Path to No-Self* and *The Experience of No-Self,* Shambhala, Boston, MA.
13. From the Gospel of Passion Sunday
14. Matt. 27:52–53
15. Gen. 1:3
16. From the Gospel of Good Friday
17. Ex. 3:7–8
18. Gospel for the Easter Vigil

19. Rev. 1:15
20. Tuesday of the Octave of Easter
21. Gospel of the Third Sunday of Easter
22. Gospel of the Third Sunday of Easter
23. Gospel of the Second Sunday of Easter
24. 2 Cor. 12:10
25. Gospel of the Third Sunday of Easter
26. Col. 3:11

CHAPTER III
 1. John 20:22
 2. Acts 1:4–5
 3. John 3:8
 4. John 17:22–23
 5. John 7:37–38
 6. John 17:21

CHAPTER IV
 1. Gospel of Fourth Sunday in Ordinary Time
 2. Gen. 1:27–31
 3. John 1:46
 4. Matt. 4:15
 5. John of the Cross, *Ascent to Mt. Carmel,* Book I, Chapter 13, 11
 6. Matt. 6:25–30
 7. Gospel of 31st Sunday in Ordinary Time
 8. Robert L. Kinast, *Caring for Society,* Thomas More Press, Chicago, IL, 1985
 9. John 5:19
10. Gospel of Seventh Sunday in Ordinary Time
11. Luke 7:38
12. John Crossan, "In Parables," p. 52
13. Gospel of 16th Sunday in Ordinary Time
14. Matt. 13:44
15. Matt. 13:45
16. Gospel of 33rd Sunday in Ordinary time
17. Gospel of Fifth Sunday in Ordinary Time
18. Gospel of Fifth Sunday in Ordinary Time
19. Gospel of 19th Sunday in Ordinary Time
20. Gospel of 14th Sunday in Ordinary Time
21. 1 Cor.

APPENDIX II
 1. *Music from Taize,* Vol. I and II, publ. By G.I.A. Publications, Inc., 7404 S. Mason Ave., Chicago, IL 60638

BIBLIOGRAPHY

■

McGinn, Bernard, ed. *The Presence of God: A History of Western Mysticism*. Vol. 1, *The Foundations of Mysticism*. New York: Crossroad, 1991.

———. Vol. 2. *The Growth of Mysticism*. New York: Crossroad, 1994.

———. Vol. 3. *The Flowering of Mysticism*. New York: Crossroad, New York, 1998.

Merton, Thomas. *The Wisdom of the Desert*. New York: New Directions, 1970.

Thompson, William N. *Jesus: Lord and Savior*. Mahwah, N.J.: Paulist Press, 1980.

Ware, Timothy. *The Art of Prayer: An Orthodox Anthology*. Salem, N.H.: Faber & Faber, 1966.

SELECTED CLASSIC SOURCES OF THE CHRISTIAN CONTEMPLATIVE TRADITION

Cassian, John. *Conferences*. In *Western Asceticism*. Translated by Owen Chadwick. Philadelphia: Westminster Press, 1958.

Bernard of Clairvaux. *Selected Works*. Classics of Western Spirituality Series. Mahwah, N.J.: Paulist Press, 1987.

Evagrius Ponticus. *The Praktikos: Chapters on Prayer*. Translated by John Eudes Bamberger. Spencer, Mass. Cistercian Publications, 1970.

Gregg, Robert, ed. *Athanasius: Life of Anthony*. Classics of Western Spirituality Series. Mahwah, N.J.: Paulist Press, 1988.

Gregory of Nyssa. *The Life of Moses*. Classics of Western Spirituality Series. Mahwah, N.J. Paulist Press, 1978.

———. *Commentary on the Song of Songs*. Translated by Casimir McCambley. Brookline, Mass.: Hellenic College Press, 1987.

Johnson, William, ed. *The Cloud of Unknowing*. New York: Doubleday, Image Books, 1973.

Kavanaugh, Kieran, and Otilio Rodriguez, trans. *The Collected Works of John of the Cross*. Washington, D.C.: ICS Publications, 1979.

Lawrence of the Resurrection. *The Practice of the Presence of God*. Springfield, Ill.: Templegate Press, 1974.

Maximus the Confessor. *Selected Writings.* Classics of Western Spirituality Series. Mahwah, N.J.: Paulist Press, 1985.

Meister Eckhart. *Sermons and Treatises.* 3 vols. Translated and edited by M. O'C. Walshe. Shaftesbury. UK: Element Books, 1987.

Pseudo-Dionysius. *The Complete Works.* Classics of Western Spirituality Series. Mahwah, N.J.: Paulist Press, 1987.

Ruusbroac, John. *The Spiritual Espousals and Other Works.* Classics of Western Spirituality Series. Mahwah, N.J.: Paulist Press, 1985.

Teresa of Avila. *The Interior Castle.* Classics of Western Spirituality Series. Mahwah, N.J.: Paulist Press, 1979.

Thérèse of Lisieux. *The Story of a Soul.* Translated by John Clarke. Washington, D.C.: ICS Publications, 1976.

William of St. Thierry. *Commentary on the Song of Songs.* Kalamazoo, Mich.: Cistercian Publications, 1969.

SELECTED CONTEMPORARY EXPRESSIONS OF THE CHRISTIAN CONTEMPLATIVE TRADITION

Bokenkotter, Thomas. *Church and Revolution.* New York: Image Books, 1998.

Funk, Mary Margaret, *Thoughts Matter: The Practice of the Spiritual Life.* New York: Continuum, 1998.

———. *Tools Matter for Practicing the Spiritual Life.* New York: Continuum, 2001.

Green, William. *When the Well Runs Dry.* Notre Dame, Ind.: Ave Maria Press, 1985.

Hall, Thelma. *Too Deep For Words.* Mahwah, N.J.: Paulist Press, 1989.

Johnston, William. *The Mysticism of the Cloud of Unknowing.* Trabuco Canyon, Calif.: Source Books, 1987.

Keating, Thomas. *Intimacy with God.* New York: Crossroad, 1994.

———. *The Human Condition.* Mahwah, N.J.: Paulist Press, 1999.

———. *The Better Part.* New York: Continuum, 2000.

———. *Fruits and Gifts of the Spirit.* New York: Lantern Books, 2000.

———. *St. Thérèse of Lisieux.* New York: Lantern Books.

Maloney, George A. *Prayer of the Heart.* Notre Dame, Ind.: Ave Maria Press, 1981.

Marion, Jim. *Putting on the Mind of Christ.* Charlottesville, Va.: Hampton Roads Publishing Company, 2000.

Merton, Thomas. *New Seeds of Contemplation.* New York: New Directions, 1972.

———. *Contemplative Prayer.* New York: Doubleday, Image Books, 1971.

Nemeck, Francis K. and Marie T. Coombs. *Contemplation.* Wilmington, Del.: Michael Glazier, 1984.

Pennington, Basil. *Centering Prayer.* New York: Doubleday, Image Books, 1980.

St. Romain, Philip. *Here Now in Love.* Liguori, Mo.: Liguori Publications, 2002.

THE PSYCHOLOGY OF THE SPIRITUAL JOURNEY

Assagioli, Robert. *Psychosynthesis,* New York: Penguin Books, 1965.

Bradshaw, John. *Bradshaw on: The Family.* Deerfield Beach, Fla.: Health Communications, 1988.

Campbell, Peter and Edwin McMahon. *Bio-Spirituality*. Chicago: Loyola University Press, 1983.

Keyes, Ken, Jr., and Penny Keyes. *Handbook to Higher Consciousness*. Berkeley, Calif.: Line Books, 1975.

May, Gerald. *Will and Spirit*. New York: Harper & Row, 1983.

———. *Addiction and Grace*. San Francisco: Harper & Row, 1988.

Schaef, Anne Wilson. *When Society Becomes an Addict*. San Francisco: Harper & Row, 1987.

———. *Co-Dependency*. San Francisco: Harper & Row, 1986.

Underhill, Evelyn. *Practical Mysticism*. London, 1914.

Washburn, Michael. *The Ego and the Dynamic Ground*. Albany, New York: State University of New York Press, 1988.

Wilber, Ken. *Up from Eden*. Boulder, Colo.: Shambhala, 1981.

———. *No Boundary*. Boulder, Colo.: Shambhala, 1979.

———. *Sex, Ecology, Spirituality*. Boston: Shambhala, 1995.

———. *In the Eye of Spirit*. Boston, Shambhala, 1997.

CONTEMPLATIVE OUTREACH NATIONAL/INTERNATIONAL OFFICE
Provides:

Networking • assistance in establishing local Centering Prayer programs • on-going Centering Prayer groups • books, audio, and video tapes • Centering Prayer retreat directors • newsletter

If you would like to learn Centering Prayer, host a workshop, identify local contacts, or merely want more information, contact:

Contemplative Outreach Ltd.
10 Park Place—Suite 2-B
P.O. Box 737
Butler, NJ 07405
Phone: 973-838-3384
Fax: 973-492-5795
E-mail: *office@coutreach.org*
www.contemplativeoutreach.org